George Oliver

The revelations of a square

Exhibiting a graphic display of the sayings and doings of eminent free and accepted masons

George Oliver

The revelations of a square
Exhibiting a graphic display of the sayings and doings of eminent free and accepted masons

ISBN/EAN: 9783337711917

Printed in Europe, USA, Canada, Australia, Japan

Cover: Foto ©Suzi / pixelio.de

More available books at **www.hansebooks.com**

THE

REVELATIONS OF A SQUARE;

EXHIBITING A

GRAPHIC DISPLAY OF SAYINGS AND DOINGS

OF

EMINENT FREE AND ACCEPTED MASONS,

FROM THE

REVIVAL IN 1717 BY DR. DESAGULIERS, TO THE REUNION IN 1813 BY THEIR R.H. THE DUKE OF KENT AND SUSSEX.

BY

GEORGE OLIVER, D.D.,

AUTHOR OF "THE HISTORICAL LANDMARKS OF FREEMASONRY," ETC., PAST D.G.M. OF THE GRAND LODGE OF MASSACHUSETTS, U. S., PAST D.P.G.M. OF LINCOLNSHIRE, AND HONORARY MEMBER OF VARIOUS LODGES IN EVERY QUARTER OF THE GLOBE.

Miscuit utile dulci.—Hor.

NEW YORK:
MASONIC PUBLISHING AND MANUFACTURING CO.,
430 BROOME STREET.
1866.

PREFACE.

FREEMASONRY, like all other sciences, is a system of progression. Something more is required to constitute a bright Mason than a knowledge of the elements of the Craft. A carpenter may know the names of his tools, and have acquired some dexterity in their practical use; but this will not enable him to build a house, or to construct a common dressing-case.

If any one is desirous of being a Mason, in the strict sense of the word, he must make himself acquainted with something more than words, signs, and tokens. The three stages of initiation can no more convert a man into a Mason, than the indenture of an apprentice can make him a mechanic.

He must read and meditate, study with care and attention the history and doctrines of the Order, and attend his Lodge with the utmost regularity, that he may become familiar with its discipline by actual personal observation.

There is no Royal road to Freemasonry.

The Gordian knot can be untied by diligence and application alone, and he who is ambitious to share in the honours of Masonry, must work his way up the ladder step by step, with patient assiduity; and, "forgetting what is behind, he must press forward toward the mark" he aims at, and his mental exertions will not fail of their reward.

The contents of this book will economize the labour of his researches, by placing before him the gradual progress of Masonry from small beginnings to its present extension and prevailing influence in every country on the face of the habitable globe. And, which is of still greater importance, it will make him familiar with the doctrines and practices, manners and customs of the Fraternity, and its master minds in times when its purity had undergone no change.

It will be evident to the most casual observer, that the information contained in this work could not have been acquired by the most industrious and persevering observation of a single life, even though it might be extended to an extraordinary length, because it consists principally of private anecdotes, which could only be known by personal communication with the parties. And, accordingly, it is the result of an experience extending over three successive generations.

The facts are these: My lamented father, who died a few years ago, at the advanced age of ninety-two, was made a Mason, as I have reason to believe, in the year 1784. He was very methodical in all his transactions; and, being a masonic enthusiast, he noted down in a diary, expressly devoted to that purpose, under a vivid recollection of the facts, whether they were witnessed by himself or communicated to him by others, every event or conversation that struck his fancy as being either singular, characteristic, or important in the working of the Craft.

By this process he preserved several interesting conversations of our distinguished Brethren in the eighteenth century, which would otherwise have been irrecoverably lost. Added to this, he was acquainted, in the early part of his life, with an intelligent Brother who was initiated by Dr. Manningham in 1740, and personally knew Brothers Desaguliers, Anderson, Martin Clare, Hutchinson, Calcott, Preston, and all the great lights of that period. He was, although advanced in years when my father knew him, full of anecdote; and having been an attentive observer of passing occurrences, my father derived a fund of valuable knowledge from his communications, which he committed to writing as he received them, and the MS. came into my hands a short time before his death. It contains many curious particulars, some of which are now made public for the first time. In fact, I do not believe there is in existence so good an account of the masonic practice of that century, as is contained in this manuscript.

For this reason the following pages must not be accounted fabulous and without authority, because its contents are communicated through an imaginary medium; for the author is in possession of authentic vouchers for every transaction. It is true the language has been corrected, and in many cases, the dialogue amplified and extended, but he is not aware that a single event has either been misrepresented or heightened in colouring or perspective. They will contain a true picture of the manners, customs, usages, and ceremonies of successive periods during the eighteenth century, drawn from the actual working of Lodges, and enlivened by numerous anecdotes of the master spirits of the several ages in they respectively flourished; and, under whose active and judicious superintendence, Freemasonry reaped vast improvements, and attained a high preponderating influence and merited celebrity.

The book will, therefore, unquestionably prove a welcome addition to the meagre history of Masonry during the same period, which proceeded from the pens of Anderson, Noorthouck, and Preston, and constitute almost the only records to which we can refer for a knowledge of the very important events that distinguished Freemasonry from the revival to the reunion of the ancient and modern sections.

It will be observed that the author has mentioned many peculiar usages and customs which the present system of Masonry does not tolerate; but being characteristic of the period, they will be, notwithstanding, an acceptable boon to the accumulating stores of masonic literature. With our present lights, the inexperienced Mason may be inclined to ridicule the practices of a bygone age, and treat its peculiar doctrines as so many improbable fictions; but he should remember that the best Masons of the days here referred to had not dipped so deeply, as we have had the good fortune to do, into the recondite interpretation of the mysteries which they transmitted to posterity; and that, consequently, their customs and amusements took a tone from the peculiar constitution of society, and bore a patent resemblance to those of the numerous clubs and coteries which occupied the leisure and divided the attention of the gentlemen of "Merrie England" in the eighteenth century.

It will not be an uninteresting recommendation of this little work, to state that all the books and pamphlets, both for and against the Order, and all the pretended disclosures of our secrets, which were incessantly puffed by our opponents, and purchased with avidity, and read with eagerness by the vast multitude of cowans, who were desirous of becoming acquainted with the mysteries of Masonry without the ceremony of initiation, that were published in England during the entire century, have been noticed. The author is not conscious of any omission. He believes that no book or paper, which possessed the slightest pretensions to publicity, has escaped his researches.

With these brief explanations, the author presents his work to the Fraternity, in the hope that it may not be altogether unworthy of their acceptance. It would probably have never seen the light, had not a portion of it, some few years ago, appeared in the pages of the "Freemasons' Quarterly Magazine and Review." And it was so generally approved, that many kind, and perhaps partial, friends expressed an anxious desire to see it in a perfect form. If it should be found to possess any degree of interest, the author disclaims all share of the credit, except for performing the more humble duty of arranging materials which had been already collected, and putting them into a readable form. The task was simple—its execution easy; and if the reader finds as much pleasure in its perusal as the author has had in its compilation, he will consider himself amply repaid for his labour.

GEO. OLIVER

SCOPWICK VICARAGE,
December 6, 1854.

CONTENTS.

LIST OF ILLUSTRATIONS.

THE

REVELATIONS OF A SQUARE.

CHAPTER I.

THE REVIVAL.—DR. DESAGULIERS.

1717—1722.

"I could a tale unfold."—Shakespeare.

"Dost feel a wish to learn this thing of me?"
Titania.

"Hoc est
"Vivere bis, vitâ posse priore frui."—Martial.

A friend and Brother, who resides in town, knowing that I am somewhat of a dabbler in antiquities, forwarded to me, some time ago, an old Silver Square, which he told me had the reputation of having been used in one of the earliest Lodges after the revival of Masonry in 1717. Of course I found it an object of great interest, and value it accordingly. Although a good deal battered, the inscription is still distinctly visible. On one limb of its upper face is the following legend—

Keepe within Compasse;

and on the other—

Acte on ye Square.

At the angle of junction is a rude heart with the letter J on it. The reverse is blank, with the exception of two small old English capitals C. W. at the angle.

The jewel is soon described; but how am I to pourtray my feelings, when, with the instrument lying on the table before me, I called up the spirits of the dead, and contemplated scenes of bygone times—the working of Lodges—the solemn Labours and convivial Refreshments which this small token had witnessed—the racy jest and sparkling wit which set the table on a roar, after the hours of business were past. This was the age when the facetious Doctor Sheridan reduced punning to a system, and it was practised by rule and compass: and, therefore, we may readily believe that the Lodges had their share of it. "O!" I exclaimed aloud, "if this square could speak, what interesting scenes it might reveal, and how it would enlighten us about the doings of Freemasonry at the time of its revival!"

I had been sitting late one evening in contemplation of the scenes which took place in the palmy days of Masonry, when Desaguliers, Payne, Anderson, Lamball, Morrice, Timson, and their compeers were at the helm of affairs. A dull and dreamy sensation came over me, and I saw, or fancied I saw, the Square, which had just been reposing motionless before me, raise itself up, with great solemnity, on the exterior points of its two limbs, which seemed to assume the form of legs. Body it had none, but the heart, which was delineated at the angle, put forth two eyes, a snub nose, and a mouth—a sort of amplification of the letter J. I could trace the features distinctly, as we see the figure of a human face in the fire on a winter's night.

While I was considering what all this could mean, I heard a small thin voice pronounce my name. To say I was merely surprised at this unexpected phenomenon, would be too tame an expression—I was utterly astonished and confounded. I rubbed my eyes and looked round the room. Everything appeared exactly as usual—no change could I perceive; the fire burned brightly; the books covered the walls; the candles cast their usual light; and the ticking of the spring clock over my head preserved its usual monotony. I began to fancy I had been mistaken, when my name was again uttered by the same unearthly voice, and there stood the little fellow, as if determined to indulge in some demoniacal soliloquy to which I was constrained to listen. At length it communicated its intention by saying—"Attend to me, and I will realize all your wishes, by enlightening you on the subject of your meditations, and giving you the benefit of my experience; but first let me caution you not to utter a single syllable, for if you do the charm will be broken; the sound of the human voice silences me for ever.

"I was originally the property of a Brother whose extensive genius has invested his name with immortality —Sir Christopher Wren, Grand Master of Masonry at the latter end of the seventeenth century, which fell into desuetude when King George I. had the impolicy to supersede this great man in favour of Bro. W. Benson, and so disgusted him with the world, that he declined all public assemblies, and amongst the rest, relinquished his connection with Freemasonry. The Craft refused to meet, or hold any communication with the new Grand Master, and Masonry languished for several years, till it was supposed to be extinct; and Dr. Plot exulted in the idea that he had given it its death-blow by some ill-natured animadversions in the History of Staffordshire.[1]

"In the year 1712, a person of the name of Simeon Townsend published a pamphlet, which he entitled, 'Observations and Enquiries relating to the brotherhood of the Freemasons;' and a few others had been issued on the decline of the Order, as if triumphing in its fall.[2] About this time, Dr. Desaguliers, a Fellow of the Royal Society, and Professor of Philosophy, was gradually rising into eminence. In the course of his scientific researches, the above works fell into his hands. He did not find

[1] "The Natural History of Staffordshire," by Robert Plot, Oxford, 1686. In this attack on the Order, the Doctor says, very illogically, that "one of their articles is to support a Brother till work can be had;" and another is "to advise the Masters they work for, according to the best of their skill, acquainting them with the goodness or badness of the material, &c., that Masonry be not dishonoured; and many such like." He then concludes by saying, that "some others they have that none know but themselves, which I have reason to suspect *are much worse than these;* perhaps as bad as the history of the Craft itself, than which there is nothing I ever met with more false or incoherent." See the entire argument in the Gold. Rem., vol. iii., p. 37.

[2] These were—"A short Analysis of the Unchanged Rites and Ceremonies of Freemasons:" London, Stephen Dilly, 1676. "The Paradoxal Discourses of Franc. Mercur van Helmont, concerning the Macrocosm and Microcosm, or the Greater and Lesser World, and their Union; set down in Writing by J. B., and now published:" London, Freeman, 1685. "A Short Charge," O.D.A.A.M.F.M.R.O.: 1694. "The Secret History of Clubs, particularly of the Golden Fleece; with their Original, and the Characters of the most noted Members thereof." London, 1709.

them very complimentary to the Fraternity, but they excited his curiosity, and he was made a Mason in the old Lodge at the Goose and Gridiron in St. Paul's Churchyard, and subsequently removed by him to the Queen's Arms Tavern in the same locality, where the Grand Lodges were afterwards very frequently held.[3] The peculiar principles of the Craft struck him as being eminently calculated to contribute to the benefit of the community at large, if they could be re-directed into the channel from which they had been diverted by the retirement of Sir Christopher Wren. Dr. Desaguliers paid a visit to this veteran Freemason, for the purpose of consulting him on the subject. The conversation of the Past Grand Master excited his enthusiasm, for he expatiated with great animation on the beauties of the Order and the unhappy prostration which had recently befallen it. From this moment, the doctor determined to make some efforts to revive Freemasonry, and restore it to its primitive importance.

"You may perhaps be inclined to inquire," said the Square, very naively, "how I became acquainted with these facts, as I was then quietly reposing in the drawer of a cabinet along with Sir Christopher's collection of curiosities. The truth is, that the venerable old gentleman had taken a liking to Dr. Desaguliers, and presented me to him with the rest of his Masonic regalia. From henceforth I was privy to all the doctor's plans; and as he soon rose to the chair of his Lodge, I had the advantage of hearing almost every conversation he had with his Masonic friends on the subject nearest to his heart, which generally occurred in the Lodge, with your humble servant at his breast suspended from a white ribbon. Every plan was carefully arranged, and the details subjected to the most critical supervision before it was carried into execution; and by this judicious process, his schemes were generally successful. Thus, having been in active operation from a period anterior to the revival of Masonry, I have witnessed many scenes which it may be both amusing and instructive to record, as the good may prove an example worthy of imitation, and the evil, should there be any, may act as a beacon to

[3] It is now called the Lodge of Antiquity.

warn the unwary Brother to avoid the quicksands of error which will impede his progress to Masonic perfection.

"Bro. Desaguliers having intimated his intention of renovating the Order, soon found himself supported by a party of active and zealous Brothers, whose names merit preservation. They were Sayer, Payne, Lamball, Elliott, Gofton, Cordwell, De Noyer, Vraden, King, Morrice, Calvert, Ware, Lumley, and Madden. These included the Masters and Wardens of the four existing Lodges at the Goose and Gridiron, the Crown, the Apple-tree, and the Rummer and Grapes; and they succeeded in forming themselves into a Grand Lodge, and resumed the quarterly Communications, which had been discontinued for many years; and having thus replanted the tree, it soon extended its stately branches to every quarter of the globe.

"There was no code of laws in existence at the period to regulate the internal economy of the Lodges except a few brief By-laws of their own, which, in fact, were little more than a dead letter, for the Brethren acted pretty much as their own judgment dictated. Any number of Masons, not less than ten, that is to say, the Master, two Wardens, and seven Fellow Crafts, with the consent of the magistrate, were empowered to meet, and perform all the rites and ceremonies of Masonry, with no other authority than the privilege which was inherent in themselves, and had ever remained unquestioned. They assembled at their option, and opened their Lodges on the highest of hills or in the lowest of valleys, in commemoration of the same custom adopted by the early Christians, who held their private assemblies in similar places during the ten great persecutions which threatened to exterminate them from the face of the earth.

"But as this privilege led to many irregularities," continued my companion, "and was likely to afford a pretext for unconstitutional practices, it was resolved that every Lodge to be hereafter convened, except the four old Lodges at this time existing, should be legally authorized to act by a warrant from the Grand Master for the time being, granted to certain individuals on petition, with the consent and approbation of the Grand Lodge in Communication; and that without such warrant no Lodge should be hereafter deemed regular or constitutional. And a few years later Bro. Desaguliers proposed in Grand Lodge that a code of laws should be drawn up for the better government of the Craft.

Accordingly, at the annual assembly on St. John's day, 1721, he produced thirty-eight regulations, which passed without a dissentient voice in the most numerous Grand Lodge which had yet been seen, conditionally, that every annual Grand Lodge shall have an inherent power and authority to make new regulations, or to alter these for the real benefit of this ancient Fraternity; provided always *that the old landmarks be carefully preserved*, and that such alterations and new regulations be proposed and agreed to at the Quarterly Communication preceding the annual Grand Feast; and that they be offered also to the perusal of all the Brethren before dinner, in writing, *even of the youngest apprentice*, the approbation and consent of the majority of all the Brethren present being absolutely necessary to make the same binding and obligatory These constitutions were signed by Philip, Duke of Wharton, G.M., Theophilus Desaguliers, M.D. and F.R.S., the Deputy Grand Master, with the rest of the Grand Officers and the Masters and Wardens, as well as many other Brethren then present, to the number of more than a hundred.

"The convivialities of Masonry were regulated by the ancient Gothic charges, which directed the Brethren to enjoy themselves with decent mirth, treating one another according to their ability, but avoiding all excess, not forcing any Brother to eat or drink beyond his inclination, according to the old regulation of King Ahasuerus—not hindering him from going home when he pleases, &c.: you remember the charge?"[4]

I nodded acquiescence. The Square took the alarm, and hastily said—"Do not forget our compact; if you speak, my revelations are at an end. To proceed:—

"I can testify to the convivial propensities of the Brethren of that day. Dermott did not libel them when

[4] In the year 1755, the Earl of Caernarvon being G. M., it was ordered that no Brother, for the future, shall smoke tobacco *in the Grand Lodge*, either at the Quarterly Communication or the Committee of Charity, till the Lodges shall be closed. In private Lodges it was a constant practice.

he said, 'Some of the young Brethren made it appear that a good knife and fork, in the hands of a dexterous Brother, over proper materials, would sometimes give greater satisfaction, and add more to the conviviality of the Lodge, than the best scale and compass in Europe.'

"Bro. Desaguliers was elevated to the throne of the Grand Lodge in 1719, and proclaimed Grand Master on the day of St. John the Baptist. He effected great improvements in the Order during his year of office; and yet all the record which he thought proper to make of his Grand Mastership was, that 'being duly installed, congratulated, and homaged, he revived the old peculiar toasts or healths drank by Freemasons;'[5] and it was agreed that when a new Grand Master is appointed, his health shall be toasted as Grand Master elect. Bro. Desaguliers was peculiarly active in the improvement and dissemination of Masonry at its revival, and, therefore, merits the respectful and affectionate remembrance of the Fraternity. He devoted much of his time to promote its best interests; and being the Master of several Lodges, I had a fair quantity of experience in a small space of time, and I can confidently affirm, that though the public records of Masonry say so little of the acts of this worthy Brother, there were many traits in his character that redound to his immortal praise. He was a grave man in private life, almost approaching to austerity; but he could relax in the private recesses of a Tyled Lodge, and in company with Brothers and Fellows, where the ties of social intercourse are not particularly stringent. He considered the proceedings of the Lodge as strictly confidential, and being persuaded that his Brothers by initiation actually occupied the same position as Brothers by blood, he was undisguisedly free and familiar in the mutual interchange of unrestrained courtesy. In the Lodge, he was jocose and free hearted, sang his song, and had no objection to his share of the bottle, although one of the most learned and distinguished men of his day. He delivered public lectures on experimental philosophy, an unusual practice for a dignified clergyman in those days, and showed him to be many years in advance of the intelligence of the age when he flourished.

"Our business, however, is with Dr. Desaguliers, as

[5] Anderson's "Constitutions," ed. 1838, p. 110.

the chief agent in the revival of the ancient and honourable Institution of Freemasonry. He brought his private Lodges into such repute, and particularly that holden at the Goose and Gridiron, that it was placed at the head of the list of Lodges; and a law was unanimously agreed to, that the Grand Master should be proposed and elected there, before he became eligible for the appointment or the Grand Lodge. It was supposed at the time that he was the author of that famous paper which so thoroughly refuted the absurd allegations of Dr. Plot against the Order.[6] It is true I heard it applied to him several times, but he uniformly disavowed it, although it was generally believed that there was no other living Mason who could have done it so well.

"As a proof of his attention to discipline and propriety of conduct, I give you an anecdote. On a certain occasion, which I perfectly remember, I witnessed the initiation of a noble lord, which was performed with great solemnity by Dr. Desaguliers; and his lordship, though only a youth, appeared very much impressed with the ceremonial. But when the refreshment was introduced, and the severity of discipline somewhat relaxed, his lordship, according to a habit then very much in vogue, occasionally intermingled his conversation with an oath. This passed at first without notice, as the vice of swearing was common both to peer and peasant. Now you are aware, I dare say, that the opening formula in those days was, 'forbidding all cursing, swearing and whispering, all religious and political disputes, together with all irreligious and profane conversation, under no less penalty than what the by-laws shall prescribe, or a majority of the Brethren shall think proper to impose.' Profanity, therefore, was a violation of Lodge rules, although they were not remarkable at that period for their stringency; but the frequent repetition of the interdicted words, created an unfavourable sensation, which was not much to his lordship's credit. Bro. Desaguliers said nothing, how much soever he might be disgusted. At length his lordship appealed to the chair for the confirmation of some opinion.

" 'I say, doctor,—d—me, don't you hear,—I ask your

[6] "A Detection of Dr. Plot's Account of the Freemasons."—See "The Golden Remains," vol. iii., p. 31.

pardon for swearing!' After this had occurred more than once, Bro. Desaguliers rose from his chair with a dignity which he well knew how to assume when circumstances called for it, and said,—

"'My lord, you have repeatedly violated the rules of the Lodge by your unmeaning oaths; and more than this, you have taken some pains to associate me personally with your profanity, by your frequent appeals to the chair. Now, my lord, I assure you, in answer to those appeals, that if God Almighty does not hear you, I will not tell him!'

"The peer was silenced, the Brethren pleased, and I must say I was proud of the Master. Another time he said to a person of equal rank, who was an adept in the reigning vice, 'My lord, if you thought you were honouring God, you would not swear so furiously."[7]

I assure you, sir, that Masonry, as then practised, was a fascinating pursuit, although its technicalities were somewhat different from those of more modern times. For instance, what you call the Great Lights were denominated Furniture with us; the three *moveable* Lights were explained to mean the same as your three *lesser* ones, and were, indeed, the same in every particular; and we had three *fixed* Lights, or imaginary windows in the east,

[7] Do not let me incur the imputation of libelling the manners of the eighteenth century by the above anecdotes, for they are strictly true. Swearing was the besetting vice of the age; and Swift observes: "I cannot recollect, in this maturity of my age, how great a variety of oaths I have heard since I began to study the world, and to know men and manners.

"For nowadays men change their oaths
As often as they change their clothes."

And he gives a case in point. "I remember an officer who had returned from Flanders, sitting in a coffee-house near two gentlemen, whereof one was of the clergy, who were engaged in some discourse that savoured of learning. This officer thought fit to interpose; and professing to deliver the sentiments of his fraternity as well as his own, turned to the clergyman, and spoke in the following manner:—'D—n me, doctor, say what you will, the army is the only school for gentlemen. Do you think my Lord Marlbrough beat the French with Greek and Latin? D—n me, a scholar, when he comes into good company, what is he but an ass? D—n me, I would be glad, by G—, to see any of your scholars, with his nouns and his verbs, and his philosophy and trigonometry, what a figure he would make at a siege, or a blockade, d—n me!'"

west, and south, which are now, I believe, discarded. Again, Wisdom, Strength, and Beauty, according to ancient usages, were represented, not as at present by three pillars or orders of architecture, but by the two pillars of Solomon's Porch, and the Blazing Star, the left-hand pillar being the symbol of Wisdom, that on the right hand Strength, and the Blazing Star in the centre, Beauty.

"The discipline of Masonry was always, as far as I could learn, essentially democratic, and the revivalists took especial care to make no innovations in the original plan. All power was committed to the members of Lodges; and even, as we have just seen, the newly initiated entered apprentices had a vote in Grand Lodge. In the popular government of Athens, it was an unalterable law, that all the citizens in turn should be distributed in the courts of justice; and on the same principle the Brethren of each Lodge choose their Master *by ballot*, who appoints his officers from amongst themselves, and these are its representatives in the General Assembly or Grand Lodge. And, as in all the democratic institutions of antiquity, a senate was appointed to prepare all motions and proposals before they were submitted to the decision of the General Assembly of the people; so we have committees nominated for the same purpose.

The Chief Governor of the Craft is annually elected by the delegates from the Lodges; and in imitation of the practice at Thurium, the office was scarcely ever conferred twice on the same person, because if such a practice had been admitted, it was thought that other persons of equal worth would be thus excluded from an honour which ought to be equally accessible to all.

"The general laws of Masonry, however, were but loosely administered. It was provided 'that no Brother should belong to more than one Lodge within the bills of mortality;' but little notice was taken of that absurd law, for it was violated with impunity by D. G. Masters Desaguliers and Martin Clare, and many others. And, again, instances occasionally occurred where a Grand Master continued in office for more than a year; but the Society generally suffered by substituting the exception for the rule, as in the case of Lord Byron, who was Grand Master from 1747 to 1752, and never attended a Grand

Lodge between those periods, which caused Masonry tc languish for want of an active and attentive patron.

"Again, with reference to private Lodges; no candidate could be admitted as a Mason, nor could any one become a member without the scrutiny of the ballot box; and so imperative were the laws respecting secret votes, that it was provided 'that when any Brother is proposed to become a member, and any person to be made a Mason, if it appears, upon casting up the ballot, that they are rejected, no member or visiting Brother shall discover, by any means whatever, who those members were that opposed his election, under the penalty of such Brothers being forever expelled the Lodge (if members), and if a visiting Brother, of his being never more admitted as a visitor, or becoming a member; and, immediately after a negative passes on any person being proposed, the Master shall cause this law to be read, that no Brother may plead ignorance.

"After all—I speak from experience," the Square continued,—"the real exercise of power was generally in the hands of a few individuals, and sometimes of a single person, who, by his influence, was able to dispose of every motion at pleasure. This superiority was exercised in succession, during the eighteenth-century, by Brothers Desaguliers, Manningham, Dunckerley, Hesletine, and White.

"In these happy times—they were times of real enjoyment—labour was conducted with great seriousness; and perhaps you will be surprised, when I tell you—and if you are not, there are those in this latitudinarian age who *will*—that the Book of Common Prayer, according to the rites and ceremonies of the Church of England, was an established Lodge book, as it was considered to contain all the moral principles of the Order. And, in the examinations,[8] Brothers Desaguliers, Anderson, and Payne,

[8] In these early times there were no Lodge Lectures, (so called), but their places were supplied by "Examinations" of the same nature and tendency, but infinitely more brief and technical. I subjoin a few of these examination questions from the oldest formula in my possession, which I have reason to believe was used during the G. Mastership of Archbishop Chichely, in the reign of Henry VI. "Peace be here."—*A.* I hope there is. *Q.* What o'clock is it?—*A.* It is going to six, or going to twelve. *Q.* Are you very busy?—*A.* No. *Q.*

placed the following passages as unalterable landmarks to designate the religious character of the Order.

"'Why due east and west?

"'Because all Christian churches and chapels are, or ought to be so.

"'What does —— denote?

"'The Grand Architect of the Universe, or Him that was taken up to the topmost pinnacle of the Holy Temple.'

"During this period the Fraternity had signs, symbols and tokens of recognition, which are become obsolete, and I question whether your brightest Masons know that they were ever in existence. But, as the principal object of my Revelations is to make you acquainted with the sayings and doings of the Fraternity in the eighteenth century, I will reproduce a few of their peculiarities for your delectation. For instance: the symbols of the four Cardinal Virtues were delineated by an acute angle, variously disposed. Supposing you face the east, the angle symbolizing Temperance will point to the south (>). It was called a Guttural. Fortitude was denoted by a saltire or St. Andrew's Cross (×). This was the Pectoral. The symbol of Prudence was an acute angle, pointing towards the south-east (7), and was denominated a Manual; and Justice had its angle towards the north (<), and was called a Pedestal or Pedal.

"Many of our tokens of recognition, under the presidency of Sir Christopher Wren," said the Square, "were curious and significant; but they were discontinued about the middle of the century, and are now, I believe, entirely forgotten. As they are excluded from the present system of Masonry, there will be no impropriety in enumerating them. They were ten in number. 1. Ask how do you do. The Brothers present drink to each other. 2. Inquire in what Lodge they were initiated. 3.

Will you give or take?—*A.* Both; or which you please. *Q.* How go Squares?—*A.* Straight. *Q.* Are you rich or poor?—*A.* Neither. *Q.* Change me that?—*A.* I will. *Q.* In the name of the King and Holy Church, are you a Mason?—*A.* I am so taken to be. *Q.* What is a Mason?—*A.* A man begot by a man, born of a woman, brother to a King. *Q.* What is a fellow?—*A.* A companion of a Prince. *Q.* How shall I know you are a Freemason?—*A.* By signs, tokens, and points of my entry, &c., &c.

Take up a stone and ask what it smells of. 4. By making a square with the feet. 5. Strike with the right hand the inside of the fourth finger of the left thrice. 6. Stroke the two first fingers of the right hand thrice over the eyelids. 7. Take off your hat with two fingers and thumb. 8. Turn your glass downwards after drinking. 9. In shaking hands, touch the wrist three times with the forefinger. 10. Whisper—the Masters and Fellows of the Worshipful company greet you well.

"Refreshment was a genuine feast of reason and flow of soul. Punning, however it may be condemned and sneered at by the fastidious scholar of the nineteenth century, as being a worthless and contemptible pursuit, was extensively practised according to the category laid down by Swift and Sheridan; and many a witticism have I heard uttered, which created the most uproarious mirth; for loud laughter was not inconsistent with the manners of an age when high jinks, in a sister country, possessed attractions which led, as Sir Walter Scott expresses it, 'the best educated and gravest men in Scotland gradually on, from wisdom to mirth, and from mirth to extravagance.'

"One evening, as these choice spirits sat around the table after supper—and suppers, I must tell you, in those halcyon days, generally terminated the business of the Lodge,—Brothers Lamball, Sorell, Beloe, Ware, Madden, Villeneau, Noyes, Cordwell, Salt, Gofton, Senex, Hobby, Mountain, and a few others being present with the W. M., all celebrated Masons, whose names are well known to the Craft, Brother Lamball, who was an incorrigible laugher, and that in no very mild tone of voice, being tickled by some witty remark, indulged his propensity in a regular horse-laugh. Brother Madden rose with much gravity, and addressing the chair, said,—

" 'R. W. Sir, did you ever hear a peaceful *lamb bawl* (Lamball) so vociferously?'

" 'No,' said Bro. Desaguliers, 'but I've heard a *mad'un* (Madden) make an ugly *noise* (Noyes).'

" 'Oh,' rejoinded Bro. Sorell, 'let him ride his *hobby* (Hobby) quietly, his lungs will be no worse for *wear* (Ware).'

" 'Ah,' Bro. Ware snapped in, 'particularly if the colour of his hobby be *sorrel* (Sorell). Ha! ha! ha!'

" 'The lamb had better go to *sea next* (Senex) and then he may *bellow* (Beloe) against the roaring of the *salt* (Salt) waves as they dash upon the *mountain* (Mountain),' shouted Bro. Hobby.

" 'Well,' replied Bro. Lamball, 'I shall never quarrel with any Brother who holds the *cord well* (Cordwell—*cable tow*) for this or anything else, provided he does not call me a *villain O* (Villeneau). Ha! ha! ha!'

" 'I shall not, Brothers and Fellows,' responded Bro. Villeneau, 'question your good faith, although you carry on so briskly a *Pun—ic* war.'

" 'A truce to your wit,' Bro. Madden interposed. 'I *thirst* to mend my simile."

" 'Nay,' said the W. Master, 'if Bro. Madden *thirsts*, why there's an end of it.'

" 'Oh, ho!' echoed Bro. Noyes, 'if a *pun is meant*, I move that we inflict the usual *punishment*.'

" 'Why, then,' says the chair, "we will replenish the glasses, and try to quench Bro. Madden's *thirst* with a *toast*.'

"Now, all this may appear very puerile to you, sir, but I assure you it is a correct sample of the wit of the age, and formed the staple commodity of a lively conversation at taverns and clubs, which were then the resort of the highest nobility and gentry in the land."

CHAPTER II.

ATTACK AND DEFENCE.—DR. ANDERSON.

1722—1740.

"The end and moral purport of Masonry is to subdue our passions, not to do our own will; to make a daily progress in a laudable art; to promote morality, charity, good fellowship, good nature and humanity."—ANDERSON.

"She is the brightness of the everlasting LIGHT, the unspotted Mirror of the power of God, and the Image of his Goodness."—SOLOMON.

"In vain would Danvers with his wit
Our slow resentment raise;
What he and all mankind have writ,
But celebrates our praise.
His wit this only truth imparts,
That Masons have firm faithful hearts."
SECRETARY'S SONG.

THE success that attended the re-establishment of Masonry," my strange companion continued, "created a very great sensation, and raised up a host of opponents, who either envied the popularity of the Fraternity, or were desirous of diverting it into some other channel; for the uninitiated were piqued at the respect and attention which it attracted so universally; and more particularly when the nobility began to interest themselves in its promulgation. Many were the consultations which were held in the Lodge on this subject. Dr. Anderson, Grand Warden in 1723, had now become an active colleague of Grand Master Payne and Dr. Desaguliers, who held the office of Deputy Grand Master, and was installed into the chair of Hiram Abiff in the same year; and with the assistance of other eminent Craftsmen, it was formally deliberated which of three proceedings it would be most expedient to adopt in this emergency. Brothers Lamball, Noyes, and Villeneau were of opinion that the most dignified method of treating the absurd publications of those cowans who distributed their anonymous effusions through the country, would be by silent contempt; others proposed ridicule as the most efficient weapon; while Brothers Desaguliers and Anderson thought that the interests of Masonry would be more effectually served by some public and authorised statement of their proceedings,—by an avowal of the real objects of the Institution, and an explanation of the principles on which it is founded. And this course was finally agreed on.

"Accordingly, these two learned Brothers entered on the work with great zeal and assiduity. Bro. Desaguliers, in 1721, made a public profession of a Mason's faith, in an Oration, which was printed and distributed plentifully both in the metropolis and provinces;[1] in which he enlarged on the re-organization of the Grand Lodge, and stated *seriatim* the peculiar benefits, both moral and intellectual, which may be derived from a regular attendance on the duties of a Lodge. And Bro. Anderson published a well-written pamphlet on the rise and progress of the Order, and its application to the practical sciences.[2]

"In the same year, September 2nd, the Duke of Montague being Grand Master, and Bros. Villeneau and Morrice Grand Wardens, a Grand Lodge was holden at the King's Arms Tavern, St. Paul's Churchyard, at which Bros. Desaguliers, Payne, and Anderson, were ordered to examine the old Gothic Constitutions, and to digest the same in a new and better method; and at the succeeding Grand Lodge, in December, a committee of fourteen expert Brethren was appointed to revise the manuscript when completed, and to make their report accordingly. In pursuance of this order, our worthy Bros. Desaguliers, Payne, and Anderson, commenced their proceedings by searching for manuscripts and authorities in every part of the kingdom where they were supposed to exist. They

[1] An eloquent Oration about Masons and Masonry. Delivered 24th January, 1721.

[2] "On the Rise and Progress of Freemasonry." The Rev. James Anderson, D. D., was minister of the Scots Presbyterian Church, in Swallow-street, Piccadilly, and well known in those days amongst the people of that persuasion, resident in London, by the name of Bishop Anderson. He was editor of the "Diplomata Scotiæ, and Royal Genealogies;" a learned man, who unfortunately lost a considerable part of his property in the South Sea bubble of 1720. He had issue a son and a daughter, the latter of whom married an officer in the army.

communicated with many Lodges under the Constitutions both of York and London, and in most cases were successful in the search; yet a few instances unfortunately occurred where certain fastidious Brethren took the alarm, and committed many valuable manuscripts to the flames concerning ancient usages, regulations of Lodges, Charges, and secrets,—particularly one written by Nicholas Stone, who was Grand Warden to Inigo Jones,—lest they should fall into the hands of our friends, and be submitted to public inspection in a printed form.

"At one of our Lodges, when this design was in progress, Bro. Payne expressed his indignation at the superlative folly of those misguided Brothers in no measured language; and it was seriously debated whether it would not be expedient, for the purpose of preventing a repetition of the offence, to move a vote of censure against them in the ensuing Grand Lodge for contempt. This was decided in the negative, as it was considered to be inquisitorial, and alien to the general design of Masonry, for the Grand Lodge to interfere with the disposal of private property.

"It was agreed, however, at the same Lodge, that the R. W. Master, Dr. Desaguliers, should move 'that the ancient office of Stewards be revived to assist the Grand Wardens in preparing for the feast, and in other things appertaining to the annual general assembly of Masons. Bro. Desaguliers accordingly proposed the appointment of twelve Brethren for those purposes; and the motion was unanimously agreed to. At the same Grand Lodge it was reported by the committee that they had perused Bro. Anderson's manuscript containing the History of Masons, the Charges, Regulations, and Masters' Song; and, after some amendments, had approved of it. In consequence of this favourable report, the Brethren requested the Grand Master to order it to be published; and its appearance produced a wonderful impression on the public mind, and insured the triumph of the Craft.[3]

"At a Grand Lodge in the same year, the Duke of Buccleugh, G. M., seconded by Dr. Desaguliers, pro-

[3] "The Constitutions of Freemasonry; containing the History, Charges, Regulations, &c., of that most Ancient and Right Worshipful Fraternity. For the Use of the Lodges:" London, printed by Will. Hunter, for John Senex and John Hooke, 1723.

posed a scheme for raising a fund for the relief of distressed Brethren, and a committee was appointed on the spot to consider what would be the most effectual means of carrying it into execution. This was the origin of the Fund of Benevolence, for which the Fraternity are indebted to the amiable disposition, coupled with the indefatigable exertions of Brother Desaguliers; and the operation of the project proved so beneficial to the general interests of the Order, that it was publicly announced in Grand Lodge, that ingenious men of all faculties and stations, being now convinced that the cement of the Lodge was love and friendship, earnestly requested to join the Society, which soon flourished in harmony, reputation, and numbers. Noblemen and gentlemen of the highest rank—learned men, merchants, and clergymen, found in the Lodge a safe and pleasant relaxation from intense study, or the hurry of business, without any intermixture of politics and parties. New Lodges were constituted,[4] which the Grand Master and his deputy visited in person, and found in them a peaceful asylum, free from the turmoils and disputes by which all other societies were characterised and deformed.

"But I can assure you, sir, that the opponents of Freemasonry, although at their wit's end, were determined not to die without a struggle[5]. They circulated all manner of ridiculous reports about the practices of Masons in Tyled Lodges, which were thus commented on by a Brother who was a member of our Lodge, in an address to the R. W. M., when the subject was mooted in open Lodge. I cannot recollect the whole of his speech; but he said, amongst other acute observations, which excited the unfeigned applause of the members: 'Though we envy not the prosperity of any society, nor

[4] Not only in this country but on the continent, and these latter unfortunately became a fruitful source of innovation. In 1725, the Chevalier Ramsay introduced his Royal Arch and other manufactured Degrees into a Lodge, under an English warrant held in the Rue de Boucheries at Paris, which was presided over by Lord Derwentwater: where they were practised as legitimate Masonry. Ramsay tried to introduce them into this country, but failed. See more of this in the Hist. Landmarks, vol. ii., Lect. xxv., Part I., p. 32.

[5] They published about this time, "Observations and Critical Remarks on the new Constitutions of the F. M., written by James Anderson, etc." London, 1725.

meddle with their transactions and characters, we have not met with such fair treatment from others; nay, even those that never had an opportunity of obtaining any certain knowledge of us, have run implicitly with the cry, and, without fear or wit, have vented their spleen in accusing and condemning us unheard, untried; while we, innocent and secure within, laugh only at their gross ignorance and impotent malice. Have not people in former ages, as well as now, alleged that Freemasons in their Lodges raise the devil in a circle, and when they have done with him, that they lay him again with a noise or a hush, as they please? How have some of our maligners diverted themselves with the wild story of an old woman between the rounds of a ladder! Others will swear to the cook's red-hot iron or salamander for marking an indelible character on the new-made Mason, in order to give him the faculty of taciturnity. Sure such blades will beware of coming through the fingers of the Freemasons?'

"Not contented with having circulated these *viva voce* calumnies," the Square continued, "pamphlets began to fly about in every form, denouncing the proceedings of Masonry;[6] and several newspapers of the day joined in

[6] In 1724, a year after the appearance of the new Book of Constitutions, we have the following pretended revelation of its secrets:— "The Grand Mystery of Free-Masons discovered; wherein are the several Questions put to them at their Meetings and Installations: as also their Oath, Health, Signs, and Points to know each other by. As they were found in the custody of a Free-Mason who dyed suddenly; and now published for the Information of the Publick:" London, printed for J. Payne, near Stationers' Hall. Fòlio. Price Sixpence. To the second edition were annexed "Two Letters to a Friend." The first concerning the Society of Freemasons; the second giving an account of the Gormagons. London, printed for A Moore, 1725. Folio. Price One Shilling. The Fraternity will thank me for presenting them with the introduction to this catch-penny, as it will show how coarsely the enemies of Masonry endeavoured to accomplish their ends. "There was a man at Louvaine who proclaimed that he had, with great toil and difficulty, overcome and tamed, and was ready at his booth to show, at the rate of six stivers a-piece, that most hideous and voracious monster, the common disturber of mankind, especially in their adversity. People flocked from all parts to see this monster. They went in at the fore door, and after they had seen the creature, went out at the back door, where they were asked whether the monster were worth seeing? But as they had, at their admittance, promised to keep the secret, they answered that it was a very wonderful creature. By some accident, however, it was divulged that this wonderful creature was a Louse!!!"

the cry, for it contributed materially to the sale of the sheet. Are you aware, sir, what very poor productions these periodicals were? Do not speak! Well, then, I'll tell you. They consisted of two leaves of pot paper, and were dreadfully stupid; barren, sir, very barren of news; and, therefore, the present popularity of Masonry was a god-send; and the writers did not fail to improve the occasion by inventing any sort of nonsense, which they nicknamed 'the doings of Masonry in secret Lodges;' and the more ridiculous the imputation, the greater was the demand for the paper.[7] Danvers, a writer in the 'Craftsman,' so far exceeded his fellow-journalists in absurdity, as to have written a prosy article for the purpose of proving that those who hanged Capt. Porteous, of Edinburgh, were all Freemasons, because they kept their own secrets;[8] and, therefore, the sapient writer concluded the perpetrators must be Masons, inasmuch as they were never found out.[9]

"The Fraternity were much amused with these abortive attempts to prejudice them in public opinion; and I have heard them sing the Sword Bearer's Song, as a glee for three voices, and full chorus, with shouts of laughter and applause.[10] But the Brethren took no

[7] Some of these amusing periodicals were called, "The Daily Post," "The British Plaindealer," "The Daily Journal," "The Post Boy," in which it is asserted that "The Freemasons put out a sham discovery to invalidate their revelations; but the only genuine discovery is in 'The Post Boy' and 'The Flying Post.'"

[8] This circumstance is referred to in our motto.

[9] "Craftsman," 16th April, 1736, No. 563. And see Sir Walter Scott's "Heart of Midlothian."

[10] This song being read with the above explanation in view, will be seen in a new and interesting light.

"To all who Masonry despise,
This counsel I bestow:
Don't ridicule, if you are wise,
A secret you don't know.
Yourselves you banter, but not it—
You show your spleen, but not your wit.

"Inspiring virtue by our rules,
And in ourselves secure,
We have compassion for those fools
Who think our acts impure.
We know from ignorance proceeds
Such mean opinion of our deeds.

"If union and sincerity
Have a pretence to please,
We Brothers of Freemasonry
Lay justly claim to these.

official notice of them, as they were considered too contemptible to merit their serious attention. Nor did they esteem the philippic of Dean Swift worthy of any reply, as it was evidently written for a satirical purpose.[11]

"At length, however, these attacks assumed a form which it was thought necessary to counteract in some public manner. One gentleman (for they were mostly anonymous) wrote a pamphlet containing a critical review of the History of Masonry;[12] another printed what he called an account of the ceremonies of initiation,[13] which brought out a third, called the Freemason's

To State disptutes we ne'er give birth;
Our motto friendship is, and mirth.

"Then let us laugh, since we've imposed
On those who make a pother,
And cry, 'The secret is disclosed
By some false-hearted Brother.'
The mighty secret's gained, they boast,
From 'Post Boy' and from 'Flying Post.'"

[11] As may be understood from the following specimen:—"As to the secret words and signals used among Masons," he says, "it is to be observed, that in the Hebrew alphabet there are four pair of letters, of which each pair are so like that, at the first view, they seem to be the same. Beth (ב) and Caph (כ), Gimel (ג) and Nun (נ), Cheth (ח) and Thau (ת), Daleth (ד) and Resch (ר); and on these depend all their signals and gripes. Cheth and Thau are shaped like two standing gallowses of two legs each; when two Masons accost each other, one cries Cheth, and the other answers Thau, signifying that they would sooner be hanged on the gallows than divulge the secret. Then again, Beth and Caph are each like a gallows lying on one of the side posts, and when used as above, imply this pious prayer: "May all who reveal the secret hang upon the gallows till it fall down.' This is their Master secret, generally called, the Great Word. Daleth and Resch are like two half gallowses, or a gallows cut in two at the cross stick at the top, by which, when pronounced, they intimate to each other that they would rather be half hanged than name either word or signal before any other but a Brother so as to be understood. When one says Gimel, the other says Nun; then the first again, joining both letters together, repeats three times Gimel Nun, Gimel Nun, Gimel Nun; by which they mean that they are united as one in interests, secrecy, and affection."

[12] "Observations and Critical Remarks on the New Constitutions of Freemasonry."

[13] "The Secret History of Freemasonry, being an accidental Discovery of the Ceremonies made use of in the several Lodges, upon the Admittance of a Brother as a Free and Accepted Mason," &c.; with the Charge, Oath, and private Articles given to him at the time of his admission. Printed from the old original Record of the Society; with some observations, reflections, and critical Remarks

Accusation and Defence, which, in fact, had already appeared in the 'Post Boy;'[14] and in 1726 an oration, in which these attacks were alluded to, was delivered by the Junior Grand Warden of the York Masons, in the presence of Charles Bathurst, Esq., the Grand Master, which was ordered to be printed.[15] A speech was also published as delivered at Carmarthen in 1728;[16] and another writer thus speaks of some objections which were made against the Craft:—'Others complain that the Masons continue too long in the Lodge, spending their money to the hurt of their families, and come home too late—nay, sometimes intoxicated with liquor! But they have no occasion to drink much in Lodge hours, which are not long; and when the Lodge is closed (always in good time) any Brother may go home when he pleases: so that if any stay longer, and become intoxicated, it is at their own cost, not as Masons, but as other imprudent men do, for which the Fraternity is not accountable; and the expense of a Lodge is not so great as that of a private club. Some observing that Masons are not more religious, nor more knowing, than other men, are astonished at what they can be conversant about in Lodge hours! but though a Lodge is not a school of divinity, the Brethren are taught the great lessons of religion, morality, humanity, and friendship; to abhor persecution, and to be peaceable subjects under the civil government wherever they reside; and as for their know-

on the new Constitution Book of the Free Masons, written by James Anderson, A. M., and dedicated to the Duke of Montague by J. Desaguliers, LL. D., Deputy Grand Master. With a short Dictionary of private signs and signals. The second edition. London, printed for Sam. Briscoe, at the Bell-Savage, 1725.

[14] "The Freemasons' Accusation and Defence, in Six genuine Letters between a Gentleman in the Country and his Son, a Student in the Temple, wherein the whole affair of Masonry is fairly debated, and all the Arguments for and against that Fraternity are curiously and impartially handled." London, Peele and Blandford, 1726.

[15] "A Speech delivered to the Worshipful and Ancient Society of Free and Accepted Masons, at a Grand Lodge held at Merchant's Hall, in the City of York, on St. Thomas's Day, December 27, 1726. The Right Worshipful Charles Bathurst, Esq., Grand Master. By the Junior Grand Warden." London, 1729.

[16] "A Speech delivered at a Lodge held at the Carpenter's Arms, the 31st December, 1728, by Edw. Oakley, late Prov. Senior Grand Warden in Carmarthen."

ledge, they claim as large a share of it as other men in their situation.' Beyond these fugitive attempts, I did not hear that anything was done at present to rebut the slanders which were so freely circulated to the prejudice of the Craft.

"At length, in 1730, a man of the name of Prichard, an unprincipled and needy Brother, concocted a book which contained a great deal of plausible matter, mingled with a few grains of truth, which he published under the name of 'Masonry Dissected,'[17] and impudently proclaimed in his dedication that it was intended for the information of the Craft.[18] And to show his learning, he

[17] "Masonry Dissected; being a Universal and Genuine Description of all its Branches, from the Original to this Present Time: as it is delivered in the constituted regular Lodges, both in City and Country, according to the several Degrees of Admission; giving an impartial Account of their regular Proceedings in initiating their New Members in the whole Three Degrees of Masonry, viz., I. Entered Prentice; II. Fellow Craft; III. Master. To which is added, The Author's Vindication of Himself. By Samuel Prichard, late Member of a constituted Lodge. London, 1730. Fourth edition, London, J. Wilford, 1731. Eighth edition, London, J. Thorbuck, 1737. Thirteenth edition, London, Chandler, 1774. Twenty-first edition, London, Byfield and Hawkesworth, 1787. It was translated into Dutch, French, and German. The former had this title:—"Prichard het Collegie der Vrije-Metselaars ontledt, of een algemeene en opregte Beschrijving van alle derzelves Soorten, van desselfs Oorsprong tot op de Jegenwoordige Tyd." Utrecht, 1734. The French edition had this title:—"La Réception mysterieuse de la célèbre Societe des Francs-Maçons, contenant une Relation générale et sincere de leurs Cérémonies. Par Samuel Prichard, ci devant Membre d'une Chamber de la meme Confrairie. Traduite de l'Anglais éclaircie par des Remarques critiques, suivie de quelques autres Pieces curieuses, relatives à la Grande Bretagne, avec des Observations Historiques et Geographiques." A Londres par la Compagnie des Libraries, 1737. And the German edition was thus announced:—"Die zunft der freien maurer, oder, allgemeine und aufrichtige Beschreibung aller derselben Gattungen, von ihrem Ursprunge bis auf jetzige zeit. Als em Unpartheyischer Bericht ihrer Handlungen bei Aunehm und Einweihung ihrer neuen Gleieder, und den drei unterschiedenen Stuffen derer Mäurer. Ans Licht gegeben durch Samuel Prichard, vormaligen Glied einer Zunfft Kammer. Ans der fünften Englishchen Auflage übersetzt 1736. Analysirt in den Actis Hist. Eccles. 1738, im Anhange von 1736."

[18] I subjoin this precious dedication. "To the Worshipful and Honourable Fraternity of Free and Accepted Masons. Brethren and Fellows.—If the following sheets, done without partiality, gain the universal applause of so worthy a society, I doubt not but their general character will be diffused and esteemed among the remaining

asserted in his preface that 'from the accepted Masons sprang the real Masons, from both sprang the Gormagons, whose Grand Master, the Polgi, deduces his original from the Chinese, whose writings, if to be credited, maintained the hypothesis of the Pre-Adamites, and consequently must be more antique than Masonry! The most free and open society is that of the Grand Kaiheber, which consists of a select company of responsible people, whose chief discourse is concerning trade and business, and promoting mutual friendship without compulsion or restriction.' !!! [19]

"What do you think of this, sir? Was not this information truly wonderful? The public thought so. They said—'It must be this—it can be nothing else; it is, as we always supposed, a whimsical cheat, supported by great names to seduce fools, who, once gulled out of their money, keep the fraud secret to draw in others.' And accordingly the book had an enormous and rapid sale, for four editions were called for in the first year of its publication, so open is poor John Bull to imposition. Its success stimulated others to follow in the same track, and three or four pretended revelations of Masonic secrets issued from the press simultaneously.[20]

"It was now considered necessary to disabuse the public mind; and for this purpose Dr. Anderson was directed by the Grand Lodge in 1738 to prepare a defence of the Order against the calumnies which had been so industriously circulated to its prejudice.. Several pamphlets had already appeared, as the Oration of the celebrated Martin Clare, J. G. W., in 1735, before the Grand Lodge;[21] the 'Freemasons' Pocket Companion,' by Dr.

polite part of mankind; which I hope will give entire satisfaction to all lovers of truth; and I shall remain, with all humble submission, the Fraternity's most obedient humble servant, Sam. Prichard."

[19] There is a degree or society of this nature in the United States, called the Secret Monitor, which was established for the purpose of enabling its members to assist each other in their commercial transactions.

[20] 1. "The Secrets of Masonry made known to all Men, by S. P., late member of a constituted Lodge. To which is added, The Author's Vindication of Himself." London, Thorbuck, 1737. 2. "The Mystery of Masonry." London, Thorbuck, 1737. 3. "The Mysterious Receptions of the celebrated Society of Freemasons; containing a true Account of their Ceremonies." London, 1737

[21] "An Address made to the Body of Free and Accepted Masons.

Smith;[22] and the 'Freemasons' Vade Mecum;' but this latter book was condemned by the Grand Lodge as 'a piratical silly production, done without leave,' and the Brethren were warned not to use it, nor encourage the sale thereof.

"In the meanwhile, Dr. Anderson wrote his celebrated Defence of Masonry, in which he treated the work of Prichard with great consideration.[23] He took his stand on high ground—gave his adversary every fair and reasonable advantage, by assuming that if all he had advanced were correct, still Masonry would be an admirable institution, and answered his book *seriatim* like a gentleman and a scholar. When the Defence came out, and the subject was canvassed in the Lodge, some thought he had conducted the dispute with greater mildness than the fellow deserved; but Brother Anderson contended—and truly, as I thought at the time—that 'it would be giving our opponents too serious an advantage to treat their productions, how absurd soever they might be, either with flippancy or severity.'

"He commenced the Defence by conceding certain points which were thought to be discreditable to the Order. 'Let,' says he, 'for once, this dissection contain all the secrets of Freemasonry; admit that every word of it is genuine and literally true, yet, under all these concessions—under all disadvantages and prejudices whatever, I cannot but still believe there have been impositions upon mankind more ridiculous, and that many have been drawn into a society more pernicious.' He then proceeded step by step to prove its manifold advantages; and admitting that 'although Masonry has in some circumstances declined from its original purity, by running in muddy streams, and as it were under ground, yet notwithstanding the great rust it may have contracted, and the forbidding light in which it is placed by the Dissector, there is still much of the old fabric remaining; the essential pillars of the building may be

assembled at a Quarterly Communication, holden near Temple Bar, December, 11, 1735." Translated into French and German.

22 "The Freemasons' Pocket Companion, by W. Smith, D. D." Thorbuck, London, 1736.

23 A Defence of Masonry, occasioned by a pamphlet called Masonry Dissected, by James Anderson, D. D. 1730.

discovered through the rubbish, though the superstructure be overrun with moss and ivy, and the stones by length of time disjointed. And, therefore, as the bust of an old hero is of great value among the curious, though it has lost an eye, the nose, or the right hand, so Masonry, with all its blemishes and misfortunes, instead of appearing ridiculous, ought, in my humble opinion, to be received with some candour and esteem, from the veneration to its antiquity.'

"The effect of this Defence was electrical. It was universally read and admired; and though the attacks on Masonry were still continued,—for while the cowan was willing to purchase, false Brethren would always be found who were ready to sell; they attracted the attention of none but the very lowest classes of the people. One of the most eminent members of the Craft, on a visit at our Lodge, paid Dr. Anderson a very high compliment when proposing the thanks of the Fraternity for the service he had rendered to Masonry by the publication of the Defence. He said—'The Freemasons are much obliged to the generous intention of the unbiassed Author of the Defence; though some think the ingenious Defender has spent too much fine learning and reasoning upon the foolish Dissection that is justly despised by the Fraternity, as much as the other pretended discoveries of their secrets in public newspapers and pasquils, all of a sort, for all of them put together do not discover the profound and sublime things of old Masonry; nor can any man, not a Mason, make use of those incoherent smatterings (interspersed with ignorant nonsense and gross falsities) among bright Brothers, for any purpose but to be laughed at; our communications being of a quite different sort.' The motion of thanks, as you may suppose, was carried by acclamation.

"I have said more about this Defence," continued my extraordinary companion, "than may be necessary on any future publication, because it constitutes the first attempt on record to explain the real working of the machinery of the Order.[24] Poor Prichard had the auda-

[24] The curious reader may find the entire Essay in the first volume of "The Golden Remains," p. 47; and it is of such sterling excellence as will amply repay a diligent perusal.

city to publish a reply,[25] but he soon found, by the stinted sale of his book compared with the rapid demand for his former production, that Dr. Anderson had spoiled his trade, and that no one now gave him credit for veracity. He had confessed himself to be a perjured man; and it proved fatal to his reputation. From being a whale among the minnows, he dwindled into a minnow among the whales; and having once sunk into contempt and insignificance, he was heard of no more.

"Dr. Anderson's Defence was followed by an anonymous work, called 'The Beginning and First Foundation of the most worthy Craft of Freemasonry,' published in 1739; and a French writer, whose book was translated into English, although not very complimentary to the Order in general, admits 'that the prince and the magistrate here lose nothing of that homage due from their inferiors. Nothing is banished but discord and quarrelling, which, if one moment raises, the next extinguishes, and this principle of union and society with which each Brother is impressed, becomes the principle of peace and quietness, which he preserves without any alteration until the time when he is required to throw it off, only for the purpose of rendering it more universal and more durable. What I have just said of the calmness and tranquillity which reigns in the Order of Freemasons will, without doubt, appear to some an incomprehensible paradox; but I will proceed, and their surprise will increase, when they know that this union is carried to such a pitch, that if two Masons, without knowing each other, should quarrel and fight with the sword,—upon an intimation that they were both Masons, the fury and rage which before animated the combatants, would in an instant give place to the most sincere reconciliation, and the most tender friendship; and this, if any signs should escape either of them, so that his adversary should only suspect him to be a member of the same Order with himself, his anger would instantly cease, and, upon an explanation, a thousand embraces and expressions of regard would quench the boiling fury, which but a moment before had consigned one or both to sure destruction.'

25 "Masonry further Dissected." London, 1738.

"The Book of Constitutions becoming scarce in the year 1737, Dr. Anderson, who had assisted in the former work, prayed for the favour of reprinting it, with the transactions of the Society down to the year 1738. This being complied with, and the copy delivered, the management of it at the press was entrusted to him. The manuscript being approved, the following Resolution was unanimously agreed to:—

"Whereas, at the Grand Lodge, on 24th February, 1734–5, the Earl of Crauford, Grand Master, being in the Chair, Bro. James Anderson, D.D., having represented that a new Book of Constitutions was become necessary, and that he had prepared materials for it, the Grand Master and the Lodge ordered him to lay the same before the present and former Grand Officers, as in the Grand Lodge Book. And our said Bro. Anderson, having submitted his manuscript to the perusal of some former Grand Officers, particularly our noble Bro. Richmond, and our Bros. Desaguliers, Cowper, Payne, and others, who, after making some corrections, have signified their approbation, and having next, according to the foresaid order, committed his manuscript to the perusal of the present Grand Officers, who, having also reviewed and corrected it, have declared their approbation of it to the Grand Lodge assembled in ample form on the 25th of January, 1737–8; the Grand Lodge then agreed to order our said Bro. Anderson to print and publish the said manuscript or new Book of Constitutions. And it is hereby approved and recommended as the only Book of Constitutions, for the use of the Lodges of the Free and Accepted Masons, by the said Grand Lodge, on the said 25th January, 1737–8, in the vulgar year of Masonry, 5737–8.[26]

[26] Anderson, in his Dedication to the Prince of Wales, says, "Your Royal Highness well knows that our Fraternity has been often patronised by royal persons in former ages, whereby architecture early obtained the title of the 'Royal Art;' and the Freemasons have always endeavoured to deserve that patronage by their loyalty. For we meddle not with affairs of State in our Lodges, nor with any thing that may give outrage to civil magistrates, that may break the harmony of our own communications, or that may weaken the cement of the Lodge. And whatever are our different opinions in other things, leaving all men to the liberty of conscience, as Masons we harmoniously agree in the noble science and the royal art, in the

"About this time I had the high honour of witnessing some regal initiations. His Royal Highness Francis Stephen, Duke of Lorrain, received the two first degrees of Masonry at the Hague, by virtue of a deputation from Lord Lovel, G.M., for a Lodge there, of which Dr. Desaguliers was the Master; and subsequently he was raised to the third degree, along with his Grace the Duke of Newcastle, at Houghton Hall, in Norfolk, the seat of Sir Robert Walpole. This was in 1731. A few years later, viz., on the 15th November, 1737, an occasional Lodge was opened at Kew, Dr. Desaguliers being the Master, and Bros. Gofton and King the Wardens, where his Royal Highness Frederick, Prince of Wales, received the two first degrees, and in due time was raised to the degree of a Master Mason in the same place, and by the same Officers, although it was not usual to raise a Brother in a private Lodge, nor in Grand Lodge, till he was elected to the Chair. The Grand Master, however, had the power of dispensing with this rule, and also of making Masons when and where he pleased.

"According to an apocryphal legend of Masonry, which it is as well to know, although impracticable in later times, the ancient Masons were enjoined to initiate their candidates at the *third*, *sixth*, and *ninth* hours only; for which custom they assigned these reasons: that it was at the *third* hour of the day that the Holy Ghost descended on the Apostles at the Pentecost;[27] at the *sixth* hour Peter went up to the house-top to offer his prayers to God, when he was favoured with a celestial vision;[28] and at the *ninth* hour Peter and John went to the Temple for the same purpose, and then and there healed a man who had been lame from his mother's womb.[29]

"Dr. Desaguliers having been a Fellow of the Royal Society for some years, the energies of his mind were now directed to other pursuits, and he resigned the Chair as Master of the Lodge; in consequnce of which your humble servant, being a moveable jewel, fell into other hands. The Doctor made many important improve-

social virtues, in being true and faithful, and in avoiding what may give offence to any powers round the globe, under whom we can peaceably assemble in *ample form*."

[27] Acts ii., 1. [28] Ibid. x., 9. [29] Ibid. iii., 1.

ments in mechanics and communicated some curious papers, which are printed in the Philosophical Transactions. He published a valuable course of Experimental Philosophy in two volumes, 4to., and contributed greatly to the scientific knowledge of the age in which he lived.[30]

"The career of this worthy Brother was marked by many essential benefits to Masonry. He established several new Lodges, and based them on such sound principles, that one of them at least is in existence at this very day. The Strong Man Lodge was numbered 68 in the lists of 1738, 1764, and 1767, and was established according to the former authorities, 2nd February 1733, and by the latter, February 17th, 1734.[31] Its origin is somewhat extraordinary, and worth hearing.

[30] The following sketch of this eminent Mason's life may be interesting. He was the son of a French Protestant clergyman, and born at Rochelle on the 12th March, 1683. His father came to England while he was an infant, and having taught him the classics, sent him to finish his education at Christ Church, in Oxford. In 1702 he was so far distinguished as to be elected, on the retirement of Dr. Keil, to read courses of experimental philosophy in Hart Hall. He settled in Westminster on his marriage in 1712, and continued his philosophical lectures there. Two years later he was named a F. R. S., to which he contributed a great number of papers on scientific subjects. About this time we find him flourishing under the patronage of the Duke of Chandos, who presented to him the living of Edgware; and he was appointed chaplain to H. R. H. Frederick Prince of Wales. After having acquired a world-wide reputation as a zealous and talented Mason, he removed to lodgings over the great piazza in Covent Garden, and carried on his lectures till his death in 1749. He was a member of several foreign literary societies, and a corresponding member of the Royal Academy of Sciences at Paris. He obtained from many competitors the Prize given by the King of France for the best treatise on Electricity. He published a "Course of Experimental Philosophy," 2 vols. 4to.; and an edition of "Gregory's Elements of Catoptrics and Dioptrics," with an Appendix, containing an account of Reflecting Telescopes. 8vo.

[31] It appears by the Records of Grand Lodge, that a warrant, bearing date the 2nd day of February, 1734, was issued under the seal of Masonry, enabling certain Brethren therein named to open and hold a Lodge of Freemasons at the Ship Coffee House, Hermitage Bridge, London, to be called "The Strong Man Lodge," which was numbered 110; but, by the general closing up of the list of Lodges in the year 1740, it became No. 98. By the closing up of the list of Lodges in the year 1756, it became 68. In the year 1770 the said Lodge became 57. By the closing up of the list of Lodges in the year 1781, it became No. 44; and by the same process in the

"About the year 1730, or it might be a year or two later, the attention of Brother Desaguliers was attracted by reports of the great strength and muscular power of a man named Thomas Topham, who kept the Red Lion public-house, nearly opposite the old hospital of St. Luke, and was called, by way of eminence, the STRONG MAN. It appears that he settled down in this locality, from its vicinity to the famous ring in Moorfields, where athletic exercises were performed,—such as boxing, wrestling, sword-play, and cudgelling, under the superintendence of Old Vinegar, whom I remember well. As was his name so was his nature. A most truculent-looking fellow, with a flat nose, swelled cheeks, low forehead, broad across the back, shoulder-of-mutton-fists, and the strength of a giant; and yet Topham found no difficulty in lowering his pride; and he overthrew him in the ring as if he had been made of cork, amidst the shouts and halloos of the fancy, and to the supreme delight of those whom the potency of Old Vinegar had hitherto forced to succumb.

"The first public feat which Bro. Desaguliers saw Topham perform for the purpose of actually testing his strength was this. A powerful cart-horse was harnessed and placed on one side of the low wall which then divided the upper from the lower Moorfields, and Topham on the other. Taking hold of the end of the traces, the fellow planted his feet firmly against the wall, and told the spectators to flog the horse, which they did, without producing any effect; for the biped proved to be the most powerful animal of the two. He afterwards pulled against a pair of horses; and Dr. Desaguliers was firmly persuaded that 'if placed in a proper position, he would have sustained the efforts of four horses, without the least inconvenience.' I have witnessed several other instances of his personal strength," continued the Square, "but the repetition of them will not be interesting to you.

"Poor Topham! With all his strength he was as

year 1792, it became No. 41. In consequence of the union of the two Fraternities of Freemasons on the 27th day of December, 1813, it became, and is now registered in the books of the United Grand Lodge, No. 61; and meets at the Swan Tavern, Mansel-street. Goodman's Fields, London.

meek as a lamb, and a perfect slave at home, for his termagant helpmate led him a very unquiet life; and, in the end, ruined him, and forced him from his dwelling. It was at this point of time that Dr. Desaguliers became his friend and patron; for, as a Professor of Experimental Philosophy, he took great interest in his performances. He placed him in another public-house at the Hermitage, with the sign of the Ship; and, after making him a Mason, established a Lodge at his house as a means of increasing his business by the introduction of his friends. And, I must say, the Lodge was well conducted, with Bro. Desaguliers at its head as the Master; and increased rapidly in numbers and respectability. Its cognizance was the redoubtable Thomas Topham matching his strength against that of a horse, with his feet propped by the fragment of a wall; and its name, THE STRONG MAN LODGE. Topham, however, unfortunately took to drinking, and the business fell into other hands; but the Lodge prospered, and was considered a crack establishment when the poor fellow and his patron were no more."

CHAPTER III.

PROCESSIONS.—MARTIN CLARE, A. M.

1740—1747.

"Regard not who it is that speaketh, but weigh only what is spoken."—HOOKER.

"All such things as are either secret or manifest, them I know." —SOLOMON.

"You shall understand, my dear friends, that amongst the excellent acts of that king, one above all hath the pre-eminence. It was the erection and institution of an Order, or Society, which we call Solomon's House, the noblest foundation (as we think) that ever was upon earth, and the lantern of this kingdom. It is dedicated to the study of the works and creatures of God."—LORD BACON.

"THE Brother, whose property I had now become," continued the Square, "was Master of the Lodge No. 2, at the Horn Tavern, New Palace Yard, Westminster, the old Lodge which formerly met at the Rummer and Grapes, and he was an expert ruler. He ——." (Here the Square communicated several particulars about the method of conducting a Lodge in those times, which, though very curious and important, I am bound to hold sacred, as I cannot make them public without incurring the penalty of the unfortunate Prichard. It appears that the Master was a strict disciplinarian, and, under his instructions, the Brethren made a rapid progress in the knowledge of Masonry, although he entertained some absurdities which he communicated only to a few select Brothers in private; one of which, not being of any great importance to Masonry, I may mention without violating a sacred pledge. For instance, he taught them that Adam, our first parent, constructed a stone in the form of an oblong square, or double cube, and placed it over the grave of of his beloved son Abel, who had been slain by his brother, inscribed with the history of the transaction in hieroglyphical characters; and this, he told them, was the origin of the same custom amongst the Egyptians! I had great difficulty here to restrain myself from uttering an exclamation. The principal symbol which it contained, was the Mark placed on the forehead of Cain by the finger of God, viz., the TAU CROSS,—the emblem of life. And thus this protective landmark was communicated to mankind, that no one might violate the divine command by depriving him of existence. And our imaginative Master was bold enough to add, that this mark was the talisman used by Moses to protect the Israelites from the devastations of the destroying angel in the wilderness of Arabia.)

"Although the Master was inflexibly rigid," my companion continued, "in the discharge of his duty, and in exacting from others the same rule of conduct which he imposed on himself, yet, when the Lodge was closed, and supper placed on the table—hey presto!—he was quite another man. No one was more jocose or full of spirits than he was. He sang a good song, cracked his joke, and was the life of the company. No prosy speeches would he allow, for he said time was precious at that hour of the night, and he was determined to make the most of it. As an agreeable relaxation, he introduced an amusement called 'crambo,' a practice which contributed to the merriment of the Lodge, during the hours appropriated to refreshment, for many years. You don't know what it is? Then I'll tell you. The Master starts the game with a line of poetry, ending with some rhyme which is capable of considerable extension; and each Brother, under a fine—which in those days was an extra glass of punch—was obliged to improvise a corresponding verse in the same measure, and terminating in the same jingle. For instance, to give you an example in point; one evening, after supper, the Brethren were in a merry cue, and the game commenced by an observation of the Master respecting a young lady of good fortune, a friend of his, whom he was afraid was about to sacrifice herself to a fellow who had no real regard for anything but her money; and was consulting with his friends what they would advise as the most effectual means of extricating her from his toils, when the following *crambonian* category was elicited amidst roars of laughter:—

"'His name's Mr. Power,' says the Master;

"'Then tell Mr. Power,' Dr. Anderson began,

"'That she has no dower,' chimed in Bro. Villeneau;

"'And he'll speedily cower,' Bro. Noyes added;

"'And droop like a flower,' said Bro. Gofton;

"'His forehead will lower,' Bro. Morrice snapped in;

"'And he'll look very sour,' shouted Bro. Lamball, with a vociferous ha! ha! ha!—in which the whole company participated with a hearty good-will.

"'He'll forsake her snug bower,' resumed Bro. De Vaux;

"'And he'll grin, gape, and glower,' said Bro. Revis, the Grand Secretary;

"'He'll be off in an hour,' added Bro. Dr. Schomberg;

"'And away he will scour,' replied Bro. Shergold;

"'Defying her power,' lisped Bro. Sir J. Mansell, in his very mild tone of voice; and 'Well done, Mansell,—ha! ha! ha!' made the glasses on the supper-table jingle with the concussion.[1]

"The Master was fond of a song, as I have already observed," my informant continued; "and, as hard drinking was the vice of the times, the following chorus was a favourite with the Lodge:—

"He that will not merry merry be,
With a generous bowl and a toast,
May he in Bridewell be shut up,
And fast bound to a post.
Let him be merry merry there,
And we'll be merry merry here;
For who does know where we shall go,
To be merry another year![2]

[1] In the old MS. from which much of the above "Revelations" has been extracted, my late father, the Rev. S. Oliver, says, that when a young man he was acquainted with an aged Mason, who was initiated in the year 1740, and he told him that this amusement was common in the Lodges of that period. And he gives a few specimens, amongst which is the above. I subjoin a crambo by Dr. Sheridan, the friend of Swift, under date of 1736, which is somewhat better:—

"Our river is dry,
And fiery the sky:
I fret and I fry,
Just ready to die;
O, where shall I fly,
From Phœbus's eye?
In bed when I lie,
I soak like a pie;
And I sweat, and I sweat,
Like a hog in a sty!"

The French Bouts Rimés were something similar to this.

[2] The whole song may be found in the Glasgow edition of "The Freemason's Pocket Companion," 1771

"Thus the song, the toast, the jest, and merry laugh passed away the time till midnight was announced from the neighbouring church clock; and then hats, swords, and canes were in requisition, for the party was broken up at once by the Master's 'right word and point of a Mason—Adieu.' The Lodge prospered under his judicious management.

"While embodying these transactions in your imagination, I must caution you," said the Master's Jewel, which I found to be rather facetiously inclined, "not to raise up before your mind's eye an assembly of Brethren habited in the costume to which you have been habituated; for if you, sir, in your present dress, had made your appearance among them, you would have created shouts of more extatic laughter than either punning or crambo. No, sir, you must see them as they actually were, if you would form a true idea of the scene. They wore square-cut coats and long-flapped waistcoats with pockets in them; the coats had long hanging cuffs, and the skirts were stiffened out with buckram and wire, to show the hilt of the sword. They had lace neckcloths and ruffles; blue or red silk stockings, with gold or silver clocks, drawn over the breeches to meet the pocket-flaps of the waistcoat, and gartered below the knee; square-toed and short-quartered shoes, with high red heels and small silver buckles. Then they had on various kinds of wigs, and small three-cornered hats laced with gold or silver, and trimmed with feathers; all formal, clean, and spruce, and in every respect a striking contrast to the fashionable costume of the present day." The Square then proceeded with its revelations.

"My next move was to the breast of a very showy and self-sufficient gentleman,—a man of ample fortune, but very superficial, and famous for nothing but his versatility and want of firmness. He seldom knew his own mind on any given subject whether in religion or politics, for eight and forty hours together. To-day he was a Whig, to-morrow a Tory, and the next something very different from both. In religion he was sometimes high church, sometimes low church, but more frequently neither one nor the other. In a word, he was unanimously pronounced a universal genius! I have known many universal geniuses in my time, though, to speak my mind freely, I never knew one who, for the ordinary purposes of life, was worth his weight in straw; but, for the government of a Lodge, a little sound judgment and plain common sense is worth all the sparkling genius that ever wrote poetry or invented theories. He was exceedingly fond of trying philosophical and political experiments; and having stuffed his head full of scraps and remnants of ancient republics, and oligarchies, and aristocracies, and monarchies, and the laws of Solon, and Lycurgus, and Charondas, and the imaginary commonwealth of Plato, and the pandects of Justinian, and a thousand other fragments of venerable antiquity, he was for ever bent upon introducing some one or other of them into use; so that between one contradictory measure and another, he entangled the government of the Lodge in more knots during his administration than half-a-dozen successors could have untied.[3]

"He had been a Junior Warden under Dr. Desaguliers; but that discerning Brother entertained some doubts whether his pretensions were sterling, and, therefore, hesitated to promote him to a higher and more responsible office. His imperfections soon manifested themselves, and the Brethren who placed him in the chair lived to repent of their choice. He formed several magnificent schemes for the advancement of Masonry, but did not possess sufficient stability to carry them into effect; like the Dutch mountebank who took a run of three miles to leap over a hill, but changing his mind during this preliminary step, when he arrived at its foot, he sat quietly down and declared himself unable to accomplish the feat. Or like the Uperephanos of Brathwait,

"He still thought,
That the world without him would be brought to nought,
For when the dogge-starre raged, he used to cry,
'No other Atlas has the world but I.
I am only Hee, supports the state;
Cements divisions, shuts up Janus' gate;
Improves the public frame, chalks out the way
How princes should command—subjects obey—
Nought passes my discovery, for my sense
Extends itself to all intelligence.'"

[3] A passage similar to the above may be found in Knickerbocker's description of William the Testy; and we must leave it to the reader to determine whether Washington Irving had it by communication with our *Γνωριομα*, or whether we copied it from him.

"This wonderful man piqued himself on his oratorical powers, and frequently wearied the patience of the Brethren by his dull and unmeaning harangues on the most trifling subjects. I remember on one occasion some topic was under discussion—I think it was on the propriety of masonic processions—which had been a fruitful subject of ridicule to the wits of London. A great difference of opinion prevailed amongst the Craft on this question, and our Lodge was so nicely balanced in point of numbers, pro and con, that any Master of common understanding would have found no difficulty in turning the scale in favour of his own views, on which side soever it might be. In this exigency what did our sapient Master do? Why, he made a speech, in which he took a view of the arguments on both sides of the question, and proceeding carefully by the strictest rules of logic, and a display of the soundest erudition, but all to no purpose, he balanced them so equally that every Brother in the Lodge congratulated himself that his opinions would be triumphant; and when the Master sat down, I heard him whisper to a Brother on his right hand, 'Now, do you know, from what I have said, which side of the question my own opinion favours?'—'Indeed, I confess myself at a loss to determine.'—'Then I have accomplished my point,' replied this sapient officer, 'for my ambition was to make a speech which should please both parties.' And when the question was put to the vote, he found himself in a minority. Not very complimentary to his tact and judgment, was it?

"Our politic Master was, at this time, building a handsome mansion at the west end of the town, and when it was nearly completed, he boasted one evening, in a set speech, of the pure Augustan style in which his dining-room was to be finished and decorated, in all the antique splendour that Gothic architecture could furnish. It was to be a perfect gem; and in the peroration of his speech, he announced his intention of opening it with a grand masonic dinner, to which he invited all the members then present. The announcement was, of course, received with cheers. Amidst the acclamations of the Lodge he sat down, and a Brother whispered in his ear, 'When do you think it will be finished?'—'Never for that purpose,' replied the Master.

"This erudite chief had concocted a notable scheme for distinguishing his year of office as a remarkable epoch, which had caused him more anxiety to bring into a disposable form, than any other subject he was ever known to entertain. It was an invention peculiarly his own, and he plumed himself upon it with more than common pride. In introducing it to the notice of the Lodge, his opening speech was flowery and rhetorical. He denominated his plan a grand panacea which would obviate all objections to Masonry, and create a universal sensation in its favor. 'The idea,' he said, 'is novel, pleasing, and practicable; it has never entered the head of mortal Mason, and I am the only individual who has been inspired with the vast design. My star is in the ascendant, and I do not doubt but a niche in the temple of fame is reserved for me, as the author of a magnificent project, which will render Freemasonry the envy of all other social institutions.'

"He went on in this style for a considerable length of time, the Brethren waiting with commendable patience for the development of his proposal. And what do you think it was? You cannot guess, and so I may as well tell you at once; it was a MASONIC BALL!!! The Brethren were taken by surprise at this unexpected announcement, so alien to the genuine principles of Masonry, and scarcely knew what to say. After they had recollected themselves by a pause of a few minutes' duration, the absurdity of the proposal struck them as so perfectly ridiculous, that, though from motives of decorum and respect for the Chair, they endeavoured to stifle their sense of the ludicrous, the effort was unsuccessful, and they gave vent to their feelings by a loud and universal peal of laughter, which they found it impossible to restrain.

"'A what?' shouted Bro. Lamball, 'A masonic ball?' which was succeeded by another general laugh. And Bro. Villeneau repeated the lines from Phædrus:

> 'Mons parturibat, gemitus immanes ciens;
> Eratque in terris maxima expectatio;
> At ille murem peperit;'

which was the signal for cachinnation the third.

"'On what law of Masonry do you found the legality of your scheme?' said Bro. Morris.

"The R. W. M. was unable to furnish either law or precedent for his delectable scheme, and, therefore, he staved off the enquiry by demanding in return: 'On what law do you found the legality of Refreshment?'

"'On the second clause of the sixth Ancient Charge,' said Bro. Morris.

"At length Bro. Desaguliers, who happened to be present, rose with great gravity, and addressing the Chair, said:

"'R. W. Sir, the proposal you have just submitted to the Lodge is so thoroughly alien to the principles of Masonry, that I am scarcely surprised at the indecorous exhibition we have just witnessed, but which, I hope, for the credit of the Lodge, will never be repeated while the S. Warden's column is in the ascendant. Supposing, for the sake of argument, that the Brethren were inclined to indulge you by acceding to your unprecedented proposition, they would be incapable of executing the design, without committing a gross violation of the general Constitutions of the Order. Are you aware, R. W. Sir, that a standing law provides that it is not in the power of any man, or body of men, to make any alteration or innovation in the body of Masonry, without the consent first obtained of the Grand Lodge? and this, Sir and Brother, would be an innovation which no Grand Lodge could ever be found to sanction or approve.'

"After Dr. Desaguliers had thus expressed a decided negative opinion on the subject, the Master, sufficiently mortified, withdrew his motion, and we never again heard of the anomaly of a masonic ball.

"But a truce to this gossip. I turn to the literary proceedings of the period, for I was now appropriated by the celebrated Martin Clare, *A. M.*, *F. R. S.*, D. G. M. in 1741, who had already distinguished himself by his zeal and intelligence on several occasions, and had done good service to Masonry by an address, which has been already referred to. In this document he made a few observations on those improprieties which are most likely to discompose the harmony of a Lodge; and then proceeded to show at large what the errors and deviations were which it would be desirable to avoid by a society of gentlemen, united by the bonds of brotherhood, and under the strictest ties of mutual love and forbearance.

"His grave and quiet method of delivery made a strong impression on the audience; and its conclusion, in these impressive words, was received with loud approbation: 'It has been long,' said he, 'and still is, the glory and happiness of this Society, to have its interests espoused by the great, the noble, and the honoured of the land. Persons who, after the example of the wisest and the grandest of kings, esteem it neither condescension nor dishonour to patronize and encourage the professors of the Craft. It is our duty, in return, to do nothing inconsistent with this favour; and, being members of this body, it becomes us to act in some degree suitable to the honour we receive from our illustrious head. If this be done at our general meetings, every good and desirable end will very probably be promoted among us. The Craft will have the advantage of being governed by good, wholesome, and dispassionate laws; the business of the Grand Lodge will be smoothly and effectually carried on: your Grand Officers will communicate their sentiments, and receive your opinions and advice with pleasure and satisfaction; particular societies will become still more regular, from what their representatives should observe here. In a word, true and ancient Masonry will flourish; and those that are without, will soon come to know that there are more substantial pleasures to be found, as well as greater advantages to be reaped, in our Society, orderly conducted, than can possibly be met with in any other bodies of men, how magnificent soever their pretensions may be; for none can be so amiable as that which promotes brotherly love, and fixes that as the grand cement of all our actions; to the performance of which we are bound by an obligation, both solemn and awful, and that entered into by our free and deliberate choice; and as it is to direct our lives and actions, it can never be too often repeated, nor too frequently inculcated.'

"At this time rumours were whispered in the Metropolitan Lodges, that the Order was subjected to great persecutions in Switzerland,[4] Germany,[5] Italy,[6] France[7] and Holland;[8] and that edicts and decrees were thundered out against it in all those countries; and although it was admitted that nothing had been discovered in the behaviour or practices of the Fraternity contrary to the public peace, or to the duty of good subjects, yet the several governments were, nevertheless, determined that the Lodges of Freemasons should be entirely abolished.

"These unprecedented measures excited in the English Fraternity such a feeling of disgust, that a few influential Brethren united themselves together for the purpose of considering what would be the most eligible and effectual method of showing the utter absurdity and impolicy of such a line of conduct; and in 1739 a pam-

[4] The magistrates of Berne issued an ordinance in these words:— "We do, by these presents, henceforth and for ever forbid, annul, and abolish the Societies of Freemasons in all our territories and districts, to all persons that now are, or shall hereafter come into our dominions; and we do ordain and decree. that all those our citizens and subjects who are actually known to be Freemasons, shall be obliged immediately *to abjure by oath* the engagement they have taken in the said society without delay. And all persons who shall frequent such assemblies shall be subject to a fine of 100 crowns without remission, and be incapable of holding any place of trust, benefit, or employment whatever."

[5] The persecutions in Germany were occasioned by the jealousy of some ladies belonging to the court, who being disappointed in their endeavours to obtain a knowledge of the secret through the agency of certain persons whom they induced to be initiated for that purpose, inflamed the mind of the empress against the society. But the persecution was defeated by the emperor himself, who undertook to be responsible for the conduct of the Masons in their Lodges, and to redress any grievances of which they were found guilty.

[6] A papal Bull of this period (1738) commanded all persons to abstain from the society of Freemasons, under a penalty of 1,000 crowns of gold, and incurring excommunication *ipso facto*, from which no one was able to give absolution but the Pope himself.

[7] In the year 1737 a persecution was commenced, under the plea that the pretence of secrecy might be used to cover some dangerous design which might affect the religion, the peace, and prosperity ot the kingdom.

[8] An edict was issued by the States of Holland, intimating that although they had not discovered anything in the behaviour or practice of the Freemasons contrary to the peace of the republic, or to the duty of good subjects, they were resolved, nevertheless, to prevent any bad consequences that might ensue from such conventions, and, therefore, commanded that they should be entirely abolished.

phlet, written in French, was published in Dublin,[9] under the title of 'An Apology for the Society of Freemasons.' It appeared in the same year in an English form, translated, as was generally supposed, by Martin Clare. It created a great sensation, and promoted the translator to the office of D. G. M. He had been already officially authorized to revise the Lodge Lectures, and to make such alterations and improvements as, in his judgment, the present state of the Order might require, always preserving inviolate the ancient landmarks. And his version of the Lectures was so judiciously drawn up, that its practice was enjoined on all the Lodges under the Constitution of England; and all former Lectures were abrogated, and pronounced obsolete.

"In this formula, the symbol of a point within a circle was introduced for the first time; and it is a singular fact, that although the original interpretation was simple enough, yet several meanings were soon attached to it by fanciful expositors, differing in reference, but agreeing in fact. And this diversity of opinion, as I should conceive," my companion added, with some allusion to my own individual judgment, "constitutes one of the peculiar excellences of the Craft; for, however the definition may have been amplified and extended, the results, when the several arguments were wound up and applied, pretty nearly corresponded with the original application of Martin Clare. For whether the point be Time, as some think, and the circle Eternity, or whether the former be an individual Mason circumscribed by the circle of virtue, the result will be the same; for virtue is boundless as universal space; and as the body of man may be accounted a fit representative of Time, so is his soul of Eternity. In the same Lectures, the numbers 3, 5, and 7, were applied, in strict conformity with ancient usage, to the Trinity, the Senses, and the Institution of a Sabbath. The Jewish Masons subsequently (for we had no Hebrews amongst us at that period), repudiated this primitive application, and substituted the following:—

[9] "An Apology for the Free and Accepted Masons, occasioned by their persecution in the Canton of Berne; with the present state of Masonry in Germany, Italy, France, Flanders, and Holland. By J. G., D.M.F.M." Dublin, Patrick Odoroko, 1739.

'Three rule a Lodge,—in allusion to the most sacred parts of the Temple of Solomon; viz., the Porch, the Holy Place, and the Holy of Holies. Five hold a Lodge, in reference to the sacred treasures of the *Sanctum Sanctorum*, viz., the Ark of Alliance, the Golden Censer, the Sacred Roll, the Rod of Aaron, and the Pot of Manna. Seven make a Lodge perfect, in allusion to the seven chief Degrees conferred by King Solomon, and to the years employed in building the Temple.'

"At the Grand Lodge, when Martin Clare was appointed Deputy Grand Master, I recollect perfectly well the Festival was celebrated in Haberdashers' Hall, March 19, 1741, several old Masons being present, including Past Grand Masters Payne, Desaguliers, the Earls of Loudon and Darnley, and the Marquis of Caernarvon, with a numerous train of noble and worthy Brothers, and several distinguished foreign members of the Craft. The twelve Stewards, and a great number of other Brethren, in their proper clothing, waited on the Earl of Morton, Grand Master Elect, at his house in New Bond Street; and after being there entertained at breakfast, had a public procession to Haberdashers' Hall, in carriages, attended by three bands of music. At the Hall gate, the Stewards received the cavalcade, and conducted the Grand Officers through the Hall into an inner chamber, the Deputy Grand Master carrying the Grand Master's Jewel. Here the Grand Lodge was opened, and our friend Martin Clare was publicly complimented by the Grand Master, and also by Bros. Payne and Desaguliers, the latter of whom moved a vote of thanks to him for his new version of the Lectures, in which he pronounced them to be a lively elucidation of the most ancient method of working a Lodge.

"The above ceremonial, and another of the same kind in the following year, each of which was attended with a public procession in coaches, originated a caricature and broadside, which were published in ridicule of the proceedings. The former was entitled, 'The solemn and stately Procession of the Scald Miserable Masons, as it was martialed on Thursday, the 18th day of this instant April;' and the latter was headed, 'A geometrical view of the Grand Procession of the Scald Miserable Masons, designed as they were drawn up over against Somerset House in the Strand, on the 27th day of April, 1742.'[10] And what sort of a procession do you think it was? You shall hear.

"First came two Tylers, in yellow cockades and liveries; then the Apprentices, armed with drawn swords to keep off all cowans and listeners; after which came the band of music, consisting of four cows' horns, as many tea-canisters, filled with broken glass, four shovels beaten with brushes, two double-bass dripping-pans, a frying-pan, a salt-box, and a pair of tubs for kettle-drums. Then followed six lean horses with funeral habiliments, and the arms of Hiram Abiff, a brick waggon for a hearse, on which was a bier of tubs covered with a chimney-sweeper's cloth, and on each side was a double rank of Brethren, bearing escutcheons, and other funereal symbols.[11] After this came another band of music similar to the above, the performers being mounted upon donkeys. Then the Grand Sword Bearers preceding the Grand Master[12] in a dust-cart, and followed by the Grand Offi-

[10] A few additional passages in this amusing paper, which produced a great deal of uproarious mirth amongst the Fraternity at the time, may not be unacceptable by way of note. It commenced with a "Remonstrance of the Right Worshipful the Grand Master of the Scald Miserable Masons, in which he claims a seniority over all other societies, whether Grand Volgi, Gregorians, Hurlothrumbians, Ubiquarians, Hiccubites, Lumber Troopers, or Freemasons; and disclaims all relation or alliance whatsoever with the latter Society, because, as he asserts, it would tend to the sacrifice of his own dignity, the impeachment of his understanding, and the disgrace of his solemn mysteries."

[11] The entire description runs thus: "Six stately unfledged horses, with funeral habiliments and caparisons, carrying escutcheons of the arms of Hyram Abyff; viz., a Master's Lodge, drawing, in a limping, halting posture, with solemn pomp, a superb open hearse, nine feet long, four feet wide, and having a clouded canopy, inches and feet innumerable in perpendicular height, very nearly resembling a brick waggon. In the midst, upon a throne of tubs raised for that purpose, lays the corpse in a coffin, cut out of one entire ruby; but, for decency's sake is covered with a chimney-sweeper's stop cloth, at the head a memorable sprig of cassia. Around in mournful order placed, the loving, weeping Brethren sit with their aprons—their gloves they have put in their pockets; at the top and at bottom, on every side, and everywhere all round about, this open hearse is bestuck with escutcheons and streamers, some bearing the arms, and some his crest."

[12] "The equipage of the G. M.," so runs the document, "being

cers[13] in carts, each drawn by four donkeys; the procession closing with probationists and candidates.

"This good-natured burlesque afforded the Craft much amusement; but in the year 1745 it was followed by an actual procession, got up by some unfaithful Brethren who had been disappointed in their expectations of the high offices and honours of Masonry, and had enlisted a number of low characters and buffoons in a scheme to exhibit a mockery of the public processions of the Craft. But while these proceedings were a source of mirth to the gaping crowd, the Fraternity were disgusted, and determined in future to confine their operations within the limits of their own assembly; and the Grand Festival itself was suspended for several years.

"At one of our Lodges during the Mastership of Martin Clare, a question was mooted respecting the meaning of the sixth Ancient Charge: 'No private piques, no quarrels about nations, families, religions, or politics, must be brought within the door of the Lodge; for, as Masons, we are of *the oldest Catholic religion* above hinted;' which refers to the following passage in the first Charge: 'In ancient times the Christian Masons were charged to comply with the Christian usages of each country, where they travelled or worked; but Masonry being found in all nations, even of divers religions, they

neatly nasty, delicately squalid, and magnificently ridiculous beyond all human bounds and conceivings. On the right the G. M. *Pony*, with compasses for his Jewel, appendant to a blue ribbon round his neck. On the left, his Excellency —— Jack, with a square hanging to a white ribbon, as G. M. elect; the Hon. Nic. Baboon, Esq., S. G. W., with his Jewel, being the Level, all of solid gold and blue ribbon; Mr. Balaam von Asinam, J. G. W., with his Jewel, the Plum-Rule."

13 "*Attendants of honour.* The G. Sw. B. carrying the Sword of State. It is worth observing that this sword was sent as a present by Ishmael Abiff, a relation in direct descent to poor old Hyram, King of the Saracens, to his Grace of Watlin, G. M. of the Holy Lodge of St. John of Jerusalem in Clerkenwell, who stands upon our list of Grand Masters for the same year. The G. Sec. with his insignia, &c. Tickets to be had for 3 megs a carcass to scran the paunum boxes, at the Lodge in Brick Street, &c. NOTE.—No gentlemen's coaches or whole garments are admitted in our procession or at the feast." Copies of the caricature have been published by Hone in England, and Clavel in France; the former professing to have taken his version from the original Broadside: and the latter from the collection of Bro. Morison of Greenfield, but they differ in many essential particulars.

are now only charged to adhere to *that religion in which all men agree*.'[14]

"A Brother present opened the Book of Common Prayer, which was always in the Lodge, and explained the phrase, *oldest Catholic religion*, by a reference to the *Te Deum* composed in the 4th century by St. Ambrose—'The Holy Church *throughout all the world* doth acknowledge Thee;' concluding that it must mean Christianity, which was typified in the two earliest dispensations known in the world, viz., those of the Patriarchs and the Jews; when Martin Clare delivered his opinion in words to the following effect: 'I have had several long and interesting conversations with Bros. Payne, Desaguliers, and Anderson on this very subject: and it is evident from their researches, that the belief of our ancient Brethren favoured the opinion that Masonry is essentially Christian; that it is indebted to Christianity for its principles; that in all ages the English Fraternity consisted exclusively of Christians; and that, therefore, the religion in which all men agree was the Christian religion. The ancient Charges, which are now before us, were extracted from old masonic records of Lodges, not only in Great Britain, but in foreign countries; and at the time when those records were originally compiled, the religion in which all men agreed was the general religion of Christendom—of the Holy Church throughout all the world, which, as has justly been observed, the *Te Deum* pronounces to be Christianity. The most ancient manuscript which passed through the hands of Bros. Desaguliers and Anderson during their researches, gives a decided affirmation to this doctrine, as may be gathered from the following passage:

Bysechynge hym of hys hye grace,
To stonde with zow yn every place,
To conferme the statutes of kynge Adelston,
That he ordeynt to thys Craft by good reson,
Pray we now to God almyght,
And to hys swete moder Mary bryght,
That we mowe kepe these artyculus here,
And these poyntes wel al y-fere,
* * * * *
And as thou were of a mayd y-bore,
Sofre me never to be y-lore;

[14] See the Ancient Charges in "Anderson's Const." Ed. 1738.

But when y schal hennus wende,
Grante me the blysse withoute ende;
Amen! amen! so mot hyt be.

This manuscript is supposed to have been compiled in the time of Athelstan, and I should, therefore, conceive its authority to be decisive.'

"In the above-mentioned year I had passed to a new Master and a new Lodge; and the first conversation I heard was on the subject of a pretended revelation of Martin Clare's revised lectures and ceremonies, in a book called 'The Testament of a Mason;'[15] where it was feigned that the formula had been found amongst the papers of a deceased Brother high in office, and, consequently, might fairly be presumed to contain the real secrets of the Order. The question was asked, Who is the author? and it was subsequently traced to one of the unfaithful Brothers who had been disappointed in his expectations of being nominated to a Grand Office.

"During the same year, if my memory be faithful, a Brother was introduced into our Lodge, whose name was Coustos. He was a foreigner, and not wanting in assurance. A great sensation, however, was created, when he exhibited some scars which betokened very severe wounds, that had been inflicted, as he affirmed, by torture in the Inquisition, at Lisbon, to extort from him the secrets of Freemasonry. It appeared, by his own account, that he had resisted both persuasion and force; and that his final escape out of their hands was owing to the interposition of the British Consul. Subscriptions were entered into in order to enable the sufferer to publish his account of the whole affair, which accordingly came out in the following year, and put a considerable sum of money into his pocket."[16]

15 "The Testament of a Freemason; ou, le Testament de Chevalier Graaf." Brussels, 1745.

16 "The sufferings of John Coustos for Freemasonry, and for refusing to turn Roman Catholic, in the Inquisition at Lisbon." London, 1746. Bode, 1779. Birmingham, 1790. Hull, 1811. London, Spencer, 1847.

CHAPTER IV.

THE SCHISM.—DR. MANNINGHAM.

1747—1760.

"She teacheth Temperance and Prudence, Justice and Fortitude, which are such things as men can have nothing more profitable in their life."—SOLOMON.

"Thys booke is not for every rude and unconnynge man to see, but to clerkys and very gentylmen that understands gentylnes and scyence."—CAXTON.

"Conscia mens recti famæ mendacia ridet."—OVID.

"I HAVE been thinking, sir," the Square continued, "how very extraordinary it is that the French Masons, as intelligence was brought over to this country from time to time, should have been so blind to the truth, or so ignorant of the legitimate principles of our divine Order, as to have instituted infidel societies in many of their chief cities, and invested them with the name of Masonry; for such were the various Elus or Elected Masons, as they styled themselves, which about this time were springing up, like noxious weeds, all over the continent of Europe. But it is still more strange that any of the English Fraternity should have been so indiscreet as to have admitted their claims to brotherhood. In the year 1747, one of our members produced in the Lodge a pamphlet which had just made its appearance in London, as a translation from the French, professing to reveal the veritable secrets of the Order,[1] by describing the revised Lectures and ceremonies; and was, in fact, a catchpenny publication, written to pander to the morbid appetites of the curious, who are ever in search of the means of procuring illegitimate and doubtful intelli-

[1] "L'Adepte Maçon, or the true secret of the Freemasons." London, 1747.

gence respecting the mysteries of Freemasonry, when the end might be obtained in a more satisfactory manner by the honourable process of initiation. No notice, however, was taken of it, and I passed quietly through two or three hands, of whom I have nothing particular to say, till I was placed on the breast of Dr. Manningham, Deputy Grand Master, a London physician of great eminence, who proved a very active Master of the Lodge, and under his rule we rapidly increased in numbers and respectability.

"This worthy Brother had already distinguished him self as a Mason, and established a powerful influence amongst the Fraternity; and about this time he contributed, by his able and judicious conduct, to restore harmony to the Craft, which had suffered considerably from the apathy of Lord Byron, the Grand Master, who, for four years together, had neither held a Grand Lodge nor nominated a successor. The Fraternity being thus neglected, several old Masons, with Past Grand Master Payne at their head, held a private meeting to consult on the safest and most legitimate method of proceeding in the present emergency. Bro. Payne proposed that a public meeting of the Brethren should be called, by advertisement, to deliberate on the propriety of proceeding to the election of a new Grand Master. He admitted that it was a strong measure, but thought that the exigency of the case would justify it. Dr. Manningham, being present, observed that he was afraid it would be a breach of masonic law; and if not, it might tend to introduce a party spirit amongst the Brethren, which is always more easily evoked than subdued. He promised, however, to communicate with the Grand Master on the subject, and assured them that a Grand Lodge should be convened at the usual time of the year, and a successor elected conformably to ancient practice. With this promise G. M. Payne professed himself to be content; and thus the breach was healed by a judicious application of the laws and principles of Masonry.

"Dr. Manningham was a *bon vivant*, as, indeed, all men were who had any pretensions to move in good society. He would have lost caste if he had been otherwise; for the only alternative a gentleman had in these days, at a dinner or tavern party, was to get drunk, or give mortal offence to his entertainer.[2] On this principle, the suppers after Lodge hours were devoted to social enjoyment. The song, the toast, and the racy jest went round merrily; and often, to say the truth, the Brethren exceeded the bounds of moderation. And it is scarcely to be wondered at, when conviviality was so fashionable amongst the higher classes of society. It was considered a mark of distinction to be called a three-bottle man, and a disgrace to retire from the dinner-table sober. I have seen a great deal of it amongst Masons, and have heard many anecdotes of the same vice in men eminently gifted with great and commanding talents.[3] There was some truth in Hogarth's representation of the Free and Accepted Masons in his picture of 'Night,' where the Master of a Lodge, Sir Thomas Veil, appears in a state of intoxication, and with a broken head. This picture was much talked about, and, although it was considered a libel on the Fraternity, it was a representation founded on undeniable facts.

"Notwithstanding these circumstances, there existed a high tone of morality amongst the Masons of that period. 'I should like to be made a Mason,' said a friend of Dr. Manningham to him one day. He was a

[2] A sermon was preached by Robert Harris, of Trinity College, Oxford, dedicated to the Justices of the Peace in Oxfordshire, who were notoriously hard drinkers, in which he says, "In drinking there is art, and in the world it is become a great profession, regulated by laws and ceremonies. There is drinking by the *foot*, by the *yard*, by the *dozen*, by the *score*; for a *wager*, for *victory*, *man against man*, *house against house*, *town against town*, and how not?"

[3] "Sir Richard Steele spent half his time in a tavern. In fact, he may be said to have measured time by the bottle; for it is on record that, being sent for by his wife, he returned for answer, that he would be with her in half a bottle. The like may be said of that great genius Savage the poet; and even Addison was dull and prosy till he was three parts drunk. It is also recorded of Pitt, but I cannot vouch for the truth of it, that two bottles of port wine per diem were his usual allowance; and that it was to this alone he was indebted for the almost superhuman labour he went through during his short, but actively-employed life. His friend and colleague, Harry Dundas, the ancestor of Earl Zetland, went the same lengths. Sheridan, latterly, without wine, was a driveller. He sacrificed to it talents such as no man I ever heard or read of possessed; for no subject appeared to be beyond his reach. The learned Porson was a drunkard, and so was Robert Burns the poet."—(Fraser's Mag., vol. xi., p. 730.)

city tradesman. 'I think it would be of service to my trade.' 'Is that your sole motive?' asked the doctor. 'Yes.' 'Then,' he replied, 'I would advise you to reconsider the matter, and relinquish all idea of becoming a Brother of the Craft, for I shall think it my duty to inform the Brethren what your motive is, and you are certain to be rejected.'

"We heard, about this time, that certain Jews were implicated in the unauthorised innovations of our continental Brethren, if, indeed, they were not the chief movers of them, as was asserted by some authorities;[4] and it was the first notice we ever received of the descendants of Abraham being admitted to a participation in our Christian privileges. From their success in procuring initiation into the surreptitious Masonry of the continent,[5] the English Jews soon became successful candidates for admission into our symbolical Order; for it was justly contended that, as Jews were not excluded from attending Christian churches, it would be impolitic and uncharitable to close a Christian Lodge against them. From that period they have been received into Masonry as members of an universal Order, whose principles, like those of the Christian religion, are destined to cover the earth as the waters cover the sea.

"Rumours now arose, whence originating no one could discover, that Freemasonry was exclusively a Jewish institution; and the proposition formed a prolific subject of discussion amongst us. At length an eminent Jew offered himself as a candidate for initiation in our Lodge; and being a reputable and intelligent man, he was, of course, accepted; and then we discovered the grounds on which the arguments for the Jewish origin and application of Masonry were based. One evening, in a numer-

[4] About this time, the Council of Emperors of the East and West, at Paris, granted a patent to a Jew, named Stephen Morin, deputing him a Grand Inspector-General for the purpose of propagating the hauts grades "in other countries beyond the seas;" meaning in the New World. (Thory, Act. Lat., tom. i., 78.)

[5] We have the evidence of Thory (Acta Lat., tom. i., 78), that at this period France abounded in Lodges, with surreptitious Constitutions, false titles, Charters antedated, and delivered by pretended authorities; being not unfrequently fabricated by the Lodges themselves; and even constituting Mother Lodges and Chapters without the slightest legal sanction.

ous Lodge, Dr. Manningham expatiated largely, in his lecture, on Faith, Hope, and Charity, as virtues equally of Masonry and Christianity. When the lecture was ended, our Hebrew Brother observed that, in his opinion, Faith, Hope, and Charity had no existence in ancient Masonry. He contended that as Solomon built the Temple at Jerusalem, which forms the great allegory of the Order, and as he was the first and chief of the three Grand Masters, it follows that Masonry must be a Jewish establishment, and consequently inapplicable to the reception of virtues which are peculiar to any sectarian religion.

"Dr. Manningham admitted that the argument was specious, and might have the effect of convincing some few superficial Brethren, but it was not sound; for, he observed, if Masonry be Jewish, it is not only sectarian, but of the most exclusive character; for Palestine was but a flower-garden compared to the rest of the world, and its population as to numbers perfectly insignificant. And if Solomon's Grand Mastership be esteemed of any importance in the decision of this question, it will be found an unfortunate argument, for the weight of evidence is decidedly against it. It is true that Solomon was a Jew, but his two colleagues were heathens, worshippers of Hercules and Astarte, and addicted to the practice of the spurious Freemasonry of Tammuz; and, therefore, if this reasoning be of any value, it will tend to prove that Freemasonry is a heathen rather than a Jewish institution, because Paganism furnished two out of three chief rulers in Masonry.

"'But,' Dr. Manningham continued, 'although Solomon was a Jew, and could speak of trees, from the cedartree that is in Lebanon, even unto the hyssop that springeth out of the wall; and also of beasts, and of fowl, and of creeping things, and of fishes, he was profoundly ignorant of the science of architecture. He understood natural history perfectly, but we do not find that he was celebrated for a knowledge of Operative Masonry. And if he was unacquainted with this sublime science, much less could any of his subjects establish a claim to such an excellent knowledge. In fact, if he had possessed, in his own dominions, artists and workmen sufficiently talented to have erected a temple to the true God, he would not have solicited the aid of foreigners and worshippers of false deities. The ancient Jews were confessedly ignorant of Masonry, and, therefore, the two Hirams were the persons principally engaged in the execution of this great work. They collected together the scattered bands of their countrymen, the Dionysiacs, from Egypt and other countries, and, dividing them into three parties, stationed one in the forest of Lebanon, another in the stone quarries, and the third in the clayey ground between Succoth and Zeredathah, while Solomon merely furnished the superior and inferior labourers for the work, under the direction of Prince Adonhiram. I cannot understand, therefore, how the above argument can be urged with any degree of confidence in favour of the hypothesis that Freemasonry is a Jewish institution.'

"Our Hebrew Brother was too tenacious of the truth of his argument to abandon it without an effort, and he triumphantly contended that as the Tabernacle and Temple, with their appendages, are constituent and indispensable objects of illustration in the system of Freemasonry, its Levitical origin is thereby unequivocally proved.

"Dr. Manningham denied the premises, on the ground that the application of these religious edifices in the lectures of Masonry is merely symbolical of a better and more perfect dispensation. 'In a word,' he continued, 'if Masonry be *universal*, it can only be applied to a *universal* religion which, Judaism confessedly is not. And, therefore, it follows, that, if there be a religion which, in God's good time, shall embrace all mankind, and bring them into one fold under one shepherd, *that* is the religion in which all men will ultimately agree. It is a consummation to which every true Mason looks forward with delight, as a season when a universal religion shall cement all mankind in the bonds of a universal Brotherhood; when the dove shall hold out the olive-branch of peace to all the kindreds of the earth; when swords shall be beat into ploughshares; when nation shall not rise against nation, neither shall there be war any more. This completion of the everlasting design of the Most High will render masonic secrecy unnecessary, and Christ shall be all in all.'

"The Jew persisted that, in applying Masonry to

Christianity, we placed ourselves in a worse situation than in admitting its Jewish tendency, because its universality was thus destroyed by the adoption of a principle exclusively sectarian.

"'What,' Dr. Manningham replied, 'sectarian to assimilate a universal system to a universal religion?'

"'But I deny,' said the Jew, 'that Christianity is a universal religion. I believe that Judaism is the only true way of worshipping God, and that it will ultimately prevail over all others.'

"Dr. Manningham here referred to the book of Common Prayer, which always lay on the table, and read from the seventh article as follows: 'The Old Testament is not contrary to the New; for in both everlasting life is offered to mankind by Christ, who is the only mediator between God and Man; and the law given from God by Moses, as touching ceremonies and rites, does not bind Christian men.' He admitted that it may be perfectly consistent in a Jew to apply Masonry to the requirements of his own religion; but, he said, it was impossible for the Christian to copy his example. And for this plain reason. If he be firmly persuaded that Christianity is a uuiversal religion, which he must be if he believes the Gospel to be true, he cannot, without inconsistency, affirm, that by making Masonry a Christian institution, its universality is affected. If, on the contrary, he really thinks that Freemasonry is a Jewish institution, he must necessarily believe in the eternity of Judaism, and is, of course, a doubtful Christian, because St. Paul affirms that the Levitical institutions were abolished by the mission of Jesus Christ.

"'But,' said the Jew, reserving his strongest argument to the last, 'What can the repeated references in Freemasonry to the Great Creator of the Universe, JEHOVAH, the Tetragrammaton of the Jews, mean, if they do not point out the Jewish origin of Masonry?'

"'These references,' Dr. Manningham replied, 'are decisive of the question at issue. T. G. A. O. T. U. is an undoubted landmark of ancient Masonry, acknowledged at the revival in 1717, and explained in the authorized lectures to mean, HIM *that was placed on the topmost pinnacle of the Temple:* and it is not possible by any process of reasoning to apply it otherwise than to Christ, without questioning the truth of Sacred Writ; for no other person that the world ever saw had been placed in that position. It follows, therefore, that the founder of Christianity constitutes an authentic and unalterable landmark of ancient Masonry. Read,' continued the Master, 'read the fundamental principles of the Order, as recorded in a manuscript in the Royal Library, said to have been originally written in the tenth century, of which I have here a copy.' And he produced the transcript, from which he read the following passage, amidst a variety of directions to the Craft, all to the same purport:—

"Into the churche when thou dost gon,
Pulle uppe thy herte to Crist, anon!
Uppon the rode thou loke uppe then;
And knele down fayre on bothe thy knen;
Then pray to hym so hyr to worche,
After the lawe of holy churche,
For to kepe the commandmentes ten,
That God gaf to alle men;
And pray to him with mylde steven
To kepe the from the synnes seven.

"'Such were the landmarks of Masonry in the time of Athelstan,' Dr. Manningham concluded, 'when the first English Grand Lodge was established at York, and they are unalterable, and continue the same yesterday, to-day, and for ever.'

"The Jew was silenced, but not convinced.

"You see, sir," my strange instructor proceeded, "that this point was argued dogmatically by our intelligent Master; and he had an undoubted right to do so, for he was not only the representative of WISDOM, but had also the advantages of study and experience. The subject was repeatedly discussed in our Lodges, and I have heard the opinions of every Mason during the eighteenth century who held any authority in the Craft, and they all agreed in the above interpretation of the connection between Freemasonry and the religion in which all men agree.

"During the Mastership of Dr. Manningham, the great gun of the opponents of Masonry, called Jachin and Boaz, made its appearance,[6] and passed through numer-

[6] "Jachin and Boaz, or an authentic key to the door of Freemasonry, both ancient and modern. Calculated not only for the instruc-

ous editions. Its success stimulated other speculators to follow in the same track, and spurious rituals flooded the community like an inundation.[7] The number of competitors in the field served to neutralize each other's claim on public credence. They differed on many material points, and, therefore, the conclusion to which the public very naturally came was, that if any one of them was true, all the rest must necessarily be false, and as none knew whether any, or which, was the real Simon Pure, it followed that all might be fabrications to impose on the credulous reader absurd ceremonials and fictitious secrets, for the base purpose of putting a few pounds into their own pockets.

"This was the argument used by Dr. Manningham to induce the Brethren to treat these furtive attempts with silent neglect. 'I should like to know,' he said one evening, when the matter was under consideration in the Lodge, 'I should like to know the real object of those who read these compilations. If they were really desirous of becoming acquainted with the secrets of Masonry, our Lodges are at hand; no man of character and purity of motive is refused; and, by initiation, he will become legitimately acquainted with the design and character of the Order. At all events, no one possessed of a rational judgment can safely rely on the information communicated by these unauthorized publications. Those who are merely desirous of enjoying a laugh at the dignified proceedings of a venerable Institution, will find their purpose sufficiently answered by a perusal of these pre-

tion of every new made Mason, but also for the information of all who intend to become Brethren." London, 1750. Fifth edition, London, Nicol, 1764. Other new editions by the same printer in 1776, 1777, 1779, 1788, 1791, 1794, 1797. New York: Berry, Rogers, and Berry, 1793. London, Newbury, 1800. The 21st edition, London, Dewick, 1805; and other editions were printed in London in 1811, 1812, 1814, and 1825.

[7] The following works were published almost simultaneously: "Le Maçon démasqué, ou le vrai secret des F. M. mis au jour dans toutes ses parties avec sincérité et sans déguisement." London, 1751; Berlin, 1757; Frankfort and Leipsig, 1786. "The Thinker upon Freemasonry;" "The Ghost of Masonry;" "The Mason's Creed;" "The Point of a Mason, formed out of his own materials;" and "A Discovery of the Secrets of Masonry," published in the "Scots Magazine" for 1755, and repeated in the "Edinburgh Magazine," for October, 1757.

tended revelations;[8] although we are justified in entering our protest against the exhibition of such a vitiated taste, and leaving them to luxuriate in the mire of their own prurient errors.'

"A Charge was delivered about this time at Gravesend,[9] in which the subject of Masonic revelations was examined. But Dr. Manningham adopted a more effectual method of neutralizing these absurd attempts to impose on the public, and disturb the harmony of the Craft. In his capacity of Deputy Grand Master, he visited the Lodges in every part of London and its suburbs, or whereever else his presence was thought necessary, correcting errors, settling disputes, redressing what was amiss in the execution of the laws, repressing irregularities, and offering for the consideration of the Brethren the most prudent advice, alike for their future observance, and conducive to their lasting advantage. And the whole of his proceedings were characterized by such a display of candour and affability, as advanced his popularity to the highest pitch, and greatly endeared him to the Fraternity at large.

[8] The satires of Dean Swift on Freemasonry are the most entertaining, and the most harmless. I have already alluded to them in a previous chapter (p. 21), and the following extract from the celebrated "Tripos," supposed to have been delivered at a commencement in the University of Dublin, will be found amusing. "It was lately ordered that, for the honour and dignity of the University, there should be introduced a society of Freemasons consisting of gentlemen, mechanics, porters, parsons, ragmen, hucksters, bailiffs, divines, tuckers, knights, thatchers, coblers, poets, justices, drawers, beggars, aldermen, paviours, skulls, freshmen, bachelors, scavengers, masters, sow-gelders, doctors, ditchers, pimps, lords, butchers, and tailors, who shall bind themselves by an oath never to discover their mighty no-secret; and to relieve whatsoever strolling distressed Brethren they meet with, after the example of the Fraternity of Freemasons in and about Trinity College, by whom a collection was lately made for, and the purse of charity well stuffed for a reduced Brother. Tam liberâ potitus contributione, frater scoundrellus sarcinulas suas discessurus colligit, et vultu hilari, ori solito quadrangulum transit, &c., &c.; proh dolor, inter partes au nobiliores, au posteriores nescio privatum fraternitatis notavit signum (Anglice, the Freemason's mark). Quo viso, Dii boni, quanto clamore totam infecit domum. Ter et sæpius pulsavit pectus, exsangues dilaniavit genas, et eheu nimium dilaceratas dilaceravit vestes. Tandem vero paulo modestius insaniens hujusmodi versiculus ridiculum effudi dolorem."

[9] "Charge delivered to the Brethren assembled at Gravesend on the 29th of June, being their first meeting after the Constitution of their Lodge." London, 1751.

"These visitations had become absolutely necessary for the purpose of discountenancing some gross improprieties which, at this period, were practised with impunity. Some unworthy Brethren, who had been excluded from their Lodges for transgressing the general laws of Masonry, endeavoured to convince the public that they were good and worthy Brothers, by opening surreptitious Lodges, and making Masons, as if they had official authority from the G. Lodge at York for such a prostitution of masonic privileges. These innovations, as might be expected, produced the most disastrous results, and were the commencement of that unhappy schism which divided the Society into two sections for more than half a century.

"At this period we had no authorized form of prayer to be used at initiations, which led to some slight irregularities since the admission of Jewish Brethren. Each Master of a Lodge had been left to his own discretion in this particular, although the general practice was, to select an appropriate form from the Liturgy of the Church. Dr. Manningham saw the evil, and determined to apply a remedy. He consulted with Dr. Anderson on the subject, and together they drew up a prayer for that particular ceremony, which was submitted to the Grand Lodge for its sanction; and that being obtained, Dr. Manningham introduced it in person to the metropolitan Lodges, by whom it was gratefully received. From thence it spread into the provinces, and was generally adopted throughout the kingdom.[10]

[10] This prayer continued in use till the time of Preston, who altered, without improving it. It was printed in the "Freemasons' Pocket Companion," and other masonic publications. I subjoin the form: "Most Holy and Glorious Lord God, thou Architect of heaven and earth, who art the giver of all good gifts and graces; and hath promised that where two or three are gathered together in thy name, thou wilt be in the midst of them; in thy Name we assemble and meet together, most humbly beseeching thee to bless us in all our undertakings: to give us thy Holy Spirit, to enlighten our minds with wisdom and understanding; that we may know and serve thee aright, that all our doings may tend to thy glory and the salvation of our souls. And we beseech thee, O Lord God, to bless this our present undertaking, and to grant that this our Brother may dedicate his life to thy service, and be a true and faithful Brother amongst us. Endue him with Divine wisdom, that he may, with the secrets of Masonry, be able to unfold the mysteries of godliness and Christianity. This we humbly

"In contravention of the pretended revelations of masonic secrets, it was asserted by an intelligent Brother that he was able, with a few masonic implements—that is, two squares and a common gavel—to convey any word or sentence to a skilful and intelligent Freemason, without speaking, writing, or noise, and that at any given distance, where the parties can see each other, and be able to distinguish squares from circles.[11] And another Brother, to the same effect, said, 'If a Christian, Jew, Turk, or Brahmin should meet together, and if they are Masons, they will no sooner tread upon the Level, than its magical and secret spring throws up a Perpendicular, and they are instantaneously found upon the Square; and these men, although ignorant of each other's language, will communicate their thoughts intelligibly, with no other assistance than the three Grand Pillars of hearing, seeing, and feeling.' And they challenged any charlatan who pretended to reveal the secrets of Freemasonry, to show by what process this was effected.

"The Craft, as you are well aware," continued my garrulous companion, "was now divided into two sections, a schism having taken place in the Order, in consequence of a few suspensions and expulsions for irregularities; and a hostile Grand Lodge was established in London, which charged the Constitutional Grand Lodge with being a self-constituted assembly, defective in numbers, form, and capacity, and stigmatized its members with the offensive appellation of *modern Masons*.[12] This caused some little sensation, and produced two or three anonymous works in 1752–4.[13]

"At the Grand Lodge, 29th November, 1754, Dr. Manningham brought the subject forward, and made a formal complaint that certain Brethren had associated themselves together under the denomination of *ancient Masons*, and declared themselves independent of the Grand Lodge, refusing obedience to its laws, and repudiating the authority of the Grand Master. He said that some notice ought to be taken of these proceedings, for

beg, in the name and for the sake of Jesus Christ, our Lord and Saviour, Amen."—See the original in "Scott's Pocket Companion." Ed. 1754.

[11] "Ahiman Rezon." Ed. 1813, p. xii.

[12] See Ibid. p. viii.

[13] A Masonic Creed, with a curious Letter by Mr. Locke. 1754.

the purpose of discouraging such irregular meetings, not only because they were contrary to the laws and an insult to the Grand Master, but also as they tended to introduce into the system of Masonry novelties and conceits inconsistent with its true principles, thus insinuating that there had been other societies of Masons of a different nature to our own ancient and honourable Order.

"The question being put, that this new society was an innovation on the ancient system of Masonry, it was carried in the affirmative, with only one dissentient voice. Dr. Manningham then moved, that the consideration of the irregular proceedings of the offending Brethren might be postponed till the next Quarterly Communication, hoping that a thorough sense of their misconduct, and a determination not to persist in it, would, in the meantime, manifest itself, and reconcile them to the Grand Lodge; which was unanimously agreed to.

"I was fortunate enough to be present at these discussions, and therefore have no hesitation in communicating them to you as unquestionable facts. Now it so happened that some of the Brethren of the Lodge No. 94, meeting at the Ben Jonson's head, Spitalfields, had been on the continent, and had brought from thence the rituals of the Ecossais, the Elu, and Ramsay's Royal Arch, which they practised secretly every third Lodge night, under the designation of ancient Masonry. This was soon whispered abroad, and Dr. Manningham, with a few other Brethren, in the course of their visitations, called at the Lodge on one of its peculiar nights, and were refused admittance. This produced a complaint at the next Grand Lodge; and, in addition to a severe vote of censure on the members of the Ben Jonson's Lodge, it was commanded that any Brother of the Order should be eligible for admission into that Lodge as a visitor on any of its regular nights.

"The offending members affected to consider this order a species of oppression to which they were not inclined to submit, and they drew up and published a Manifesto,[14] in which they accused the Grand Lodge of partiality, innovation, and deviation from ancient Land-

[14] "Manifesto and Mason's Creed." London, 1755.

marks, and publicly renounced their allegiance to it Several passages from this book were read in Grand Lodge, and I remember one paragraph from the Preface particularly; it was as follows: 'Whereas the genuine spirit of Masonry seems to be so greatly on the decline, that the Craft is in imminent danger from false Brethren: and whereas its very fundamentals have of late been attacked, and a revolution from its ancient principles, etc., it has been thought necessary, by certain persons who have the welfare of the Craft at heart, to publish the following little pamphlet, by means of which it is hoped the ignorant may be instructed, the lukewarm inspirited, and the irregular reformed.'

"Rather a bold beginning, was it not?

"How far this ill-judged pamphlet produced these effects it will not be difficult to pronounce; and in the Lodge I heard but one opinion of it. Certain it is that the Grand Lodge, on St. John the Baptist's day, 1755, passed unanimously the following resolution: 'Ordered, that the Brethren complained of at the last Quarterly Communication, persisting in their disobedience to the determination of the Grand Lodge, their Lodge, No. 94, held at the Ben Junson's Head, Pelham street, Spitalfields, be erased from the Book of Lodges, and that such of the Brethren thereof who shall continue those irregular meetings be not admitted as visitors in any Lodge whatever.'

"These decisive and vigorous proceedings," said the Square, "increased the schism, and appeared to render a reunion impracticable. And, indeed, the refractory Brethren understood it to be so, for they immediately took measures for the permanency of their new branch of the Order, by constituting a Grand Lodge, and issuing warrants for private Lodges, and thus commenced the practice of a species of Masonry unknown in former times. They instituted a novel degree, which they called the Royal Arch, compounded out of a portion of the third degree, and from various continental innovations, which gave them a vast advantage in the minds of curious and unthinking persons, over the pure ancient system practised by the old Grand Lodge, inasmuch as it held out the prospect of superior information, and a greater insight into the design of ancient Freemasonry.

There are some reasons, however, for believing that this schism was beneficial, rather than otherwise, to the cause of genuine Freemasonry. Indeed, this was the opinion of Dr. Hemming, and he publicly asserted, at the reunion of the two Grand Lodges in 1813, that it had done a great deal of good, by introducing a spirit of inquiry which proved favourable to its general interests. And we do not find that its 350 or 400 Lodges had any effect in reducing the members attached to the constitutional Grand Lodge; for they continued to increase by gradual and certain steps, and it maintained its rank, in the face of every opposition, with becoming dignity. There can be no doubt but the prevalence of schism on the continent of Europe laid the foundation for this unnatural division of English Masonry into two hostile parties; but, as the dispute was conducted with moderation on both sides, it soon subsided, and the two Grand Lodges proceeded in their respective careers in peace, harmony, and brotherly love.[15]

[15] See the "Historical Landmarks of Masonry," vol. ii., p. 58; and "First Letter to Dr. Crucefix," by the Author.

LIBRARY OF THE UNIVERSITY OF CALIFORNIA

CHAPTER V.

TESTS AND QUALIFICATIONS.

ENTICK, HESLETINE, CALCOTT, HUTCHINSON.

1760—1769.

"Maçonrye beeth the skylle of Nature, the understondynge of the myghte that ys hereynne, and its sondre werkynges."—OLD MASONIC MS.

"She knoweth the subtilties of speeches, and can expound dark sentences; she forseeth signs and wonders, and the events of seasons and times."—SOLOMON.

"Some folks have with curious impertinence strove,
From Freemasons' bosoms their secrets to move,
I'll tell them in vain their endeavours must prove;
Which nobody can deny."
MASONIC SONG.

"IN revealing some of the peculiar practices of Masonry in the eighteenth century, which, I am persuaded, are not clearly understood," continued the Master's Jewel, "I must caution you against confounding the pursuits of labour with those of refreshment, for they were perfectly distinct. Labour was an exclusive employment practised by Masons alone, while the amusements which attended the latter were common to many other convivial societies, and were regulated in accordance with the customs of the day. Grave business being closed, wit and good humour reigned triumphant, and the Brethren indulged themselves with a zest and freedom which distinguished no other community. Amongst Free and Accepted Masons, harmony and brotherly love were alike cherished and enforced; and disputes and quarrels seldom deformed the chaste enjoyments of the festive board. But I am truly concerned to say that, in some of our Lodges, Masonry was deformed by the unnatural attempt to blend these two divisions of masonic employment, which were never intended to coalesce; and the fatal consequences of such a course will too plainly appear by sundry revelations which I shall feel bound to make in the period now under consideration.

"In the eighteenth century the Lodge expenses were constructed on the most economical scale. The initiation fees ranged from one to two guineas, exclusive of the registration fee; and the quarterages were from 2*s.* 6*d.* to 5*s.*, including suppers. Under these circumstances, it required the exercise of great caution and discrimination to prevent the introduction of improper persons. And, accordingly, we had a clause in our Bye-Laws—which, indeed, was pretty general amongst the Fraternity—to the following effect:—'And whereas the Craft hath suffered greatly in its reputation and happiness by the admission of low and inferior persons, no ways fit to become members of our ancient and honourable Institution, whereby men of rank, quality, knowledge, and education, are often deterred from associating with their Brethren at their public meetings: it is hoped that every Brother who is desired to propose any person will be particularly careful that he is one in all respects suitable to the Venerable Society he is to become a member of; one whose temper and disposition may cement the harmony of the Lodge, and whose conduct and circumstances in life are such as may not tend to diminish the credit of it.

"In the choice of a Master, it was recommended in the Bye-Laws that abilities should be preferred to seniority or station in life; but this rule was not always observed, and the Lodges occasionally fell into inefficient hands, to the depreciation of their character, and the diminution of their numbers. In many Lodges it was the practice to elect the Master, Treasurer, Secretary, and Tyler, by ballot; nor did the former possess the privilege of nominating any officer, except his senior Warden, lest he should possess an undue authority over the Brethren; and, therefore, the senior Warden appointed his junior, and both were then invested by the Master. Decorum was enforced by a rigid exaction of fines, which were frequently directed to be paid in wine or spirits, to be consumed then and there by the Brethren present.[1] And as the Lodges were generally held at an inn, or tavern, the landlord, to whom the furniture usually belonged, possessed considerable influence in the Society, and was in a position to subject the Brethren to great inconvenience if they presumed to interfere in the slightest degree with his views of profit or emolument. From these causes, added to the universal license of the times, they were induced to indulge in excesses which transgressed the bounds of moderate conviviality, and brought discredit on the Order. This compulsory practice became at length so burdensome, that a clause was introduced into the Bye-Laws, by direction of the Grand Lodge, that 'no landlord or master of the house where a Lodge shall be held shall be permitted to have any other share in the furniture and property of the Lodge than as an individual member.' By the genial operation of this rule the above nuisance was considerably abated.

"The period I have passed over in the preceding chapter produced several authentic publications on the subject of Masonry, which were read in the Lodges for the edification of the Brethren.[2] The 'Ahiman Rezon'

[1] Thus in an old minute book belonging to the Witham Lodge, Lincoln, we find the following entries in the Bye-Laws:—"The Master, if present, or his Wardens, in his absence, shall regularly open and close the Lodge at the appointed hours. Or if all of them happen to be absent, the member who was last Master, or for want of a person who hath passed the Chair, the last Warden present is to do the same, and during the Lodge hours shall promote the business of the Craft; so that there may be one EXAMINATION, at least, gone through on every Lodge night, or the persons so neglecting *shall forfeit a bottle of wine, to be drank by the Brethren after the Lodge is closed, to make them some part amends.* Not fewer than three leaves, part of the Constitutions of the Fraternity, shall be read immediately after opening the Lodge, on every Lodge night, by the Master, his Wardens, or their Official, or by some other Brother present by their appointment, under the penalty of *one bottle of wine to be paid as aforesaid.* No Brother made in another Lodge shall be passed Master in this Lodge under half a guinea, *to be paid for the entertainment of the Masters present.*

[2] These were—"A Charge delivered at the King's Arms, in Helston, Cornwall, on Tuesday, April 21st, 1752, by Isaac Head." "A Search after Truth: a Sermon, delivered at Gloucester before the Lodge, No. 95:" 1752. "A Pocket Companion, and History of Freemasonry, containing its Origin, Progress, and Present State; the Institution of the Grand Lodge of Scotland; Lists of the Grand Masters and other Officers of the Grand Lodges of Scotland and England an Abstract of their Laws, Constitutions. Customs, Charges, Orders

was also published for the use of the seceders, and was adopted by the schismatical Grand Lodge, as its Book of Constitutions.[3] At this period our Rev. Bro. Entick engaged in the laudable design of counteracting the repeated attempts that had been made to throw Masonry into confusion, and contributed several valuable additions to masonic literature. He was, in his turn, the Master of our Lodge, and I glittered on his breast for three consecutive years. His habits were grave and sober; but he was a good Master, and a fair disciplinarian, popular amongst the Craft, an expositor of Masonry in many printed works, and at the same time he preserved his status in the Grand Lodge, which is more than Capt. Smith, Preston, Whitney, and some other popular Brethren, were fortunate enough to accomplish at a subsequent period. He published two several editions of the Book of Constitutions,[4] and preached many sermons on Free-

and Regulations, for the Instruction and Conduct of the Brethren." By Jonathan Scott. London: Baldwin, Davey, and Law, 1754; Second edition, 1759; Third edition, 1764. To this latter edition were appended many other particulars for the use of the Society.

[3] "Ahiman Rezon, or a Help to a Brother; showing the Excellency of Secrecy, and the First Cause or Motive of the Institution of Masonry, the Principles of the Craft, and the Benefits from a Strict Observance thereof; also the Old and New Regulations. To which is added, the greatest Collection of Masonic Songs." By Bro. Dermott. London: Bedford, 1756; Second edition, London, 1764; Third edition, London, Jones, 1778; Fifth edition, Dublin, 1780; Sixth edition, by Bro. Harper, London, Burton. 1800; Seventh edition, London, 1807; Eighth edition, London, 1813; Ninth edition, London, Asperne, 1836. "The Mariland Ahiman Rezon; containing the History of Masonry, &c." Baltimore, 1799. Freemasons' Library, and General Ahiman Rezon." By Samuel Cole, Baltimore, 1817. "Ahiman Rezon abridged and digested." By W. Smith, D.D. Philadelphia, 1783. "Charges and Regulations of the Society of Free and Accepted Masons; extracted from Ahiman Rezon, under the sanction of the Prov. Grand Lodge of Halifax, in New Scotland." Halifax, 1786. It was answered in a book called "A Defence of Masonry, as practised in the Regular Lodges, both Foreign and Domestic, under the Constitution of the English Grand Master. In which is contained a Refutation of Mr. Dermott's absurd and ridiculous Account of Freemasonry, in his book entitled 'Ahiman Rezon,' and the Several Queries therein reflecting on the Regular Masons considered and answered." London, Flexney and Hood, 1765.

[4] "The Constitutions of the Ancient and Honourable Fraternity of Free and Accepted Masons; containing their History, Charges, Regulations, &c. Collected and digested by order of the Grand Lodge, from their Old Records. For the Use of the Lodges By

masonry, which ought to have been preserved, as they did honour both to his head and his heart.[5] I must confess I had a great respect for Bro. Entick. He was an active man, and a dear lover of Masonry; and I was exceedingly sorry when fate, in the shape of a vote of the Lodge, threw me into other hands.

"After this I passed two years of severe probation, for the Masters were inefficient, and the Brethren began to be very slack in their attendance; in fact, at the close of the year, our Lodge was *hors de combat*. The latter of these worthies was inordinately addicted to the prevailing convivialities of the age, and introduced amongst us the exploded custom of drinking and smoking in open Lodge, an evil practice, destructive of all scientific investigation. I admit that he was not a solitary exception to the standing order, that, 'no Brother do presume to come into the Lodge intoxicated, or on any account whatever to call for wine or liquors in open Lodge, but to address himself to the stewards or wardens, who, if they think it necessary, will give their orders accordingly,' for there were many existing Lodges whose sole business appeared to be sensual indulgence, but they were carefully avoided by every sincere friend of the Order. Many protests were entered against the practice by the remaining few discreet members of our Lodge without effect: the nuisance was not abated; and even the lecture—when we had the good fortune to hear one—was delivered amidst volumes of smoke, which rivalled in intensity the reeking impurities of a burning prairie, and interrupted by frequent calls to the land-

James Anderson, D. D. Carefully revised, continued, and enlarged, with many additions, by John Entick, M.A." London, Baldwin, Davey, and Law, 1756. "The Constitutions, &c." By J. Entick, M.A. A new edition, with Alterations and Additions, by a Committee appointed by the Grand Lodge. London, Johnston, 1767. "Appendix to the Constitutions of the Society of Free and Accepted Masons." 1776.

[5] "The Free and Accepted Mason described, in a Sermon preached at St. Stephen, Walbrook, June 25, 1750, by John Entick, A.M." London, Scott, 1750. "The Free and Accepted Mason truly stated." Preached by J. Entick, from Acts xxviii., 22. "A True Representation of Freemasonry; in a Lecture, delivered at the King's Head Lodge, in the Poultry, London, March 20, 1751, by J. Entick, A.M." "A Caution to Free and Accepted Masons; a Sermon preached at St. Mildred, in the Poultry, Oct. 26, 1752, by J. Entick, A.M." London, Scott, 1752.

lord for beer and strong waters, and the jingling of pots and glasses! Forgetting the *favete linguis* of the old mysteries, the enjoyment of every Brother seemed to centre in himself alone; and this unhallowed triad of lecturing, smoking, and drinking at one and the same time, bestrode the Brethren like the old man of the sea on the neck of Sinbad, and they possessed no means of liberation but by dissolving their connection with the Lodge; and thus the Institution was deprived of some of its most valuable members.

"This R. W. M., whose name, for various reasons, I have purposely omitted to mention, as if determined to give the Lodge its *coup de grâce*, introduced a contest for superiority between the old and several young members, who understood very imperfectly the true principles of the Order, and entered warmly into the dispute for the sake of excitement and mischief. The juniors were at first always defeated in the numerous motions and subjects of discussion which they nightly poured forth upon the Lodge, with as little judgment as Sancho Panza exhibited in the application of his proverbs; but being encouraged by the Master, they succeeded in procuring an accession to their numbers by the introduction of candidates for initiation, till, at length, the old members were in a minority. The undisguised marks of triumph which the juniors displayed, so disgusted their more sedate Brethren, that they dropped off gradually, until the Lodge was left to the sole management of the injudicious Master, and his superficial associates. I need not tell you the result. After the pæans of victory had subsided, and the excitement of the contest was at an end, these boon companions found Masonry but a dull affair, and soon followed the example of those worthy Brethren whom they had driven from the Lodge, by discontinuing their attendance; until, at length, we received a summons, dated 17th October, 1776, and signed 'Samuel Spencer, Grand Secretary,' requiring us, under the penalty of erasure, to show cause, at the ensuing Quarterly Communication, why the Lodge had not been represented in Grand Lodge for the last two years, and no subscriptions paid. Fortunately, the remaining few members who had faithfully adhered to the Lodge amidst all its fluctuations,—if not by actual attendance, at least by continuing on the books,—interfered, and by inviting an active and scientific member, Bro. James Heseltine, who had served the office of Warden under Bro. Entick, to take the chair, restored the peace and unanimity of the Lodge.

"Many of the continental fancies and innovations, extracted from the Jewish Talmuds, and introduced into their surreptitious Masonry, were much talked of in our Lodges at this period; and some of them were absolutely incorporated into our symbolical ritual, which was one reason why an authorized mode of working was considered by all genuine Masons to be essentially necessary. The rage for *something new* in England, as formerly in Athens, was not easily suppressed, and a knowledge of these traditions was deemed indispensable for every Brother who was ambitious of enjoying the reputation of being an adept in Masonry. One of these traditions you will like to hear, as it continued for a great length of time a cherished figment amongst us. It refers to the history of the Foundation Stone of Solomon's Temple, which was traced in the legend from Enoch through Noah, Abraham, and Solomon, to the apostate Emperor Julian by the following process. They described it as a double cube, every side, except the base on which it stood, being inscribed. The first face of the cube was said to have been engraved by Noah with an instrument of porphyry when the Ark was building; the second, by Abraham, with *the horn of the ram*—credat Judæus!—which was substituted for his son on Mount Moriah! the third, with a porphyry tool by Moses; the fourth, by Joshua; and the fifth by Hiram Abiff, before it was deposited in its final bed at the north-east angle of the Temple. Having been placed by Enoch in the basement of his subterranean edifice, it was discovered by Noah, and used as an anchor to fix the Ark on Mount Ararat. Abraham took it thence to Mount Moriah, where it constituted the altar on which he offered Isaac. It formed the pillow of Jacob when he saw his celestial vision of the ladder, and accompanied him in all his wanderings. He bequeathed it to Joseph in Egypt, who directed it to be placed over his grave. Moses took it with him, at the great deliverance, into the wilderness of Arabia. He stood upon this remarkable stone when the Red Sea was divided, and when the Amalekites were defeated; knelt on it when the Tables of the Law were delivered on Mount Sinai; and finally commended it to the care of Joshua, who built his altar on it at Mount Ebal. It was deposited in the Sanctuary at Shilo, until the Temple was erected at Jerusalem, when Solomon directed it to be placed in the foundation as the chief corner-stone. Here it remained undisturbed either by Zerubabel or Herod, as it was destined to defeat the insane attempt of Julian to rebuild the Temple, which it effected by destroying his workmen through the agency of fire.[6]

"A similar fiction about the Rod of Moses was also imported from the Continent, which was traced from the Paradisiacal Tree of Knowledge;[7] another about the institution of Templary, which, as it was said, had its origin in Egypt before the Exodus;[8] that Moses and Aaron, having been initiated into its mysteries, brought it with them into Judæa; that thence it passed through the two St. Johns to the Crusades, &c.; and a fourth, about the imaginary travels of Peleg, and the erection of his triangular Temple.[9] We had another, which recounted the pseudo-history of Hiram Abiff; and many similar ones, which it would be a waste of time to mention. It may be necessary to add, that these fables were not countenanced by any but some young and inexperienced Brethren, who were ambitious of being accounted cleverer and brighter Masons than their fel-

[6] These legends are equally apocryphal with those of the Scottish fabulists about the same stone. They feign that, from the time of Jacob, who used this stone for a pillow, it was preserved in Spain till Gathol, king of the Scots, ruled over Gallicia, and that he used it for a throne. That Simon Brech, another Scottish monarch, about 700 years before Christ, or about the time when Rome was built, conveyed it into Ireland, where it remained for three or four centuries before it was translated into Scotland. When there, it was installed in the Abbey of Scone, as a palladium, and enclosed in an oaken chair by king Kenneth, on which the following verse was engraven:—

> "Ni fallat fatum, Scoti quocunque locatum.
> Invenient lapidem, regnare tenentur ibidem."

This stone and chair were deposited in Westminster Abbey, A.D. 1296, where they still remain. *Utrum horum mavis accipe!*

[7] This legend may be found in the Hist. Landmarks, vol. ii., p. 599.

[8] Ibid., vol. ii., p. 24.

[9] Ibid., vol. i., p. 63.

lows. And you would have been astonished to see the absurd airs of importance which the possessors of these fabulous conceits assumed when the conversation of a Lodge happened to turn upon the abstruse subject of cabalistical acquirements."

My tongue itched to inquire into the particulars of the history of Hiram Abiff, and I had some difficulty to restrain my curiosity. My companion observed the movement, and interpreted it correctly. "You wish to learn something of the reputed private history of this eminent Freemason," he said; "but I am not quite sure that I shall be able to gratify your curiosity, for conjecture, after all, is no great authority. You shall hear some of the legends, however, if it will afford you any satisfaction. Our continental Brethren identified Hiram Abiff with Jesus Christ, and endeavoured to prove that his history was an allegory of the Crucifixion. They contended that the word הירם meant, *He that existed from all eternity*—T. G. A. O. T. U.—Christ;[10] and asserted that in ancient times seven days was the legitimate interval between the ceremony of raising a candidate, and communicating to him the secrets of a Master Mason, in allusion to the period of mourning for his death, which, amongst the Jews, was seven days, as in the recorded instance of the lamentations of Joseph for his father Jacob; and the same period intervened between the resurrection of Christ and his public appearance to his disciples to remove the unbelief of Thomas. And in recounting the history of Masonry, they feigned that the art and mystery of the Order was first introduced at the building of the tower of Babel; and from thence handed down by Euclid, a worthy and excellent mathematician of Egypt; that he communicated it to Hiram Abiff, under whom, at the building of the Temple of Solomon, was an expert architect called Mannon Grecus, who, travelling westward after the Temple was completed, taught the art of Masonry to Carolus Marcel, King of France, from whence it was transplanted into

[10] The passage in my authority is thus stated: "When we divide the word הירם Hiram into two syllables הי־רם Hay-ram, the translation of this word is, He who exists, &c., which explains the Master's Sign."

England in the time of Athelstan, who commanded the Brethren to assemble annually in the city of York!

"They further stated, that the Stylus with which Hiram Abiff drew his plans and designs, and engraved that mysterious diagram on the foundation-stone of the Temple, which is now known as the 47th Proposition of Euclid, was found on his person at his raising, and was ordered by Solomon to be placed in his monument. I omit the fable of his marriage with the sister of Prince Adoniram, his death, burial, monument, obelisk, with its circles, squares, and columns, and Solomon's bitter mourning, together with the distraction and suicide of his widow, because, I dare say, you are heartily sick of this absurd jumble of truth and fiction, where Euclid is made contemporary with the dispersion from Shinar, and Hiram Abiff brother to the Carthaginian Hanno.

"Our Brethren, however, amidst all their fondness for continental innovations and Jewish legends, were not so ungallant to the softer sex as to introduce that graceless illustration of the Valley of Jehoshaphat, or the holy ground on which the Lodge is placed, that was used by the French Masons, viz., as 'a place of peace, harmony, and concord, where cock never crows, women never brawl, nor lion ever roars.'"[11]

Here I was about to violate our compact by repudiating the application of these puerilities to the Masons of the present day, when my mentor hastily moved one of his limbs forward, with an admonitory swagger, and cried out, "Hold! speak not, answer not; the sound of the human voice will annihilate my colloquial powers! I acquit you of any participation in these fabulous inventions. They were excusable a century ago, when the million could neither read nor write, and were obliged to take on credit every vague assertion of those who had the advantage of mental culture; and, therefore, you need not wonder that in times when the fables of King Arthur and his Raven, the Seven Champions, Mother Shipton, and the Predictions of Nostrodamus and the Double-thumbed Miller, were implicitly credited, there

[11] The ladies of France amply revenged themselves by instituting a Freemasonry of their own, and every principal town in France soon exhibited its Lodge of Adoption.

should be found many believers in the spurious legends of continental Masonry.[12]

"I have taken the liberty of digressing at this particular period," continued the Square, "because I have nothing favourable to reveal respecting the transactions of our Lodge under an inefficient Master; but when I passed to Brother Hesletine, our numbers were soon recruited. It is true, masonic impostors and masonic pretenders were numerous and active; but our R. W. M. was ever on the alert, and knew all the vulnerable points of the enemy's position. Thus he was able, by a series of judicious and well-timed exposures of the iniquity of the one and the moral degradation of the other, to silence the gainsayers, and put the scoffers to open shame. He made them feel that men who are willing to prostitute their time and talent for the questionable purpose of gratifying a prurient curiosity, are open to the operation of public opinion, which, when rightly directed, is sure to cover them with confusion and disgrace.

"Brother Hesletine was extremely anxious that the Craft should enjoy the blessings of uniformity in discipline and work. And to contribute to the accomplishment of so desirable an end, he spared neither time nor expense; and not only visited every London Lodge, but made excursions to the most distant parts of the island. Wherever he heard of a Lodge which was celebrated for either the one or the other, that Lodge was certain of a

[12] Amongst the continental Masons of this period, and I believe also in the United States, the following vocabulary was used:—1. Initiated. 2. Passed. 3. Raised. 4. *Mark Master*, Congratulated. 5. *Past Master*, Presided. 6. *Most Excellent Master*, Acknowledged and Received. 7. *Royal Arch*, Exulted in a Chapter. And further, an assembly of *Knights Templars*, was called an Encampment; of *Knights of the Red Cross and Prince of Jerusalem*, a Council; of *Knights of the Christian Mark*, a Conclave; of *Illustrious Knights*, a Grand Chapter; of *Knights of the East and West*, a Grand Council; of the *Grand Patriarch. Prince of Libanus*, a College; of *Chief of the Tabernacle*, a Sovereign Council; of *Prince of the Tabernacle*, a Hierarchy; of *Knights of the Brazen Serpent*, a Court of Sinai; of *Prince of Mercy*, the Third Heaven; of *Sovereign Commander of the Temple at Jerusalem*, a Court; of *Kadosh*, Areopagus; of *Princes of the Royal Secret*, a Consistory; of *Rose Croix*, a Sovereign Chapter; of *Grand Inquisitor Commander*, a Sovereign Tribunal; and of *Sovereign Grand Inspector-General*, a Convocation.

visit from him. He became acquainted with all the different systems of work which presented themselves to his notice, accompanied by their respective Tests or Examination Questions, and he found that every variety of lecture was in practice which had been used from the time of Desaguliers and Anderson to the moment of inquiry. It is a great pity," the Square apostrophized, "that these important marks of distinction were not considered as unalterable as the S. T. & W. A collection of them would, I should think, be a great curiosity; and if you will listen attentively, I will repeat them from Brother Hesletine's notes."

Observing that I took up my pen to jot them down, the Square hastily added, "Hold, hold! my good friend! mind what you are about! I feel myself authorised, without any indiscretion, to communicate to you, *vivâ voce*, both the questions and the answers of these curious Tests; but whether, consistently with your O. B., you can commit to paper anything more than the simple questions, which, of themselves convey no information, is for you to determine, when you have taken a deliberate view of the moral responsibility attached to such an act."

Having said this, my strange companion receded a few steps, to allow me time for deliberation; and the wisdom of his remark appearing incontestable, I determined to act on his advice, and take down the questions only. The Square then proceeded.

"The Tests of Masonry were at that time generally denominated Examination Questions, and may be considered, not merely as curious illustrations of individual feeling at the consecutive periods of its onward progress, but as absolute landmarks to distinguish true from pretended Freemasonry, which were periodically considered necessary by the master minds who successively appeared on the masonic stage; and being arbitrary in their character, were occasionally changed, that the impostor might be more easily detected, and the cowan more effectually exposed.

"The most ancient formula," said the Square, "that I ever heard mentioned by Sir C. Wren, was that which he himself used, and he pronounced its origin to be of a remote and unknown antiquity. The questions were fifty in number, and all of the greatest importance. These were reduced to fifteen when used as a preliminary examination, thus:—1. What o'clock is it? 2. How go Squares? 3. Which is the point of your entry? 4. How many particular points pertain to a Freemason? 5. How many proper points? 6. Why do odds make a Lodge? 7. What Lodge are you of? 8. Where is the Mason's point? 9. Who rules and governs the Lodge as its Master? 10. How many angles in St. John's Lodge? 11. How many steps belong to a right Mason? 12. Give me the solution? 13. What is the Jerusalem Word? 14. What is the Universal Word? 15. What is the right word or right point of a Mason? These Tests ought never to have been altered, because every answer is a landmark.

"The succeeding formula was introduced by Desaguliers and Anderson at the revival in 1717; and though not destined to a very long reign, they were perspicuous and expressive, and a brief summary of their contents were embodied in the following Tests:—1. I. T. B. G. C. T. H. A. T. E. 2. What is the place of the senior apprentice? 3. What are the fixed lights? 4. How ought the R. W. M. to be served? 5. What is the punishment of a Cowan? 6. What is the bone bone-box? 7. How is it said to be opened? 8. By what is the key suspended? 9. What is the proper clothing of a Mason? 10. What is a Mason's brand? 11. How high was the door of the middle chamber? 12. What does this stone smell of? 13. Can you tell me the name of an E. A. P., of a F. C., and of a M. M.? 14. H. T. W. P. O. T. T. P. O. T. T.

"The Lectures or Examinations having been remodelled about the year 1730 by Martin Clare, he thought it expedient to alter the Tests; and his category was approved by the Grand Lodge. It was as follows:— 1. Whence came you? 2. Who brought you here? 3. What recommendation do you bring? 4. Do you know the secrets of Masonry? 5. Where do you keep them? 6. Have you the key? 7. Where is it deposited? 8. When you were made a Mason, what did you consider most desirable? 9. What is the name of your Lodge? 10. Where is it situated? 11. What is its foundation? 12. How did you enter the Temple of Solomon? How many windows did you see there? 14. What is the duty of the youngest apprentice? 15. Have you ever worked as a Mason? 16. What did you work with? 17. Salute me as a Mason.

"This arrangement lasted ten years, and was superseded by an improved series of Examination Questions promulgated by Dr. Manningham, and adopted by most of the metropolitan and several provincial Lodges. Be careful that you take them down correctly, for they are so ingeniously constructed, that the omission or alteration of a single word may cause a mystification that will not be easily unravelled. 1. Where were you made a Mason? 2. What did you learn there? 3. How do you hope to be rewarded? 4. What access have you to that Grand Lodge? 5. How many steps? 6. What are their names? 7. How many qualifications are required in a Mason? 8. What is the standard of a Mason's faith? 9. What is the standard of his actions? 10. Can you name the peculiar characteristics of a Mason's Lodge? 11. What is the interior composed of? 12. Why are we termed Brethren? 13. By what badge is a Mason distinguished? 14. To what do the reports refer? 15. How many principal points are there in Masonry? 16. To what do they refer? 17. Their names. 18. The allusion.

"These Tests continued unaltered down to the period of which I am speaking. A very talented Mason was now rising into notice, who was destined to effect organic changes in the system. I shall reveal his improvements in due course; and he is introduced here simply because he was the author of a brief paper of questions, which he considered more characteristic than any that had preceded them. I allude to Brother Dunckerley, a name which will live as long as Masonry shall endure. His Tests were only ten in number, but each possessed a significant reference to some important landmark of the Order. 1. How ought a Mason to be clothed? 2. When were you born? 3. Where were you born? 4. How were you born? 5. Did you endure the brand with fortitude and patience? 6. The situation of the Lodge? 7. What is its name? 8. With what have you worked as a Mason? 9. Explain the Sprig of Cassia. 19. How old are you?

"About this period," the Square proceeded to say, "a young man named Preston anneared in town from the north, and was initiated in an Athol Lodge, where he displayed such extraordinary intelligence and zeal as elicited the applause of all classes of the Fraternity. Our R. W. M., Bro. Hesletine, heard of his fame, and sought his acquaintance. An attachment sprang up between them, which produced some extraordinary results. Bro. Hesletine induced him to dissolve his connection with the Athol Masons, and to legitimatize himself in a constitutional Lodge. This young man, as the first fruits of his labours, placed in the hands of our R. W. M. a new arrangement of the Tests, which, though not actually introduced till a later period, were read in the Lodge, and highly approved by the Brethren. He divided them into three sections of seven questions each and they contained, as you will hear, some novelties. *First Section.*—1. Whither are you bound? 2. Are you a Mason? 3. How do you know that? 4. How will you prove it to me? 5. Where were you made a Mason? 6. When were you made a Mason? 7. By whom were you made a Mason? *Second Section.*—1. From whence come you? 2. What recommendation do you bring? 3. Any other recommendation? 4. Where are the secrets of Masonry kept? 5. To whom do you deliver them? 6. How do you deliver them? 7. In what manner do you serve your Master? *Third Section.*—1. What is your name? 2. What is the name of your son? 3. If a Brother were lost, where should you hope to find him? 4. How should you except him to be clothed? 5. How blows a Mason's wind? 6. Why does it thus blow? 7. What time is it? [13]

"In this country, in accordance with ancient practice, we admit only three degrees; but on the continent the

[13] To complete this catalogue of masonic Tests it might seem necessary to subjoin the Qualification Questions of Hemming and Shadbolt. But these are so well known amongst the Craft that it would be a work of supererogation to insert them here. And it would savour of egotism if I were to introduce a series of Questions which I myself arranged a few years ago for the same purpose. They consist of nine sections; *i. e.* three to each Degree, containing eighty-one questions in the whole, or nine to every section; systematically constructed on the principle of trichotomy, and prominently exhibiting most of the chief Landmarks of antiquity. Thus each one of our Triad of Degrees has a triad of sections; and the Questions in each section are a triad of triads; having been studiously arranged in a trinal form. I have found them in practice exceedingly useful, being acquired with great facility, and easily retained in the memory.

list was swelled out to the enormous category of twenty degrees of Apprentice,[14] twenty-three of Fellowcraft,[15] and sixty of Master.[16] Although such innovations were prevalent in France and Germany, and found their way secretly amongst ourselves, yet they received no sanction from the masonic authorities, and the Fraternity were cautioned to beware how they introduced any of the foreign fallacies into their Lodges. In many cases, however, curiosity prevailed over expediency, and individuals received them as genuine masonic truths, and had no little pride in their acquisition.

"About this time a remarkable Essay, on the applica-

[14] These were, besides the simple E. A. P. of primitive Masonry, an Apprentice Architect; App. Perfect Architect; App. Prussian Architect; Cabalistic App.; Coen App.; App. of Paracelsus; Egyptian App.; Secret Egyptian App.; Female Egyptian App.; Scotch App.; Scotch Trinitarian App.; Hermetic App.; Male App.; Female App.; Adoptive App.; Mystical App.; App. Philosopher of the number nine; App. Hermetic Philosopher; App. Philosopher of the number three; and the Theosophic App.

[15] For the second degree they admitted a Fellowcraft Mason; F. C. Architect; F. C. Perfect Architect; F. C. Prussian Architect; Cabalistic F. C.; F. C. Coen; F. C. of Paracelsus; Scotch F. C.; Scotch Trinitarian F. C.; Egyptian F. C.; Hermetic F. C.; Mystic F. C.; F. C. Hermetic Philosopher; F. C. Philosopher by the number three; F. C. Sublime Philosopher by the number three; F. C. Philosopher by the number nine; F.C. by the number fifteen; Theosophic F. C.; Biblical F. C.; Discrete F. C.; Female F. C.; Female Egyptian F. C.; and Obligated F. C.

[16] And as a corollary to these fictitious degrees, they had an English Master; a Little English Master; Ancient M.; Grand Architect M.; Perfect Architect M.; Prussian Architect M.; M. by the number fifteen; M. of all degrees; Cabalistic M.; Coen M.; Crowned M.; M. of the Key of Masonry; M. of English Lodges; M. of French Lodges; Mark M.; M. of Paracelsic Masonry; M. of Neapolitan Chapters; M. of Legitimate Lodges; M. of Masters; Most High and Puissant M. of Masters; Perfect M.; Perfect M. of Secrets; Perfect English M.; M. of Egyptian Secrets; M. of Hermetic Secrets; Scotch M.; Egyptian M.; Elect M. of nine; Little Elect M.; M. in Israel; M. in Perfect Architecture; Hermetic M.; Illustrious M.; Illustrious M. of the number fifteen; Illustrious M. of the Seven Cabalistic Secrets; Irish M.; Perfect Irish M.; Puissant Irish M.; Provost Irish M.; Symbolic M.; Mystic M.; M. by Curiosity; Perfect Hamburg M.; Particular M.; Past M.; M. of Hermetic Philosophy; Philosophical M. by the number three; Philosophical M. by the number nine; Pythagorean M.; Four Times Venerable M.; Royal M.; Wise M.; Secret M.; Illustrious Symbolical M.; Sublime Ancient M.; Theosophic M.; M. ad vitam; True M.; and Absolute M.

tion of Geometry to the requirements of moral duty, was circulated amongst the Lodges.[17] It was adapted to symbolical Masonry alone, and was generally attributed to the pen of Bro. Dunckerley. But in 1768 a severe attack on Masonry was commenced by an anonymous writer, who published a pamphlet under the extraordinary title of "Masonry the Way to Hell,"[18] which created some sensation amongst the Metropolitan Craft, and produced a paper war. I remember hearing a discussion on the subject in our Lodge. Some Brethren were inclined to understand it as a serious attack on the Order, while others considered it only as an ill-natured joke; however, it was concluded that the only way of ascertaining the real sentiments of the author would be to feel his pulse by a reply. Bro. Thompson was, therefore, deputed to answer it, which he admirably effected;[19] and another reply came from a quarter with which our Lodge had no connection.[20] The author of the obnoxious pamphlet did not respond, and it was believed that his conscience accused him of having basely slandered a benevolent institution, and that he thought it expedient to atone for his calumny by silence; and the controversy—if it may be called by that name—terminated with a pamphlet bearing the triumphant title of "Masonry the Turnpike-Road to Happiness in this Life, and Eternal Happiness hereafter."[21]

"Amidst all this trifling, the age was not barren in legitimate and well-authenticated publications on pure Masonry.[22] But the gem of the period was the Candid

[17] See the Golden Remains, vol. i., p. 15.

[18] "Masonry the Way to Hell; a Sermon, wherein is clearly proved, both from Reason and Scripture, that all who profess the Mysteries are in a State of Damnation." London, Robinson and Roberts, 1768.

[19] "Remarks on a Sermon lately published, entitled 'Masonry the Way to Hell;' being a Defence of that Order against Jesuitical Sophistry and Calumny. By John Thompson." 1768.

[20] "An Answer to a certain Pamphlet, lately published under the solemn Title of 'A Sermon, or Masonry the Way to Hell.' By John Jackson, Philantropos." 1768.

[21] London, Bladon, 1768.

[22] "Love to God and Man inseparable; a Sermon before the Masons." 1765. "Charge to the Wolverhampton Lodge." 1765. Masonic Sermon, by the Rev. Thomas Bagnall." 1766. "On the Government of the Lodge; delivered before the Brethren of St. George's Lodge, No. 315, Taunton. By John Whitmash." 1765.

Disquisition of Wellins Calcott,[23] in which he has traced primitive Masonry from its origin; explained its symbols and hieroglyphics, its social virtues and advantages; suggested the propriety of building halls for the peculiar and exclusive practice of Masonry, and reprehended its slanderers with great but judicious severity; for the unprincipled charlatans were still working at their masked battery, catering for the morbid curiosity of the profane world, and their shafts flew in clouds about our heads.[24]

In 1769, our R. W. M. was appointed to the office of Grand Secretary, by the Duke of Beaufort, and in that capacity I accompanied him on a visit of inspection into the north of England; and we found considerable variations in the several systems of working amongst the

[23] "A Candid Disquisition of the Principles and Practices of the Most Ancient and Honourable Society of Free and Accepted Masons; together, with some Strictures on the Origin, Nature, and Design of that Institution. By Wellins Calcott." London, 1769.

[24] The following spurious publications were supplied about this time to gratify the curiosity of the uninitiated:—"The Secrets of Masonry revealed; by a disgusted Brother. Containing an ingenious Account of their Origin, their Practices in the Lodges, Signs, and Watchwords, Proceedings at the Makings, &c." London, Scott, 1759. "Allegorical Conversations organized by Wisdom." Hiram, or the Grand Master Key to the Door of both Ancient and Modern Freemasonry; being an accurate Description of every Degree of the Brotherhood, as authorized and delivered in all good Lodges. Containing more than any Book on the Subject ever before published. By a Member of the Royal Arch." London, 1764. Second Edition, London, Griffin, 1766. "An Institute of Red Masonry." 1764. "Shibboleth; or every man a Freemason." 1765. "Solomon in all his Glory, or the Master Mason; being a true Guide to the inmost Recesses of Freemasonry, both Ancient and Modern. Containing a minute Account of the Proceedings. By T. W. Translated from the French Original, published at Berlin, and burnt by Order of the King of Prussia, at the Intercession of the Freemasons." London, Robinson and Roberts, 1766. Second Edition, London, 1768. "The Three distinct Knocks, or the Door of the Ancient Freemasonry opened to all Men, neither naked or clothed, barefooted nor shod; being an universal Description of all its branches, from its first use to this present time, as it is delivered in all Lodges. By W. O. V. M." The sixth Edition. London, Sergeant, 1767. Seventh Edition, London, 1768. Eighth Edition, Clench, 1811. Ninth Edition, London, Hughes, 1825. "The Freemason stripped naked; or the whole Art and Mystery of Freemasonry made Plain and Easy to all Capacities, by a faithful Account of every Secret, from the first making of a Mason till he is completely Master of every Branch of his Profession. By Charles Warren, Esq., late Grand Master of a regularly constituted Lodge in the City of Cork." London, Isaac Fell, 1769.

Brethren of different localities. At the Lodge No. 209, holden at the Plume of Feathers, Bridge street, Chester, we inspected a curious floor-cloth, which had been painted only a short time previous, and contained some reference to the masonic innovations of France and Germany. It consisted of a Mosaic pavement, accessible by three steps, marked AUDI, VIDE, TACE, with the five-pointed blazing star in a circle occupying the centre, flanked by two Corinthian pillars, on the summit of which were placed the sun and moon. The plinth of the sinister column was charged with a diagram, representing, probably, the Mark key-stone, while that on the dexter-side of the pavement was occupied by a ladder in clouds. Each of these pillars was attended or guarded by a naked sword, the one pointed, and the other flaming, to represent Justice and Mercy, together with a Level and Plumb. Over the pavement, and resting on the pillars, was an arch inscribed SIT LUX ET LUX FUIT, with a double key-stone supporting a sphere, and upon it the head of the Redeemer, as T. G. A. O. T. U., surrounded by a nimbus; beneath which was an altar supporting the Holy Bible, placed on a cushion, flanked by masonic emblems. Amongst the clouds above the arch, there appears a radiated triangle, with the word יהוה. At the base of the floor-cloth are three objects; the one an oblong square chest, or Lodge, with an endless serpent on its lid, and the word *ΑΒΡΑΞΑΣ* in front; the centre, a cube, with the three masonic colours, and word אגלא (AGLA,) one of the cabalistic names of the Deity; and the other, a tumulus, with the sprig of Cassia. Above them, the following inscription, *ΘΕΟΝ ΣΕΒΟΥ ΞΕΝΟΥΣ ΞΕΝΙΖΕ.* I remember this floor-cloth distinctly, for it underwent a very particular examination;[25] and Bro. Hesletine took a sketch of it, and delivered a lecture on its peculiarities when he returned to town.

"From Chester we proceeded to Barnard Castle, in the county of Durham, where we found Masonry shining with unsullied lustre, under the active superintendence of Bro. Hutchinson, who worked the details after a per-

[25] This floor-cloth is now in the Cestrian Lodge at Chester; of which my friend, Bro. Willoughby, of Birkenhead, has kindly favoured me with a sketch.

fect model. He delivered his own Lectures, Charges, and Orations, strictly adhering to the ancient landmarks of the Order; and his example was followed by the Masters of other Lodges, who visited the Barnard Castle Lodge for the advantage of his instructions. Many of these detached pieces appeared in print,[26] and were so much admired for the pure principles of Masonry which they enunciated, that the Fraternity at length requested Bro. H. to make a selection from his Lectures, and publish them in a permanent form. He complied with the request, and produced a volume of such surpassing interest, that, after going through many editions,[27] it still retains its value, and is read with avidity by all who are desirous of information on the sterling and unchangeable doctrines of the Order."[28]

[26] See my edition of the Spirit of Masonry, which includes all the works of Bro. Hutchinson.

[27] "The Spirit of Masonry, in Moral and Elucidatory Lectures, by W. Hutchinson." London, Wilkes and Goldsmith, 1775. Second Edition, Carlisle, Jollie, 1795; Third Edition, Carlisle, 1802; Fourth Edition, Edinburgh, MacEvan, 1813; Fifth Edition, Carlisle, 1814; Sixth Edition, London, 1815. Other editions have been published, and the last contains all Bro. Hutchinson's detached pieces. London, Spencer, 1843.

[28] In an Address, prefixed to the second edition, he says, with his usual benevolence of character, "I have been induced to give this edition to the press for the purpose of relieving the family of a worthy but indigent Brother, *by the whole profits of the subscription and sale;* and doubt not that the motive to the present publication will procure it the attention of the Brethren of this excellent Institution . . . . It is hoped that these Lectures may serve to detect the wretched artifices used by wicked men to impose upon the world; and may also excite in the Fraternity the due exercise of those moral works which our profession enjoins."

ERSITY OF CALIFORNIA

CHAPTER VI.

IT RAINS!—DUNCKERLEY.

1770, 1771.

"Do good to theim that ben nedy, and that shall pleyse me more and be better to the than yf thou fastyd xl. yere on brede and water. Do good to thy power in all yt thou may, and put pease and love amonge thy neyghbours, and it shall pleyse me more and be better to the than if thow were every day rauyssht to heaven."—*The Prouffytable Boke for Mannes Soul.*—WYNKIN DE WORDE.

"Cryst then of hys hye grace,
Zeve zow bothe wytte and space,
Wel thys boke to conne and rede,
Heven to have for zowre mede!
Amen! amen! so mot hyt be,
Say we so alle per charyte."
OLD MASONIC MS.

"Thy watchful EYE, a length of time,
The wondrous circle did attend;
The glory and the power be thine,
Which shall from age to age descend."
DUNCKERLEY.

THE Square thus moralized in continuance of its Revelations:—

"The mind of man is an inscrutable mystery, past finding out. Talk of the mysteries of Freemasonry, they are nothing to the enigma of the human mind. There are so many springs of thought—so many motives of action, that positive results can never be divined by any series of preconceived notions. If a locomotive is out of order, the engineer will speedily set it to rights: if a vessel has lost its helm, the shipwright will restore it safe and sound; but if a man's ideas become disarranged, it is twenty to one whether they ever resume their original tone. In the course of my experience, I have witnessed many well-regulated Lodges; but the end has been attained by so many different processes, that I have often wondered how they should happen to conduce to the same harmonious conclusion.

"Bro. Hesletine was a good Master; and so was his successor, although differing *toto cœlo* from each other in character and style of government. The former being appointed to the high office of Grand Secretary, in May, 1769, I was transferred, at the ensuing election of officers, to a young but very zealous Mason, named Dagge, who had served as a warden in the Caledonian Lodge, holden at 'The Ship,' in Leadenhall street. Being in easy circumstances, he devoted the greater portion of his time to the study of Masonry, and the duties of the Lodge; and as industry generally produces excellence, he soon became a proficient in the art.

"It will be plainly seen that Bro. Dagge had a great affection for the Order; and if his enthusiasm did not, like that of the Spanish Don, cause him to mistake windmills for giants, Benedictines for enchanters, and a flock of harmless sheep for an army of 'divers and innumerable nations,' bristling with lances, and advancing, with banners displayed and trumpets sounding to the charge, it sometimes led him into ludicrous situations. He would, occasionally, when he had an hour to spare, get the key of the Lodge-room from Mrs. Kitching, the woman in whose custody it was deposited, and, locking himself in, would open the Lodge, lecture the empty benches with becoming gravity, close the Lodge, lock the door, and take his departure, very much edified with this supererogatory exercise.

"This occurred so often in the early part of his career as Master of the Lodge, that two or three of his most intimate friends concocted a scheme for detecting him in the fact. Having arranged their plans, with the assistance of Mrs. Kitching, they watched his motions, and very soon had the satisfaction of surprising him in the act of riding his hobby at railroad speed. When he next called for the key,—after pretending to search for it, first in one place, then in another,—the woman said, 'Oh, I remember, I swept out the Lodge, and dusted the furniture yesterday, and forgot to lock the door; I must have left the key in the lock. You will find the door open, sir.' The door, indeed, was open, but the key had been removed; and consequently he was unable to secure himself, as usual, from interruption. He cared very little for this, as he had not the slightest anticipation of being intruded on. He placed me on his breast, and mounting his rostrum before the pedestal, opened the Lodge, and commenced the first lecture, addressing his imaginary Wardens and Brethren, with all due seriousness and decorum, with

"'Bro. Senior Warden, where did you and I first meet?' and the worthy lecturer went swimmingly on through the first three sections.

"While he was thus pleasantly engaged, Mrs. Kitching, the agent of mischief, sent a message to the conspirators, to apprise them that the mouse was in the trap. By the time they were assembled below, Bro. Dagge had got into the marrow of his subject, and was enlightening the benches and tables on the theological virtues, with his mind wholly wrapped up in the fascinating employment, when, at a pause in the discourse, he fancied he heard something like a suppressed titter. No—it could not be: his ears had deceived him. He looked at the entrance-door from the Tyler's room,—it was closely tyled: he listened,—all was silent, and he resumed the thread of his argument, on the chequered scenes of life figured in the Mosaic pavement of the Lodge. 'To-day success may crown our labours, while to-morrow we may be suddenly surprised,'—again the same noise was repeated. 'What can it be?' said Bro. Dagge to himself; 'Oh, some people in the garden below. I wish Mrs. Kitching would be more on her guard.' Satisfied with this conclusion, he started off again in full career. 'Then let us ever act according to the dictates of reason and religion, and cultivate harmony, maintain charity, and live in unity and brotherly love!'

"At this point the door opened, and in walked three Brethren, with Mrs. Kitching at their heels, freely indulging in the laugh they could no longer restrain. 'Capital!' they shouted. 'Ah! Dagge, my boy!' exclaimed Bro. Hesletine, 'I am glad to see you in harness! Take care the hobby does not throw you!'

"'R. W. Sir,' said Bro. Rowland Berkeley, who was one of the party, with an appearance of great respect, 'we hope the Brethren are edified.'

"'They are very silent and attentive,' said Bro. Bottomley, 'as in duty bound; and are, no doubt, considerably benefitted by such a learned dissertation.'

" 'Aye,' rejoined Bro. Hesletine; 'sure never R. W. M. was blessed with such an obedient Lodge of Brethren. There is not a scabbed sheep amongst them. Hope you will favour us with a touch of your quality, R. W. Sir.'

" 'What have you done with the key?' Mrs. Kitching slily asked, with a mischievous leer at her companions. 'I hope you have not taken it out of the lock, for I don't see it there.'

"This brought on an uproarious peal of laughter from the conspirators, as Bro. Dagge descended from his elevation to meet his brother officers.

"He met the joke," said the Square, "with his usual good nature, for he was too enthusiastic to care anything for their jeers. *Finis coronat opus* was his motto, and he worked it out famously. Freemasonry was his hobby. He rode it hard, and it mattered little who saw him mounted. And this is the feeling which leads to success and eminence, as it actually did in his case, for he rose to the office of S. G. W. in 1778.

"At the expiration of Bro. Dagge's year, during which the circumstances of the Lodge were greatly improved, I had the good fortune to fall into the hands of the most eminent Mason of the age," my garrulous companion continued,—"Bro. Thomas Dunckerley, an expert Master, and a good tactician. He was supposed to be the natural son of King George II., and his manners did not belie his breeding.[1] He was a perfect gentleman and a ripe scholar,

[1] The anecdote is too interesting to be passed over in silence. It is thus related by his biographer: "In the year 1760, on his return from the siege of Quebec, an event happened which could not but fill him with astonishment; as it placed him in a new and most extraordinary point of view. A lady, receiving the sacrament on her death bed, made a declaration in all the awful solemnity of the occasion, by which it appeared that Bro. Dunckerley owed his birth to the first Personage in the kingdom; and Nature was determined that it never should be questioned."—(F. M. Mag., 1793, p. 378.) And those who have seen his portrait, which now occupies a prominent situation in the Preparing Room of the Royal Cumberland Lodge, at Bath, have been struck with the resemblance which it bears to the Royal Family now on the throne of England. Bro. Dunckerley, on this discovery, adopted the Royal Arms, with the bend sinister for distinction, and assumed, in his confidential correspondence, the name of Fitz-George,

combining a knowledge of science and philosophy with grace and dignity of deportment, and the uniform practice of every moral and religious duty. At the period now under consideration, he was a student at one of the inns of court, and was in due time called to the bar.[2]

"Though conversant in scientific and philosophical researches, he was of too virtuous and vigorous a frame of mind, and too well grounded in his religious and moral principles, ever to suffer philosophy to lead to infidelity; but all the Christian truths received his most hearty concurrence, and all the Christian virtues his constant practice.

"In the Lodge he intermingled the *fortiter in re* so judiciously with the *suaviter in modo*, that, while the Society over which he presided was in the highest state of discipline, there was an ease and comfort amongst the Brethren which elevated the character of the Lodge, and procured for us the honour of many distinguished visitors, who all admired the quiet and easy deportment of Bro. Dunckerley in the chair, and the orderly and respectful conduct of the Brethren.

"In conducting the business of the Lodge, Bro. Dunckerley did not content himself with the usual commonplace demonstrations contained in the Lodge lectures, but, like a skilful navigator, boldly launched forth into unknown seas, in the hope of discovering regions hitherto unexplored, where he might work a virgin soil in search of unfolded riches, or detect the germ of new and interesting sources of knowledge. And he was eminently successful; for he discovered and brought to light a hidden vein of science, which had escaped the penetration of all the eminent men who had preceded him in the same track. His indefatigable exertions and self-devotion

and the motto, FATO NON MERITO. I have in my possession, by the kindness of Bro. Percy Wells, the present W. M. of the Royal Cumberland Lodge (1854), a genuine impression of his seal.

[2] At the demise of George II., which happened almost at the moment of the above disclosure, his friends, who were of high rank, laid his case before the new king, who generously allowed him £100 a year, which was subsequently augmented to £800, out of the privy purse; and this, with the profits of his profession, put him into easy circumstances; and it is due to his memory to add, that his charities were boundless, and the destitute Brother never applied to him in vain.

to the holy cause soon advanced him to the greatest dignities Freemasonry had it in her power to bestow.

"By the indefatigable assiduity of this truly masonic luminary, Masonry made considerable progress, not only within his own province of Hampshire, but in many other counties in England. In grateful testimony of his zealous exertions for many years to promote the honour and interest of the Society, the Grand Lodge conferred upon him the rank of Past Senior Grand Warden, and that in all processions he was entitled to take place next the present Senior Grand Warden for the time being.

"He was also Provincial Grand Master for the city and county of Bristol, the counties of Dorset, Essex, Gloucester, Hereford, Somerset, Southampton, and the Isle of Wight; Grand Superintendent and Past Grand Master of Royal Arch Masons for the city and county of Bristol, the counties of Dorset, Essex, Gloucester, Hereford, Kent, Nottingham, Somerset, Southampton, Surrey, Suffolk, Sussex, and Warwick, under the patronage of His Royal Highness the Duke of Clarence; and Most Eminent and Supreme Grand Master of Knights of Rosa Crucis, Templars, K. H., &c., of England,[3] under His Royal Highness Prince Edward, Patron of the Order.[4]

"Bro. Dunckerley was well known as a Mason," the Square continued, "and had acquired a competent general knowledge of the Craft before the period in which I am introducing him to your notice, for he delivered a Charge at Plymouth in 1757 on the Light and Truth of Masonry,[5] which in a printed form spread through the

[3] Bro. Dunckerley introduced a revised Lecture into the military degrees, which was received into the several Encampments under the designation of "Dunckerley's Sections." A copy of this document has been placed in my hands by Bro. Wells, and I find it concise, but perfectly comprehensive and intelligible. He has also favoured me with an impression of the Official Seal which he used to verify his documents as G. M. of Templars. and Rosa Crucis.

[4] "These masonic titles show the high sense which the G. Lodge entertained of his abilities and exertions; the great trust reposed in him by the Heir Apparent and his illustrious Brothers; and the very great esteem and regard with which he is honoured (we had almost said adored) by hundreds of Brethren in the above-mentioned counties."—(Freemasons' Mag., 1793, p. 377.)

[5] "The Light and Truth of Masonry explained; being the substance of a Charge delivered at Plymouth in April, 1757. By Thomas Dunckerley." Davey and Law, 1757. See Golden Rem., vol. i., p. 137.

length and breadth of the land, and will be known and admired as long as Masonry endures. I had the gratification of being present at its delivery, and can assure you that the exquisite grace of the orator, and the rich modulation of his musical voice, entranced the hearers. The feelings of the Brethren were wound up to such a pitch of intensity that a pin might have been heard to drop in the midst of that numerous assembly. There was silence in heaven for the space of half an hour.

"After this time he saw a great deal of service as an officer in the navy, and was at the taking of Quebec. The roar of cannon, and the outcry of bloody conflict, however, proved insufficient to stifle the still, small voice of benevolence and peace which reigned triumphant in his bosom; and he had only returned to this country a short time before he was induced to accept the office of R. W. M. of our Lodge. He delivered two other addresses,—one at Marlborough,[6] and the other at Colchester,[7] which increased his popularity as a Mason, and were printed and extensively circulated amongst the Craft.

"Bro. Dunckerley was the oracle of the Grand Lodge, and the accredited interpreter of its Constitutions. His decision, like the law of the Medes and Persians, was final on all points both of doctrine and discipline, and against it there was no appeal. His views of Masonry were liberal, and he despised sectarian controversy. He frequently visited the *Ancient* Masons' Lodges for the purpose of ascertaining what was the actual difference between the two systems, as Lawrence Dermott, in the Ahiman Rezon, had confidently boasted of the superiority of their mode of work over that which was recommended by the legitimate Grand Lodge; and he carefully culled its flowers, and transplanted them into Constitutional Masonry; for he actually found amongst the ancients, to his undisguised astonishment, several material innovations in their system, including some alteration of

[6] September 11, 1769.

[7] "A Sermon preached at St. Peter's Church in Colchester, June 24, 1777. By W. Martin Deake; before the Provincial Grand Master and the Grand Lodge of Essex. To which is added, a Charge, by Bro. Dunckerley, and an Address, by Bro. Henry Chalmers." Colchester, 1778.

the Old Landmarks, and a new application of the Master's Word. As John Wesley is said to have observed, when he adopted some popular ditty to his collection of hymns,—'It is a pity the devil should monopolize all the best tunes,' so our Bro. Dunckerley, how loudly soever the self-styled *Ancients* might blow their schismatical trumpet, and proclaim the exclusive excellence of their schism, resolved that they should not appropriate to themselves a single pearl of any real value towards the elucidation of the Craft. And hence, when he was authorized by the Grand Lodge to construct a new code of Lectures by a careful revision of the existing ritual, and a collation of all the ancient forms, he executed the task so well, that the Grand Lodge adopted it without alteration, and enjoined its practice on all the Lodges under its jurisdiction.

"These were the palmy days of Masonry," said the Square, exultingly, "and it is doubtful whether it has ever been in greater repute than under the direction of this learned and philosophical Brother. In one instance, he certainly laid himself open to the charge of building on another man's foundation, for he reconstructed Dermott's Royal Arch, and introduced it into the Grand Lodge of England. It was a bold attempt; but from the patronage of the Duke of Clarence, united with his own influence in Grand Lodge, it was eminently successful. I cannot deny but it was an innovation, for it absolutely disarranged the Landmarks, by transferring the Master's Word to a subsidiary Degree. And so it was generally considered at its first introduction. It was like grafting a crab upon an apple-stock. But time has effected wondrous changes. The crab has ripened into a most delicious fruit, and the improved Royal Arch Degree is now considered the perfection of Masonry.[8]

"Bro. Dunckerley found among the ancient Masons a French work, which, taken as a corollary to their professions of superior antiquity, constituted a curious anomaly that is deserving of a passing notice, its professed object being to rebut the claims of Masonry to a high antiquity,

[8] I have in my possession a copy of the R. A. Lecture which was introduced by Bro. Dunckerley into Grand Lodge on the above occasion. It is a curious and interesting document, as constituting a fair evidence of the nature of R. A. Masonry at its commencement in 1740.

and to limit its existence to the last two hundred years. The author confidently asserts that it was a purely English invention, never contradicted by the Fraternity when speaking with each other in confidence, and tacitly acknowledged by all foreign Lodges, which are nothing more than branches from this original stock. And he asks triumphantly, 'But what happy mortal amongst the English has been able so to interest the heavens in his favour, as to gain the glorious title of founder of this Order? There are few who will guess at him from the hints I have given, yet still fewer who, like him, could penetrate into the very heart of man, could trace all its windings, and draw from him all his thoughts; fewer who, like him, could at one glance discern the advantages of such an Institution, the means of establishing it with success, and of making it useful to his political and religious designs. There are few whom (as the poet says) Jupiter eyes so partially, as suddenly to dispel the night which environs them, and bringing them into light, to show them truths concealed from others under shadows and hieroglyphics. In a word, it wanted a CROMWELL to insure success. A genius so vast as his could alone embrace a project of such importance, and contrive the means of supporting it, until its final and surprising execution astonished the world by a most terrible metamorphosis. If we refer to the masonic deliberations of those days, we may discover in them storms continually increasing, and powers sleeping on the very verge of a precipice. . . . . The Order frequently changed its name in the first year of its formation. That which it now bears was the first; its partisans afterwards called themselves Levellers, then Independents, afterwards Fifth Monarchy Men. At last, they resumed their original name of Freemasons, which they keep to this day. They had a standard upon which was a lion *couchant*, to designate the lion of the tribe of Judah, with this motto,—WHO SHALL DARE TO ROUSE HIM UP?'

"What do you think of this, sir? But more extraordinary things are yet to come. The author gives the following unique application of the symbolical Temple of Solomon: 'The Society adopted the Temple of Solomon for its symbol, because it was the most stable and the most magnificent structure that ever existed, whether we consider its foundation or superstructure; so that of all the societies men have invented, no one was ever more firmly united, or better planned, than the Masons. Its chief aim is to conciliate and tame the passions, to establish among men the spirit of peace and concord, which may render them impenetrable to the feelings of hatred and dissension, those bitter enemies which poison the best of our days;—to inculcate sentiments of honour and probity, which may render men more attentive to their respective duties;—to teach a dutiful obedience to the orders of parents and princes;—to support towards one another the tender relation of Brothers, by which name they address each other;—and, in a word, to form an admirable sect, whose only aim is liberty, love, and equality. If this interpretation should not be to the taste of the candidate, or if he feels any repugnance to adopt it, they well know how to reply in a manner still more artificial. The Temple of Solomon, then, signifies nothing more than a Temple sacred to the Virtues, which are practised by the Society in the greatest perfection; a dungeon destined for the vices, where these monsters groan under the most rigorous confinement. . . . . . The edifices which Freemasons build are nothing more than virtues or vices to be erected or destroyed; and in this case heaven only occupies their minds, which soar above a corrupted world. The Temple of Solomon denotes reason and intelligence, &c.'[9]

[9] It is believed that this authority, and a few other writers of the same school, induced the English Opium Eater to assert, in the *London Magazine* for 1824, as *a fact established upon historical research*, "that before the beginning of the 17th century, no traces are to be met with of the Masonic Order." And he adds, "that although the Arabs have been the instructors of the moderns in mathematics, astronomy, astrology, medicine, materia medica, and chemistry—and although it is very probable that from the Arabs might have originally proceeded the conceit of physical mysteries without the aid of magic, such as the art of gold-making, the invention of a panacea, the philosopher's stone, and other chimeras of alchymy which afterwards haunted the heads of the Rosicrucians and the elder Freemasons; but of cabalism and theosophy, which occupied both sects in that early period, the Arabs as Mahometans could know nothing. I am willing to concede," he concludes, "that alchymists, cabalists, and dealers in the black art, there were unquestionably before the 17th century, but not Rosicrucians and Freemasons, connected into a secret Society and distinguished by peculiar characteristics."

"We had once a rich scene in our Lodge, during Bro. Dunckerley's Mastership, which carries with it a useful lesson, and ought not to be disregarded," proceeded my gossipping companion, who, like the barber in the Arabian Nights, would not suffer anybody to talk but himself "A stranger presented himself as a visitor, was examined, and admitted. He proved to be of a respectable standing in society, although on the present occasion he lent himself to the perpetration of a very disreputable affair; and the R. W. M., with all his tact and discrimination, was very nearly outwitted. An ancient law of Masonry provided that no visitor, however skilled in the art, shall be admitted into a Lodge unless he is personally known to, or well vouched and recommended by, some of the Brethren then present. Many occasions arose in which it had been deemed expedient to remit the strict observance of the rule, and such had been the case in the present instance. The intruder, however, had not occupied his precarious position more than five minutes, before a venerable Brother called aloud,—'IT RAINS!'

"Brother Dunckerley's presence of mind did not forsake him in this emergency, and he gravely demanded of the visitor,—'Where were you made a Mason?'

"The answer was at hand. 'In a Lodge at the King's Head, Gravesend.'

"This reply betrayed him; the daw was stripped of his borrowed plumes. The Brethren rose simultaneously from their seats in some degree of unnecessary alarm, like a flock of sheep in the presence of a strange dog.[10]

"Indeed, if the Wandering Jew had appeared among them in *propriâ personâ*, they would scarcely have exhibited a more urgent demand for his summary expulsion than was implied in the loud and universal murmur of disapprobation which was heard from every part of the Lodge. The intruder was perplexed; he saw his error, but knew not the remedy: and when the R. W. M. quietly observed: 'Now, sir, will you be kind enough to favour us with your version of the story,' he replied, in the language of Canning's Knife Grinder:—

[10] The Square is inclined to be facetious here. A strange dog (*κυων*), filling the flock with apprehension, is brought forward as an apt comparison to the appearance of a strange eaves-dropper (cowan) amongst the Brethren of a Tyled Lodge.—P. D.

"'Story!—Lord bless you!—I have none to tell! I was anxious to see a Lodge of Brethren at work; and one of your seceding Members furnished me with answers to a few questions which he said would be proposed in the Tyler's room, and for a frolic I was determined to test their truth, as, at the very worst, I could only be rejected, which I did not conceive would be either a disappointment or a disgrace; for, to say the truth, I scarcely expected to gain admittance into the Lodge.'

"What was to be done? The dilemma was pressing, and various opinions were proposed and discussed, while the delinquent was securely locked up in the preparing-room, and left in darkness to his own agreeable reflections. The confusion in King Agramante's camp, so well described by Ariosto, where one said one thing and another the reverse, may convey some idea of the consternation which ensued. All spoke together, and the reins of authority seemed to have been unnaturally snapped asunder; for the R. W. M. had retired with his Wardens behind the pedestal, leaving the Brethren in the body of the room to denounce or threaten at their pleasure; and their objurgations were rather amusing than otherwise. One or two young members, in the exuberance of their zeal, thoughtless and ill-judging, like sailors at the prospect of a wreck breaking open the spirit-room, jumped upon the benches, like Victor Hugo's scholars in Notre Dame,[11] vociferating,—'Out with him! Down with the intruder! Turn him out!'

"Others were more moderate. One Brother observed, in a deprecatory tone of voice: 'He ought not to have been admitted.' A fat Brother, with a red face peering from under a periwig and *queue*, who had not taken the trouble, amidst all this excitement, to move from his seat, quietly asked, 'Who examined him?' And others, acting under the impulse so universally displayed by the young men on the bench, were clamorous that the watch should be called in, and the intruder transferred to the round-house.

"Meanwhile, Bro. Dunckerley had matured his plan, and having ascended into the chair, and given the signal which appeased the tumult, and brought every Brother to his seat in a moment, he said:—

[11] The Square anachronizes.—P. D.

"'Brethren,—I need not tell you that we are placed at this moment in a situation where a false step may involve not only this Lodge but the entire Craft in unknown difficulties. It was the maxim of Socrates,—it is well to punish an enemy, but it is better to make him your friend. Now we must not content ourselves with asking who examined him? or why he was admitted? for he is actually amongst us; and it is too late to prevent the intrusion. And if we were to adopt that worthy Brother's advice who recommended him to be turned out, the matter would not be greatly mended;—the principal difficulty would still remain. I conceive, therefore, that the wisest course we can pursue under these untoward circumstances will be, to use our best endeavors towards converting this temporary evil into a permanent benefit, as the bee extracts honey from the most poisonous flowers, by transforming the unwelcome cowan into a worthy Mason. For this purpose I propose that—if his station in life be not objectionable—the provision of our bye-laws respecting the admission of candidates be suspended in this single instance, and that he be initiated on the spot.'

"The proposition was regularly seconded by the S. W., and was unanimously agreed to; and the intruder was again introduced by the Senior E. A. P., for we had in our Lodges at that time neither Deacons nor Inner Guard. The R. W. M. first examined him as to his residence, trade, and respectability of character; and these inquiries being satisfactorily disposed of, the question was proposed, whether he would adopt the alternative of being made a Mason, to avoid the disgrace of being posted as an impostor.

"He said nothing could be more acceptable to his wishes. In fact, it was the very proposal he intended to make himself, as an atonement for his error, and a means of wiping away his disgrace. He accordingly received the first degree, and not only proved an excellent and zealous Mason, but in due course rose to the chair of the Lodge.

"The origin of the above significant watchword," continued the Square, prosingly, as if he was taking credit to himself for communicating some very important secret which was known to none but himself,—"Don't speak!" —he ejaculated, in a sharp and eager tone of voice, as I exhibited indications of a reply,—"Don't speak, and you shall hear! In our time, a cowan, or over-curious uninitiated person, who was detected in the fact of listening, or attempting to procure, by any undue means, a knowledge of the peculiar secrets of Masonry, was termed an eavesdropper, from the nature of the infliction to which he was subjected. He was placed under the eaves of a house in rainy weather, and retained there till the droppings of the water ran in at the collar of his coat, and out at his shoes, and, therefore, the phrase, '*it rains*,' indicates that a cowan is present, and the proceedings must be suspended.

"Bro. Dunckerley always endeavoured to keep the Lodge in good humour, and it was seldom, indeed, that he was unsuccessful. He adopted a very judicious method of lecturing, which never failed to interest the most careless Brother. His lectures were often delivered extemporaneously, and interspersed with amusing anecdotes. He knew the value of that Horatian maxim, *Misce stultitiam consiliis brevem*, and used it with a most beneficial effect. He was an acquaintance of the celebrated lexicographer Dr. Johnson; and I remember, on some particular occasion, when the Lodge was remarkably full, he entertained the Brethren, at the close of a copious illustration of the Theological and Cardinal Virtues, with the following characteristic sketch. A person in company with Ursa Major, as the learned doctor was sometimes denominated, said he had been so unfortunate as to displease Dr. Johnson, and, wishing to reinstate himself in his good opinion, thought he could not do it more effectually than by decrying such light amusements as those of tumbling and rope-dancing. In particular, he asserted that a rope-dancer was, in his opinion, the most despicable of human beings. Johnson (awfully rolling himself as he prepared to speak, and bursting out into a thundering tone) said, 'Sir, you might as well say that St. Paul was the most despicable of human beings. Let us beware how we petulantly and ignorantly traduce a character which puts all other characters to shame. Sir, a rope-dancer concentrates in himself all the Theological and Cardinal Virtues. We will begin with Temperance. Sir, if the joys of the bottle entice him one inch beyond the line of sobriety, his life or his limbs must pay the forfeit of his excess. Then, sir, there is Faith without unshaken confidence in his own powers, and full assurance that the rope is firm, his temperance will be of little advantage; the unsteadiness of his nerves will prove as fatal as the intoxication of his brain. Next, sir, we have Hope: a dance so dangerous who ever exhibited unless lured by the hope of fortune or fame? Charity next follows: and what instance of Charity shall be opposed to that of him who, in the hope of administering to the gratification of others, braves the hiss of multitudes, and derides the dread of death? Then, sir, what man will withhold from the funambulist the .praise of Justice, who considers his inflexible uprightness, and that he holds his balance with so steady a hand as neither to incline to the one side or the other? Nor, in the next place, is his Prudence more disputable than his justice. And, sir, those who shall refuse to the rope-dancer the applauses due to temperance, faith, hope, charity, justice, and prudence, yet will scarcely be so hardened as to deny him the laurels of fortitude. He that is content to totter on a cord while his fellow-mortals tread securely on the broad basis of *terra firma*—who performs the jocund evolutions of the dance on a superficies compared with which the verge of a precipice is a stable station, may rightfully snatch the wreath from the conqueror and the martyr—may boast that he exposes himself to hazards from which he might fly to the cannon's mouth as a refuge or a relaxation! Sir, let us now be told no more of the infamy of the rope-dancer!'

"The masonic career of Bro. Dunckerley was brilliant as the stately progress of a comet amidst the permanent orbs of heaven; and he was regarded, according to the testimony of an eminent contemporary, as a great masonic luminary. He was truly a Master in Israel; and, by the powerful efficacy of his moral example, controlled the destinies of the Order, which

——'From pole to pole,
Its sacred law expands,
Far as the mighty waters roll,
To bless remotest lands.'

And his memory will be dear to every true-hearted Brother as long as Masonry shall endure. When his year of office expired, the Brethren earnestly entreated him to retain possession of the chair; but his public duties left him no time to devote to the business of a private Lodge, and he felt himself obliged to decline the offer, although he expressed his extreme reluctance to dissolve his connection with a Society of Brethren, amongst whom he had enjoyed so many hours of unalloyed happiness.

"He did not, however," the Square continued, as if he knew not when he had said enough in praise of this distinguished Brother, "he did not cease to evince, on all occasions, an anxious desire to promote the sacred cause of Masonry long after his resignation of the Chair of our Lodge; and under his able superintendence the affairs of his Provinces were prosperous and well managed;[12] for

[12] Amongst other instances of benefits which were derived from his zeal and activity as a P. G. M., may be mentioned with commendation, his resuscitation of the old Lodge, No. 59, according to the authority of the engraved Lists, but numbered 39 in the printed Quarterly Communications, holden at the White Bear in Bath, which was established May 13, 1733, and its union with the Royal Cumberland Lodge in that city, No. 309, in 1784. The latter had been recently instituted by himself; and he projected the junction to enable it to take precedence in the Province by the adoption of the former number, which, at the closing up of the Lists of Lodges in 1792, was advanced to No. 36. I have the pleasure of offering to my readers the following reminiscence of this eminent Mason, extracted from the private MSS. of Bro. Charles Phillott, a banker in Bath, who was initiated by Bro. Dunckerley, and proved, for many years, an active and zealous member of the Lodge. It appears to have been the first meeting after the union of the two Lodges.

"At a Lodge of Free and Accepted Masons called the Royal Cumberland Lodge, held at the Bear Inn, in the city of Bath, on Wednesday, the 11th day of August, 1784, pursuant to a Warrant of Dispensation for that purpose, under the hand and seal of Thomas Dunckerley, Esq., Provincial Grand Master for the counties of Essex, Gloucester, Dorset, and Somerset, bearing date the 7th day of August, 1784. The following Brethren were assembled.

"Brother Thomas Dunckerley, P. G. M.—M. pro tem.
" William Street, S. W.—pro tem.
" Milborne West, J. W.—pro tem.
" Thomas West, T.—pro tem.
" Harry Atwood, } Members of the said Lodge.
" Philip George, }
" John Smith, P. G. Sy. }
" Thomas Woolley, P. G. Stew. } Visitors.
" Peter Appleby, P. G. Stew. }
" William Birchall. }

"A Lodge of the first degree was opened in due form, and it was

Freemasonry was all in all to Bro. Dunckerley, whether as an employment, an amusement, or a medium for the practice of every moral and social duty. He gave numerous masonic parties at Hampton Court, where he resided, to eminent Brethren in all classes of society, amongst whom I could name, if I were so disposed, many estimable men, whose virtues shed a lustre on their rank and title; and where was the Brother who did not covet the honour of a card to these most agreeable reunions? Nor did his profuse hospitality, though it trenched awfully on his purse and his time, prevent his regular attendance on the public meetings and festivals of the Craft, and particularly in those provinces where he held rank. But it made him poor. And, coupled with his liberality, which never suffered a needy Brother to apply in vain, his pecuniary difficulties ceased only with his life. *Quando ullum inveniemus parem?* He died at Portsmouth, A.D. 1795, at the age of 71 years, universally lamented by the Fraternity."[13]

proposed and unanimously agreed that Charles Phillott, of the said city of Bath, Banker, be made a Mason. He was called in; received the first degree, and *the Lodge was then closed.* After which a Lodge of the second degree was opened, when our Brother Charles Phillott was passed, and the Lodge closed."

[13] A writer (Fidus) in *The Freemasons' Quarterly Review*, 1842, exclaims, when recording this event, "Alas! for human nature! Bro. Dunckerley's masonic example was lost on his son, who embittered the last years of his existence. Extravagance straitened the means—disorderly conduct afflicted the mind of the fond, unhappy parent. Every means were tried ineffectually to reclaim the wretched son. At his father's death, there being no provision left, he became a wanderer and an outcast. At last he became a bricklayer's labourer, and was seen carrying a hod on his shoulders, ascending a ladder! This poor fellow's misfortunes and misconduct at length terminated, and the grandson of a king died in a cellar in St. Giles's."

LIBRARY OF THE UNIVERSITY OF CALIFORNIA

CHAPTER VII.

DISCIPLINE.—DR. DODD

1772—1777.

"Sezets, senhors, e aiats pas;
So que direm ben escoutas;
Car la lisson, es de vertat,
Non hy a mot de falsetat."

RAYNOUARD.

"Silent be they, and far from hence remove,
By scenes like ours not likely to improve;
Who never paid the honour'd muse her rights,
Who senseless lived in wild, impure delights;
I bid them once, I bid them twice begone,
I bid them thrice, in still a louder tone:
Far hence depart, whilst we with voice and song,
Our solemn feast, our tuneful nights prolong."

ARISTOPHANES.—*Beloe's Translation.*

"Freemasonry annihilates all parties, conciliates all private opinions, and renders those who, by their Almighty Father, were made of one blood, to be also of one heart and one mind;—Brethren bound, firmly bound together by that indissoluble tie, the love of their God, and the love of their kind."—DR. DODD.

"IT was the observation of a wisdom greater than man can boast," said the Square, resuming its Revelations, "that a house or kingdom divided against itself cannot stand; and experience proves the soundness of the axiom. This proverb may be applied with great propriety to an institution whose members are segregated from the rest of the world by obligations, customs, and laws of a peculiar nature, yet retain their independence of character by a perfect freedom of thought and action. In such a society a judicious ruler is absolutely essential, not merely to its prosperity, but to its very existence. If the shepherd be careless or inefficient, the flock will be scattered abroad. It will be in vain to apply stimulants. All love for the institution will vanish if it lack the food which gives it vitality and freshness.

"Unity is the mainspring of Freemasonry. Destroy that, and the machinery will fall in pieces. The divine science will be unattractive, if divested of its divinity or vivifying power. When the soul has departed, the body becomes a putrid mass of worthless carrion. It will be a difficult matter to preserve the links in the chain of unity unbroken, unless the Master pursue an accommodating policy, which may cause the Brethren to be mutually pleased with each other's society, accompanied by an inflexible regard to discipline, which, while it allows freedom of action, will preserve inviolable the respectful submission that is due to the chair, as its undoubted and unalienable prerogative.

"These remarks," continued the Square, "have arisen out of the condition of our Lodge at the point of time to which events have gradually conducted us; for I have now the misfortune to record another melancholy instance of mismanagement and its consequences; which will show that a man may be extremely clever and intelligent in the ordinary business of life, and yet be incapable of conducting the affairs of a Lodge, so as to produce unanimity amongst the Brethren, and prosperity to the Institution.

"Our next Master, who was installed on St. John's day, Dec, 27, 1771, as Bro. Dunckerley's successor, was a medical practitioner of some repute. Being an intelligent young man, and fond of Masonry, he had passed through the preliminary offices creditably, and had not only acquired a competent knowledge of the Lectures and ceremonies, but to a certain extent possessed the confidence of the Brethren.

"But, alas! my friend, with all this sail, he wanted ballast. Like Sterne's *Yorick*, he was utterly unpractised in the world; and at the age of thirty, knew just about as well how to steer his course in it, as a romping, unsuspicious girl of thirteen. His great failing was a constitutional infirmity which biased his judgment with respect to the progress of time. *Tempus fugit* was no motto for him. He could not understand it. And, consequently, he seldom kept an appointment with any degree of punctuality. His friends and patients had frequent occasion to complain of neglect and disappointment in expected professional visits, and the receipt of medicine.

In a word, procrastinotian became a habit, and he strove not to conquer it.

"When first installed into the Chair of our Lodge, he appeared likely to realize the expectations of his supporters, and prove an excellent and irreproachable Master. But it was soon found that he had no firmness of character. Serious personal disputes were allowed to be introduced into the Lodge, which, finally, deprived him of the power to command. And the reins of authority being once relaxed, confusion usurped the place of order, —discussion was confined within no decent limits,—the disputants were clamorous to be heard,—all spoke together,—sometimes half a dozen Brethren being on their legs at once, till the Lodge became a type of Bedlam. Some Brethren were expelled, others withdrew, and Bro. Dunckerley soon ceased to attend in his place.

"The *corpus delicti* was in the R. W. M., who was frequently admonished in private by some judicious friends; but he was as obstinate as the Abbess of Andouillet's mules. You might bou, bou, bou,—fou, fou, fou,—gre, gre, gre,—tre, tre, tre,—to all eternity; he was perfectly insensible to every thing but his own egregious vanity; and even if you gave him a smart cut with the whip, to rouse his sluggish zeal into activity, he would merely switch his tail,—the mule was still a mule,—and remained so to the end of the chapter.

"I have mentioned his want of punctuality," said the Square. "This was another failing which produced strange consequences; but it appeared to be insuperable, and not to be suppressed. After a few months, he began to be a quarter of an hour, then half an hour behind his time, sometimes an hour. This conduct, as it was nightly repeated, disgusted the Brethren; and they gradually dropped off, when the Master did not appear at the time named in the summons. They refused to wait, because it introduced another evil of no small magnitude; it delayed the closing of the Lodge to an untimely hour, which proved a source of great inconvenience to many of the old members.

"This unpropitious course was continued, until, from a Lodge of thirty or forty Brethren, in constant attendance, which was the usual average number during Bro. Dunckerley's rule, they dwindled away to such an extent, that when the R. W. M. made his appearance, an hour, perhaps, too late, it frequently happened that he did not find a sufficient number of Brethren present to perform the opening ceremony; and they were obliged to separate, weary and dissatisfied.

"Several of the members, recollecting the example of Bros. Dagge and Dunckerley, exerted their influence to prevent the consequences of such extraordinary conduct; but the new R. W. M. was too much wedded to his own system of mismanagement to listen to their suggestions. He knew no law but his own will and pleasure, and the Brethren had only this alternative,—to succomb or secede; and many of them chose the latter. They gave him every fair chance to retrieve his error; but nothing could rouse him from his lethargy; and the utter dissolution of the Lodge was anticipated, unless some alteration took place in his conduct.

"It is evident," the Square continued, "that he was exceedingly annoyed at this gradual defalcation of the Brethren, because, at length, to the astonishment of every member present, he made the following extraordinary proposition from his place in the Lodge: 'That in future, every officer who is not in attendance before the expiration of five minutes beyond the prescribed time of opening the Lodge, shall be subject to a fine in the following proportion. The R. W. M. half a crown; the Wardens one shilling each; and the inferior officers sixpence for each offence; and that the operation of the law commence on the next Lodge night, whether it be a Lodge of emergency or otherwise.'

"This proposition was, of course, carried *nem. con.*, and the only wonder was, that he should emanate from the Chair, as it was universally believed that he had made a rod for his own back, and that he would be the first, and perhaps the only delinquent. And to establish the decree more firmly, like the law of the Medes and Persians, which altereth not, he called on the secretary to hand him the minute-book, and he made the entry with his own hand, and read it publicly in the ears of all the Brethren.

"On the next Lodge night," the Square went on to say, "the Brethren were all present at the time named in the summons, except the R. W. M.; and after waiting a full hour, he made his appearance, as usual, in a very great bustle, and opened the Lodge. As soon as the minutes of the last Lodge had been read and confirmed, an aged Brother rose, and observed that, as the R. W. M. had broken his own law, it was only just that he should pay the penalty, and requested him to hand over to the treasurer the sum of half a crown, to give effect to his own proposition, and as an example to other Brethren who might violate the rule in future. The R. W. M. replied without hesitation, that he had been professionally engaged, and, therefore, was not liable, and that if another word was said about the matter he would vacate the chair, and withdraw himself from the Lodge, as a subscribing member, which, he added, in its present divided state, would effectually extinguish it.

"At this announcement the Brethren were surprised and disgusted, and several members rose and protested against the conduct of the R. W. M., as equally unmasonic and ungentlemanly. The Master was loud in his reply, and so were they in the rejoinder. And after this extraordinary display of weakness and petulance combined, the Brethren vanished as rapidly and certainly as the sparks from a sheet of paper consumed by fire, after the blaze is exhausted; and a few only were left to sustain the integrity of the Lodge.

"From this unfortunate dispute, the Lodge with difficulty recovered. The meetings became gradually smaller and more 'beautifully less,' until the Lodge drew to an end, like a tale that is told. And this once celebrated Society would have been an extinct tradition, if extraneous aid had not been secured to prevent so sad a catastrophe. But, fortunately, there came to the rescue, at the last extremity, a popular and talented Brother, who restored the equipoise, and saved the Lodge from dissolution.

"In the preceding Revelations," the Square continued, "you will not fail to have remarked that the Lodge had undergone many vicissitudes, but never, till this present year, did it approach so nearly to the verge of complete decay. In fact, a preliminary meeting of the Brethren was held, as the year drew towards its conclusion, to determine whether it would not be expedient to resign the Warrant, and unite with some other Lodge, as several of the members had already done, when a Brother incidentally mentioned the popularity of Dr. Dodd, and expressed his regret that he was not a member; for it appeared to him indubitable, that, if this celebrated Brother were elevated to the Chair, the Lodge would not only be saved, but also restored to its former state of solvency.

"The hint was taken, and a deputation was commissioned to invite Dr. Dodd to become a member of the Lodge, and to accept the office of its R. W. M., as he had already acted in that capacity more than once in other Lodges, with distinguished success.

"Now, I need not tell you," said the Square, parenthetically, "that Dr. Dodd was an eloquent and talented man, and an assiduous and zealous Mason. He had long been a popular preacher, and his learning and zeal recommended him to the notice of his superiors in the Church. His activity and promptitude in advocating charitable institutions became proverbial; and whenever it was found necessary to replenish the funds of a benevolent establishment, the suggestion was,—'Ask Dodd to preach for it;' and the experiment was generally attended with success. The honours of his profession were not denied him: for he was Rector of Hockliffe and Winge, Prebendary of Brecon, Chaplain to His Majesty, and Grand Chaplain of Free and Accepted Masons.

"The deputation consisted of Brothers Captain George Smith, Minshull, and Dr. Sequiera; and when these worthy Brothers arrived at Dr. Dodd's residence, the rev. gentleman was mounting his horse at the door; but, at the request of the deputation, with all of whom he was on terms of intimacy, he threw the reins to his servant, and entered the house in their company.

"On being admitted, the subject of their mission was opened by Captain Smith with becoming gravity and respect. He stated, in energetic language, the continued prosperity of the ——— Lodge under several eminent Masters, and particularly Bros. Desaguliers, Manningham, and Dunckerley; touched with great delicacy on the most glaring instances of mismanagement committed by the present R. W. M., whose tenure of office was, fortunately, on the eve of expiring, and the consequent prostration of the Lodge by the secession of its most valuable members, all, or the greater part of whom, he said, would certainly return, if the Lodge should be able to resume its functions under an efficient Master, whose popularity and position in the Order might have a tendency to restore its primitive reputation as one of the oldest Lodges on the list, and the possessor of this,—the jewel of Sir Christopher Wren,—exhibiting me," added the Square, with no little pride, "else how should I have been able to detail the particulars of this important interview? And Captain Smith concluded by expressing a hope that Bro. Dodd would accede to the unanimous wishes of all the old members, and accept the office of R. W. M. of the ——— Lodge.

"The Rev. Doctor replied that, although his time was rather limited, as he had a sermon to preach for an interesting charity on that very day, and that, in fact, he ought to be on his journey, yet he hoped to be able to spare half an hour for deliberation. 'But you will pardon me,' he added, 'if,—while I express my gratification at the preference you have shown me,—I hesitate before I finally consent to take upon myself the responsible duty you propose, under circumstances so difficult and adverse as those you have had the candour to explain. I am not altogether ignorant of the unpropitious management of the Brother to whom you have alluded, and deeply regret that a young man of estimable character and high attainments should be so inconsiderate as to compromise himself and you by a succession of injudicious acts, which, I am sure, on mature consideration, his conscience cannot approve.

"'However,' he continued, 'the mischief, it appears, has been inflicted, and it only remains to consider how we are to provide an effectual remedy. You are pleased to think it possible that I may be instrumental in the restoration of the Lodge to its primitive *statu quo*, which was rather high. If I were fully assured that such would be the result, I might be induced to 'gird up my loins' to the task; but I am afraid, from your own showing, that several of your most influential members have no only withdrawn from the Lodge, but have taken a final leave of it, by actually uniting themselves to other more flourishing societies; and they might feel great delicacy in dissolving their new connection to return to the embraces of their first love. It is, therefore, probable that, in anticipating the re-union of all the old members, you have taken too wide a margin. Nor can you be ignorant that, without their concurrence and active co-operation, our prospects of a successful issue may reasonably be considered doubtful. But,' he added, abstractedly, and half aloud, 'dissolve,—a Lodge like this dissolve,—it must not be, it cannot be permitted, although the chances appear to be against it.'

"'Help us, then, with your influence and experience, my good Brother,' said Dr. Sequiera. 'You will have the most animating prospect of success. The difficulty to which you have alluded has been foreseen, and measures have been taken to test its accuracy. Several of the seceding Brethren have been applied to personally to ascertain their sentiments on this point, and, with few exceptions, they have all expressed their approbation of the proposed plan to resuscitate the Lodge, and have pledged themselves to reunite with the Brethren, on receiving an assurance that a Brother of Dr. Dodd's eminence shall have been elevated to the chair.'

"Not to detain you longer on this point," the Square continued, swinging itself majestically round on one of its silver limbs, "as I have many other revelations of great importance to make respecting the doings of Masonry in the eighteenth century, I will merely add that, after a few other minor objections had been disposed of, Dr. Dodd consented to be put in nomination for the chair of the Lodge at the ensuing choice of officers; for, he said, it would be discreditable to the Order to suffer such a Lodge to fall without an effort being made in its behalf. It may be needless to add, that he was elected unanimously, and was installed on St. John's day, 1772.

We found," said the Square, "the new R. W. M very methodical in all his masonic arrangements; and hence, you may be certain that his Lodge was placed at once under a systematic mode of management. He used to say that, as the R. W. M. represents the rising sun, he ought to make his appearance in the east with the unvarying regularity which his protoype displays. And, accordingly, the following routine was always punctually observed. He opened the Lodge at the exact hour and minute expressed in the Bye-laws; and from this practice he never, on any occasion, deviated. When the Lodge was open, and the Officers at their post, the Secretary was desired to read the Minutes of the last Lodge, which were then formally put for confirmation. If there happened to be an initiation, passing, or raising, on the books, it took precedence of all other business, and preparations were immediately made for introducing the candidate. After the ceremony was over, any motion, of which notice stood on the book, was entertained, and temperately discussed. Then followed a lecture, adapted in length to time, for the J. W. was called on to exercise his peculiar duty at nine o'clock precisely. At the expiration of half an hour, which was spent in cheerful conversation, song, and toast, the R. W. Master's gavel struck one, and was followed by a dead silence,—the Lodge was called from refreshment to labour, with the proper ceremonies; and the R. W. M. was prepared to receive propositions of candidates, notices of motions, or any general observations for the benefit of Masonry in general, or that particular Lodge; and at ten the Lodge was closed, and the Brethren departed to their own homes,—except at the quarterly suppers, which were conducted with the same order and decorum, and broke up at midnight.

"The consequences of this system of regularity," the Square continued, "were soon visible in the increase and improvement of the members; and many of the Brethren became so well acquainted with the ritual, and understood the ceremonies so perfectly, as to be fully equal to the duties of the chair; although, for the succeeding three years, no one would accept the office of R. W. M. under an apprehension that the retirement of the present Master might perchance deteriorate from the popularity which the Lodge had so deservedly attained under his judicious management. It is true that Dr. Dodd frequently expressed a wish to resign the chair at the expiration of his year of office, but he was always re-elected without a dissentient voice.

"And what was the secret of this continued popularity?" said the Square, interrogatively. "I can tell you. It was comprised in a single word—DISCIPLINE. He would never overlook an infringement of the Bye-laws. On that point he was inflexible. Discipline, he said, was the cement of the Order. Once relax your discipline, and the whole fabric will soon be dissolved. Loosen the cement of the Lodge, and the building will fall to the ground. The result of this management was, that, during the time he held his high office, there was not a single dispute in the Lodge; and all differences of opinion were settled so amicably, as to give entire satisfaction to all the parties concerned.

"He never paraded himself to the prejudice of others, but embraced every opportunity of 'conferring honour where honour was due.' Deserving Brethren were brought prominently forward, as objects of esteem and confidence; and all masonic rewards were accessible to the industrious Brother, without regard to his situation in life, provided he were a good and worthy man in his social relations. The Lodge might be compared to a hive of bees. All were equally industrious; every Brother discharged, with assiduous punctuality, his individual duty, without reference to others; order and harmony prevailed amidst the multifarious employment; no jostling, no interference with each other's work,—all united in the one great labour of increasing the stock of honey, until the hive was abundantly stored with its golden sweetness.

"Now, although the attainments of Dr. Dodd in Masonry were of the highest order, he assumed no airs of superiority, and was ever ready to communicate knowledge to all who were willing to receive it. His conduct in the chair was mild and dignified; and, although he sustained its authority by suppressing at once and firmly all attempts at insubordination or infraction of the Constitutions, he never took advantage of his power to promote any private purposes of his own, or to silence a temporary opponent by harshness of manner, or an undue exercise of the authority vested in him as the Chief. In a word, the work of the Lodge was scientifically arranged; and a judicious division of labour did not fail to produce a harmonious result.

"During the mastership of Dr. Dodd," the Square continued, "a circumstance occurred which I must not pass over in silence, as it displays a discriminating liberality equally with a high sense of duty towards a Brother suffering under unmerited distress and persecution. We had at this time a member whom I will call Bro.

Watson. He had been in reputable circumstances during the early part of his life, but, through unavoidable misfortunes, he had gradually declined, until, at length, he found it difficult to provide for the necessities of his family. As he had been for many years a consistent member of the Lodge, and uniformly active and zealous, he was held in great esteem by the Brethren at large.

"It so happened that he had given mortal offence to a certain attorney, who was the most artful of dodgers (excuse the phrase, but it is not misapplied,) and the *magnum opus* of sheriff's officers; for he was the son of a bumbailiff, and had been the drudge of an attorney's office for a dozen years to earn his articles. This worthy menaced poor Bro. Watson with ruin, whenever a chance might arise for effecting it; and every one that knew him was satisfied *à priori* that he would keep his word. Years passed over without any such chance occurring. At length, however, Bro. Watson fell into insuperable difficulties, and, in an unfortunate moment, accepted from the vindictive lawyer a loan of twenty pounds. Like the deadly boa-constrictor, he then proceeded to wind his loathly coils about his prey, that no hope might remain of liberation or escape.

"To secure his victim, he had delayed his vengeance, that it might be the more certain and inevitable. Under the pretence of friendship, and pity for the poor man's necessities, he declined, for three years together, to receive interest for his money, on the pretext that the payment might be inconvenient; but, at the end of that time, he sent in a bill for principal, interest, and law expenses, amounting to thirty pounds, with an intimation, that if the mony was not paid forthwith, he would arrest him and throw him into gaol.

"This was the trump-card,—you shall hear how he lost the game.

"The above gentle intimation was received by Bro. Watson a few days before our regular monthly meeting; and, as the fact became known amongst the Brethren, the Lodge was numerously attended. After the usual business had been disposed of, the R. W. M. requested Bro. Watson to state his case, which he did in simple and affecting language,—for he was not eloquent,—and the sympathy of the Brethren was only equalled by their disgust at the pettifogger's crooked and disgraceful policy.

"When Bro. Watson concluded, Dr. Dodd rose gracefully from his chair, and taking out his purse, announced that he was about to place five guineas in the hands of the Treasurer, as the nucleus of a subscription, to liberate their unfortunate Brother from the fangs of his persecutor, expressing, at the same time, a hope that the Brethren would be willing to second his endeavours, and commending to their consideration the atrocity of the attempt, and the extreme suffering to which it would subject his wife and children, should they permit it to be successful. 'Whether the attorney winces or winces not, is a matter of little moment,' continued the worthy Doctor. 'Let the money be paid, and our worthy Brother be rescued from his pitiless clutches.'

"The appeal was responded to with enthusiasm; and it was at once and unanimously determined to save our hapless Brother from destruction. For this purpose, twenty guineas were subscribed on the spot; and it was resolved *nem. dis.* that the balance should be taken from the Lodge fund, as a loan, to be repaid on a future day, and the debt discharged without the slightest delay.

"The Master and Wardens called on the attorney the very next day for that purpose; and it is impossible to express the astonishment which he displayed at hearing that the money had been raised in the Lodge on the previous evening as a voluntary offering to relieve the wants and alleviate the distresses of a worthy and meritorious Brother. He could scarcely believe that such a disinterested instance of benevolence was possible; but, when convinced, by ocular demonstration, that it did really exist, could only say—and the expression was attended with a most remarkable contortion of visage when he found his vengeance so effectually defeated—'Aye, this is the *curse* of Masonry!'[1]

"A few weeks, or it might be months, afterwards," my gossipping companion went on to say, "our R. W. M. was requested to preach a sermon in St. Paul's church, at Deptford, for the benefit of some masonic charity—I forget what it was—and an assertion which he made from

[1] A literal fact.

the pulpit, that Freemasonry, according to its present management, is almost exclusively a Christian institution, gave rise to an interesting discussion respecting the tendency of the Order towards Christianity, when practised in a Christian country.

"At the next Lodge, when the R. W. M. made the customary inquiry, whether any Brother had anything to propose for the good of Masonry in general, or this Lodge in particular? a young man named Franco, who attained the rank of President to the Board of Grand Stewards in 1780, rose and said, that he had an observation to make, with permission of the Chair, which he trusted would neither be out of order, as coming within the category of *religious disputes*,—which was far from his intention,—nor uninteresting to the Brethren.

"Leave being granted, Bro. Franco proceeded to express a doubt whether such a prayer as we now use at the initiation of a candidate, concluding with the words: '*Endue him with divine wisdom, that he may, with the secrets of Masonry, be able to unfold the mysteries of godliness and Christianity. This we humbly beg in the name and for the sake of Jesus Christ our Lord and Saviour*,' can be reasonably applied to an universal institution like Freemasonry, which deduces its origin, not only from a period long anterior to the advent of Christ, but beyond the reach of all accredited history. He could not but conclude such an appropriation to be sectarian; and he had been much surprised to hear the same doctrine publicly advocated from the pulpit by an eminent Christian minister. This observation produced a debate.

"The defence of the Order," continued the Square, "was in good and sufficient hands. The R. W. M. immediately rose with great solemnity, and said: 'Brethren, in reply to our worthy Brother's observation, I will take this opportunity of explaining my views respecting the nature and character of Fremasonry as a religious and moral institution. You are all aware that the revivers of our symbolical Order, at the beginning of the present century, applied themselves with great diligence to the collection of ancient documents and charges; and, amongst the rest, they found the identical prayer that was used in the Lodges of those worthy and inimitable artists who built our noble ecclesiastical edifices; and Brothers Desaguliers and Anderson exercised a sound discretion in retaining it in our improved ceremonial as a landmark or beacon, to point out to succeeding ages the religious character of the Institution. And for this reason I did not hesitate to affirm my belief from the pulpit that Freemasonry, as it is received in this country, is essentially—although, perhaps, not exclusively—Christian. I am not, indeed, ignorant that an adverse opinion, unknown in former times, has recently been started, on the assumption indicated by Bro. Franco, that the Order originated long before the Christian era. Although a question of great importance, I considered it of too exclusive a nature for discussion in a pulpit discourse, which is more particularly intended for general edification. But, as we have a little spare time, if Bro. Franco will state his objections in detail, I will endeavour, as far as my abilities extend, to satisfy his inquiries, and give him the advantage of my own researches on this momentous subject.'

"Bro. Franco expressed his gratification at the courtesy of the R. W. M., and added, that nothing would afford him greater pleasure than to be enlightened on such an intricate inquiry. He was mistrustful of his own ability to contend with such a learned man and excellent Mason as Dr. Dodd, and should content himself with simply naming an argument which appeared to militate against the Christian hypothesis. He confessed he had not thought very deeply on the subject, but he would suggest, for the consideration of the Brethren, whether Masonry, being coeval with the building of the Temple at Jerusalem, which was erected by the Jews, must not of necessity be a Jewish institution; and, if this be admitted, it cannot possibly have any connection with Christianity, although practised by Christians in common with the twelve tribes of Israel. If it be indebted to the latter for its existence, and its landmarks be unalterable, its fundamental principles must be exclusively Jewish.

"Bro. Dodd replied, that he conceived the argument to be based on a fallacy arising out of an erroneous view of the facts. 'A very slight insight into the design of Freemasonry will show,' he said, 'that, although its morality is more particularly adapted to the genius of Christianity than to any other religion,[2] it is, in reality, neither exclusively Jewish, patriarchal, nor Christian, but cosmopolite; and, amongst all peoples where it ever flourished, it inculcated the morality of their peculiar religion, and selected its patrons, or parallels, from eminent men of their own tribe and kindred. Thus, for example, amongst the Noachidæ, the parallels of Masonry were Noah and Abraham; subsequently, Moses and Solomon were substituted; and the Christians chose the two St. Johns.

"'This,' he continued, 'was, beyond all doubt, the doctrine promulgated by Grand Masters Sayer and Payne, and their associates Desaguliers and Anderson, at the revival, and established as a permanent and unalterable landmark of the Order. Freemasonry would sink into disrepute if it were degraded into a religious sect. How it could enter into Bro. Franco's imagination that Freemasonry is a Jewish institution, I am at a loss to conjecture, for the Jews never practised Masonry themselves, or encouraged it in others; and it may be safely conjectured that, even at the present day, there are not a dozen Jewish Masons in England, and at the revival, in 1717, there was not one in all the world. As a Christian, and an unworthy member of the Church, I believe Jesus to be the Son of God; and, as He has said that His religion shall ultimately be "one fold under one shepherd," I believe that Christianity, like the rod of Moses, will swallow up all others; and that Jew and Gentile, Greek and barbarian, bond and free, will embrace this universal system, and Christ shall be all in all. And I confess I

[2] A writer of the last century expresses himself thus on this important subject. "Masonry received its finishing touches, its grand completing stroke in the glorious display of the Christian Revelation. Every Christian grace enters into the true masonic character. The doctrines, even the most peculiar and sublime doctrines of Christianity, as some of these have been termed, are regarded as holy, and just, and true, in our Lodges. I may add also that they are illustrated in such a manner as to tend to the settling the pious mind on the firm basis of a consistent, orthodox belief. It is our principal endeavour to form our minds into the sublimest conceptions of the Divine Being, and to the most implicit and regular obedience of all his dispensations and precepts; and we are, therefore, sensible that nothing conduceth so well to the accomplishment of these important ends as the sincere profession of Christianity."

was not prepared to hear a professing Christian cast a reflection on his Redeemer, by doubting the universality of his religion, and pronouncing it to be nothing more than a sect.'

"Here the R. W. M. resumed his seat," said the Square, "and Bro. Dunckerley rose, and, addressing himself to the chair, observed that he concurred in pronouncing the general construction of Masonry to be cosmopolite, and, consequently, democratic; yet he would submit to the consideration of the Lodge, whether the Lectures which we use are not essentially Christian.[3] He conceived that the exclusive appropriation of Masonry to the Jews, according to Bro. Franco's hypothesis, would be a far greater error than making it altogether Christian; because, amongst the many hundreds of Christian Lodges, which are spread over the four quarters of the globe, it is very doubtful whether there be a single Jewish Lodge in existence. 'Besides,' he added, 'what claim can the Jews, as a nation, have to be conservators of an institution which they certainly never practised, if we except a few Grand Superintendents and the Entered Apprentices, during the seven years which were occupied in preparing the materials for, and building the Temple at Jerusalem? The expert Masons, the Fellowcrafts, and Masters, were the Dionysiacs, *i. e.* Tyrians and Egyptians; and they were ranged in separate Lodges, under Hiram Abiff, Tito Zadok, and their fellows. When the Temple and Solomon's other buildings were finished, I cannot find that these accomplished men held any further communication with the people of Israel; but spread themselves abroad, and practised the art amongst other nations, till their posterity became famous as the *Collegiæ Fabrorum* of Rome, from whom the Freemasons of the middle ages, who built our matchless churches and cathedrals, received it, and transmitted it faithfully to us.'

[3] The writer above quoted says further: "The truly enlightened, the highly *exalted* Brethren, must perceive, and will cheerfully allow, that the further we proceed in our masonic course, the deeper must be our veneration for the Sacred Scriptures; and in proportion as we study the mysteries which it contains, so shall we be convinced of the importance and beauty of the grand doctrines of the Christian system. With these doctrines the most sublime of our Symbols hold a perfect unison; and I may add that the latter elucidate the former with a strong and pleasing lustre."

"'The argument appears clear and decisive,' said the R. W. M., 'and if Bro. Franco does not see it in the same light, perhaps he would have the kindness to state his peculiar opinions, as I am curious to hear what can be said on the opposite side of the question.'

"Bro. Franco, being thus appealed to, put the objection in another form. 'I argue,' said he, 'as an humble follower of Jesus, who was born a Jew and died a Jew. During his lifetime, he publicly acknowledged that Moses, and the prophets, and the kings of Israel, were his predecessors in the great scheme which he himself accomplished. But while I believe in Jesus, I cannot close my eyes to the fact that these very predecessors were the original founders of Freemasonry, and, therefore, though adopted by Christians, it has no claim to a Christian origination.'

"Dr. Sequiera then rose," said the Square, 'and submitted to the chair that the argument used by Bro. Franco was not sustainable. 'Christ,' he said, 'had no predecessors. He himself asserted that he existed before Abraham; and our great patron and parallel, St. John, says that he was not only before the worlds, but that he was the Maker of them. It is evident, therefore, that this Divine Being was anterior to Solomon, or Moses, or Abraham, or Noah, or Adam, the first created man. I consider it an open question,' he continued, 'whether the origin of Masonry may be dated from the building of Solomon's Temple, or from some earlier period; but, at all events, it cannot be an institution exclusively Jewish,—because the Mosaic dispensation itself was not that universal religion which it was predicted should ultimately "cover the earth as the waters cover the sea." That system was only intended by the Most High to be temporary, and was strictly limited to the period when "the sceptre should depart from Judah," and the Messiah be commissioned to usher in a more perfect dispensation, which, in God's good time, should supersede every other system, and bring all mankind into the sanctuary of Christ.'

"Bro. Franco explained, and expressed his curiosity to know with what propriety, under these circumstances, Freemasonry can be termed a universal institution.

"'For this reason,' said Capt. Smith, 'because it is an appendage to a universal religion, of which those of the patriarchs and Jews were only types and symbols, and were never intended to be final. And this accounts for the introduction into our lectures of all the chief types of Christ contained in the Sacred Records. For instance, one of our masonic landmarks refers to Moses at the Burning Bush, where Jehovah commanded him to take the shoes from off his feet, because the place where he stood was holy. From this spot he was divinely commissioned to deliver the children of Israel from their Egyptian bondage. And when thus miraculously liberated, they were led by the self-same Shekinah, who was no other than the Second Person in the Sacred Trinity, whom we Masons denominate T. G. A. O. T. U.'

"Bro. Franco would not confess himself conquered," said the Square, "but continued the battle with great gallantry. He urged that a single historical fact introduced into the Lectures, by accident probably, could be no valid proof of a general principle. 'Bro. Dunckerley has asserted that the Lectures are, as a whole, if I understood him correctly, essentially Christian. That learned Brother will not, I trust, consider me intrusive, if I request his proofs of that important fact.'

"Bro. Dunckerley immediately replied that nothing would afford him greater pleasure than to convince Bro. Franco of the real tendency of the Lectures, which, he might safely say, he had studied with the utmost attention. 'The prayer which Bro. Franco has referred to is not the only one which was in use amongst our ancient Brethren; but being the best adapted to the revised order in a Protestant country, it was agreed by the Grand Lodge to incorporate it into the ceremonial as an unalterable landmark, in preference to others, which were more peculiarly allied to the Romish ritual.'

"'Perhaps,' interposed Bro. Franco, 'our learned Brother would favour us with a specimen of these masonic prayers.'

"'With great pleasure,' Bro. Dunckerley replied. 'One ancient masonic invocation was in this form. *Pray we to God Almigghty and to hys swete moder Mary.* Another runs thus, *Jhesu, for thyn holy name, schulde me from synne and schame.* Others ran in a similar strain. It will, therefore, be seen that the most comprehensive formula was adopted, and has ever since been retained in use.

The Lectures of Masonry,' continued Bro. Dunckerley ' are full of landmarks which refer to the subject under discussion. The sacrifice of Isaac on Mount Moriah was an indisputable type of the great atonement; and this constitutes an unalterable landmark to consecrate the floor of our Lodges. The construction of the Tabernacle in the wilderness is another landmark to account for the masonic custom of building our Lodges due East and West; and the Tabernacle and its appendages were all symbolical of corresponding events in the Christian dispensation.[4] The H. P. was a type of Christ, and the blood of the covenant was a symbol of his blood shed upon the Cross. Why need I enumerate those other landmarks of Masonry which bear an undoubted reference to Christ and his religion, when you are all as familiar with them as myself? And I think, when Bro. Franco considers seriously these striking coincidences, he will find it impossible to put any other construction on the design of the masonic system, than as a development of the chief truths of our most holy faith, leading to the inculcation of a pure morality, and the duty of doing to others as we would have them do to us.'[5]

"The R. W. M. then rose and said, 'I appeal to the

[4] These Lectures had some odd fancies about Aaron's Rod, which were ultimately transferred to a separate degree. "The blossoming and bearing fruit of Aaron's Rod show how quickly those who are called by grace should blossom and bear heavenly fruit, and become faithful watchmen and seers of the night. This fruit points to Christ our Saviour, of whom Moses was a type, he being the shepherd and bishop of our souls; leading his children like tender buds growing up in spiritual and Divine knowledge; sweet blossoms of that spiritual Rod expanding with the fragrance of grace. The ripe fruit referred to the able ministers of the New and Old Testaments, whose office it is to withstand gainsayers. Their shells are hard, but their kernels abound in sweet doctrine, refreshing to the soul, the heavenly fruit of righteousness, provoking to obedience and love. Again, as those almond nuts did not perish, but were continually on the Rod, and laid up in the Ark of the Covenant, so neither shall the Word of the Gospel, or the work of Grace in the hearts of the faithful, wither away; but every branch in Christ, shall not only, like Aaron's Rod, bring forth fruit, but have life more abundantly."

[5] A masonic writer of this period makes the following judicious remark: "We know, and dare venture to declare to all the world, that no man can be a consistent Freemason who denies a Divine revelation; *even that revelation which is professed by Christian believers*, and in the state of immortality which that revelation holds out to us." —(Freemasons' Mag., vol. i., p. 384.)

Brethren present, whether these are not the received doctrines of the Order, as they are inculcated in all our Lodges.'

"The Brethren responded unanimously by the usual token of concurrence, and Bro. Franco found himself in a minority of one.

"When Dr. Dodd retired from office, at Christmas, 1775, he had created amongst the Brethren a great veneration for his untiring zeal in promoting the general interests of the Craft; for his liberality in maintaining the hospitality of the Lodge, and for those social qualities which chastened and enlivened the banquet. He had restored the Lodge to its primitive *status*, and had earned golden opinions from every class of the Brethren; and, like a successful gladiator, he was invested with the Rudis amidst the acclamations of his fellows.

"In the year 1776," continued my amusing companion, "I had the gratification, under a new Master, of witnessing the most magnificent spectacle it is possible to conceive; for it realized the gorgeous description of the Arabian Tales. I refer to the solemn dedication of Freemasons' Hall.[6] The numerous band of Grand and

[6] As it may happen that many Brethren do not even know when Freemasons' Hall became the place of meeting of the Grand Lodge of England, it may be satisfactory to them to be furnished with the following document, recorded in Noorthouck's Consts., p. 312. During the ceremony of laying the Foundation Stone, the Grand Secretary read the inscription on a plate, which was then deposited in the stone as follows:—

"Anno regni Georgii tertii quindecimo
Salutis humanæ MDCCLXXV, mensis Maii die
Primo
Hunc primum lapidem,
Aulæ Latomorum,
(Anglicè, Free and Accepted Masons)
Posuerit
Honoratissimus Rob. Edv. dom. Petre, baro
Petre, de Writtle,
Summus Latomorum Angliæ Magister;
Assidentibus
Viro ornatissimo Rowlando Holt, Armigero,
Summi Magistri deputato;
Viris ornatissimis
Joh. Hatch et Hen. Dagge,
Summis Gubernatoribus;
Plenoque coram Fratrum concursu;

Past Grand officers, in full masonic costume ; the galleries crowded with ladies of rank and fashion, presenting the appearance of a magnificent *parterre* decorated with a galaxy of exotic flowers dazzling to the eye ; a hundred musicians, vocal and instrumental, placed in the orchestra; the Masters and Wardens of private Lodges arranged, like a holy Sanhedrim, in order of precedency upon the benches on the floor; added to the splendid and tasteful decorations in the Hall itself,—produced a *coup d'œil* which exceeds my powers of rhetoric to describe.

"It was a superb sight to behold the Brethren, invested with the badges and appendages suitable to their rank, entering the hall from the committee-room, and proceeding to the throne of Solomon, compass the room three several times to sweet and heavenly music, amidst the waving of handkerchiefs and scarfs from the ladies in the galleries. The Grand Tyler led the way ; then followed the Lodge, covered with white satin, borne by four serving Brethren ; after which, the corn, wine and oil, in covered vessels of gold and silver, carried by Master Masons of good standing in the Order, followed by the members of the Hall Committee, and the Brethren of the Alfred Lodge, Oxford, two and two, in their academical dress, surmounted by the insignia of their several offices.

"But it will be an unnecessary waste of time," the Square interjected, parenthetically, "to describe the order of a procession which must be perfectly familiar to you. When the preliminary ceremonies were completed, and the Lodge placed in the centre of the Hall ; when the three lesser lights, with the gold and silver pitchers

Quo etiam tempore regum, principiumque
Virorum favore,
Studioque sustentatum.—Maximos per
Europam
Honores occupaverat
Nomen Latomorum,
Cui insuper nomini summum Angliæ
Conventum præesse fecerat
Universa Fratrum per orbem multitudo,
E cœlo descendit.
Γνῶθι Σεαυτόν."

The dedication of this building took place on the 23rd of May 1776.

containing the elements of consecration, were placed thereon: when the three great lights on a velvet cushion were deposited upon the pedestal in solemn silence, then did the heart of every Brother present rebound, like the war-horse at the thrilling blast of the trumpet, on hearing the simultaneous burst of harmony from the orchestra, which introduced the opening symphonies of the foundation-stone anthem,

'To heaven's High Architect, all praise,' &c.

which was sung by Mr. Hudson, of St. Paul's Cathedral, the choruses being filled up by the whole band.

"The ceremony, I assure you, sir, was very imposing; and although the eye was satiated with the gorgeous display, and the ear delighted by the sweet influence of music, yet the heart of every person in this vast assembly was carried away by the oration of the Grand Chaplain, our late R. W. M. Dr. Dodd, whose matchless eloquence of language and grace of delivery riveted the attention of his audience. And when he pronounced any particularly fine passage, with all the energy of enthusiasm, the acclamations were unbounded; and the conclusion of the address, after a deep silence of a few seconds, was hailed with such peals of enthusiastic cheering, as have scarcely ever since been heard within the walls of Freemasons' Hall. The triumph of the orator was complete.[7]

"It is a day to be remembered, not only on account of the real interest attached to the ceremony, but from the importance of its results; for it constitutes the first onward step that had been taken since the revival to place Freemasonry on a permanent footing, as one of those beneficial institutions which reflect so much glory on the island of Great Britain, and mark its inhabitants as a people celebrated for works of munificent benevolence and unostentatious charity.

"This was the closing scene in the popularity of the unfortunate Dr. Dodd. But as the above oration will convey his name as a Mason to all posterity, when the evidences of his excellence as the Master of a Lodge

[7] This Oration may be found in the "Golden Remains," vol. ii., p. 205.

would be buried in oblivion if I had not thus placed it on permanent record by revealing the particulars to you, I will briefly fill up, for your satisfaction, the general outline of his history; for I remember him well, and he is entitled to pity and commisération..

"His career, though brilliant, was brief; for an insatiable craving for popularity was his rock ahead, and embittered his otherwise unstained course. To this unworthy object he sacrificed talents of a high order, fame, honour, reputation, and character. *Dum vivimus, vivamus*, was his motto, and in the auction of life, he bid freely for a short and merry lot. The admiration which his eloquence commanded was amply sufficient to buoy him up with bright anticipations of still higher preferment, and he might have succeeded to the full extent of his wishes, had he possessed a common share of prudence. But he was too thoughtless, open-hearted, and impatient to wait the slow and steady progress of events. Public applause was the idol before which he bowed the knee—riches and honours were the objects of his ambition; and, as might be expected, his deities were unpropitious; they deserted him in his need, and disgrace and death followed in their train.

"He was fond of expensive amusements," continued the Square, "too fond, alas! for his peace of mind, or for the continuance of his popularity; and he entered more freely than became his cloth into the licentious pleasures of the times, and lived in a lavish profusion, which his limited means did not justify. Thus, when his creditors were clamorous for a settlement of accounts which he did not possess the means of liquidating, he became restless and morose, and resorted to unlawful practices for the purpose of recruiting his exhausted finances.

"The fact is, he mistook his vocation. If a tailor were to undertake the building of a church, or a stonemason the construction of a court dress, they would both undoubtedly fail, and subject themselves to derision and contempt. Neither ought a clergyman to meddle in secular affairs, and particularly with the abstruse and dangerous practice of dabbling in bills and acceptances. Our unhappy Brother was too thoughtless to foresee the probable consequences of such a course; and in an evil hour, to the universal sorrow and regret of all his friends, he forged a cheque on Lord Chesterfield, his former pupil, for £4,200, in the hope of being able to redeem it before it became due. This hope failed him—his Lordship was inexorable, and poor Dodd being capitally convicted of the forgery, was deprived of his chaplaincy, and expelled by the Grand Lodge; and, notwithstanding the most energetic exertions were used for a commutation of the sentence, he suffered the extreme penalty of the law."[8]

[8] The celebrated Dr. Johnson was one of his friends, and he has left behind him the following testimony to his merits as a Christian divine. "Of his public ministry the means of judging were sufficiently attainable. He must be allowed to preach well, whose sermons strike his audience with forcible conviction. Of his life, those who thought it consistent with his doctrines, did not originally form false notions. He was at first what he endeavoured to make others; but the world broke down his resolution, and he in time ceased to exemplify his own instructions. Let those who are tempted to his faults tremble at his punishment; and those whom he impressed from the pulpit with religious sentiments, endeavour to confirm them by considering the regret and self-abhorrence with which he reviewed, in prison, his deviations from rectitude."

CHAPTER VIII.

DISPUTES.—WILLIAM PRESTON.

1777—1779.

"Arma virumque cano."—VIRGIL.

"Pardon thine enemy, and have manliness of heart enough to do him good. This generous sacrifice, one of the most exalted precepts of religion, will awaken in thee the most benignant sensations; thou wilt represent the image of the Deity, who with adorable kindness pardons the errors of men, disregarding their ingratitude, and pours down his blessings upon them. Always recollect that this is the most glorious victory thy reason can obtain over the brutal instincts; and thy motto be—'A Mason forgets only injuries, never benefits.'" —MASONIC EXHORTATIONS: *From the German.*

"I object to you strongly on the score of your processions; and I object to you still more decidedly on the score of your secret. You are a secret society, held together by a stringent oath; now I hold that wherever there is mystery there is iniquity."—*The Anti-Masonic Vicar, in "Stray Leaves."*

IN the earliest part of my existence," the Square continued, "I heard the venerable and excellent Bishop Hall preach, and he said, very strongly, in his usual antithetical manner, 'One man may kindle a fire which all the world cannot quench. One plague-sore may infect a whole kingdom. One artful partisan will do more to seduce others into evil, than twenty just and upright men.'

"This truth will be amply verified in the following Revelations: for I have now before me the irksome task of communicating the particulars of an unhappy dispute between our oldest Lodge and the Grand Lodge itself. The recollection of it is by no means pleasing; but as a most indefatigable and successful Mason, whose name will descend with honour to posterity, was a party in the quarrel, it must not be suppressed, for every event in the career of such a man cannot fail to be interesting to the Fraternity.

"As a moveable Jewel," continued the Square, "I became the property of Bro. Preston, in the year of poor Doctor Dodd's misfortune. He had served the office of R. W. M. of the Lodge of Antiquity, in the preceding year, when he published a new edition of his celebrated Illustrations of Masonry.[1] I assure you, sir, Bro. Preston was no common man. He was a Scotchman by birth, and came to London in the year 1760, soon after which he was initiated in a Lodge, meeting at the White Hart, Strand, under the Constitution of the *Ancients*, as they denominated themselves, although in reality, their system had not been in existence more than thirty years, and arose, as I have already intimated, out of a schism in, and secession from, the Grand Lodge of England. There, however, Bro. Preston first saw the light. But, being doubtful, on their own showing, whether the Brethren with whom he was associated were not acting in defiance of legitimate authority, he left them and procured admission into a regular Constitutional Lodge, at the Talbot, Strand.[2] From this time he devoted his attention to the

[1] "Illustrations of Masonry, by William Preston." London, Williams, 1772. Second Edition, London, Wilkie, 1775. Third Edition, translated into German by Meyer, Stendal, Frauzen, and Grosse, 1776. Fourth Edition, 1780. A new Edition, with additions, London, Wilkie, 1781. A new Edition, London, Wilkie, 1788. Another Edition, London, 1792. Ninth Edition, London, 1799. Tenth Edition, London, Wilkie, 1801. "Illustrations of Masonry, selected from Preston, Hutchinson, and others; to which is prefixed the Funeral Service, and a variety of other Masonic Information. By John Cole." London, Jordan, 1801. The first American Edition, Alexandria and Fredricksberg, Coltorn and Stewart, 1804. Twelfth Edition, London, Wilkie, 1812. "Illustrations of Masonry, by the late W. Preston; with Additions and Corrections, by Stephen Jones, P. M. of the Lodge of Antiquity." Thirteenth Edition. London, Whitaker, 1821. Fourteenth Edition, with additions to the present time, and copious Notes, by the Rev. G. Oliver, D. D. London, Whitaker, Treacher and Co., 1829. Fifteenth Edition, London, Whitaker, 1840.

[2] The account of this transaction given by his biographer, Brother Stephen Jones, is as follows:—"Soon after his arrival in London, a number of Brethren from Edinburgh resolved to institute a Freemason's Lodge in the city, under the sanction of a Constitution from Scotland; but not having succeeded in their application, they were recommended by the Grand Lodge at Edinburgh to the Ancient Grand Lodge in London, which immediately granted them a dispensation to form a Lodge, and to make Masons. They accordingly met at the White Hart, in the Strand, and Mr. Preston was the second

principles of the Craft as enunciated in its Lectures, and succeeded in effecting a beneficial improvement in the details of the Order.

"It will be worth our while to retrograde a little in point of time, for the purpose of recording the progress of his exertions.

"At this period a literary taste was beginning to display itself amongst all classes of society, and Bro. Preston thought that if Freemasonry was to preserve its standing it must spread its roots and expand its branches deep and wide, for the purpose of extending its capabilities to meet the exigencies of the times. To promote this salutary end, and to rescue the Order from the charge of frivolity, he gave up a considerable portion of his leisure to a revision of the Lectures.

"He commenced his design by holding private meetings with his friends once or twice a week to effect their improvement, on which occasion all the existing rituals were discussed with every possible care and attention, until, by the assistance of some zealous friends, whom he had deputed to visit a variety of Lodges in different parts of the kingdom, for the purpose of gaining information, he succeeded in arranging and digesting the whole of the First Lecture. To establish its validity, he resolved to submit the progress he had made to the judgment of the Society at large, and on Thursday, May 21st, 1772, he gave a banquet, at his own expense, at the Crown and Anchor Tavern, in the Strand, which was honoured with the presence of the Grand Officers, and many other eminent and respectable Brethren.

"At his request, the Brethren assembled early," said the Square, "and Bro. Preston opened the business of the meeting in words to this effect:

"'Brethren and Friends,—I should scarcely have taken the liberty of soliciting your attendance here this

person initiated under that dispensation. The Lodge was soon after regularly constituted by the officers of the Ancient Grand Lodge in person. . . . At length Mr. Preston, and some others of the members, having joined a Lodge under the regular English Constitution, at the Talbot Inn, in the Strand, they prevailed on the rest of the Lodge to petition for a Constitution. Lord Blaney, at that time Grand Master, readily acquiesced with the desire of the Brethren, and the Lodge was soon after constituted a second time in ample form by the name of the Caledonian Lodge."

day, had I not conceived that the general interests of Masonry might reap essential advantages from a convocation of the chief Members of the Craft, to consider and deliberate on a measure which could not take the initiative in Grand Lodge. I allude to a revision of our Lodge Lectures, which, I think, ought to keep pace with the gradual advancement of other branches of Science, that the Fraternity may be furnished with an adequate motive for the exercise of their assiduity and zeal. Freemasonry is the friend of Industry, and being rather chary of her favours, will not dispense them to the indolent or indifferent Brother. If he be either too proud to learn, or too listless to attend to the general and particular business of the Lodge, there is good reason to believe that he will never be a bright and intelligent Mason. It would have been better not to have sought admission amongst us, than by a want of diligence to have rendered his initiation unproductive of solid advantages. Whatever is worth doing at all, is worth doing well; and no one can ever attain excellence in any art, human or divine, without an anxious development of the principles on which it is founded. His heart must be in the work, or he will never succeed; and Masonry will yield neither bud, nor blossom, nor fruit,—he will neither understand its objects, nor participate in its advantages. With the name of a Mason, he will remain ignorant of its secrets, and incapable of estimating their value.

"'This is one chief reason why so many nominal Brethren exist amongst us, who know no more of the aim and end of the Institution than if they had never seen the light. The bright rays of truth and wisdom which illuminated their initiation, have been quenched in darkness, and they have sacrificed, at the unholy shrine of indolence, such advantages as no other Institution has the power of offering for their acceptance.[3]

[3] What are these advantages? An American writer, Bro. G. F. Yates, thus explains them:—"In the most remote times, even as in the present, the preservation of the arts and sciences was not the exclusive object of Freemasonry. The doctrines of the unity of the Godhead, the knowledge of the true God, life and immortality beyond the grave, and of universal love, were taught in our mysteries; *that love which is real Christianity, has ever been, and is now, the grand object of our Order in all its departments.*"

" 'This vapid and unsatisfactory state of things, Bro. Preston continued," said the Square, " 'if I am not mistaken, would be greatly ameliorated by a reconstruction of the Lectures, and by investing them with new charms, more interesting to the imagination and more pleasing to the mind. Presuming, therefore, that the object of the numerous and talented band of Brethren, who have done me the honour to meet me this day for the purpose of mutual instruction, is a desire of improving the mind and enlightening the understanding, it becomes my duty to explain the motives which have induced me to take the liberty of soliciting your attendance at my School of Instruction, and to offer some plain suggestions by which a knowledge of the Science may be attained.

" 'The first and most indispensable requisite for becoming a good Mason, is regularity of attendance on the duties of the Lodge, which will open to the view, like the gradual approach of light to cheer and invigorate the earth on the refulgent morning of a summer's day, an increasing development of the bright rays of science, till the splendour of truth irradiates the mind, as the bursting forth of the orb of day spreads its glories over the face of heaven. The instruction of the Lodge is delivered orally; and as, therefore, it can only be secured by hearing, every Lecture neglected by absence or inattention strikes a link from the chain of knowledge. Besides, punctuality will receive an additional reward by infusing that degree of ardour which is necessary for the attainment of excellence. The erection of a magnificent building is not the work of a day; the sacrifice of time and labour, the exercise of wisdom, strength, and beauty, patience, and consideration, are necessary to complete the edifice in all its fair proportions. So in Masonry, no one can store his mind with scientific knowledge by any other process than the just application of patient industry, untiring assiduity, and a powerful inclination to excel; for there is no royal road to science. The more frequently a Brother appears in the Lodge to witness its proceedings, the greater will be his love of Masonry, until zeal will ripen into enthusiasm, and prepare him for promotion to the highest honours of the Craft. Every Free and Accepted Mason, therefore, who desires to understand the elementary principles of the Order, should be earnest in acquiring a competent knowledge of the Lectures. As in all other sciences, this can only be accomplished by a gradual process. He must take care not to begin where he ought to finish, for many excellent and well-intentioned Brethren have failed by falling into this fatal, though very common error.'

"Bro. Preston," said the Square, "then entered on an explanation of the process which he had adopted in collecting information, and arranging the various modes of working used in different parts of the kingdom, into a connected and intelligible form;[4] and stated that his present object was to submit to the judgment of the meeting the result of his labours, that he might have the benefit of their united opinion on the details of the First Lecture, which was all that he had hitherto been able to accomplish.

"'I need not inform you,' he continued, 'that the Degrees of Masonry are progressive. I have constructed the series on such a principle, that the preliminary clauses of the First Lecture are simply elementary. They commence by a process which is calculated to fix certain leading principles indelibly in the mind, as stepping stones to conduct the student gradually to a perfect understanding of that which is to follow. My first object was a revival of the Tests. These I have distributed into three sections, each containing seven questions. It is true, they convey intrinsically no great amount of information, but they lead to matters of more importance, which would be imperfectly understood without their assistance.'

[4] "Wherever instruction could be acquired," his biographer says, "thither he directed his course, and, with the advantage of a retentive memory, and an extensive masonic connection, added to diligent literary research, he so far succeeded in his purpose as to become a competent master of the subject. To increase the knowledge he had acquired, he solicited the company and conversation of the most experienced Masons from foreign countries; and, in the course of a literary correspondence with the Fraternity at home and abroad, made such progress in the mysteries of the Art, as to become very useful in the connections he had formed. He has frequently been heard to say, that in the ardour of his inquiries, he has explored the abodes of poverty and wretchedness, and, where it might have been least expected, acquired very valuable scraps of information. The poor Brother, in return, we are assured, had no cause to think his time or talents ill bestowed."

"Here," said the Square, "Bro. Preston repeated the formula,[5] and then proceeded:—

"'A competent knowledge of some such series of examination questions, adapted to each of the Three Degrees, constitutes an indispensable qualification for the progress of the candidate from one step to another; and I attach so much value to their acquirement, that, as the Master of a Lodge, I never, on any occasion, pass the candidate to a superior Degree until he has displayed a correct knowledge of these certain tests of his understanding and zeal. And as every Brother is thus necessarily acquainted with them, the candidate will find many opportunities of receiving instruction in private before he appears in the Lodge, to assert his claim to another Degree.

"'After I had arranged these Tests to my satisfaction,' Bro. Preston continued, 'I then girded up my loins to the still more arduous task of remodelling the whole Lecture, with a careful eye to the ancient landmarks. This was a work of time and patient industry. And when I had completed a digest of the entire Lecture, I found that it had extended to a much greater length than I anticipated; and, therefore, in order to facilitate its acquirement, it became necessary to re-arrange the whole into convenient portions, not only to assist the memory, but also for the accommodation of Masters of Lodges, who, when pressed for time, might not be able to deliver the entire Lecture.

"'For this purpose I have divided it into sections, and subdivided each section into clauses, a disposition which has simplified the subject, and reduced it into a compass so narrow and easily accessible, that the application of a very small portion of industry and zeal will suffice for mastering a competent knowledge of this Lecture, although it embodies the chief mysteries of the Craft, together with its reference to science and morals.

"'I have no hesitation in saying, that any Brother who shall persevere for a few months in studying this ritual, and shall faithfully apply it to its legitimate purpose, will become an ardent admirer of the Science, and reap essential benefits from its practice; while, on the

[5] The questions may be found on page 77, but the answers cannot be committed to print.

other hand, if any Brother shall rest contented with a knowledge of the few conventional signs and tokens by which we are distinguished as a body of men set apart from the rest of mankind for the purposes of benevolence and charity, and seek no farther privilege than the right of sharing in our convivialities, his reward will be carnal instead of intellectual, and he will have nothing but sensual pleasure for his pains, which may be purchased in other societies at half the expense, and without the trouble and formality of masonic initiation.'

"At this point," the Square continued, "Bro. Preston deliberately repeated the entire Lecture from end to end, amidst the reiterated applauses of the Brethren. And the commendations were not unmerited, as every one who is acquainted with the formula will readily admit. Numerous explanations were required by Brothers Dillon, D. G∴ M., Sir Peter Parker, S. G. W., Rowland Berkeley, G. Trea., and Bro. Hesletine, G. Sec., who were all present, as well as most of the Grand Stewards." But these particulars, though the Square might consistently reveal them to me, cannot be placed on record here.

"After the Lecture had been discussed *seriatim*, and approved," said the Square, "Bro. Preston concluded with an oration, which was printed in the first edition of his celebrated masonic work.

"The Brethren then adjourned to the banqueting-room, where they found a band of music, and a table spread with every delicacy the season could afford. It was, indeed, a most magnificent affair, and nobly did Bro. Preston regale his friends. After the table was cleared, and dessert and wine introduced, the conversation took its tone from the especial business of the day, and, considering the talents and high station in Masonry of the company present, was an intellectual treat of no common order.

"These preliminary exertions on the part of our worthy Brother," said my amusing companion, "I became acquainted with incidentally, for they occurred before I had the honour of being introduced to him. His singular activity and vigour in the government of a Lodge were celebrated throughout the Fraternity, and had contributed to heap honours and commendations upon him, to which I must add, in justice to his memory, he was fairly entitled. When I was first suspended from his collar, he held the office of Deputy G. Sec., which occupied much of his time. He executed the chief part of the correspondence; entered the minutes; attended committees; issued summonses; drew out and printed abstracts of petitions; compiled the calendars, &c.

"All this labour he performed gratuitously for two years, and he was further employed by the Hall Committee to search the Grand Lodge Books, and make condensed extracts from the minutes, and to arrange and digest them as an appendix to a projected Book of Constitutions. Such an incessant demand on his time was prejudicial to his health, and a transient dispute with Bro. Heslotine, the G. Sec., originating in some misunderstanding about the publication of his Illustrations of Masonry, induced him to resign the office. The circumstances which led to this unfortunate disagreement are easily enumerated.

"The Grand Secretary, with a view to the publication of an improved edition of the Book of Constitutions, which should bring down the history of Masonry to his own time, had selected Bro. Preston, whose popularity was in its zenith, as the most eligible person he could employ to carry the design into execution. For this purpose he was allowed a free inspection of all papers, documents, and evidences belonging to the Grand Lodge. But it so happened, that while Bro. Preston was thus engaged, the Grand Secretary became acquainted with a Barrister of Bernard's Inn, called Noorthouck, who was a member of the Lodge of Antiquity. Being a facetious, free-witted, and amusing fellow, full of anecdote, and possessing a fund of general information, the G. Secretary became fascinated by his vivacity and ready wit. The consequence was, that, as the compilation of the Book of Constitutions was likely to be attended with considerable emolument, Bro. Hesletine was desirous of associating him with his deputy as a joint partner in the undertaking. But as the latter had already incurred all the heavy labour in selecting, copying, and embodying the records into historical form, in the hope that he should be ultimately remunerated for his trouble, he declined the offer, and Bro. Noorthouck was intrusted with the sole execution of this important work.

"When Bro. Preston found," the Square continued, "that he was excluded from all participation in the honours and rewards which he had confidently anticipated would result from the great inconvenience and loss of time to which he had been subjected in the preparation of materials for the undertaking, he expostulated warmly, and, perhaps, intemperately, against such a flagrant act of injustice, and threw up the office of D. G. Sec. in disgust.

"'By my faith,' said Bro. Preston one evening, when the matter was discussed in open Lodge, 'I would not have held the D. G. Secretaryship on such terms another hour,—no, not if Hesletine were incapable of finding a substitute. He might, for aught I care, have done the work himself.'

"It was an imprudent word, and, being repeated to Bro. Hesletine, was warmly resented. Whether Bro. Preston refused to give up the materials which he had collected with so much labour or not, I could never discover; but it is highly probable he withheld them, as the G. Sec. was mortally offended, and determined within himself that such contumacy should not remain long unpunished.

"An opportunity soon presented itself; and Bro. Preston was arraigned before the Grand Lodge for an alleged breach of the laws of Masonry. The grounds of the proceedings which were instituted against him were simple enough in their nature and origin, but they produced very serious effects. The facts were these. It had been determined unanimously by the Brethren of the Lodge of Antiquity, at a full meeting, holden on the 17th of December, 1777, that at the annual festival, on St. John's day, a procession should be formed to St. Dunstan's Church, a few steps only from the Mitre Tavern, where the Lodge was held, to hear a sermon from Bro. Eccles.[6]

[6] Bro. Preston gives the following account of this transaction:—'The Master of the Lodge, Bro. Wilson, called upon me, and requested my assistance in procuring the Church. We waited on Bro. Noorthouck, at his chambers, and he acquiesced in our proceedings. Some private conversation ensued in regard to the propriety of advertising; and no material objection occurring, it was agreed to insert the following in the papers—'FREE MASONS. A Sermon will be preached before the R. W. Master, Wardens, and Brothers of the Lodge of Antiquity, by the Rev. Mr. Eccles, Rector of Bow, and

"When the day arrived, and preparations were made for the ceremony, a protest against the procession was entered by Bro. Noorthouck, the Treasurer, and Bro. Bottomley, Past Treasurer of the Lodge; in consequence of which the Brethren abandoned the design, and did not proceed to the church in masonic costume, as was originally intended, but clothed themselves in the vestry-room; and, being only ten in number, they all sat in the same pew. Bro. Eccles gave them an appropriate discourse; and, divine service being ended, the Brethren crossed the street in white aprons and gloves. This was construed into a grave offence against the standing rules of the Order.

"Bro. Noorthouck did not attend the ensuing Lodge, but he sent a strong remonstrance against the proceeding, and threatened to bring the matter before the Grand Lodge, if the Lodge of Antiquity did not, then and there, pass a resolution affirming that, as a Lodge, they not only totally disapproved of and repudiated the transaction, but also absolutely censured and condemned the ten individuals engaged in the (so called) procession for such an unwarrantable breach of masonic law.

"Bro. Bottomley was intrusted with the resolution, and proposed it in form. The Brethren were taken by surprise; but the motion being duly seconded, it was of course submitted by the Master to the deliberation of the Lodge, and a debate ensued.

"On this evening a distinguished visitor was present, in the person of Capt. George Smith, an active and zealous Mason, who was on terms of intimacy with the Grand Master, and the personal friend of Bro. Preston. He had studied Masonry both at home and abroad, and was presumed to be well acquainted with the Laws and Constitutions of the Order. Eminent in masonic attainments himself, he was ever ready to estimate and proclaim the same excellence in others. Belonging to an honourable profession, he was too chivalric to allow passion or prejudice to interfere with justice and equity, nor would he suffer the weak to be oppressed without

Chaplain to that Lodge, on Saturday next, the 27th inst., being the festival of St. John the Evangelist, at St. Dunstan's Church, Fleet street. Service to begin at 11 o'clock.' "

lending a helping hand, even though his exertions in their behalf might chance, like the seventh bullet in 'Der Freischütz,' to recoil upon himself.[7] In the present case, he was impressed with the idea that the charge against his friend was too trifling for any serious notice; and he determined to use an effort for its defeat. For this purpose he craved permission of the R. W. M. to offer an opinion on the question at issue, which would have been readily conceded, if Bro. Bottomley had not entered a protest, alleging that, as a visitor, he had no voice there. Capt. Smith bowed to the decision, and informed the Chair that he should content himself with watching the proceedings in silence.

"'You may watch as you please,' Bro. Bottomley added, 'so long as you have the kindness to refrain from speaking. You are not a Member, and have no vote here.'

"It was an unpropitious commencement," the Square continued, "and I should gladly conceal the subsequent proceedings, if I consulted my own inclination. The debate continued to a late hour. Bro. Bottomley persisted in his argument, that the act of appearing in public decorated with masonic badges constituted an infraction of the spirit, if not of the actual letter of the law,, and merited censure.

"'As to the fact,' said Bro. Buchanan, 'we do not deny it. We did appear in masonic clothing. But if any person chanced to see us, which is not proved, during the half-minute employed in crossing the street, he passed on without either notice or remark, and, therefore, it is evident we attracted no extraordinary observation.'

"'How know you that?' Bro. Rigg asked, sneeringly.

"'Because,' Bro. Buchanan replied, 'I can use my eyes.'

"'If your eyes,' Bro. Rigg responded, 'serve you no

[7] The Square once more anachronizes. But I suppose we must excuse the lapse, on the Horatian maxim, "*quando bonus dormitat Homerus.*"—P. D.—[An error, with submission to the above erudite authority; for the Square appears to be wide awake. Though recording the past, he is represented as an existing reality; and a reference to any transaction of more recent date than the period of which he treats, is, therefore, grammatically correct.—Ed. *F. Q. M. & R.*]

better than your judgment, there will be some danger in intrusting your veracity to their keeping.'

"This was sharp practice," continued the Square, "and Bro. Wilson, the R. W. M., thought it time to interfere. 'Come, come,' said he, 'this language is not masonic, and is a greater breach of the law than walking ten yards in a white apron. Let us, by all means, have order in our debates, whatever may be the ultimate decision. The question before the Lodge is, whether we are inclined to repudiate or discountenance the Brethren who attended Divine Service in St. Dunstan's Church, on St. John's day?'

"'With submission, R. W. Sir,' Bro. Bottomley objected, 'the resolution which I have had the honour to propose refers not to the men so much as to the measure. The Lodge is called on to discountenance the breach of masonic law committed on that occasion.'

"'If this be the real question at issue,' said Bro. Preston, 'it is first incumbent on you to prove that it *was* a breach of masonic law; for no man, devoid of prejudice, would be capable of affirming that the law respecting processions actually debars the Members of any private Lodge from offering up their adorations to the Deity in a public place of worship, in the character of Masons, under the direction of their Master. The very idea of such restriction would be the height of absurdity, and could not be admitted by any person who professed himself a friend to the Society. Example will ever exceed precept, and it is surely commendable to see a Lodge of Masons patronizing the established religion of their country, and thus recommending the practice of piety and devotion to their fellow-subjects. Besides which, the Lodge of Antiquity has its own peculiar rights, formally secured to it, at the revival in 1717, when the present Grand Lodge was established; and we are determined to preserve them inviolate. And I again affirm that no existing regulation was infringed, even if it be admitted—which is very questionable—that the Grand Lodge is empowered to make laws binding upon a Lodge which has acted on its own independent authority from a period long anterior to the existence of that body.'

"This avowal," said the Square, "was received with so much applause, that Bro. Bottomley exclaimed, 'Ay, those are the sentiments which we are determined to rebut, be the consequence what it may. I affirm that the Grand Lodge is, absolutely, and to all intents and purposes, infallible; and its dictates, whether for good or evil, must be obeyed, even by the Lodge of Antiquity, though it *was* in existence before the reconstruction of the Grand Lodge.'

"'Keep your temper, I beseech you, Bro. Bottomley,' said the R. W. M., mildly, 'we are assembled to deliberate, and not to indulge in personalities and recrimination: otherwise, I shall be under the painful necessity of closing the Lodge without coming to a decision.'

"The Master's authority, however, was not sufficient to stem the tide, and the debate became so stormy, that he had great difficulty in keeping order. At length the question was put from the Chair, and it was negatived by a majority of eighteen against four.

"This decision was so unpalatable to the accusing Brethren, that, at the ensuing Grand Lodge, a Memorial, signed by John Bottomley, John Smith, William Rigg, and John Noorthouck, was presented, stating that a flagrant outrage had been committed against the Institution by the Master, Wardens, and some of the Brethren of the Lodge of Antiquity, principally instigated by the persuasion and example of Bro. Preston, its Past Master, who, at a recent Lodge, violated his duty as a Mason, by justifying public processions, and claiming for that Lodge an inherent right to act in such affairs without the authority of the Grand Lodge, and questioning the power of that Body to interfere in the private concerns of a Lodge which was alleged to possess a prescriptive immunity from its jurisdiction.

"In consequence of the above charges, Bro. Preston was summoned to appear before the Committee of Charity, to answer any complaint which might be preferred against him.[8] In the intermediate period, however,"

[8] The above memorial was replied to officially by the Master, Wardens, and Brethren of the Lodge to the number of eighteen, all of whom appended their signatures. They stated that, on the occasion alluded to, "there was no formal masonic procession; and that a few Brethren only walked across the street from the church to the Mitre Tavern, the distance being scarcely a dozen yards, in their clothing and Jewels as individuals. Masons were not indiscrim-

the Square continued, "the Grand Secretary was implored by several Brethren, who were personally uninterested in the dispute, to use his influence with the memorialists, for the peace and reputation of the Order, to induce them to withdraw their charges, as he must see that it was simply a frivolous and vexatious attack on an individual who had rendered great services to Masonry. Unfortunately the application was disregarded.

"Bro. Preston attended the Committee on the 30th of January, 1778, and was charged with asserting that the Lodge of Antiquity possessed exclusive privileges of its own, independent of the Grand Lodge; and he was called on to retract that opinion publicly, and to declare that it was equally untrue and inadmissible.

"In reply to this demand, Bro. Preston rose and said:—'Right Worshipful Sir,—In answer to the charge which you have now preferred against me, I beg leave respectfully to declare that whatever private opinions I may entertain on the prescriptive immunities of the Lodge of Antiquity, they have always been inoperative; and I have never attempted to prejudice the Brethren against their obedience to the Grand Master. As to the abstract question of retracting an opinion, I cannot understand how that is possible, unless I am convinced of my error; and I submit that, as a Free and Accepted Mason, I am fairly entitled to the right of self-judgment; but I pledge my honour that it shall never disturb the tranquillity of the Craft.'

"Notwithstanding this open and candid declaration,"

nately collected from a variety of Lodges, with a view of exposing the insignia of the Order to gratify a private inclination for masonic display, or to amuse the rabble, as the memorialists allege; the character of the profession was not disgraced by imprudence or indiscretion; there was no private interest to serve, no peculiar passion to gratify; the number of Brethren did not exceed ten, all of whom were members of the Lodge; their behaviour was suitable to the business in which they were engaged; and they, therefore, submit their case to the consideration of the Grand Lodge, in the hope that the conduct of the memorialists will be considered illiberal; their reflections on Bro. Preston as ungenerous and ill-grounded; and their proceedings dictated by a warmth of temper not altogether consistent with their professed knowledge of the principles of Masonry; and that, in consequence thereof, their complaint will be rejected as frivolous."

said the Square, "the Committee came to the following resolution, after a long and warm debate.

"'It having been represented to us that Bro. Preston, the Past Master of the Lodge of Antiquity, believes and teaches that an inherent right is vested in that Lodge, by virtue of its immemorial Constitution, to discharge the duties and practise the rites of Masonry on its own sole authority, and that it is not in the power of the Grand Lodge to infringe on its privileges; it is Resolved, that as Bro. Preston refuses to retract the said false opinion, he be, and hereby is, expelled the Grand Lodge, and declared incapable of attending the same, or any of its Committees.'

"You will remember, sir," said the Square, swinging playfully round on his dexter limb, "that I was present on all these occasions, and, therefore, may be fairly presumed to state the matter correctly. At the next meeting of the Lodge of Antiquity, the R. W. M. complained of the unusual harshness of the decision, and said,—'I appeal to you all, whether, from the number of years Bro. Preston has been actively engaged in Masonry, the pains and diligence he has used in promoting the general designs of the Order, the many valuable members he has introduced, to the amount of upwards of three hundred in number, of which Masonry and the Grand Lodge have reaped all the benefit, and Bro. Preston nothing, added to the time and money he has expended in masonic pursuits, the present transaction is not a very ungrateful and inadequate return for his services.'

"The Brethren answered in the affirmative, and advised Bro. Preston to memorialize the Grand Lodge to withhold its confirmation of the sentence. He took their advice; and at the next Quarterly Communication a motion was made to that effect, and a hot debate ensued, in which several members took a part; but as the enemies of Bro. Preston appeared to be the most numerous party, the Deputy Grand Master proposed a compromise, to the effect that if Bro. Preston would sign a document recanting his opinions respecting the presumed rights of the Lodge of Antiquity, the sentence pronounced by the Committee of Charity should be formally quashed. Bro. Preston hesitated about subscribing to a dogma which he did not believe; but, being pressed by his friends, he complied with the requisition, and signed the document.

"The sentence of expulsion was thus evaded," continued the Square, "but it produced consequences which were never anticipated, even by the Deputy Grand Master himself.

"At the next meeting of the Lodge of Antiquity, Bro. Bottomley contended that Bro. Preston no longer possessed the power of speaking or voting in any regular Lodge, being restricted by his subscription to the above document; and moved that Bro. Preston should sign in the minute-book a declaration to the same effect with that which he had signed at the last Quarterly Communication. The question was put, and negatived by a great majority.

"Bro. Preston then said, that if the declaration he had signed, at the pressing entreaty of his friends, was intended to debar him from the privilege of speaking and voting in his own Lodge, he should immediately write to the Grand Secretary, and withdraw his subscription. Accordingly, the next day he wrote to Bro. Hesletine, stating that he had affixed his name to the declaration, by the advice of his friends, for the sake of peace, although his private opinions on the subject remained unchanged; but as he had been informed, to his great surprise, by Bro. Bottomley, that it was considered in the light of a virtual expulsion from the Order, he had come to the determination of withdrawing his subscription from the document.

"Poor Bro. Preston," continued the Square, "was placed on the horns of a dilemma. If his subscription remained untouched, the expulsion was *virtual;* if he withdrew it, the former sentence remained in force, and the expulsion was *actual.*

"Nor did the proceedings terminate at this point. For Bro. Preston was once more summoned before the Committee to answer a protest against the proceedings of the Lodge of Antiquity, and other complaints which had been exhibited against him.

"At this meeting," said the Square, "the Deputy Grand Master occupied the chair, and Bro. Preston was permitted to enter on his defence. He made a long and admirable speech, in which he contended that the Grand

Lodge was not competent to enter a protest against the proceedings of a private Lodge; and called upon the Grand Secretary to say whether a single precedent to that effect could be found on the books of the Grand Lodge from its first establishment to the present time. And if no precedent could be adduced, he hoped the present process would be rejected as informal.

"This able and conclusive defence," the Square continued, "was followed by a desultory conversation, in which all the principal parties to the dispute, on both sides, delivered their opinions freely. There was a clash of arms—loud words—but no bones broken. The case was so clear that the Committee came to no formal resolution on the subject; and Bro. Preston and the members of the Lodge of Antiquity withdrew—not, it is true, singing *Te Deum*—but without having any censure passed on their conduct, and scarcely able to ascertain correctly why they had been summoned to attend. They flattered themselves, however, that, after this vapid exhibition, the unpleasant subject would be allowed to sink quietly into oblivion.

"Alas," said the Square, "they were never more mistaken. At the very next Quarterly Communication, Bro. Hull, a Past Grand Warden, and Clerk in the Salt Office, moved, that, in the opinion of this Grand Lodge, Bro. Preston had been the promoter and instigator of all the measures taken by the Lodge of Antiquity, in derogation of the authority of the Grand Master, and calculated to bring the Grand Lodge into contempt with the Brethren.

"This motion was intended as a preparatory step to a new censure on his conduct; and being immediately seconded, it would have been put to the vote at once by the Deputy Grand Master, if some of the Brethren had not desired to be heard against it. While the matter was in the course of discussion, Bro. Hull was advised by some Brethren, who were under the apprehension of being in a minority, to withdraw his motion. The evening being now far advanced, and two other motions having been quashed by the D. G. M. on account of their tendency to revive the dispute, it was imagined that nothing further would be heard respecting the Lodge of Antiquity or its members; and on this presumption many of the most attached friends of Bro. Preston retired.

"But at this late hour," the Square continued, "a motion was made, and duly seconded, to the effect, that the Hall Committee be continued with its usual powers, except that Bro. Preston's name be excluded; for it was thought by his adversaries that if this were carried, it would be tantamount to actual expulsion. The proceeding was not strictly regular; but as all advantages in strategy are accounted fair, the resolution, though combated by Bro. Preston, with his usual tact and ability, and though the Deputy Grand Master, perceiving its tendency, and feeling confident that it proceeded from an unfriendly spirit, observed that unless the Brother could be prevailed on to withdraw his motion, he should be obliged, though reluctantly, to submit it to the decision of the Grand Lodge, it was persisted in; and the question being put, it was carried in the affirmative, and Bro. Preston was excluded from the pale of Masonry.[9]

"The R. W. M., Officers and Brethren of the Lodge of Antiquity," the Square proceeded to inform me, "felt the indignity, which had been cast upon them by these proceedings, so warmly, that, at the very next Lodge, they expressed their sentiments on the subject, in a manner not to be mistaken, by the expulsion of the three chief agitators, Bros. Bottomley, Noorthouck, and Brearly. They passed a unanimous resolution, in which they pronounced the late transactions of the Grand Lodge to be a violation of their inherent rights; declaring that from henceforth the Lodge of Antiquity renounced all communication with that body; and that they would for the future act on their own legitimate authority, as an immemorial Institution.[10]

[9] Bro. Preston published a brief account of these transactions in a pamphlet, which he called "A State of Facts, 1778," for private distribution amongst his own particular friends. It was, I believe, never published; but the above particulars have been gathered partly from that authority.

[10] Bro. Preston thus laments this unfortunate schism. "The Lodge of Antiquity having expelled three of its Members for misbehaviour, the Grand Lodge interfered, and, as was thought, without proper investigation, ordered them to be reinstated. With this order the Lodge refused to comply, the Members conceiving themselves competent and sole judges in the choice of their own private Members. . . . Matters were carried to the extreme on both sides, resolutions precipitately entered into, and edicts inadvertently issued, memorials and remonstrances were presented in vain, and at last a rupture ensued.

"For ten consecutive years this arrangement continued undisturbed; and the Lodge of Antiquity held on its course, independently of either of the rival Grand Lodges which were at the head of the two sections into which English Masonry was divided. During the period o. Bro. Preston's exclusion he seldom attended a Lodge; but devoted his attention to other literary pursuits, which contributed more essentially to his advantage. To the Lodge of Antiquity, and to ours," said the Square, "he continued warmly attached; and it was a matter of deep regret with many of the best friends of the Institution, that so useful and zealous a Brother should have had occasion to withdraw his active co-operation from a Society to which he had proved himself a diligent and faithful advocate.

"At length," the Square continued, "in the year 1787, when the metropolitan Fraternity had become grieved and disgusted at this unsatisfactory state of things, so disreputable to the Order, and his Royal Highness the Duke of Cumberland was Grand Master of Masons, he was earnestly entreated to interfere. Under his superintendence, therefore, the case of Bro. Preston and the Lodge of Antiquity was submitted to the consideration of the Grand Lodge in a better spirit; and that body at once rescinded all the former proceedings, reinstated the Lodge of Antiquity in all its masonic privileges, and restored Bro. Preston to his dignities and honours. And, to the unfeigned joy of all the Fraternity, this eminent Brother, like the sun bursting through a bank of clouds, once more resumed his usual activity in the sacred cause of Masonry. He revived the Order of Harodim, and instituted a Grand Chapter, where the Lectures of Masonry were periodically illustrated by the Companions. Over this Chapter the Right Hon. Lord Macdonald presided as Grand Patron; and James Hesletine, William

The Lodge of Antiquity pleaded its immemorial privileges, published a manifesto in its vindication, notified its separation from the Grand Lodge, and avowed an alliance with the Grand Lodge of all England, held in the city of York. The Grand Lodge, on the other hand, enforced its edicts, and expelled several worthy Brethren from the Society for refusing to surrender the property of the Lodge to persons who had been regularly expelled from it. This produced a schism which lasted for ten years."—(Illustr. of Masonry, p. 245. Ed. 1829.)

Birch, John Spottiswoode, and William Meyrick, Esqs., as Vice-Patrons.[11]

"Through the medium of this Institution, Bro. Preston's system of lecturing became prevalent in all the Lodges both in town and country; and," the Square added, "I considered it to be a great blow and discouragement to Masonry, when the Order of Harodim was suffered to fall into desuetude, inasmuch as, while it preserved the ancient purity of the science, it refined the vehicle by which it is conveyed to the ear; as a diamond is enhanced in value by being polished."

[11] The Order is thus explained by its author. "The mysteries of this Order are peculiar to the Institution itself; while the lectures of the Chapter include every branch of the masonic system, and represent the art of Masonry in a finished and complete form. Different classes are established, and particular lectures restricted to each class. The lectures are divided into sections, and the sections into clauses. The sections are annually assigned, by the chief Harod, to a certain number of skilful companions in each class, who are denominated Sectionists; and they are empowered to distribute the clauses of their respective sections, with the approbation of the Chief Harod and General Director, among the private companions of the Chapter, who are denominated Clauseholders. Such companions as by assiduity become possessed of all the sections in the lecture, are called Lecturers; and out of these the General Director is always chosen."

SITY OF CALIFORNIA

CHAPTER IX.

FIRE!—CAPTAIN G. SMITH.

1779—1785.

"The Dove brings quiet, and the Olive peace."—PRIOR.

"Wise and learned men are the surest stakes in the hedge of a nation or city; they are the best conservators of our liberties; the hinges on which the welfare, peace, and happiness hang; the best public good, and only commonwealth's men. These lucubrations, meeting with a true and brave mind, can conquer men; and, like the basilisk, kill envy with a look."—SMITH.

"Ye dull stupid mortals, give o'er your conjectures,
Since Freemasons' secrets ye ne'er can obtain;
The Bible and Compasses are our Directors,
And shall be as long as this world doth remain."

MASONIC SONG.

AFTER the important case of Bro. Preston had been disposed of, the Square continued its revelations by quoting Plato. "This celebrated philosopher," he said, "once observed, 'that there never was an individual born into the world who did not possess some personal quality which was sure to recommend him to notice, if properly applied. If of a fair complexion, he will be considered the favourite of heaven; if black, manly; should he be hooked-nosed, it will give him an air of majesty,' &c.; and he might have said the same thing of mental qualifications, which are quite as diversified as bodily peculiari ties.

"These remarks are fully exemplified in the character of an eminent and worthy Brother, Capt. George Smith, on whose breast I was now glittering as R. W. M. of the Lodge. He was an intimate friend of Grand Master the Duke of Manchester, plain in speech and manners, but honourable and upright in his dealings, and an active and zealous Mason. As Provincial Grand Master for

Kent, he had delivered his inauguration Charge on St. John's day, 1778;[1] and drew up a code of laws for the province which was much approved.[2] In a word, he was a bright and learned Brother, although rather bibulously inclined; and in his convivial moments, he jocularly adopted the symbolical vocabulary which had become familiar to him by long practice on the continent, calling the table a *workshop;* bottles, *barrels;* glasses, *cannons,* candles, *stars,* &c.

"But this whimsicality was only indulged on occasions of festivity, and did not derogate either from the general excellence of his masonic administration, or from his personal popularity. The affairs of the Lodge were prosperous, and the Brethren were edified by his lucid disquisitions on many abstruse points which, at that period, were but imperfectly understood by any but bright Master Masons. His lectures attracted numerous visitors, and Bro. Dunckerley was one of his most intimate and esteemed friends.

"I remember," said the Square, "on a very full evening, when several distinguished Masons, Bro. Dunckerley amongst the number, were present, the R. W. M. had been lecturing on the Fellowcraft's Degree, when an interesting discussion arose, respecting the true form, destination, and emblematical meaning of the Winding Staircase; Bro. Dunckerley observing, that in his opinion some extraordinary misconception must have existed amongst the Fraternity concerning this remarkable structure, because, he said, 'it is improperly delineated in all the engravings and diagrams that I have ever seen. Its true form was undoubtedly spiral, and it was termed *cochleus* from its resemblance to a screw or worm. The number of steps assigned to it is evidently symbolical, and has varied in different ages of the Craft. At first it was 3, 5, or 7; afterwards 3, 5, 7, or 11; while it is occasionally phrased 3, 5, 7, or some greater number, which may, perhaps, be the true ancient reading. I should be glad to hear the opinion of so good a Mason as our R. W. M. on this abstruse subject.'

[1] Charge to the Lodge of Friendship at Dover, Dec. 27, 1778.

[2] Rules and Regulations for the government of the Provincial Grand Lodge of Kent. 1781.

"Being thus appealed to by name," said the Square, "Bro. Smith rose from his chair, and addressing the Brethren, he said, 'Bro. Dunckerley has correctly observed, that the form of the Winding Staircase was spiral; and I need not add, as you are all conversant with the fact, that the Masons, at the building of the Temple, are traditionally said to have made use of it when they ascended to the Middle Chamber to receive their wages. But its symbolical reference involves facts and doctrines of the greatest importance, which were taught to the Craftsmen in their Lodges. On the first step they were instructed, according to our received traditions, to reflect on the Divine Unity, and to worship JEHOVAH, the great Creator and Governor of all sublunary things. The third step suggested the Holy Trinity; the fifth referred to the orders of architecture, and the external senses; the seventh, to the liberal sciences, and to the days of labour and rest at the creation of the world; and the eleventh, to the Patriarchs after Joseph was sold into Egypt.'

"Having given this brief explanation, Bro. Preston requested permission to state his opinion, which being granted, he said, 'I am inclined to believe, R. W. Sir, that the Masons of the Middle Ages extended this symbolical comparison somewhat farther. They represented the three steps as pointing out the number of Masons who ruled the Lodge, in allusion to the three Grand Masters at the building of the Temple, viz., the Master and Wardens; the five steps to the number of Brethren who are competent to hold a Fellowcraft's Lodge, viz. the Master, Wardens, and two Fellowcrafts; the seven steps to those who are reputed to make a Lodge perfect, viz., the Master, Wardens, two Fellowcrafts, and two Apprentices; and the eleven, to the number of Apostles after the apostacy of Judas Iscariot.'

"This explanation," interposed the Square, "though forming a part of the Prestonian Lectures, is at variance with those of Dr. Hemming, which are now in use, for they exclude all religious references, and account for the symbolical steps by an allusion to simple physical causes and effects. But this interpretation receives no countenance from the established mode of lecturing used by our ancient Brethren.

"Bro. Meyrick, a promising young man," the Square continued, "who had been recently initiated, inquired of the chair whether he might be permitted to ask if any masonic traditions are in existence respecting the use and appropriation of this staircase, in connection with the upper chambers of the Temple?

"In answer to this inquiry, the R. W. M. stated that the Staircase led directly to the Middle Chamber, a fact which is attested equally by Masonry and the Holy Scriptures, although, in the former, we have introduced an entrance door, ornamented with certain hieroglyphics, which are not noticed in the latter. The old Lectures of Masonry simply say that the door was open, but closely tyled, and that the ceiling of the Chamber contained an illuminated Letter, as a sacred symbol, referring to the art by which the Temple had been built and decorated.

"To this information," said the Square, "Bro. Dunckerley added an observation on the Letter itself, which is not void of interest. He said, 'We call it the Letter Ⓖ; but, in fact, if it were really a single letter, it was the Yod within a triangle ◬, which the Rabbins call the King Name, and believe it to include all the attributes of the Deity. It will be impossible, however, to determine correctly whether the inscription in the Middle Chamber was יה or יהוה, but probably the latter; although, as the Jewish religion was typical of Christianity, the former, which meant the Messiah, would be equally appropriate; and as far as the reference to numbers extends, it might be either; for, as the former applies to 3, 5, and 7, so the latter embraced the original canon of 3, 5, 7, and 11. In this Chamber, according to the teaching of Freemasonry, the Fellowcrafts received their wages on the Square, without diffidence or scruple, from the good opinion which they entertained of their employers.

"Here Bro. Dunckerley resumed his seat; and after a short silence, Bro. Dupont rose, and stated his doubts whether these facts were well authenticated. 'As the Masons,' he said, 'were principally employed in the forest and the quarry, before the foundations of the Temple were laid, it was morally impossible that they could have received their wages in the manner indicated by the tradition; nor could the process have been adopted at all in this locality, with the Ancient Junior Warden guarding the foot, and the Ancient Senior Warden the summit of the Staircase, until the Temple was nearly completed. Some enthusiastic Brethren, as I am informed, have been so unwise as to adopt another Rabbinical fiction, and think that because the stones were hewn and squared in the quarries of Zeredatha—and that, consequently, there was neither axe, hammer, or tool of iron heard in the house, while it was building—they were not in reality so prepared by human agency, or by the use of any instrument whatever, but that all this work was performed by a worm called *Samir*, which is termed by these Brothers the *Insect Shermah*. The legend, although too absurd for belief, goes on to say, that after the materials were thus prepared, they conveyed themselves, without assistance, to Jerusalem, and were put together by angels. This fable is noticed by Bishop Patrick, who thinks that it might probably arise from the conjecture of some enthusiastic person who did not understand the meaning of the word *Samir*, which signifies a very hard stone, by the use of which other stones were cut and polished. And the emblem undoubtedly referred to the peace and harmony of the Christian Church, where all things ought to be done without dispute or contention.'

"I have been somewhat diffuse on this point," the Square continued, "for the purpose of showing you how these matters were handled in the Lodges, and by the Masons of the eighteenth century, and I now turn to other topics of a more stirring character.

"I need scarcely tell you, my dear friend, and surely I may apply that appellation to you, after so long a conference, that I had the advantage of being present at most of the Grand Lodges (for the Master of our Lodge was generally at his post), whence proceeds my universal knowledge of the transactions of the Craft. And I am now about to favour you with a fragment of secret history respecting our worthy R. W. M., of which the Fraternity in general were ignorant, because in those days the transactions of the Grand Lodge were imperfectly reported.

"He regularly attended the Quarterly Communications, and, in his capacity of Auditor of the Grand Lodge, had discovered, or fancied he had discovered (for the matter was never fully investigated) some trifling discrepancy in the Grand Secretary's accounts. He whispered his suspicions to the Grand Master, and Bro. Hesletine was mortally offended, although the insinuation applied to him only by reflection from his subordinates.

"When Achilles was affronted at the siege of Troy," said the Square, "he withdrew from the Grecian host in sullen discontent. Not so Bro. Hesletine. High in moral courage, and armed with the triple panoply of innocence, integrity, and uprightness of intention, he determined to break a lance with his military opponent at the very earliest opportunity; and the first encounter came off at the Quarterly Communication in May, 1780.

"At this Grand Lodge, the Duke of Manchester announced the nomination of our R. W. M., Capt. G. Smith, to be his Junior Warden; when the Grand Secretary entered a caveat against the appointment, on the ground that he was already a P. G. Master, which constituted, in his opinion, a disqualification for any office in Grand Lodge.

"Capt. Smith requested the G. Secretary to point out the law which rendered an office in Grand Lodge untenable with a Provincial Office, and appealed to the Brethren whether the act of impeding the Grand Master in the exercise of his undoubted privilege of nominating his subordinate officers, did not constitute a grave offence, opposed equally to the dignity of Solomon's Chair, and the courtesy due to its legitimate occupant.

"It was not a very edifying spectacle," interjected the Square, "to see two such men opposed to each other in a Mason's Lodge, the patented abode of harmony and peace. The G. Secretary was unconvinced, and persisted in his objection, because, he said, it is anomalous for any one individual to sit in Grand Lodge under two qualifications; for, if such a practice were admitted, he might claim to have two votes on every question, one in each capacity, which would be totally inconsistent with the general laws of Masonry. And, he added, as an illustration of his argument, that the Grand Master, and every Brother now present, must recollect a disgraceful transaction, which occurred only a few years ago, arising out of this very questionable practice.

"The case was this:—A noble Lord, who held a high

office in Grand Lodge, had a younger brother, who was desirous of a seat in the House of Commons. Now, it so happened, that the representation of a certain borough in a Province, for which no deputation had been granted, became vacant, by the death of one of its members. The peer immediately sent his brother down as a candidate, and procured from the Grand Master his own appointment as the Prov. G. M. In that capacity, he convened a P. G. Lodge in the borough; converted all the principal Masons who had votes into P. G. Officers; gave them a sumptuous dinner, and promised them a masonic gala on a future day. Thus, by an assumed urbanity and kindness, he reaped golden opinions from all the Brethren, and his relative was triumphantly returned in the face of a strenuous opposition.

"His lordship's zeal cooled down after his purpose had been accomplished; and the promised masonic gala was exchanged for an election ball, which so disgusted the Brethren, and offended the public, that Masonry became a by-word and term of reproach, equivalent to treachery and insincerity, and was almost extinguished in the province for several years.

" 'Such proceedings,' Bro. Hesletine continued, 'reflect disgrace on the Grand Lodge, when the offender happens to be one of its officers, because the Constitutions expressly forbid any Brother, how high soever may be his rank, to use Freemasonry as a political engine for any purpose whatever. We all know, M. W. Sir,' the G. Secretary concluded, 'that his lordship's rank prevented any official notice to be taken of the circumstances, but it created great dissatisfaction, and was universally condemned by the Fraternity, which his lordship held in sovereign contempt, after he had made Freemasonry subservient to his own private interests.'

"This being a strong case," said the Square, "Capt. Smith offered to relinquish the P. G. Mastership, if it should be the opinion of the Grand Lodge that the two offices, vested in the same person, is inconsistent with the provisions of masonic law. Bro. Hesletine's objection, however, was overruled by the Grand Master himself, who observed that, if the law propounded by the G. Secretary were sound, a Grand officer would be debarred from accepting the Chair of a private Lodge, which, equally with the office in question, gives a vote in Grand Lodge. He proceeded, therefore, to appoint Capt. Smith his Junior Grand Warden, without requiring him to surrender his Provincial office. But, at the subsequent Communication, the G. Secretary announced that Capt. Smith had relinquished the office of a Grand Warden; and it was immediately resolved, as a standing rule, that it should in future be considered a violation of the laws of this Society for any Brother to hold more than one office in the Grand Lodge at the same time.[3]

"This sparring was only preparatory to a more serious contest in Grand Lodge on the 9th of April, 1783, under a president who was not particularly favourable to Capt. Smith's views, the Earl of Effingham acting for H. R. H. the Duke of Cumberland, G. M. It appears that Capt. Smith had written or compiled a Book on Masonry, and was desirous of publishing it under the sanction of the Grand Lodge. A motion to that effect was brought forward in his absence by a friend, when Bro. Hesletine rose and observed that the application had been already entertained by the Committee of Charity, which, after mature deliberation, had resolved that it be recommended to the Grand Lodge to withhold its sanction to the work.

"This reported decision of the Committee," the Square continued, "brought on an animated debate, in which several members of the Grand Lodge took a part. In answer to a question from the Acting Grand Master, the G. Secretary admitted that no particular objection had been stated against the book; but that the sanction of the Committee had been refused on the general principle that, considering the flourishing state of the Lodges, where regular instruction and suitable exercises are ever ready for all Brethren who zealously aspire to improve themselves in masonic knowledge, new publications are unnecessary on a subject which books cannot teach. 'Indeed' he continued, 'the temptations to authorship have effected a strange revolution of sentiment since the year 1720, when ancient manuscripts were destroyed by scrupulous Brethren to prevent their appearance in a printed Book of Constitutions.'

"The Deputy Grand Master, Bro. Rowland Holt,

[3] M. S. penes me. See also Noorth. Const., p. 336.

stated, that, in his opinion, 'masonic literature ought to be encouraged; and that it was the interest, and would be the soundest policy of Freemasonry, to keep pace with the increasing intelligence of the age.'

"Bro. Burlington observed, that all masonic publications were trash.

"The Deputy Grand Master replied, rather sharply, 'But surely our worthy Brother, in his sweeping condemnation, will make an exception in favour of Anderson's Defence, and the useful publications of Calcott, Hutchinson, Dunckerley, and Preston.'

"'I make no exceptions whatever,' responded Bro. Burlington, 'for I never read a masonic book in my life, and I trust I never shall.'

"'Then,' asked the D. G. M., 'how can you conscientiously pronounce a book to be trash, which you confess you have never read?'

"Bro. Burlington found himself in a dilemma, and, being unable to return a direct answer to this home question, he cut the knot, by exclaiming, 'I hate all masonic writings!' and turned the subject from himself by asking Bro. Goldsmith what masonic books he had read.

"Bro. Goldsmith replied that he thanked God he had read nothing but the Book of Constitutions and the Ahiman Rezon.

"O! Bro. Goldsmith, Bro. Goldsmith," the Square interjected, "what a discourteous *lapsus linguæ!* Had you forgotten that the Ahiman Rezon was written expressly to denounce the very Grand Lodge in whose presence you were standing when the ungracious thanksgiving was uttered!

"The Hon. Washington Shirley, a friend of Capt. Smith's, then rose, and entered into a long defence of the proposed work, stating that it contained little more than an amplification of the subjects which had been already promulgated by Bro. Calcott, under the sanction of the Grand Master, and nine-tenths of the Craft throughout England; that, as all other sciences were freely and copiously illustrated for the general benefit of mankind, he thought Freemasonry ought to enjoy the same advantages. A mine of gold, without workmen or tools, he observed, will yield no returns; and a science, without books, is equally worthless. He felt morally certain, that genuine masonic writings would serve to disabuse the public mind, by dissipating the absurd conjectures which were fostered and encouraged by the catch-penny trash that had been spread over the face of the country under the pretext of explaining the secrets of the Order; and he thought that, as the favour of a Grand Lodge sanction had been awarded to Calcott and Hutchinson, it ought not to be withheld from Capt. Smith, who was an intelligent member of Grand Lodge, and an active and successful P. G. Master.

"The G. Secretary replied somewhat acrimoniously," said the Square, "and ventured to utter a few oblique sarcasms against Bro. Smith, which the Acting Grand Master observed would have been much better omitted: at the same time declaring himself to be unfriendly to all publications on the subject of Masonry. And the question being formally put from the Throne, was decided in the negative.

"Bro. Smith, however, published his book without the sanction,[4] and the edition was speedily exhausted; and, at the following anniversary, Bro. Hesletine resigned the G. Secretaryship.

"This decision," continued the Square, "as might be expected, had an unfavourable effect on the interests of masonic literature; and nothing was published for some years but a few single Sermons and Orations.[5] The G. Secretary, however, embraced this opportunity of bringing out his new Book of Constitutions, which had been entrusted, a few years ago, to the editorship of Bro. Noorthouck, as I have already had occasion to mention. The manuscript being now ready, it was submitted to

[4] "On the Use and Abuse of Freemasonry. By Bro. Capt. G. Smith, P. G. M. for Kent." London, Kearsley, 1783.

[5] A Sermon preached at Maidstone before the P. G. Lodge of Kent, on the Festival of St. John the Evangelist, by the Rev. Bro. Delanoy, 1781. An Oration delivered in Christ Church, Middleton, 1783. A brief History of Freemasonry, collected from the most approved authors; to which is added a Concise System of Christian Masonry, by J. Johnson, Grand Tyler and Janitor to the Grand Arch Chapter. London, Moore, 1784. On Brotherly Love, delivered at the Constitution of the Harmonic Lodge, No. 369, Dudley, by the Rev. John Hodgets, 1784.

the Hall Committee for examination and correction, and at length it received this unequivocal sanction:

"'We, the Acting Grand Master, Deputy Grand Master, Grand Wardens, and other Members composing the Hall Committee, do hereby recommend this present edition as the only Book of Masonic Constitutions for the Free and Accepted Masons; disallowing all other publications that have not the sanction of the Grand Lodge; and do warn all the Brethren against being concerned in writing, printing, or publishing any such book in their respective Lodges, as they shall be answerable to the Grand Lodge."[6]

"This, I believe," added the Square, "is the only authentic book that you have on the general history of Masonry.[7] And subsequent investigations into the true philosophy of Speculative Masonry have shown that it conveys a very imperfect, and, in many respects, erroneous view of the subject. We are not a society of Operative, but of Speculative Masons. As well might a student in divinity hope to find evidences of the Christian system of religion in the moral writings of Seneca or Plato, as the masonic tyro expect to derive a clear notion of Symbolical Masonry by the study of Noorthouck's improved edition of Anderson's History. Both would experience the mortification of disappointment. I have heard the observation of our most learned Masons on this production, and the prevailing opinion was, that Bro. Noorthouck ought to have added, at the least, a slight sketch of Speculative Masonry to Dr. Anderson's Operative History, as the intelligence of the times required some additional illustrations. For this, added to the increasing popularity of Freemasonry, demands that a clear and comprehensive history of the Order should be published by authority, explaining, in a rational and intelligent manner, without any affectation of secresy,

[6] The above sanction was signed by Effingham, A. G. M.; Rowland Holt, D. G. M.; W. Shirley, S. G. W.; W. Carrington, J. G. W., and countersigned by the Grand Secretaries.

[7] "Constitutions of the Ancient Fraternity of Free and Accepted Masons; containing their History, Charges, Regulations, &c.; first compiled, by order of the Grand Lodge, from their old Records and Traditions. A new edition, revised, enlarged, and brought down to the year 1784, by John Noorthouck." London, Rozea, 1784.

its origin and design, the utility of its mysteries, and the moral and religious references of its symbolical construction; for it is a standing disgrace to the Craft that nothing has been done for the last seventy years to remedy its glaring defects.

"Towards the close of Bro. Smith's term of office," continued the Master's Jewel, "and he occupied the chair of the Lodge for four successive years—a very rare practice, by-the-bye—several of our Members assembled in the Lodge unusually early; and some of them made their appearance before the Tyler had arranged the furniture, and disposed the jewels on the cushion of each officer's desk or altar. I had not been placed on the closed Bible in the East more than five minutes, before I became aware that something out of the common way was in agitation, but what it was I could not make out. There were present several visitors of distinction in the Craft, and little knots of four or five Brethren each were formed in different parts of the room, speaking to one another in a suppressed tone of voice.

"'We have no time to lose,' said one.

"'O, as for that,' said another, 'all is prepared.'

"'We shall make a night on't,' responded a third.

"'Is he apprised of the circumstance?' asked Bro. Dagge.

"'Certainly not,' was the answer.

"Then in another part of the room I heard Sir John Aubyn say, 'But what if he should not come?'

"'No fear of that,' was the reply of the Hon. Washington Shirley.

"'Then you intend to surprise him,' Bro. Dunckerley asked, as he stood carelessly with his elbow on the mantelpiece.

"'That is the cream of the joke,' said Bro. Crespigny; 'and I believe he has not the slightest suspicion of the treat which is prepared for him.'

"Again a third group were expressing their delight at the scheme, whatever it might be; and I heard the Deputy Grand Master, Bro. Rowland Holt, ask who were the originators of the measure.

"'Brothers Shirley, Hesletine, and Crespigny,' was the reply.

"'How?' said the D. G. M. 'Then I presume Brothers Hesletine and Smith are friends again?'

"'Perfectly so,' Bro. Vanderstop answered; 'are they not Brothers?'

"'I am glad to hear it with all my heart,' responded Bro. Holt, 'and I hope they will always continue to be so, for they are both valuable and efficient Masons.'

"What all this secret preparation was about, I could not, for the life of me, guess," said the Square, "and I began to fear something had happened which might compromise our hitherto irreproachable R. W. M., and disturb his popularity. While these thoughts were passing across my mind, I heard, in a remote corner of the room, some Brother observe, in rather a loud tone of voice—

"'What glorious spirits he'll be in when the communication is made!'

"Ha! ha! ha! was repeated in full chorus; and the laughter became general when the joke was repeated.

During these detached conversations, which continued a few minutes longer, Capt. Smith entered the room, his good-humoured countenance beaming with radiant smiles, which diffused happiness and joy, like a gush of sunshine breaking through an atmosphere of clouds. Greeting a few of the Brethren as he passed, he walked straight up to the pedestal, and gave the report. The Brethren were clothed and seated round the table in a few minutes, and the R. W. M. opened the Lodge. The minutes having been read, and no particular business appearing on the books, the Master was in the act of rising to deliver the Lecture, when he was superseded by Bro. Shirley, who said, addressing the chair,—

"'R. W. Sir, before you commence the business of the Lodge, I would request the favour of a brief hearing, as I have somewhat to communicate, which I trust will neither be disagreeable to you, or any of the Brethren present.'

"He resumed his seat," said the Square, "and Bro. Smith replied, in his usual abrupt, but exceedingly facetious manner, 'Ho, Bro. Shirley, are not you out of order?'

"'I am afraid,' Bro. Shirley responded, 'I *am* rather

out of order, but, R. W. Sir, I hope it will be considered an excusable trespass, when the nature of my communication is known.'

"'Go on, go on,' was heard in the west.

"'Order, order, chair,' from the Brethren in the south.

"The R. W. M. then said, that although Bro. Shirley's interruption was somewhat irregular, yet he should be most happy to hear his proposition, and was sure that the Brethren would entertain it with becoming dignity and seriousness.

"Bro. Shirley having thus obtained the sanction of the chair, proceeded to say, that as it was the evening of the last Quarterly supper during the presidency of their worthy and popular R. W. M., a few Members of the Lodge, himself included, as a mark of their esteem, and a grateful admission of the talent by which he had contributed so essentially to the general interests of the Society, have resolved to provide a supper at their own expense. (Hear, hear, from all parts of the Lodge.) And to invite Bro. Smith, and all the Members present, to favour us with their company, hoping that the R. W. M. will honour the banquet still further by retaining the chair, and presiding over it with that tact and good-humour which have uniformly characterized the social meetings of the Lodge when celebrated under his superintendence. And if, R. W. Sir, you will condescend to accept our offering, we further pray that, as there is no particular business on the books, you will dispense with the Lecture, and close the Lodge early, as supper is to be on the table at eight o'clock.

"This speech was loudly applauded from every quarter of the Lodge. When the acclamations had subsided, Bro. Smith rose and said—

"Ho, friend Shirley, are you there with your bears? Well, then, be it according to you wish. I thank you for the honour, and by George, our King, we'll make a night on't. If this is to be the game, away with grave business; we'll be merry for the nonce, if we never be merry again. As the old song says—

"'Adieu, sober-thinking detraction and spleen;
You ought to be strangers where Masons convene
Come, jest, love, and laughter, ye sociable throng;
You're free of the Lodge, and to Masons belong.'

"The Lodge was accordingly closed at eight, and the Brethren adjourned to the supper-room, on receiving an intimation from the Tyler, that the *work-shop* was decorated, the *stalls* placed, the *materials* spread, a *rough ashlar* on each *rag*, the *platforms* set, the *stars* shining brilliantly, *barrels of strong, weak, and yellow powder* ready for charging the *cannons*, and everything prepared for immediate *mastication.*

"The gallant captain was now in his element. He was ceremonially ushered into the supper-room by the D. G. M. and Bro. Dunckerley, and took his place amidst the cheers and plaudits of the Brethren. Everything was in order, as the Tyler had announced, and a sumptuous affair it proved to be. When the Brethren were seated, Grace was said by Bro. the Rev. Daniel Turner, of Woolwich, in the following form:—

"'*O Source of purest light! O Lord of glory! Great, incomprehensibly great, are thy handiworks! Thou gavest us, at the building of the Temple, wisdom, strength, and beauty! Thou gavest us vitality, pleasure, meat, and drink. To Thee, therefore, be glory, honour, praise, and thanks.*'

"This was the signal for action; and immediately the clatter of *swords* and *pickaxes*, *tyles* and *trowels*, was heard, and the process of mastication began.

"'I'll thank you to hand the *cement*,' says one.

"'A little of that *sand*,' says another.

"'Tyler, top the *luminaries*, but do not extinguish the *stars*,' a third called out.

"'Give me the *yellow powder*, I want to fire a *cannon*,' said the D. G. M.

"'*Rough ashlar* here,' a Brother demanded.

"'Remove this *platform*;[8] it is in my way,' shouted an obese Brother, from whose brow the perspiration fell in a copious shower, while he transferred the choicest of the *materials* from the *workshop* to his stomach; in the perpetration of which he evinced a pertinacity that displayed a mechanic perfect in the art.

"'Bro. Sequiera, do be so obliging as to favour me with that *barrel of strong powder*,' said Bro. Dunckerley.

[8] See the Historical Landmarks, vol. ii., p. 101, for an explanation of these terms.

"'Change this knife and fork,' shouted a Biother from the West.

There was a dead silence!!!

* * * * * *

"'A fine! a fine!' said the Chairman. 'Who's the delinquent?'

"He was soon discovered; the fine satisfied; and the supper proceeded through its courses, as suppers generally do, until the rage of hunger was appeased. Then the previous sounds, like the sudden subsidence of a hurricane, diminished into a peaceful stillness, interrupted only by an indistinct murmur of voices, as adjacent Brethren conversed together in whispers. The closing Grace was then delivered:—

"'*God be praised! Thou hast thought on us this day also! Be praised for this day's blessings. Oh, protect us Fatherly, according to thy grace and power, in happiness and in sorrow, in all our ways, and bless this night.*'

After this thanksgiving, the *barrels*, amply provided with *strong* and *fulminating powder*, were duly arranged; the *cannons* were set in order; the battle began in good earnest; and Bro. Smith proved himself to be an experienced commander.

"The R. W. M. issued his orders, that the *cannons* should be charged in line, and each placed in advance of the *tyle*. He then gave one report, and proposed the first toast.

"'The King, God bless him!'

"One stroke with the gavel, and the Brethren rose to their feet.

"'To arms!

"'Advance your cannons!

"'Discharge your cannons by three!

"'Fire!

"'Good fire!

"'Fire all! Quick!

* * * * * *

"'Ground your arms!

"'Advance your swords!

"'Poise your swords!

"'Salute with swords!

* * * * * *

"'Swords at rest!'

"Acclamations, three times repeated.

"I could tell you," continued the Square, "what toasts were drank, what songs were sung, and what speeches were made (though there was very little speechifying—it was all a running conversation, sparkling with wit and good humour), but the detail would not advance my design in communicating to you the peculiarities of masonic custom in the eighteenth century. It is true, the above ceremonies cannot be fairly classed amongst the legitimate usages of English Masonry, because they were practised only by a few eccentric Masters, whose popularity would bear them out in, what may be termed, an innovation. But they were occasionally sanctioned by the presence of the best and gravest of Masons in the land. The carnivals of our Brethren in Scotland at the same period, were generally enlivened by a game of High Jinks.[9] On the continent the above customs were absolutely enjoined as an indispensable part of the system,

[9] Which I take the liberty of describing by an extract from Bro. Sir Walter Scott's "Guy Mannering" (vol. iv., p. 56, Ed. 1825). "Mr. Pleydell was a lively, sharp-looking gentleman, with a professional shrewdness in his eye, and, generally speaking, a professional formality in his manners. But this, like his three-tailed wig and black coat, he could slip off on a Saturday evening, when surrounded by a party of jolly companions, and disposed for what he called *altitudes*. Upon the present occasion, the revel had lasted since four o'clock; and, at length, under the direction of a venerable compotator, who had shared the sports and festivity of three generations, the frolicsome company had begun to practise the ancient and now forgotten pastime of *High Jinks*. This game was played in several different ways. Most frequently the dice were thrown by the company, and those upon whom the lot fell, were obliged to assume and maintain, for a time, a certain fictitious character, or to repeat a certain number of fescennine verses in a particular order. If they departed from the characters assigned, or if their memory proved treacherous in the repetition, they incurred forfeits, which were either compounded for by swallowing an additional bumper, or by paying a small sum towards the reckoning. At this sport the jovial company were closely set when Mannering entered the room. Mr. Counsellor Pleydell, such as we have described him, was enthroned as a monarch, in an elbow-chair, placed on the dining-table, his scratch wig on one side, his head crowned with a bottle-slider, his eye leering with an expression betwixt fun and the effects of wine, while his court around him resounded with such crambo scraps of verse as these:—

Where is Gerunto now? and what's become of him?
Gerunto's dead, because he could not swim, &c., &c.

Such, O Themis, were anciently the sports of thy Scottish children!"

and were consequently exercised in every foreign Lodge. In the Adoptive system, the lady Masons fell cheerfully into the scheme, and during their hours of relaxation, practised the following formula. The Lodge was called *Eden;* the degrees, a *ladder;* the door, a *barrier;* the glasses, *lamps;* wine, *red oil;* water, *white oil;* bottles, *pitchers,* &c. And they applied it thus: *Trim your lamps,* meant fill your glasses; drinking was termed, *snuff your lamps;* fire, *lift up by five,*[10] &c. But to return.

"The evening passed away as most convivial evenings do pass, although with a little more license than is customary with you, for there was a freedom in the enjoyments of that period which is now unknown. Song, toast, and repartee constituted the staple of the entertainment. The following chorus was sung by all the Brethren present more than once; and the convivialities terminated at Low Twelve with the National Anthem.

'He that will not merry merry be,
With a generous bowl and a toast,
May he in Bridewell be shut up,
And fast bound to a post.

'Let him be merry merry there,
And we'll be merry merry here;
For who can know where we shall go
To be merry another year?

'He that will not merry merry be,
And take his glass in course,
May he be obliged to drink small beer,
Ne'er a penny in his purse.
'Let him be merry, &c.

'He that will not merry merry be,
With a company of jolly boys,
May he be plagued with a scolding wife
To confound him with her noise.
'Let him be merry, &c.'

"During the presidency of Capt. Smith, it was in the gloomy month of November, and the very Lodge which succeeded the above gala, if my memory does not deceive me," continued my amusing companion, "he opened the proceedings with peculiar gravity, and I was certain something extraordinary had occurred to disquiet his mind. Accordingly, after the usual routine of business had been disposed of, my anticipations were amply veri-

[10] Vid. Hist. Landm., p. 111.

fied; for he made a communication which was received by the Brethren with displeasure and regret. He told the Lodge that he had received a letter from a Brother at Aix-la-Chapelle, informing him that the Fraternity were placed in a situation of great difficulty and danger by the denunciations of the priests; and imploring advice and assistance from the English Craft. 'It appears,' he added, 'that they have been denounced from the altar under the character of villains, cut-throats, sorcerers, and incarnate fiends; and one of the priests, whose name is Louis Grumman, assured his hearers that fire from heaven, like that which destroyed the cities of the plain, in the days of Abraham and Lot, would soon descend to exterminate these imps of darkness for similar crimes.

"'These denunciations,' he continued, 'produced such a powerful effect on the populace, that every person who is suspected of being a member of the gentle Craft, is greeted in the public streets with hootings, yells, and execrations; pelted with mud and stones, and otherwise so grossly insulted that the Masons are afraid to proceed about their usual business, lest they should become the victims of a blind bigotry, which, like its author, goes about seeking whom it may devour; for the priests had threatened every person with excommunication who should consort with them, lodge them, or afford them any countenance whatever.'

"There was a solemn silence in the Lodge for some minutes' duration," said the Square, "after this afflicting intelligence had been communicated; when Bro. Rowland Holt, the D. G. M., rose, and said that he had received an official document on the same subject, with these additional particulars; that the chief magistrate of Aix-la-Chapelle, under the pretext of appeasing the priests, had promulgated the Pope's mandate against Freemasonry, which denounced the severest penalties on all persons who should either attend a Lodge, or favour the Fraternity in the slightest degree. This increased the evil; for the priest, instead of being appeased, launched his fulminations with additional fury, and excited the people to madness, by rushing through the streets, crucifix in hand, and conjuring them, by that holy symbol, to assist him in the extirpation of those devils in human shape, who were the enemies and scourge of Christianity, and under the immediate condemnation of God.[11] Bro. Holt announced his intention of bringing these untoward circumstances under the consideration of the Grand Lodge, although he expressed his doubts whether that body would be induced to interfere, in the absence of any competent authority to render its mediation efficacious.

"During Capt. Smith's Mastership," the Square continued, "the celebrated masonic impostor, Balsamo, or, as he styled himself, Count Cagliostro, flourished. He had already attempted to make London the scene of his charlataneries, but without success. His revelations respecting the Egyptian Masonry, which you will not forget was Androgyne, were discredited, and he was obliged to return to the place from whence he came. On the continent he was more successful, and found many credulous and munificent patrons. His pretensions, however, becoming at length suspected, he resolved once more to try his fortune in the English metropolis; and he inserted a public circular in the 'Morning Herald,' dated Nov. 1, 1786, in which he proposed to introduce into England his new system of Masonry, and invited

[11] These outrages happened in the eighteenth century, when the majority of the people of every nation in Europe were without the advantage of education. But what are we to think of the following denunciation, pronounced *ex cathedrâ* by a Romish Archbishop, in the month of November, 1851—the age of schools and colleges, and mental culture? "Let me admonish you again, as I have done before," says the Archbishop, in his celebrated Pastoral, "both by word and in writing, that nothing can be more fatal to charity than those secret societies which have been unhappily projected throughout many parts of Ireland. I have before declared to you—and I beg of the clergy in every parish to repeat the admonition continually—that all those who are banded together by oath in those wicked societies, under whatever name they may be called, and, also, all Catholics who join in the Society of FREEMASONRY, are subjected to the penalty of excommunication; cut off as rotten branches from the Church of God, *and if they die in this deplorable state, doomed to eternal perdition.* It is a sad calamity that a system so pernicious in its effects, and so hostile to Christian charity, should be tolerated or encouraged in any district. PAUL CULLEN, ARCHBISHOP AND PRIMATE OF ALL IRELAND." I would ask Primate Cullen how it happens that, after such a display of virtuous indignation against Freemasonry as a secret society, he should give a tacit approbation, by preserving a mysterious silence on the subject, to the Vehme Gerichte of Ribbonism, whose infamous emissaries are spread over the whole face of the land, and commit assassinations with perfect impunity.

the Craft to meet him for that purpose. It was thus expressed:—

"'*To all True Masons.* In the name JEHOVAH. The time is at length arrived for the construction of the New Temple of Jerusalem. The advertiser invites all True Masons to meet him on the 3rd instant, at nine o'clock, at Reilly's Tavern, Great Queen Street, to form a plan for levelling the foot-stone of the true and only Temple in the visible world.'

"It so happened," said the Square, "that our Lodge met on the evening of the day when the above advertisement was inserted; and it was publicly read by the R. W. M., who observed that the matter was warmly taken up by all the Brethren with whom he had conversed; and after some deliberation, it was finally agreed that a deputation should be appointed to meet him at the time and place indicated, which should consist of all the leading Members of the Lodge, and it was expected that many other Brethren would be present, which proved to be the case.

"Cagliostro was a man of good address, and of unbounded assurance.[12] He exhibited all the cunning he

[12] The following list of the works published by and respecting this impostor may be acceptable. "Opissanie prebuwania w' Mitawé is wostnaho Kaliostro na 1779 god." 1788. "Fru von der Recke Berättelse om Cagliostro's magiske Forsöck uti Mitau 1779." Stockholm, 1793. "Cagliostro démasqué à Varsovie, ou relation authentique de ses opérations alchimiques et magiques, faites dans cette capitale en 1780. Par un témoin oculaire." Lausanne, 1786. "Le Charlatan démasqué, ou les aventures et exploits du Comte de Cagliostro. précédé d'une lettre de M. Le Comte de Mirabeau." Francfort, 1786. "Des Grafen Mirabeau Schreiben uber Lavater und Cagliostro." Leipzig, 1786. "Confession du Comte de Cagliostro, avec l'histoire de ses voyages en Russie, &c." Cairo, 1787. "Memoria sulla dimora del Signor Cagliostro in Roveredo. In Italia, 1789 Liber memorialis de Caleostro dum esset Roborati. L'arrivée du fameux Cagliostro, 1789." "Compendio della vita e delle geste di Giuseppe Balsamo, denominato il Comte Cagliostro, che si è estratto dal processo contro di lui formato in Roma, l'anno 1790. In Roma, nella Stamperia della Rev. Camera Apost. 1791." "Vie de Joseph Balsamo, connu sous le nom de Comte Cagliostro, extraite de la procédure instruite contre lui à Rome, en 1790." Paris et Strasbourg, 1791. "Testament de mort, et déclarations faites par Cagliostro, de la secte des Illuminés, et se disant chef de la Loge Egyptienne, condamné à Rome." Paris, 1791. "Life of Count Cagliostro, with his Trial before the Inquisition for being a Freemason." London, 1791. These are only a few of the works which were published, particularly in Germany, respecting this very clever and successful impostor.

was master of, propounded his plan in a flourishing speech, boasted of his knowledge of the hermetic science, the philosopher's stone, and elixir of life; referred to the Czarina and the Grand Sultan as his most eminent patrons, extolled his researches into futurity, through the medium of animal magnetism, and exhibited a variety of legerdemain tricks in proof of the extraordinary powers conferred by his system of Masonry, which imposed on a few Members of the deputation, and astonished others. But he had encountered talent superior to his own, and in the end he was effectually exposed, and obliged to leave the country. His life was afterwards published, his schemes were laid bare, and he came to an untimely end."

CHAPTER X.

SECRETS.—JOHN NOORTHOUCK.

1785—1790.

"A large man he was with eyen stepe,
A fairer burgeis is ther non in Chepe.
Bold of his speche, and wise, and wel y taught,
And of manhood him lacked righte naught."
CHAUCER.

"All the plans of Freemasonry are pacific. It co-operates with our blessed religion in regulating the tempers, restraining the passions, sweetening the dispositions, and harmonizing the discordant interests of men; breathes a spirit of universal love and benevolence; adds one thread more to the silken cord of evangelical charity which binds man to man; and seeks to entwine the cardinal virtues and Christian graces in the web of the affections, and the drapery of the conduct."—HARRIS.

"Writers on Masonry, by the overwarmth of their zeal, are sometimes betrayed into the use of hyperbolical epithets, and superfluous effusions of panegyric on particular occasions, that to readers, who are not of the Fraternity, appear extravagant, and, of course, counteract their intention. If our Institution be of a laudable nature, there is less occasion to arrogate the reward of praise to ourselves; for so long as a tree is known by its fruits, the world will do us justice."—NOORTHOUCK.

"I am old enough to remember the celebrateed Dean Swift," continued the Square, in that agreeable, gossipping tone to which I had become accustomed, "and I think I have already alluded to a humorous effusion of his spleen against the Order in which I have the honour to be the representative of justice and equality. But it is not my present intention to refer to that exquisite production of his satirical genius. He wrote a book to which he prefixed the ludicrous title of *A Tale of a Tub*, which gave mighty offence to his superiors, although I really do not know why it should have had that effect—they did not understand it, perhaps—in which, amongst other severe hits at his own, as well as other churches, he represents John Calvin as saying, in reference to his father's will, *i. e.*, the Bible, '*Gentlemen, I will prove this very skin of parchment to be meat, drink, and clothes; to be the philosopher's stone, and the universal medicine.* In consequence of which raptures, he resolved to make use of it in the most necessary, as well as the most paltry occasions of life. He had a way of working it into any shape he pleased, so that it served him for a nightcap when he went to bed, and for an umbrella in rainy weather. He would lap a piece of it about a sore toe; or when he had fits, burn two inches under his nose; or if anything lay heavy on his stomach, scrape off and swallow as much of the powder as would lie on a silver penny. They were all infallible remedies.'

"You will not fail to perceive," said the Square, "that there is an abundance of matter for reflection in the above passage. It conveys the intelligible moral, that our First Great Light contains a present remedy for every affliction incident to the lot of man. And as a curious coincidence, I must further inform you that I once heard Bro. Preston make a similar remark respecting the universal application of Fremasonry; not in the same words, I admit, for they are widely different, but conveying precisely the same meaning. 'Masonry,' he said, 'gives real and intrinsic excellency to man, and renders him fit for the duties of society. It strengthens the mind against the storms of life, paves the way to peace, and promotes domestic happiness. It meliorates the temper, and improves the understanding; it is company in solitude, and gives vivacity, variety, and energy to social conversation. In youth, it governs the passions, and employs usefully our most active faculties; and in age, when sickness, imbecility, and disease have humbled the corporeal frame, and rendered the union of soul and body almost intolerable, it yields an ample fund of comfort and satisfaction.'

"I submit to your consideration," the Square continued, "whether this character of Masonry is not indelible, and of universal application in all cases and circumstances of life, whether of prosperity or adversity. Speak not!" he continued, seeing I was about to reply to his appeal—"answer not! Be dumb, or you will make me so! and I will communicate a very interesting disputation that once occurred in our Lodge, which will abundantly establish the truth of the above text. It added considerably to the reputation that Bro. Noorthouck, our new R. W. M., had already attained by the publication of his additions to Anderson's History of Masonry.

"Now, I consider it necessary," said the Master's Jewel, "to correct, *in limine*, any misconception which may have arisen in your mind respecting this eminent Brother, from the part he took in the dispute between Bro. Preston and the Grand Lodge. His conduct on that occasion, I freely admit, was open to censure; but all men are liable to view things in a distorted light when their *amour propre* is attacked. Such was the case with Bro. Noorthouck. Notwithstanding this, he was a clever and intelligent man, and an expert Mason; and his election to the chair of our Lodge was not only unanimous, but carried by acclamation. The Members were glad to enrol on their list of Masters the historian of Masonry during the zenith of his popularity.

"Bro. Preston, as I have already communicated to you, was under a cloud; but his Lectures were silently making their way amongst the Fraternity, and Bro. Noorthouck was not backward in doing them ample justice, as will be seen by the scientific conversation or dispute, as it may be more properly denominated, between himself and Bro. Mackintosh, on certain particulars which were at that time rejected by the cowan, and considered questionable even by some few imperfectly instructed Masons. Bro. Mackintosh was a literary man, and not over fond of Masonry at that time; but the arguments of the R. W. M. were so effective, that he subsequently renounced his errors, and became a useful and honoured Member of the gentle Craft.

"It so happened," said the Square, "that Bro. Mackintosh, who was desirous of testing the actual literary capabilities of Masonry, had made a motion, a few nights after Bro. Noorthouck had been installed, to the effect that *in future it should be imperative on the R. W. M., for the time being, to deliver an original Lecture on any important subject connected with the Degree in which the Lodge shall be open, at least once in every quarter; and on that night no other business shall be transacted.* The motion was duly seconded; and after considerable discussion, was negatived by a large majority.

"When Bro. Mackintosh next appeared in his place, which was not until three or four months after his motion had been defeated, there happened to be no business of any importance on the books, and the R.W.M. took the opportunity of asking him whether he was correct in supposing that he had expressed an opinion at a previous Lodge, that Freemasonry is a very frivolous pursuit, and unworthy the profession of a gentleman and a scholar.

"'You have construed my observation correctly,' Bro Mackintosh replied, 'for I have hitherto found nothing in Masonry which appears to be worthy of the great interest it has excited, or which offers an adequate return for the time and expense that are often devoted to its exemplification by some of our Brethren, from whose judgment and intelligence in other matters I should have expected better things.'

"'And yet,' the R. W. M. quietly observed, 'you have attended the Lodge with tolerable regularity. How can this be accounted for, if you do not approve of our proceedings?'

"'Why, the fact is,' he said, kindly, 'that myself, and a few other Brethren who entertain similar opinions, have made a point of attending out of respect to our late R. W. M. and yourself. We are convinced that you both believe Freemasonry to contain something more than appears on the surface; and we are willing to assist you in the development of your own principles, in the hope that we may ultimately discover what those principles are, and share with you in the benefits which they professedly confer. We believe that we may possibly be able, at some future time, to penetrate the mystery, although I am free to confess that we have very little hope of participating in the enthusiasm which you so uniformly display.'

"'It was on this account that I was desirous of coming to an explanation with you,' returned the R. W. M.; 'for, as it is unprofitable to fight with shadows, I am extremely anxious to learn the nature of the objections which are urged by those Brethren who act with you, and who form a small minority in the Lodge; and should be glad to know the peculiar causes of the disappointment of which you complain, that I may have an opportunity of endeavouring to remove them.'

"'A fair proposal,' Bro. Mackintosh rejoined, and I most gratefully accept it."

"The Brethren, you may be certain, were very attentive," said the Square, "for a masonic discussion between two such men was likely to prove exceedingly interesting. Bro. Mackintosh then stated his objections *seriatim.*

"'In the first place,' he said, 'we are dissatisfied with the Lectures; and are somewhat at a loss to discover their real object and tendency. Vapid and uninteresting in our view of the case, they appear incapable of exciting either a desire of knowledge, or an inclination to pursue investigations which are so feebly recommended, so imperfectly supported, and lead to no profitable result. They profess to explain our peculiar ceremonies, but they are too circumscribed to render the explanation satisfactory. They touch on an abundance of subjects, but always leave the inquirer in the dark. They excite expectations which are never realized; and, after having been at the trouble of sifting them completely, and come to count the gains, we scarcely find a single grain of wheat in a whole bushel of chaff.'

"'I am sorry to find that you have formed such a low estimate of our excellent Lodge Lectures,' said Bro. Noorthouck. 'You forget that they are merely elementary. They were never intended to include a full development of the system. They breathe the fresh air of the most early ages, and contain the essence of those pure principles which cemented our ancient Brethren, and gave them the influence they undoubtedly possessed over the uncultivated spirits of the age in which they lived. And in every instance where the Lectures are deficient in modern illustration, it is the admitted duty of the Master of the Lodge to amplify and explain the more occult passages, and impart to the Brethren that complete instruction and information which may supply what is wanting, and make difficult and doubtful references clear and satisfactory.'

"'There may be something in this,' Bro. Mackintosh replied; 'and, accordingly, whenever you have announced an intention of delivering an original Lecture on some particular symbol or portion of the ritual, you may have remarked that the Lodge is always well attended; but it occurs so seldom that we do not derive much benefit from the practice. Indeed, what with our numerous initiations, passings, raisings, and other routine business, I scarcely see how you can find time to repeat them more frequently. Now, as we have the Lectures tolerably well up, we cannot but consider our attendance at the Lodge, on ordinary occasions, little better than a waste of time, because we merely reiterate, parrot-like, certain words and forms with which we are well acquainted, and with but very slender prospects of increasing our masonic knowledge. It was for this reason that I submitted my motion at a late Lodge, which you defeated by a majority that gave great umbrage and dissatisfaction to many worthy Brethren who entertain the same opinions as myself.'

"'My dear friend,' said the R. W. M., 'you could not surely conceive that I would allow such a measure to become a standing law of the Lodge; it would not only increase the onerous nature of the duties attached to the chair, but prove a serious obstruction to business. These duties are plainly specified in the Constitutions of Masonry and the Bye-Laws of the Lodge, and the Brethren are incapable of imposing any additional restrictions on the chair, without an alteration of those Laws. This cannot be effected by the simple vote of a private Lodge. Place a notice on the books for a revision of the Bye-Laws, if you please; but you will not forget that all new regulations must be submitted to the approval of the Grand Master; and I have serious doubts, even if you succeeded in obtaining a majority of votes for that purpose, whether such a law as you contemplate would pass the ordeal.'

"'Then throw Masonry to the dogs—I'll none on't!' replied Bro. Mackintosh, petulantly; 'the Lodge Lectures are but chaff and bran, and of very little value.'

"'You forget, my dear Brother,' interposed the R. W. M., 'that the Lectures only profess to teach the elements of the science. You appear to view our ancient Lectures through a false and uncertain medium, like a modern freethinker. If you wish to penetrate into its more abstruse arcana, you must meditate with seriousness and attention on the several sections and clauses, for no art or mystery can be attained by a mere knowledge of its first rudiments. All human learning emanates from the alphabet, but you will not contend that an acquaintance with the alphabet alone will make you a wise or learned man. The elements of divinity are contained in the short catechism of the Church, but if your researches are not extended beyond that summary of the Christian religion, you will never become a sound divine. In like manner, the Lodge Lectures contain the leading principles of Masonry; but without something more than a mere verbal knowledge of these indispensable tests, you will never be esteemed a bright, expert, or scientific Mason.'

"'This may be all very true,' said Bro. Mackintosh, 'but if we waive this objection, which, I am free to confess, is not insuperable, still the general drift of the Institution is a mystery which I am not able to penetrate.'

"'Be it my province to enlighten you,' Bro. Noorthouck replied. 'You profess your ignorance of the real intention of Masonry; I am sorry for it. Surely you must have gathered from the Lectures, that one of its most important objects is to diffuse amongst mankind a universal principle of brotherly love and mutual goodwill, accompanied by a discriminating application of charity to worthy and deserving persons, when reduced by unmerited misfortune to distress and indigence—first, to the Fraternity, and then to all mankind. If these were our *sole* pursuits, Freemasonry, so far from being trifling and frivolous, as you and your friends appear inclined to think, is worthy of the patronage and support of the wise and good amongst every denomination of Christians. You remember the paragraph in our Lodge Lectures which illustrates the principle of universal charity? Very well; if there be any truth in that, Freemasonry cannot be surpassed by any other beneficent institution.'

"'I am well acquainted with the passage to which you refer,' Bro. Mackintosh observed, 'and as I have often witnessed its active operation, I am willing to concede that, in this respect, Freemasonry professes no more than she practises; and I make this concession the more readily from the knowledge which I possess of our public institutions—where a princely provision has been made for the permanent relief of destitute orphans, as well as for the temporary assistance of distressed Brethren. But stil. all this might be done without any affectation of secrecy; for, after all, our real, or, as you would say, peculiar secrets amount to nothing, and might be communicated to the world without any serious inconvenience—without, I may say, either injury to Masonry, or benefit to mankind.'

"'So,' Bro. Noorthouck exclaimed, 'you are offended at our secrecy! But, tell me—what would Freemasonry be—what would the world be, without its secrets? What are the councillor's wig, the physician's gold-headed cane, and the surplice and hood of the reverend divine, but secret symbols of the mysteries contained in those learned professions? What are the arts of the painter, the sculptor, and the designer, but secrets which none but the initiated can understand? And to descend lower in the scale, what are the goose and thimble of the tailor, the awl, last, and end of the manufacturer of boots and shoes, but collateral emblems of the secrets of their respective crafts, which neither you nor I are able to penetrate? Secrets! Every profession and every trade has its peculiar secrets, as well as Masonry. What was the powerful cause which produced those stupendous masses of building, blazing with all the rich results of decorative architecture, that adorn every corner of our land? It was secrecy! The Operative Masons, in those days, adopted every secret measure—even holding their Lodges in the crypts of cathedrals and churches—to prevent the great principles of their science, by which their reputation was secured and maintained, from being publicly known. Even the workmen, the Apprentices and Fellowcrafts, were unacquainted with the secret and refined mechanism which cemented and imparted the treasures of wisdom to the expert masters of the art. They were profoundly ignorant of the wisdom which planned, the beauty which designed, and knew only the strength and labour which executed the work. The pressure and counterpressure of complicated arches was a secret which the inferior workmen never attempted to penetrate. They were blind instruments in the hands of intelligent Master Masons, and completed the most sublime undertakings by the effect of mere mechanical and physical power, without being able to comprehend the secret that produced them; without understanding the nice adjustment of the members of a building to each other, so necessary to accomplish a striking and permanent effect, or without being able to enter into the science exhibited in the complicated details which were necessary to form a harmonious and proportionate whole. And so it is at the present day, and ever will be so long as the Craft shall endure. No, no, my dear Brother, you must not undervalue our secrecy, because you know that of all the arts which Masons possess, silence or secrecy constitutes their peculiar distinction.'

"'But tell me this,' said Bro. Mackintosh, 'of what real use is secrecy? If Freemasonry be truly the beneficent institution which you so loudly proclaim, and I do not question your sincerity, why not promulgate it publicly, that all mankind may participate in its advantages? We live in an enlightened age, when the secret springs of every art and science are clearly explained for public edification. The day of mysteries is rapidly passing away, and Freemasonry must, sooner or later, become a subject of open investigation—why not anticipate the period, and give it to the people at once? I ask these questions that I may be furnished with a reply when I hear them pressed by others. You may believe me when I add that this objection is more frequently advanced than you can imagine, and I confess that I have found it difficult to satisfy the scruples of many of my uninitiated friends, who have pertinaciously urged it upon me.

"'Is that all?' replied the R. W. M. 'Then I will endeavour to enlighten you; although I have often regretted that some of our obstinate opponents have not tried the experiment of initiation. They would lose nothing, at all events; and it would be a positive advantage to their argument by being able to speak from experience. But to the purpose. You infer, if I understand you rightly, that if our secrets were known, they would be much more highly estimated.'

"Bro. Mackintosh bowed.

"'Now I entertain very serious doubts on that point,' continued Bro. Noorthouck, warming with his subject. 'I think, on the contrary, that they would lose their interest, and not be prized at all. It is the expected secret that urges the candidate forward, like a well trained spaniel in search of game. The excitement is every thing. It is hope, the very ground and essence of our nature. No secrets, no candidates! I would ask you, in return, whether the secrets of Nature are more estimated by being known? Far from it. The mechanism of the growth of a flower, which was a profound secret to our grandfathers, is now becoming familiar to every boarding-school Miss. The nature and uses of electricity were a secret, until Franklin furnished mankind with a key to its elucidation; and the day will come when, by the operation of a series of discoveries and improvements, distant nations will be able to communicate with each other in an incredible short space of time. The secrets of geology are every day becoming more clearly developed. Gas and steam, those vast and irresistible agents, still remain amongst the secret operations of Nature; but, depend upon it, the experience of another age will work wonders upon them. Yet how few of the human race care about the study of those sciences, whose secrets, open to all, are really known to few, although destined to confer permanent benefits on mankind. The multitude profit by the effect, but disregard the cause. So in Masonry. The Institution is daily bestowing innumerable moral blessings on the world; while the cause, or the secret, is known only to a very small number, who are the agents by whom its benefits are disseminated. But as I see Bro. Inwood in his place, he will, perhaps, favour the Brethren with his opinion on this important subject.'

"Bro. Inwood," said the Square, "immediately rose from his seat, and said, 'R. W. Sir, I am so well convinced of your ability to defend all the salient points of our Order, that I should not have presumed to offer my opinion without a call from the Chair. In obedience, however, to your request, I will refer you to Holy Writ for a confirmation of your hypothesis that secrets excite a degree of attention when unknown, which vanishes when they are openly divulged. St. Paul told his disciples that when he was snatched up into the third heaven, he heard *unspeakable words*, which it was not lawful for a man to utter. Now it is quite clear to me that these words were calculated to excite the curiosity of the disciples to the highest pitch. And that they did so, we are furnished with abundant evidence to prove.

The speculations on these heavenly words were incessant and overwhelming, and the disciples of different classes attributed to them diverse and contradictory explanations. But it appears, after all, that the Sacred Name יהוה was the principal ingredient in this impenetrable secret. Now, my Brethren, mark the consequence; when St. John imparted to them what these mysterious words actually were, all their curiosity subsided, and they no longer felt any interest in the investigation, although it involved the solution of all their hopes, both in this world and in the next. So of the secrets of Masonry—many contradictory speculations have been urged respecting their nature and design, as witness all the charlatanarie which has been greedily devoured by the public in spurious revelations where they were said to be disclosed; but if they were really made known, and public curiosity allayed, they would be disregarded, like those stupendous phenomena, the revolutions and laws of the heavenly bodies; and all the concurrent benefits which they diffuse throughout the entire fabric of society, would gradually subside; the real would supersede the ideal, and Freemasonry, with all its advantages of sociality, brotherly love, and charity, would be swallowed up and lost.'

"'Admitting this argument to be sound,' said Bro. Mackintosh, curtly, 'how does it happen that the most lovely part of our species are formally excluded from these benefits?'

"'Aye, there it is,' replied Bro. Noorthouck, getting somewhat out of patience; 'the old hackneyed objection, if objection it be, which is greatly to be doubted. It would be more correctly termed a recommendation. What do the ladies care about being excluded from convivial societies, usually held at taverns and public-houses? The exclusion on their part is voluntary. What lady—except, perhaps, the ladies of the *pavé*—would consent to appear amongst the members of a law or medical society for instance? at a saturnalia of barristers, or at any of our well-frequented clubs? Even at a domestic dinner party, her sense of delicacy incites her to retire to the drawing-room, while the male portion of the guests take their wine with the host. Where is the female of any class that would not be ashamed of being seen amongst the Gormagons, the Pre-adamites, the

Grand Kaiheber, or any other of the legion of convivial societies which exist in this great metropolis, carousing with the members in an atmosphere redolent of the fumes of beer and tobacco? Pshaw! any decent female would revolt from such indelicate contamination; and the simple proposition of such a degrading exposure of her person, would be considered the highest insult you could offer. No, sir,' he continued, 'the ladies would hate us if we were to insist on their company at the Lodge. I admit that, a few years ago, certain empirical works on Masonry were read with avidity by a certain class of females on the continent, who were anxious to penetrate the great secret, if possible, without regard to the means; and there was even an androgyne Order formed for the admission of women; and the excitement was kept up by means of balls, feasts, and other amusements; but few were found to embrace the offer of becoming acquainted with the secret by such unauthorized practices.'

"'There may be something in what you say,' replied Bro. Mackintosh, 'for I confess that although I have frequently heard my female acquaintances say that they are dying to know the secret, I never perceived any anxiety on their part to mix with the members of the Lodge. And certainly our late experiment of a masonic ball, in imitation of the example afforded by our continental Brethren and Sisters of the Adoptive Lodges, which I implicitly believed would have the effect of conciliating our female friends, and inducing a more favourable opinion of our pursuits, was a decided failure; for we were not honoured with the presence of any ladies of good standing in society; which rather favours your hypothesis that they have no particular anxiety to assemble in our Lodges, or share in our festive celebrations.'

"'I am glad to hear,' Bro. Noorthouck replied, 'that you think these pollutions (for I cannot give masonic dancings a more favourable designation) are alien to the principles of the Craft; because you were one of the parties who forced our late masonic ball upon me. But I hope you will do me the justice to admit that I opposed it to the utmost, as an unmasonic proceeding; and only gave way in compliance with the decision of a majority of votes. But it would be a manifest injustice to charge the unhappy consequences of this disgraceful proceeding on Masonry, or to contend that the Order is responsible for the results of a false step taken in direct violation both of its principles and its laws. This ill-advised measure has caused divisions amongst ourselves which will be very difficult to heal, and pointed the finger of scorn against the Institution in a manner very little to its credit. In a word, every evil has occurred which I predicted, and several others, of which I never dreamed.'

" 'On this point,' Bro. Mackintosh rejoined, 'we are now of one mind. Experience has convinced me that such celebrations are inexpedient, to say the least of them; and I intend to propose, at some early Lodge, that they be never repeated. I am quite sure that a majority of the Brethren will carry out the vote; for most of us are utterly disgusted with the result of the experiment.'

" 'So truth prevails in the end,' the R. W. M. replied. 'The charges of frivolity which are pertinaciously preferred to the prejudice of our Institution by the outward world, the cowan, and the profane, are sufficiently numerous already; let us not add to them by the adoption of an amusement which would give our adversaries all the advantage they require to turn the tide of popular feeling decidedly against us. It would, indeed, afford a public confirmation of those vague reports which accuse us of frittering away our valuable time in a round of trifling and childish amusements, and devoting ourselves to the temptations of luxury, and the indulgence of sensual passions. Even Bro. Heidegger, the celebrated *arbiter elegantiarum* of fashion, the very prince and high priest of saltation, and enjoying the favour of the monarch—at the moment of his greatest influence with his patron the Duke of Richmond, the Grand Master of Masons, and intrusted with the sole arrangement of the Grand Lodge Festivals, would not have dared to venture on a proposition so hostile to the grave and serious principles of the Order as a masonic ball. Dancing is a solecism irreconcileable with any one point, part, or secret connected with the Institution. If once the Fraternity is so weak and inconsiderate as to give themselves up to such frivolous and unworthy pursuits, they may bid farewell to Masonry; and, uniting themselves with the *ci-devant* Gormagons, may dance under the green-wood tree.'

"'Your observations are perfectly correct,' said Bro. Franco, who rose the instant Bro. Noorthouck had resumed his chair, 'English Masonry knows nothing of a masonic ball. It is an exotic of foreign growth, and will never thrive on British soil. It may be in character with the continental Lodges of Adoption, which admit females to join in the celebration, but it can never prevail to any extent in a country where they are excluded on principle from participating in the privileges of the Order. Consider, R. W. Sir, the marked indelicacy of such a practice. The Apron is used as the emblem of separation between the intellectual and carnal portions of the human body; and, therefore, when exhibited at a masonic ball, it affords (not to say invites) each lady, in a contre-dance, a favourable opportunity of calculating, with perfect accuracy, the exact point where the intellectual ends, and the carnal begins. In France this may not create an unfavourable sensation, because the morals of the people are becoming extremely lax; but in England, where correctness of demeanour and rectitude of conduct are the sole credentials of admission into decent society, such an example is contaminating beyond all calculation. Good heavens! is it possible that the Free and Accepted Mason can be found who is capable of subjecting the refined feelings of an English woman to the degradation of a scrutiny like this!'

"Bro. Franco was warm," said the Square; "but perfectly correct. Freemasonry has no precedent for a masonic ball; and I confess I felt grieved when the experiment was determined on by the vote of a majority of the Brethren. Fortunately the attempt proved abortive, and was never repeated. To proceed.

"'Well,' Bro. Mackintosh quietly observed, 'nothing further need be said on the subject; for the question will now be finally settled so far as regards the members of our Lodge. But you will not, I am afraid, so easily dispose of the objection, that the prayers of the Lodge are offered up without any reference to the Redeemer of mankind. As Christians, we cannot well understand how this omission has been suffered to exist for so many centuries amongst those who profess themselves followers of a crucified Saviour.'

"'I am surprised,' the R. W. M. replied, 'that a man of your sense and discrimination should have been led to adopt this weak and puerile argument;' for he was somewhat piqued at the pertinacity of Bro. Mackintosh; 'but,' he continued, 'as we are now embarked in the discussion of principles, I will again take the liberty of calling on Bro. Inwood to answer this objection, as it applies more particularly to his profession than to mine.'

"Bro. Inwood replied without hesitation," said the Square: "'It is true, R. W. Sir, that the Actual Name, Jesus Christ, is not mentioned in our present formulas, as they have been revised by Bro. Preston, but why he should have omitted the primitive invocation in his new prayer, I am at a loss to conjecture, as it was always used by our ancient Brethren; and, therefore, Bro. Mackintosh is mistaken in supposing that the omission had existed for centuries. But, waiving this argument, have you never considered that the Messiah is worshipped in Christian countries under a great variety of significant appellations, all of which refer to JEHOVAH or CHRIST? In the Old Testament he is called the Voice of the Lord, the Angel of the Covenant, the Wonderful, the Councillor, the Mighty God, the Everlasting Father, the Prince of Peace, the Creator, the Sun of Righteousness, the First and the Last, Emanuel, a Shepherd, a Rock, the Branch, &c., &c. And in the New Testament he has the corresponding titles of Emanuel, a Shepherd, a Door, a Rock, the Advocate, Alpha and Omega, the Sun of Righteousness, the Builder and Maker of the Universe, a Vine, the East, the Morning Star, &c.; under any of which appellations he may be legitimately worshipped. Now I would ask Bro. Mackintosh in what Name or names our invocations are usually made?'

"'We commonly use that of T. G. A. O. T. U.,' said Bro. Mackintosh.

"'Right. And according to the teaching of Masonry, who is he?'

"'Him that was placed om the pinnacle of the Temple, at Jerusalem.'

"'Which was Jesus Christ, for no other person was ever placed in that perilous situation; and He, if we may believe the Scriptures, was the Creator or Architect of the Universal World; or, as St. Paul expresses it, *by* whom and *for* whom all things were made. But we also use the titles of Most High and Jehovah, both being the names of Christ; and amongst the diversity of appellations bestowed on him in Holy Writ, I am decidedly of opinion that the choice of our ancient Brethren was most judicious. But more effectually to convince Bro. Mackintosh of his error, I may add, that in the earliest masonic prayers on record, the invocation was invariably made in the actual name of Jesus Christ. These original prayers have been discontinued only a very few years; that is, from the time when Hutchinson introduced the following well known passage into his Lectures, which were publicly and officially sanctioned by the Grand Lodge. Speaking of the action of the Third Degree, he says,—The Great Father of all, commiserating the miseries of the world, sent his only Son, who was innocence itself, to teach the doctrine of salvation; by whom man was raised from the death of sin unto a life of righteousness; from the tomb of corruption unto the chambers of hope; from the darkness of despair to the celestial beams of faith; and not only working for us this redemption, but making with us the covenant of regeneration, whence we are become the children of the Divinity, and inheritors of the realms of heaven.

"'We Masons,' Bro. Inwood continued, describing the deplorable state of religion under the Jewish law, 'speak in figures, and say,—Her tomb was in the rubbish and filth cast forth of the Temple, and Acacia wove its branches over her monument, ακακια being the Greek word for *innocence*, or being free from sin, implying that the sins and corruptions of the old law, and the devotees of the Jewish altar, had hid religion from those who sought her, and she was only to be found where innocence survived, and under the banner of the Divine Lamb; and, therefore, as we ourselves profess to be distinguished by our Acacia, we ought to be true Acacians in our religious faith and tenets. Again; the acquisition of the doctrines of redemption is expressed in the typical character of Euramen (*Ηυραμεν*, *inveni*), and by the application of that name amongst Masons, it is implied that we have discovered the knowledge of God and his salvation, and have been redeemed from the death of sin, and the sepulchre of pollution and unrighteousness. Thus the Master Mason represented man under the Christian doctrine, saved from the grave of iniquity, and raised to the faith of salvation. As the great testimonial that we are risen from the state of corruption, we bear the emblem of the Holy Trinity, as the insignia of our vows, and of the origin of the Master's Order. At this period, also, our worthy Bro. Preston, in his code of Lectures, which have become almost universal in our Lodges, explains the number Five, in the Second Degree, by a reference to the birth, life, death, resurrection, and ascension of our Lord and Saviour Jesus Christ.'

" 'This explanation,' said Bro. Mackintosh, 'appears, *à priori*, so satisfactory, that I shall not take the trouble to examine its accuracy. But I have still another observation to make, with permission of the Chair, on a subject which I confess has created some serious misgivings in my mind, respecting the real intention of the Order at its original establishment. Perhaps some well-informed Brother will be able to explain my doubts away. But it naturally excites the apprehensions of a thinking man, when he finds the science of alchymy, or some such absurdity, anciently identified with Masonry, under the suspicious designation of Abrac, Abraxas, or Abracadabra, which is admitted by both the authorities you have just cited, viz., Hutchinson and Preston.'

" 'Your doubts would be reasonable,' the R. W. M. replied, 'if they were just; but the admission of those two great Masons is rather problematical, for they allude to them only in explanation of an ancient manuscript, said to be written in the reign of Henry VI., about the year 1430. Now, you will not forget that in the age indicated by this MS., alchymical pursuits excited the attention of kings, peers, and prelates, and actually formed one branch of liberal education. All the hidden mysteries of natural philosophy were classed under the common head of occult science, and the king's astrologer was a public officer, and formed an influential member of every royal household in Europe. But, my dear friend, the Abracadabra was unconnected with alchymy. It is an appropriation which throws us back upon the dark ages of heathen ignorance, when some philosophers con tended that fire was the chief deity; and hence, as Bochart informs us, in his "Sacred Geography,"[1] the city of Ur, in Chaldea, where, according to Jewish tradition,[2] Abraham was cast into the furnace, was so called from a word signifying LUX, *seu ignis*. They placed fire in the centre of the earth, and as the earth was thus considered the primary object round which all the celestial bodies revolved, the situation assigned to their deity was, in their estimation, the absolute axle or pivot that directed and governed the entire universe.[3] This hypothesis was in some degree conformable to the opinions of the Jews, who entertained a firm belief that JEHOVAH, who had manifested himself to their ancestors by fire, was resident in their land only, which they esteemed to be the centre or middle of the earth, and that the said axle was exactly coincident with the *Sanctum Sanctorum* of the Temple at Jerusalem. Hence they pronounced the rest of the world to be out of the pale of God's observation and protection, occupying an indefinite circle of darkness, and alienated from the light of the Most High.'

"'You are aware, of course,' said Bro. Mackintosh, 'that this interpretation was repudiated by the Basilideans.'

"'I am not ignorant of the fact,' replied the R. W. M. 'The Basilideans, and other Gnostics, being better informed than the Jews, from having been instructed in the truths of Christian revelation, fell into errors equally fatal and absurd, by an intermixture of the Egyptian philosophy with the tenets of the Christian religion. They emancipated Jehovah from the Pythagorean and Jewish centre, and confined him to the circle of the year. They endowed him with 365 attributes or emanations, one for each diurnal rotation, which were individually deified in their turn as a separate power, and invested with a corresponding name.'

"'And do you conceive this absurd doctrine to have been embodied in Masonry by our ancient Brethren?' interposed Bro. Mackintosh, 'for that is the question I am desirous to have solved.'

[1] Geog. Sacr., p. 83, ed. 1681. [2] Jerom., on Gen. xi., 31.
[3] Hist. Init., p. 63, n.

" 'Not at all,' said Bro. Noorthouck. 'The Egyptian doctrine, from which this was borrowed, appertained to the worship of Isis (a corruption, according to the Basilideans, of the name of Jesus), who was called Myrionyma, or the goddess with a thousand names, each name being a separate attribute, and proclaimed herself, as Plutarch informs us, *Sum quidquid fuit, est, et erit, nemoque mortalium mihi adhuc velum detraxit.* Apuleius introduces her as saying, "I am the queen of heaven, the mystery of the elements, the beginning of ages, the governor of the firmament," &c. And it was in imitation of this prototype that Basilides gave his 365 names to the deity, one of which—perhaps the chief—was Abraxas,[4] which, on the one hand, referred to the sun at the first hour of his rising, and, on the other, to Jesus, who is represented in the New Testament as the DAY-STAR from on high, rising in the East. Now, the Day-star is the sun, and hence he is called in another place the Sun of Righteousness.'

" 'Then what, in the name of patience,' Bro. Mackintosh hastily said—'what *was* this *facultie of Abrac*, about which so much has been said?'

" 'Be calm,' the R. W. M. answered, 'and I will tell you. The facultie of Abrac, mentioned in the MS. to which you have referred, was nothing more than the art of raising a horoscope or figure of the heavens at a certain given moment of time; and every almanac-maker at the present day is acquainted with the process, although I greatly doubt whether it ever formed a legitimate object of research in a Masons' Lodge. I am rather inclined to think that, as the MS. was only a copy of one still older, this art was inserted amongst the secret practices of Masonry by some ignorant transcriber, who fancied that being an *occult*, it must necessarily be a *Masonic* pursuit. I admit that the word Abraxas is found on some few of the Craft Lodge floorcloths, but whether the Brethren understand the facultie of Abrac literally, or whether it is intended as a name of the Mediator, I will not pretend to determine.'

[4] For a full description of the Abraxas, see my article on the subject, in the F. Q. R., for 1848, p. 376.

"'You will excuse me, I am sure,' said Bro. Mackintosh, 'if I suggest a still further question, and it shall be the last, arising out of a passage in the R. A. Lectures, where mention is made of the Soul of Nature. I confess I cannot understand it, unless it has a reference to the above subject.'

"'You are correct,' the R. W. M. replied, 'in supposing that the Soul of Nature refers to the Abraxas, for we find that name substituted for Jehovah in some of the earliest chapters. It is, in fact, a reproduction of the Platonic triangle, T'AGATHON—NOUS—PSYCHE. The Platonists believed the world or Nature to be a living animal, endued with a soul (ζωον ενψυχον); and esteemed it as a form informing the universe, or rather a Form assistant, imagining it unsuitable to its deity to be mixed with, or vitally united to the grossest sub-celestial matter, and to have perceptions of all its motions. You will find the doctrine explained in Seneca de Beneficio, in the seventh chapter of the Fourth Book. According to this philosopher, when treating of the Soul of the World or Nature, matter is eternal—T'Agathon representing the Supreme Being—Nous, or Logos, the Intellectual world—and Psyche, or Demiurgus, a sort of deputy Creator, or Soul infused into Nature, which was constructed out of pre-existent materials, called Hyle. This quaternary of the Intellectual World or Nature, T'Agathon—Nous—Psyche—Hyle, formed the Pythagorean Tetractys, and was considered equivalent to the Jewish Tetragrammaton, which may be the reason why a reference to the doctrine was improperly foisted into R. A. Masonry by our respected and intelligent Brother Dunckerley; but I conceive that no such principles were ever intended to form a characteristic portion of this exalted Order.'

"'My dear friend,' said Bro. Mackintosh, 'I confess I ought to cry *peccavi*, and apologise for the trouble I have given you. You have afforded me considerable enlightenment on these intricate subjects; and, to say the truth, I was scarcely aware that they were capable of such an elucidation. It strikes me that occasional conversations like this in which we are at present engaged in open Lodge, on doubtful or unintelligible points, would be of great service to Masonry, and confer more essential benefits on the Brethren than the eternal repetition of the usual Lodge Lectures.'

"The Brethren professed themselves to be greatly edified by the discussion," said the Square, "and Bro. Mackintosh, from that moment, became a zealous and industrious Mason, and gradually advanced to the highest honours of the Craft."

CHAPTER XI.

CHARLATANS.—ARTHUR TEGART.

1790-1794.

"Absentem qui rodit amicum;
Qui non defendit, alio culpante; solutos
Qui captat risus hominum, famamque dicacis;
Fingere qui non visa potest; commissa tacere
Qui nequit; hic niger est: hunc tu, Romane, caveto."
HOR.

"The base and vile doctrine of doing evil that good may come; or, in other words, that the end justifies the means, has also been alleged against the Freemasons. Or, rather, it is expressly asserted of the Jesuits and Illuminees, by authors who decidedly implicate and involve our Society with those corrupt associations; declaring it to be formed on the same plan, founded on the same principles, and furthering the same designs."—HARRIS.

"In mids of which depainted there we found
Deadly debate, all full of snaky hair
That with a bloody fillet was ybound
Outbreathing nought but discord everywhere."
SACKVILLE.

THE Square continued his Revelations in a moralizing spirit. "Towards the conclusion of the eighteenth century," he said, "Fremasonry had many enemies to contend with. Besides the professed Cowans, there were false Masons, seceding Masons, and Antimasons, all of whom were arrayed against the truth; but the latter were the most venomous. They attacked, with blind and indiscriminate zeal, like a bear overturning a hive of bees, unconscious of the punishment to which he exposes himself, an institution, of the design of which they were profoundly ignorant, with the avowed determination of scuttling and sinking the gallant ship. This hazy notion led them into a slough of difficulties, where every plunge they made sank them deeper and deeper in their soft and miry bed. Pope had already described them in the 'Dunciad:'—

'Here plung'd a feeble, but a desperate pack,
With each a sickly Brother at his back;
Sons of a day! just buoyant on the flood,
They number'd with the puppies in the mud.
Ask ye their names? I could as soon disclose
The names of these blind puppies as of those.'

"Nor could they be made to understand that the genius of Masonry, while pursuing her stately march of benevolence through the world, diffuses happiness wherever she appears, and scatters blessings with a liberal hand.

'Her flowing raiment pure as virgin snow
Or fabled field where fairest lilies grow,
A milk-white lamb ran sporting by her side,
As innocence her manners dignified.
Her whole deportment harmony and love,
Temper'd with meekness from the realms above.
A blazing star upon her front she wore;
A cornucopia in her hand she bore.
Where'er she trod the sciences arose;
Where'er she breath'd confusion sham'd her foes;
Dismayed they fled, nor dar'd to look behind,
For foes of her were foes of human kind.'[1]

"Although Freemasonry is thus constantly employed in performing the high behests of the Divinity, the Antimasons of a foreign land, during the period now under our consideration, succeeded in obstructing her course and, for a brief period, absolutely annihilated her existence, amidst the wild dissensions and anarchy of a blood-stained revolution. Translations of the virulent attacks of Lefranc[2] and Latocnaye[3] were freely distri-

[1] From an unpublished "Ode on Masonry," by the Rev. S. Oliver.

[2] Lefranc's work is called the "Veil withdrawn for the Curious; or, the Secret of the Revolution divulged by the aid of Freemasonry. By the Abbé Lefranc, Principal of the Seminary of the Eudists, at Caen, in Normandy." 1792.

[3] "The Philosophy of Masonry." An answer to this attack was published in the "Freemasons' Magazine" for 1793, in which the writer gives the following account of the object and design of Freemasonry:—"This sublime Institution refines society into a more beautiful and a more perfect system, by joining men together in closer and more affectionate relations than is the case in the enlarged state of social intercourse. But its grand labour to bring about this glorious end, is to make its votaries good men and true; and as the strong-

buted; the former of whom reproduced the worn-out fiction, that, on the death of a friend who had been a very zealous Mason and many years Master of a respectable Lodge, he found amongst his papers a collection of masonic writings, containing the rituals, catechisms, and symbols of every kind belonging to a train of degrees, together with many discourses delivered in different Lodges, and minutes of their proceedings. The perusal filled him, as he tells his readers, with astonishment and anxiety. For he found that doctrines were taught, and maxims of conduct inculcated, which were subversive of religion and all good order in the state;[4] and which not only countenanced disloyalty and sedition, but even invited to it. He thought them so dangerous to the state, that he sent an account of them to the Archbishop of Paris, long before the Revolution, in the hope that he would represent the matter to his majesty's ministers,

est motive to virtue, it points their view to that Temple of immortal perfection beyond the present state, where social happiness is alone complete, but which you have endeavoured to persuade men is only a visionary structure erected by artifice, and supported by superstition."

[4] Lefranc seems to have improved on the fable invented by an English charlatan, and inserted in the Preface of a pretended revelation which had been published many years before; where the author unblushingly proclaims, for the purpose, we suppose, of obviating the suspicion of perjury, the incredible fiction that he acquired his knowledge from some loose papers belonging to a merchant, to whom he was nearly related, who had been a member of the Queen's Arms Lodge, St. Paul's Churchyard. This relation dying about ten years ago, the Editor became possessed of his effects; and on looking over his papers, amongst others he found some memorandums of Masonry, which excited his curiosity so far, that he resolved to enter a Lodge without going through the ceremonies required by the Society. He first made trial on an intimate acquaintance who was a Freemason, and he readily returned the sign which was made to him. After a more particular examination on the part of his friend, as to where he was made, and when, &c., to all of which he answered with great readiness, he received an invitation to attend the Lodge as a visiting member. Elated by success, he consented to accompany his friend; and after the usual ceremony at the door, he was admitted by the Tyler, clothed himself in his apron, and took his seat as a Brother Mason. He further tells his readers that he was present at two initiations, and that the ceremonies corresponded with his deceased relative's papers. He then went to another Lodge, where he distinguished himself greatly in answering the Questions proposed by the Master, which he acquired from his friend's manuscripts of the Entered Apprentice, and Fellowcraft's Lectures.

and that they would put an end to the meetings of this dangerous society, or at least restrain its members from committing such excesses. But he was disappointed, and, therefore, thought it was his duty to lay them before the public.

"And Latocnaye," continued the Square, "treats his readers with a rigmarole story, that when he was initiated, an old gentleman asked him what he thought of Freemasonry. He answered, 'A great deal of noise, and much nonsense.' 'Nonsense!' said the other; 'do not judge so rashly, young man, I have been a Mason these twenty-five years, and the farther I advanced the more interested I became; but I stopped short, and nothing shall prevail on me to proceed a step farther.' In another conversation the old gentleman confessed that his quarrel with the Institution originated in his refusal, a long time previous, to accede to some treasonable proposals which were made to him by some members of his Lodge, ever since which he had been treated by the Fraternity with great reserve; and under the pretext of further instructions, they were anxious to soften down their seditious proposals by giving them a different explanation, for the purpose of removing the suspicions which he had formed concerning the ultimate scope of the Institution.

"Then the great guns were brought to bear on the Order," said the Square, "in the ponderous 'Proofs' of Professor Robison,[5] and the Abbé Barruel's 'Memoirs of Jacobinism;'[6] the latter of whom, with consummate skill,

[5] "Proofs of a Conspiracy against all Religions and Governments of Europe, carried on in the Secret Meetings of Freemasons, Illuminati, and Reading Societies. Collected from good authorities. By John Robison." Edinburgh, Creech, 1797. The Second Edition, with corrections and additions: London, Cadell: and Edinburgh, Creech, 1797. Third Edition, still further enlarged: London, Cadell, 1798. Fourth Edition: London, 1798. This book was translated into French, and published by Thory in 1797; into German, and published in 1800; with other editions in 1802 and 1803; and also into several other continental languages.

[6] "Memoirs, illustrating the History of Jacobinism, by the Abbé Barruel, and translated into English by the Hon. Robert Clifford." London, 1797. Second Edition: London, 1798. This extraordinary book was originally written in French. It went through several editions in that country, and was translated into most of the continental languages. In support of his theory, Barruel tells his readers that a nobleman, who had been disgusted with what he saw in the

graced a losing cause by dressing up falsehood in great eloquence of language, and gilding discomfiture with selfish adulation. These two works created an immense sensation, although they were powerfully answered by Preston,[7] Jones,[8] and other masonic worthies.

"And the task was not difficult," said the Square 'If these unprincipled charlatans, abbés, and professors, had favoured us with a few rays of truth to enlighten our progress through the vast region of darkness and error into which their copious tomes have led us, we might have afforded to excuse the evil for the sake of the good. But *obtrectatio ac livor pronis auribus accipiuntur;*[9] and instead of that, their publications present to our view one gigantic tissue of errors. False in principle, false in practice, false in facts, and false in detail, they are unpossessed of a single redeeming feature, although they passed through as many editions as 'Jack the Giant Killer' and 'Tom Thumb;' and every argument, every objection, and every surmise has been answered and refuted a thousand times over.

"As for Barruel, he was either deceived himself, or possessed with a wilful and wicked determination of deceiving others. The latter alternative appears the most reasonable; for it is barely possible that he could be misinformed on a subject, to the study of which he had devoted all his energies for the professed purpose of

Freemasons' Lodges, reported it to the minister, saying that he considered it his duty to do this, though it might probably lodge him in the Bastile. The minister turned on his heel, and said, with a smile, "Be satisfied, my friend, you shall not go to the Bastile, nor will the Freemasons disturb the state." It appears also that the king himself had been informed of those dangerous proceedings. But being easy and confident, he did not know the change which had been produced in the minds of his subjects, till his return from Varennes. Then he observed to a friend, "How does it happen that I closed my mind against this? I was informed of it all eleven years ago, and refused to believe it."

[7] "Freemasons' Magazine," and "Illustrations of Masonry."

[8] A Vindication of Masonry from the charge of having given rise to the French Revolution, in the "Masonic Essayist."

[9] "What!" cried the scholar, "have you studied the classics?" "You ought hardly to be surprised at that," replied the devil. "I speak fluently all the barbarous tongues—Hebrew, Greek, Persic, and Arabic. Nevertheless, I am not vain of my attainments; and that, at all events, is an advantage I have over your learned pedants." —ASMODEUS.

exposure and ultimate extinction. He tells his readers the improbable fiction that *initiation was absolutely forced upon him.* Hear his lachrymose confession from his own mouth, and wonder: 'During the last twenty years,' he says, 'it was difficult, especially in Paris, to meet with persons who did not belong to the Society of Freemasons. I was acquainted with many, and some were my most intimate friends. These, *with all that zeal common to young adepts*, frequently pressing me to become one of the Brotherhood; and notwithstanding my constant and steady refusal, they determined to enrol me. Having settled their plan, I was invited to dinner at a friend's house, and was the only *profane* person in the midst of a large assembly of Masons. Dinner being over, and the servants having withdrawn, it was proposed to form themselves into a Lodge, and to initiate me. I persisted in my refusal, and particularly declined to take any oath to keep those things secret which were unknown to me. The oath was, therefore, dispensed with; but I still refused. They then became more pressing; telling me that Masonry was perfectly innocent, and its morality unobjectionable. In reply, I asked whether it was better than that of the Gospel. They only answered by forming themselves into a Lodge, and commenced all those grimaces and childish ceremonies which are described in books on Masonry. I attempted to escape, but in vain; the apartment was very extensive, the house in a retired situation, the servants in the secret, and all the doors locked. I was then questioned, and my answers were given laughingly. In the end I was admitted Apprentice, and immediately afterwards Fellowcraft. Having received these two degrees, I was informed that a third was to be conferred on me. On this I was conducted into another spacious apartment, where the scene changed, and assumed a more serious appearance, &c., *Ohe, jam satis!*

"Do you believe this medley of improbabilities?' said the Square, interrogatively. "No one does. There is not a single grain of truth in this overflowing measure of chaff. Freemasonry is not a proselyting system; no zealous young adepts can press their friends to become Masons, for the candidate is bound to declare that his application is purely unsolicited, or he would be summarily rejected. Again, no Lodge can be opened after dinner in a private house, nor in the presence of a candidate before initiation; the O. B. cannot be dispensed with; the Brethren have no grimaces and childish ceremonies; nor can three degrees be conferred at one time. Such wild assertions as the Abbé has used to cajole his readers, may blind the profane and Antimason, who will complacently swallow a camel's load of the most incredible scurrility, when directed against the Institution of Freemasonry; but no man of ordinary common sense could be deluded into believing such a mendacious statement, which violates all the ordinary principles by which Masonry is regulated and knit together.

"To support his hypothesis, that the object of Freemasonry is liberty and equality, or, in other words, revolution, and the destruction of social order, Barruel used the following argument, deduced from presuming facts. 'It was on the day,' he says, 'when Louis XVI. was imprisoned by a Decree of the Jacobins, that the secret of Freemasonry was, for the first time, made public; that secret, so dear to them, and which they preserved with all the solemnity of the most inviolable oath. At the reading of this famous decree, they exclaimed, "We have at length succeeded, and France is no other than one immense Lodge. The whole French people are Freemasons, and the entire universe will soon follow their example." I witnessed this enthusiasm, and heard the conversation to which it gave rise. I heard Masons, till then the most reserved, freely and openly declare, that at length the grand object of Masonry was accomplished by the establishment of equality and liberty. "All men are now equal and brothers," they exclaimed, "and all men are free. This is the entire substance of our doctrine, the object of our wishes, and the whole of our Grand Secret." Such was the language,' says the Abbé, 'which I heard fall from the most zealous Masons; from those whom I have seen decorated with all the insignia of the highest degrees, and who enjoyed the rights of Venerables to preside over the Lodges. I have heard them express themselves in this manner before those whom Masons would call the profane, without enjoining the slightest secresy, either from the men or women present. They said it in a tone as if they wished all France should be acquainted with this glorious achievement of Masonry; as if they were to recognise in them its benefactors, and the authors of that revolution of EQUALITY and LIBERTY, of which it had given so grand an example to all Europe. *Such, in reality, was the general secret of the Freemasons.*'

"The man declares," pursued the Square, "that he saw and heard all this. Is he to be credited? I think not; or at least his testimony must be received *cum grano salis;* for it may be difficult to conjecture what kind of reverie he was in when he dreamt of such absurdities.

"Once more. He presents his readers with a pretended extract from the Lodge Lectures. Listen to it: 'Learn, in the first place,' says the Venerable to the candidate, 'that the three implements with which you have been made acquainted, viz., the Bible, the Compass, and the Square, have a secret signification, which I will explain. The Bible instructs you to acknowledge no other law than that of Adam—the law which the Almighty engraved on his heart, and is called the Law of Nature. The Compasses recall to your mind that God is the central point from which everything is equally distant, and to which everything is equally near. By the Square you learn that God has made everything equal. The Cubical Stone teaches that all actions are alike with respect to the Sovereign good. The death of Hiram, and the change of the Master's word, teach you that it is difficult to escape the snares of ignorance; and that it is your duty to show the same courage as our Master Hiram, who suffered himself to be massacred rather than hearken to the persuasion of his assassins.'

"One would think," continued the Square, emphatically, "that the simplest and most gullible Cowan in his majesty's dominion could scarcely be deceived by the relation of these gross absurdities. If Barruel believed them himself, he had more verdant reticulations on the cuticle of his brain than I gave him credit for. I am not hypercritical; but I put it to you pointedly and plainly, whether, on a fair literal and grammatical construction of his words, any resemblance, however remote, to our general illustrations, can be traced in this fanciful exposition of our highly-esteemed symbols? And it is, therefore, impossible to arrive at any other conclusion than that a wilful perversion of facts, supported by a sophistical train of reasoning, are the unstable grounds on which the Jesuit has founded a superstructure, that, like the ancient military towers called Belfroi, was intended to batter down, and level with the earth, the bulwarks of a benevolent institution, which teaches man to do justly, to love mercy, and to walk humbly with his God. The attempt, however, failed most signally, and the defamers of the Order sank into insignificance. We may, therefore, say with Dryden,—

> 'Let them rail on; let their vindictive muse,
> Have four and twenty letters to abuse,
> Which, if they jumble to one line of sense,
> Indict them of a capital offence.'

"This important subject," the Square proceeded to say, "constituted a prolific topic of conversation amongst the Craft, and it was once discussed *seriatim* by the Members of our Lodge, who expressed their opinions on it very freely. It was induced by an observation of Bro. Arthur Tegart, who was installed on St. John's day, 1793, that he had recently seen a book, published by a French emigrant, which was intended to prove that Masonry is a system of deism.

"'And to convince you, Brethren,' the R. W. M. continued, 'of the lamentable ignorance which this gentleman displays of the Institution which he professes to expose, you shall hear the account that he gives of one of the ceremonies of initiation. He tells his readers that the candidate, after having heard many threatenings against those who should betray the secrets of the Order, is conducted to a place where he sees the dead bodies of several persons who are said to have suffered for their treachery. At this point of the ceremony, he himself, as he coolly asserts, saw his own Brother bound hand and foot, and was informed that he was doomed to suffer the punishment due to this grave offence, and that it was reserved for himself to be the instrument of their vengeance, which would enable him to manifest his complete devotion to the Order. It being observed, however, that his countenance indicated extreme horror, as his Brother continued earnestly to implore his mercy, a bandage was charitably placed over his eyes, in order to spare his feelings. A dagger was then placed in his right hand, his left being laid on the palpitating heart of the victim, and he was commanded to strike. He instantly obeyed; and when the bandage was removed from his eyes, he discovered that a lamb had been substituted, although he verily believed that he had stabbed his brother. Surely, he adds, such trials, and such wanton cruelty, are fit only for training conspirators.'

"'He cannot be speaking of blue Masonry,' Bro. Pigou observed, 'for there is not a shadow of resemblance to any one of our ceremonies in the entire process.'

"'He scarcely knows what he is speaking of,' said Bro. Jones; 'but it is evident that he intends the profane world to believe that it is a faithful description of our secret rites; and to my certain knowledge there are a vast number of people that either *do*, or pretend to believe it.'

"'As they do also,' Bro. Preston interposed, 'the wild assertion of Lefranc, that while the National Assembly protected the meetings of Freemasons, it peremptorily prohibited those of every other Society. The obligation, he continues, of laying aside all stars, ribbons, crosses, and other honourable distinctions, under the pretext of fraternal equality, was not merely a prelude, but was intended as a preparation for the discontinuance of all civil distinctions, which actually took place at the very beginning of the Revolution, and the first proposal of a surrender was made by a zealous Mason. He further observes, that the horrible and sanguinary oaths, the daggers, sculls, and cross-bones, the imaginary combats with the murderers of Hiram, and many other gloomy ceremonies, have a natural tendency to harden the heart, to qualify its natural disgust at deeds of horror, and to pave the way for those shocking barbarities which made the name of a Frenchman abhorred throughout Europe. It is true, these deeds were perpetrated by a mob of fanatics; but the principles, as he informs his readers, were promulgated and fostered by persons who styled themselves masonic philosophers.'

"'Absurd!' interjected Bro. Crespigny. 'To what Quixotic projects will some persons resort in support of an untenable hypothesis. These men are labouring to promulgate an opinion that Freemasonry was the proximate cause of the Revolution in France, with which it had as little to do as in producing the general Deluge. Hoffmann, a German writer against Freemasonry, has the candour to admit that the Order had been abused and misrepresented by *the matchless villany* (these are the very words) of its opponents; and that they were perfectly unscrupulous in the invention and application of any facts or surmises, how absurd soever they might be, which promised to preserve the balance of their theory.'

"'For which purpose,' said Bro. Pigou, 'one of these worthies boldly asserts, that the President's hat in the National Assembly is copied from that of a Venerable Grand Master in a Mason's Lodge; and that the Scarf of a municipal officer is the same as is worn by an Entered Apprentice Mason. And when the Assembly celebrated the Revolution in the Cathedral of Notre Dame, he further says, its members accepted of the highest honours of Masonry, by passing under an Arch of steel, formed by the drawn swords of a double rank of Brethren.'

"'These improbable chimeras have been conjured up by Lefranc,' Bro. Jones observed, 'to excite the apprehensions of the timid, and the ridicule of the bold. Now, the alternative embraced by his hypothesis may be put in this form: he was either a Freemason or not. If the former, and had entered into solemn obligations of secresy, does the violation of those obligations afford him any claim to credence? Or is the man who fearlessly violates an oath, which, according to his own statement, is most awfully administered, likely to have any scruples of conscience respecting the truth or falsehood of his assertions, when he undertakes to publish a pamphlet *ad captandum vulgus?* If M. Lefranc never was initiated, it follows, of course, that his work must be an unauthorized fabrication. As to the stale pretext of deriving his knowledge of Masonry from a collection of papers, placed in his hands by a Brother on his deathbed—the long-hackneyed fiction is too palpable to deserve a moment's consideration.'

"Bro. Preston then appealed to the Brethren present, to say whether these books, which denounce Freemasonry as an irreligious and deistical Institution, active in promoting evil, but neutral at the least, if not hostile, to the existence of good, are not a gross and wicked libel on a Society whose foundation and superstructure are peace, harmony, and brotherly love? To submit to the powers that be; to obey the laws which yield protection; to conform to the government under which they live; to be attached to their native soil and sovereign; to encourage industry, to reward merit, and to practise universal benevolence, are the fundamental tenets of Masons; 'peace on earth and good will to man,' are their study; while the cultivators and promoters of that study are marked as patterns worthy of imitation and regard. Friends to Church and State in every regular government, their tenets interfere with no particular faith, but are alike friendly to all. Suiting themselves to circumstances and situation, their Lodges are an asylum to the friendless and unprotected of every age and nation. As citizens of the world, religious antipathy and local prejudices fail to operate, while every nation affords them a friend, and every climate a home.

"'I am obliged to Bro. Preston,' said the R. W. M., 'for his excellent eulogium—indeed, nothing less could be expected from a Brother of his eminence. But the question is, can anything be done to counteract the effect of these mendacious publications, which, like the blasting simoom of the Arabian deserts, that envelops man and beast in its deadly embrace, carry conviction to the understanding of some, overthrow the faith of others, and create doubt and suspicion in the minds of all?'

"'I rather incline to the opinion of Gamaliel,' Bro. Sir John Aubyn gravely replied; 'let them alone: if this counsel or this work be of man, it will come to nought. And I am fully persuaded that the proximate intention of all these writers against Freemasonry, is to produce an effect decidedly hostile to the lessons of peace and order which the Redeemer bequeathed as an everlasting legacy to his followers.'

"'I shall at least,' said Bro. Preston, 'discharge my own conscience, by endeavouring to furnish all right-minded men with a reply to the gratuitous and unfounded assertions of Lefranc, in a short paper on the subject, addressed to the Editor of the 'Gentleman's Magazine.'

"'I see no harm in that,' replied Bro. Dagge, 'provided it be done in a mild and gentlemanly spirit.

"'And I will take care not to exceed the bounds of the strictest decorum,' Bro. Preston rejoined.

"But all the masonic charlatans of the age," the Square continued, "and their name is Legion, were eclipsed by a working tailor of the name of Finch, who was now beginning to acquire a notorious celebrity, which was consummated a few years later by the unblushing assurance with which his pretensions were advocated. Expelled from the Order by the Grand Lodge, he commenced a system of practical Masonry on his own account, although at the best he was but *malæ fidei possessor;* and, like the fox that had lost his tail, he used every art of persuasion to induce others to cut off theirs, that his deformity might escape the censure of singularity. He succeeded in finding an abundance of ready abettors, by whose aid he reaped a golden harvest.

"Thus Masonry, appearing to be more profitable than the exercise of his needle, he determined to make the most of it; and having been furnished by Nature with an assurance equal to that of Signor Corcuela's friend in 'Gil Blas,' he did not hide his talent under a bushel, but brought it into practice with tolerable success. He commenced his career by giving private instructions in Masonry, for a con-si-de-ra-tion, and numbers resorted to him for that purpose. By some means or other, known only to himself, he had become pretty well versed in the continental fables, and by amalgamating them with English Masonry, he succeeded in exciting a prurient curiosity amongst the more inexperienced Brethren, which brought an abundance of grist to his masonic mill.

"The R. W. M.," continued the Square, "on one of our regular Lodge nights, read a prospectus, which Finch had addressed to him officially, and a brief conversation arose out of a remark of Bro. Deans on the insufferable arrogance and effrontery of that person in venturing to annoy the Lodges with his unauthorized correspondence.

"'These circulars,' Bro. Preston observed, 'which are in reality nothing more than advertisements, to promote the sale of his catchpenny publications,[10] are not only

[10] His principal works were not published till the beginning of the nineteenth century: but I insert a few of them here to render the

disseminated among the Lodges, but publicly placarded on blank walls in the purlieus of the city, in company with notices of quack medicines, blacking-pots, metallic tractors, and animal magnetism.'

"'I know the fellow,' said Bro. Pigou. 'His self-possession, under any circumstances that may arise, is worthy of a better cause. He is a nondescript in his principles, and a cormorant in his appetite for plunder. Peace and harmony have no charms for him; order and regularity are his aversion; obedience and subordination he detests; in a word, his sole object is to sink the tailor, and convert Masonry into a more profitable and less laborious employment. His needle is sharp, but he thinks himself sharper, and he has discarded the thimble for a *rig* which he fancies will be more remunerative.'

"'Besides all this,' Bro. Dean interposed, 'the man is cursed with the demon of ambition, and is desirous of being

'Jove in his chair
Of the sky Lord Mayor,'

which is but a prelude to his ultimate exposure.'

"'And it would be as well to effectuate it at once,' Bro. Dagge observed.

"'Let him alone,' replied Bro. Preston; 'let him alone. His imposture is too transparent to be of long continuance. Give him rope enough, and we shall see him, one of these fine days, gracefully dangling from his own signpost."

subject complete. (1) "A Masonic Treatise, with an Elucidation on the Religious and Moral Beauties of Freemasonry; Ziydvjxyjpix, Zqjisgstn, Wxstxjin, &c. R A— A M— R C— K S— M P— M— &c.; for the use of Lodges and Brothers in general. Dedicated, by permission, to William Perfect, Esq., P. G. M. for the county of Kent. By W. Finch, Canterbury. Please to observe that every book has on the Title-page, ty Qxzf, and Oivjjxg Qvwgzjpix." Deal, 1800. Second edition, Deal, 1802. (2) "An Elucidation of the Masonic Plates, consisting of sixty-four different compartments. By W. Finch." London, 1802. (3) "A Masonic Key, with an Elucidation. By W. Finch." Deal, 1803. (4) "The Lectures, Laws, and Ceremonies of the Holy Royal Arch degree of Freemasonry. By W. Finch." Lambeth, 1812. (5) "A new Set of Craft Lectures for the use of Lodges and the Brethren in general." Lambeth, Finch, 1814. (6) "The Origin of Freemasons, their Doctrine &c." London, 1816. He published many other pamphlets respecting the higher degrees, which it would be tedious to enumerate.

"'At least,' said Bro. Jones, 'his reputation will be thus suspended, and exposed to public derision. It will not attain a green old age, how verdant soever his credu lous disciples may at present be.'

"'More improbable things than that have occurred rejoined Bro. Pigou.

"'And yet,' the R. W. M. observed, 'his speculation promises to be successful, for he is exceedingly popular with a certain set, as many a demagogue has been before him, and will be again, so long as a dupe remains to be tormented by fictitious evils, or amused with the hope of imaginary good.

"'I confess,' said Bro. Batson, 'that my patience is severely tried, when I reflect on the self-sufficient assumption of infallibility which this ignorant empiric arrogates to himself. He boldly announces that both the *ancient* and *modern* sections are erroneous, not only in practice, but in principle; and asserts that the York system alone, which he insinuates to be something essentially different from both, is genuine. And he further proclaims, with a flourish of trumpets, that the York system of Masonry is represented in its purity by only one solitary Lodge—the glorious light of Masonry has been universally extinguished, or become like the flickering blaze of an expiring rushlight, and burns brightly in one only place—and that place—hear it, ye genii that preside over humbug and knavery, imposition and falsehood—that place—the house of William Finch, of Canterbury, and himself—save the mark—its Grand Master!!!'

"'From which metropolitical centre,' the R. W. M. interposed, 'his manifestoes and prospectuses radiate in every direction, to induce the purchase of his pretended Lectures, which are enunciated in the form of thin pamphlets, at the enormous charge of half a guinea each. And to clothe the imposture with the hope of being permanently remunerative, they are chiefly in manuscript, and ingeniously constructed on such a principle that, as I am told, a personal application to the author for their elucidation is absolutely necessary to make them moderately intelligible; and the interview can only be obtained through the medium of an additional fee.'

"'The rogue,' said Bro. M'Gillivray, 'is grasping to

receive, but always unwilling to pay. Like Billy Green, the idiot, who accosted every one he met, with 'Sir, give a penny, and I will sing you a song, but *give me the penny first*,' he stipulates in his prospectuses, as a *sine qua non*, that all payments must be made *in advance*, and all letters be post-paid.'

"'I have had the curiosity,' Bro. Batson remarked, 'to visit his crack Lodge; but my attention was excited by nothing so much as the extreme unction with which he pronounced the self-laudatory address that terminated the proceedings.'

"'And what did he say for himself?' the R. W. M asked; for he felt some slight interest in any personal anecdote of a character who had established such an unenviable notoriety.

"'It was in the style of eulogy, delivered in extremely coarse and vulgar language,' Bro. Batson replied; 'and he was a good mimic,'" the Square interposed, parenthetically. "'Brethren, my name is William Finch. I am not ashamed of it. The name of Finch will be known when those of his calumniators are forgotten. I am the true and only conservator of genuine ancient Masonry. No man understands it so well as myself. I am the greatest Mason in Europe, as all the foreign Lodges are ready to testify. Those who wish to learn the science must come to me. I alone can teach the true secrets of mysticism, cabalism, and theurgy, practised by those learned masonic bodies the Chevaliers Bienfaisants, the Amis Réunis de la Vérité, the Philalethes, and the Misraimites. They are not known to any Englishman except myself! I'm wide awake, my friends! I know a trick or two! Put down your gold, dear Brethren, and you shall see—what you *shall* see. They'll bowl me out, will they? If they succeed, my name is not William Finch. No, no, they can't do it. I should like to see them try. Ha! ha! They *have* tried more than once, and failed; and they will not do it again, I'll engage.' And thus he ran on, something in the style of Richard Brothers, the political prophet, to the edification of his youthful admirers, and the unconcealed disgust of all right-minded Brethren. *Risum teneatis amici!*

"'I have, myself, been weak enough,' said Bro. Dagge, to purchase one of his manuscripts, and I cannot say that my disappointment was altogther unexpected, when I discovered that on the most material points I was referred to other pamplets, as well as to a private interview for explanation. This course was evidently pursued with the undisguised intention of inducing the purchase of *them* also at the same price, that his nest might be effectually feathered. Well may it be said that charlatanism pays better than merit; for I soon found that it would be impossible to decipher his complicated hieroglyphics so as to understand the system, unless I had every one of his books before me, as well as the keys of his ciphers, and elucidations of his numerous blanks and spaces,[11] and even then it is doubtful whether any useful information can be extracted from their perusal; for they leave the reader nearly as much in the dark as when he commenced the hopeless task of unriddling these cabalistic productions.'

[11] Read the following delectable specimen as an example, if you can. "5 He liwvivw those t——r——g 33 to wrerdv gsvn hvoevh equally into ulfi wrerhrlmh, one of which was to go down to Qlkkz where the materials were ozmwvw for the yfrowrmt and vmjfriv, if any such nvm had yvvm gsviv at the same time to wrhxiryv gsvn they received uli zmhdvi there had, but owing to the vnyzitl they could not obtain a kzhhztv, they therefore returned into the rmgvirli kzig of the xlfm gib, those gsivv 33 then returned orpvdrhv, and on passing by the nlfgs lu a xzev by the hvz hrwv they svziw the following vcxoznzgrlmh (here follows the various vcxoznzgrlmh) they knowing by their elrxvh they were nvm lu Gbiv and by their vcxoznzgrlmh that they were the hznv, they were rm kvihfrg lu they therefore if hsvw rm and awd ulfmw the same, they then ylfmw gsvn and yilftsg gsvn yvulix K S———." Again in another pamphlet. "So r—m— and i— from the W— M— in xxx E—; xxx and c—t— txt— S. W. in the W. In xxx S— &c. (See the first part of my Union Lectures.) Once more. The origin of the M— M— O— B— is taken from a custom of the Jews when they E— i— a— S— E—, they b— f— a— B— and c— it a—; and p— b— the p— t—, they said t— l— it be done t— h—, and t— l— h— q— b— b— c— a—, who shall b— h— o—." These extracts will be quite sufficient to show that the real intention of the charlatan was to extract money from the pockets of his dupes; but I cannot refrain from giving another quotation from his pamphlet on the Royal Arch. "W— w— t— do a— in l— and unity the S— W— o— a— R— A— M— to k— a— n— t— r— i— t— a— i— t— w— unless it be when t— s— a— w— d— m— and a—. They now give the S— of S— the t— t—; which done they a— t— t— p— and S— on the f— s— of their c— s—. Z— s— I— d— t— g— and R— C— d— o— in the n— o— g. There is another method of opening the Royal Arch Chapters far more sublime than this; which may be had in MS. by application to W. Finch!!!"

"It may save trouble," the Square continued, "to sum up this impostor's history by an account of his final exposure, although it did not occur until many years afterwards, for his career was long and profitable. Success and impunity at length made him reckless and incautious, and he became so eager in the pursuit of his game, that sometimes it eluded his grasp. When he was expelled from Masonry, as I have already observed, the fellow opened a surreptitious Lodge in his own house, in accordance with a false principle, which he publicly avowed in his circulars, that every Lodge possesses an inherent power of acting on its own authority, and that any body of Masons, being not less in number than seven, are at full liberty, from their inalienable rights, to open a Lodge when and where they please, to make Masons, and perform all the rites and ceremonies of the Craft. In his own Lodge the fees were enormous, and he succeeded in finding a competent number of dupes who were weak enough to submit to the imposition.

"Now it appears," said the Square, "that he considered himself to be the sole *usufructuarius* of the property, both of his Lodge and trumpery publications; and, therefore, though he charged unprecedented prices for certain miserable engravings which were intended to elucidate his system of Masonry, yet he frequently succeeded in defrauding his workmen of the fair profits of their honest labour, by persuading them to be initiated in his Lodge. A poor fellow, named Smith, was thus victimized. When he sent in his bill for work done, Finch, as usual, favoured him with a cross account for masonic instruction. Smith refused to pay the demand, and brought an action to recover the sum of £4. 2*s*., as balance of an account for engraving and printing Finch's masonic pictures. As a set-off against this demand, Finch was imprudent enough to plead that Smith was indebted to him £16. 19*s*. 6*d*. for initiation, passing, raising, and instruction in various degrees of Masonry at the Independent Lodge in his own house. Smith brought forward Dr. Hemming, Past S. G. W., and Brothers White and Harper, the Grand Secretaries, as witnesses, who proved that Finch was not authorized to open any such Lodge, to make Masons, or to give instructions in Masonry; and that his whole system was an imposition on the public, which ought not to be suffered to exist in a civilized country, or remain under the protection of its laws.

"The judge therefore ruled," continued the Square, "that as it had been clearly proved that Finch was an impostor, his claim could not be legal; that his conduct was unjustifiable; and as he had been repudiated by the Fraternity, he stood before the Masonic world as an outlaw without a claim to protection. The jury gave their verdict accordingly for the full amount of the engraver's demand.

"In consequence of this defeat, Finch issued a manifesto, in which he made the following extraordinary disclosure, although few persons were found credulous enough to believe it. 'About four years ago,' so runs the document, 'our worthy and respectable Rabee, the Master of the Lodge at Hampton Court, was deputed by his Brethren at that place, and parts adjacent, to wait on me (W. Finch), and solicit my attendance at Hampton, to instruct the Brethren in various parts of Masonry. The evening was fixed for holding a conclave and Encampment in the degree of Knights Templars, &c., in which my assistance was most earnestly solicited, to conduct the business of the evening, and to make several Brothers Agreeably to this request, I attended; and Dr. Hemming was one of the party. He assisted me as one of my officers; acted according to my instructions; agreed with all my systems; and paid me five guineas for my trouble. Now I call upon Dr. Hemming to deny any part of this statement if he can; and had he not been so extremely officious as to have come forward in an action for debt wherein I was chiefly concerned, I should not have thus exposed him.'

"This statement, which is in every respect unworthy of credit," the Square continued, "was followed by an attempt to renew the schism, after the union between the two sections had been effected; and, for this purpose, he invited the Lodges to secede under a statement of imaginary grievances, *sustained by himself*. And, in the year 1815, he dispersed a circular amongst the Fraternity, in which he broadly asserted that 'a vast number of Brethren view with regret and concern, that since the union has taken place, the inundation of modern innova tions, and the exclusion of most of the ancient rules and ceremonies, have given such umbrage to a great number of old Masons, that nearly fifty Lodges in town and country have already withdrawn from the Union. That the union between the Athols and Moderns seems to be but a temporary measure towards the restoration of perfect harmony; for whilst they continue to deviate from the ancient landmarks, and pursue their persecutions against the R. W. M. of the Independent Lodge of Universality (himself), it only tends to widen the breach which friendly means might contribute to heal. That the Grand Lodge have violated the ancient landmarks of the Order, which they entered into with the Brethren when they constituted a Grand Lodge in the year 1717, and which bound them, by the most solemn engagements, to preserve inviolate in all time coming; and by virtue of which they were recognized as a Grand Lodge, and held their power as such, on this tenure only. By the violation of those acts, their power as a Grand Lodge cannot henceforth have any legal existence; as they have cancelled their own authority by this infraction on their own voluntary act and deed. That every Lodge may, therefore, act independently, &c.'

"And he further said, in his Preface to another publication in 1816, 'On the Origin of Masonry,'—'I am well convinced in my own mind that these individuals (Dr. Hemming and the two Grand Secretaries) would almost as soon lose their office as have the present work made public; I have, therefore, thought proper to oblige them with its publication; and since they have compelled me to withdraw the veil, I shall give publicity to several other matters that I know will prove highly acceptable to these generous gentlemen, *unless sufficient remuneration is made me for the loss sustained by their ill-judged interference.*'

"After these futile attempts, we heard no more of Bro. W. Finch. He had played out his game, and lost it. From thenceforth he degenerated into an ignoble obscurity, and died in the most abject poverty; yet, as he created some sensation at the time, I could not consistently avoid giving you a brief but connected history of his proceedings. And I have been rather more diffuse on the subject than I originally intended, for the purpose of illustrating the certain consequences of a breach of discipline, and disobedience to masonic law.

"And now," the Square continued, "after leading you, as John Bunyan did his pilgrims, through the gardens of Beelzebub, to show you the forbidden fruit, rank and unwholesome, that flourishes there—the apples of charlatanism, the grapes of Antimasonry, and the cowans' figs, not particularly wholesome, I must return to the ever-blooming delectable mountains and sunny vales, which are situate in the midst of a Lodge, just, perfect and regular, when it is open, but closely tyled.

"The eighteenth century was the age of clubs," said the Square, "and their public suppers were generally scenes of unmixed, though rather turbulent enjoyment; but there was a festive gratification thrown over a masonic banquet, which was unapproachable by any other society, Even the celebrated Heidegger, the *arbiter elegantiarum* of high life, was often heard to say, that if he had not been a Mason, he should never have had a perfect zest for the exercise of his art. It is not in the viands (they are the same everywhere), it is not the wines—we cannot boast of any superiority there. The secret may be found in the congeniality of feeling which mutually exists amongst the Brethren—knit together by closer ties—cemented by a chain of more sincere and disinterested affection—each and all being determined to give and receive pleasure—to be happy themselves, and the source of happiness to others. By this means a Lodge of true-hearted Brothers, during its hours of relaxation and refreshment, is a region of peace, and the patented abode of good temper and unmixed enjoyment.

"This result," said the Square, "arises out of a community of interests, so nicely balanced and regulated by the Constitutions of the Order, that being directed by Wisdom, supported by Strength, and ornamented by Beauty, harmony establishes itself without any artificial assistance; and the Lodge, like a well constructed machine, true in all its parts and proportions, performs its work with the most perfect accuracy and unvarying correctness. Interests seldom clash; each officer's duty being so clearly defined as not to admit of any mistake; the springs and wheels execute their respective functions so truly, as to preserve their symmetry, and contribute to the beauty, magnificence, and durability of the whole.

"This exact regularity, as I once heard Bro. Calcott say," continued the Square, "so far from occasioning a melancholy seriousness, diffuses the most pure delights; and the bright effects of enjoyment and hilarity shine forth in the countenance. It is true that appearances are sometimes a little more sprightly than ordinary, but decency runs no risk of violation; it is merely wisdom in good humour. For if a Brother should so far forget himself as to use any improper expressions, a formidable sign would immediately recall him to his duty. A Brother may mistake as a man, but he has ample means of recovering himself as a Freemason. And although order and decorum are always scrupulously observed in our Lodges, we do not exclude gaiety and cheerful enjoyment. The conversation is always animated, and the kind and brotherly cordiality that is found there, gives rise to the most pleasing reflections.

"These particulars may justly recall to our minds the happy time of the divine Astrea, when there was neither superiority nor subordination, because men were as yet untainted by vice on the one hand, and uncorrupted by licentiousness on the other."

CHAPTER XII.

COWANS.—JOHN DENT.

1794—1798

"It is frequently urged against Freemasonry, that some of those who belong to it are intemperate, profligate, and vicious. But nothing can be more unfair or unjust than to depreciate or condemn any institution, good in itself, on account of the faults of those who pretend to adhere to it. The abuse of a thing is no valid objection to its inherent goodness. Worthless characters are to be found occasionally in the very best institutions upon earth."—HARRIS.

"Nothing is more common than for giddy young men, just entering into life, to join the Society with the mere sinister view of extending their connections. Such men dissipate their time, money, and attention, in running about from one Lodge to another, where they rather aim to distinguish themselves in the licentious character of jolly companions, than in the more discreet one of steady good Masons."—NOORTHOUCK.

"Let Cowans, therefore, and the upstart fry
Of Gormagons, our well-earn'd praise deny,
Our secrets let them as they will deride,
For thus the fabled fox the grapes decried,
While we superior to their malice live,
And freely their conjectures will forgive."
MASONIC PROLOGUE, 1770.

"I REMEMBER," the Square continued, "and it is one of the earliest circumstances which has been imprinted on my memory, that after the great fire of London, 1666, when the re-edification of St. Paul's was in progress, the surveyor was setting out the dimensions of the great dome, and had fixed upon the centre, a common labourer was ordered to bring a flat stone from the heaps of rubbish (such as should first come to hand), to be laid for a mark and direction to the masons: the stone, which was immediately brought and laid down for that purpose, happened to be a piece of a gravestone, with nothing remaining of the inscription but this single word, in large capitals,—RESURGAM. This circumstance made so strong an impression on the mind of Sir Christopher Wren, that he caused a Phœnix, rising from the flames, with the motto *Resurgam* inscribed beneath, to be sculptured in the tympanum of the south pediment above the portico, as emblematical of the reconstruction of the church after the fire.[1]

"This circumstance occurred in the year 1715," the Square observed, "and referred not merely to the re-edifying of the cathedral, but also to the restoration of ancient Masonry, which was accomplished about the same period, and is supposed to have a further allusion to the revivification of the Order, by the reunion of ancient and modern Masons, that was now in progress, and actually completed within a few years from the present period. The preparations for this great event were already arranged, and our present R. W. M., Bro. John Dent, was one of the influential parties who brought it about.

"He was elevated to the chair on St. John's Day, 1794, and his inaugural address was received with acclamations. It was to this effect:—

"'Brethren, by a unanimous vote you have elevated me to the proud distinction of R. W. M. of one of the oldest Lodges on record. Invested with the Jewel of that far-famed architect Sir Christopher Wren, I will take especial care that its brilliancy shall not be sullied in my possession. I trust you will never have occasion to reflect that your confidence has been misplaced. I have too high a respect for the system to allow its beneficial operation to be jeoparded by any species of neglect or moral delinquency; and I trust, that while I adhere to the general Constitutions of Masonry, and the provisions of our Bye-Laws myself, I shall be enabled, with your kind co-operation, to prevent their infraction by others.

"'We have all much to learn,' he continued, with becoming humility, 'and it will be our own fault if we

[1] Mr. Brayley conjectures that the stone which was thus brought to Sir Christopher was the same as had been provided in commemoration of Dr. King, who preached the sermon before James the First, for promoting the rebuilding of St. Paul's; and who directed by his will that a plain stone only, with the word RESURGAM, should record his memory.

do not gladly embrace every opportunity which presents itself, in the labours of the Lodge, of improving our minds, and correcting our morals; for while Masonry tolerates private judgment in matters of religion and politics, and even forbids the introduction of questions which may produce a diversity of opinion on those exciting subjects, it enters very largely on the sacred duties of morality, and expatiates, with a pardonable enthusiasm, on almost all the Christian graces and perfections.

"'In the First Degree, we find many types of the Great Atonement, by which, according to the repeated promises made to the patriarchs and prophets in the Old Testament, original sin was to be expiated, and mankind placed in a condition of salvation. And the Lecture contains a series of significant symbols, which inculcate the morality of the New Testament. The first clause exhibits an emblem which reminds the Brethren of the necessity of observing a strict attention to silence or secrecy in their commerce with the world, because it is a Jewel of inestimable value, derived from the practice of the Deity, in concealing from his creatures the secret mysteries of his providence. And this is not only the duty of a Mason, but of every person who is desirous of maintaining a spotless reputation amongst his fellows. For instance, if a friend intrusts a secret to your keeping, it is with a tacit understanding that it shall be preserved inviolate, for a babbler or a tale-bearer is a character universally despised, and deservedly scouted from civil society. He who betrays a secret is guilty of treason to his friend. What confidence can be placed in any one who has been so indiscreet as to violate a sacred pledge? You might as well pour water into a sieve under the impression that it will not escape, as to pour your griefs and sorrows into the bosom of a man who will communicate to the next person he meets every fact which you are desirous of concealing from the world.

"'The same subject,' Bro. Dent continued, 'is recurred to in the Third Degree, where you have each undertaken to keep a Brother's secrets as carefully as you would conceal your own. And for this reason, that the betraying of such a trust might do him the greatest injury he could possibly sustain; it would be like the villany of an assassin, who lurks in darkness to inflict a mortal wound upon his adversary when unarmed and least prepared to meet an enemy. And so careful is Freemasonry in enforcing an observance of this duty, that it forms a part of the solemn obligation which every Mason enters into at his initiation, and is repeated with additional solemnity at the commencement of each degree. And it will not be too much to anticipate that by an attention to this one duty the Fraternity will prove themselves more worthy of the confidence of their friends; and the profession of Masonry will thus conduce not only to their own peace and comfort, but to the general benefit of society.

"'The E. A. P. Lecture then proceeds to explain the tendency of those expressive ceremonies which took place at your initiation, for the purpose of showing that the most minute observance was not without its moral signification, and calculated to contribute its powerful aid towards promoting the great design of the Institution, the improvement of the reasoning faculties, the cultivation of the intellect, and a gradual progress in the science of virtuous living. You are here first introduced to those Great Lights which are to be your guides and directors in passing through the chequered scenes of good and evil with which this transitory world abounds. This constitutes the abiding excellence of the Order; for an institution founded on the covenant between God and man can never be shaken, unless its peculiar principles be abandoned by an alteration of its standing landmarks. The Bible is the great charter of a Mason's privileges, and the basis on which he rests his hopes of salvation. The Square teaches us our social and relative duties, and represents the golden rule which the Redeemer proposed as the distinguishing portraiture of a Christian—viz., to do to others as we would have them under similar circumstances do to us; to render strict justice in all our undertakings, and to study to promote the blessings of order, harmony, and brotherly love.

"'Thus, my Brethren, you will perceive that Freemasonry is intended to make you just and honest in your dealings with your fellow-creatures, and to explain and simplify the duties which the Christian religion enjoins on all its sincere professors, that you may keep within Compass with all mankind as members of a common faith, in the hope of sharing the rewards which are promised to all those who nobly earn the character of good and faithful servants of T. G. A. O. T. U.'"

At this point the Square made an abrupt transition, for the purpose of favouring me with a gratuitous disquisition on the beauties of the Order. "Freemasonry," he said, "is in itself the most perfect and sublime Society existing in the world of mere human establishment. It is calculated to promote the happiness and comfort of all ranks and descriptions of men, when practised in its intrinsic purity. It is a Society of peace, where nothing is allowed to enter which may disturb the equanimity of its Members. The jarring elements of discord are banished, under the presidency of a judicious governor, whose conduct tacitly pronounces the ancient formula of exclusion,

'Procul, O procul esto profani!'

Good temper prevails, and nothing is tolerated but suavity of manners, and mutual courtesy of deportment.

"There are many methods of producing human felicity, and Masonry absorbs them all. We have science—we have morality—we have benevolence—we have brotherly love and sacred truth; and how exalted soever may be the conceptions of any individual respecting the mode of disseminating universal happiness, and producing the amelioration of mankind, his ideas may be amply developed, and his plans for the advantage of his species carried out in the comprehensive system of Masonry. All the peculiar aspirations of a Howard or a Fry are embraced in the wide grasp of masonic beneficence. Peace on earth is its object, Christian morality its practice, and the rewards of virtue its end.

"Whoever is desirous of hearing useful and salutary doctrines, should enter into a Masons' Lodge, and there his wishes will be gratified. Is he anxious to learn what will procure him the veneration and respect of his species? Let him become acquainted with the Lectures of Masonry; let him mark, learn, and inwardly digest them, and his hopes will not be disappointed. Does he require some general rules, by the use of which he may perform his duty to God acceptably?—Freemasonry will teach them. Does he wish to learn how he may profitably discharge his duty to his neighbour? Does he ardently desire the knowledge of a precept by which he may conduct himself impartially, and with strict and equal justice in all his undertakings?—Let him resort to the Lodge, and there he will be taught these invaluable maxims. Does he study to avoid the Scylla of intemperance, or the Charybdis of slander and evil speaking, that he may walk in the narrow path which will preserve his self-respect without violating the divine commands?—He may attain this comparative degree of perfection by following the teaching of Masonry."

The Square now balancing upon one leg, and spinning half round, continued, inquiringly, without expecting me to answer, but rather speaking in soliloquy—"And what do you think the cowans and opposers of Masonry say to the above statement? Why," he answered, as he completed the circle, "they triumphantly urge—If this be true, why do you keep it to yourselves?—why do you not reveal it for the benefit of mankind? And if it be *not* true, why do you so pertinaciously assert and reiterate a falsehood? There's your dilemma—shake yourselves clear of it if you can.

"Why, a mere tyro," said the Square, "would easily avoid its formidable horns, by merely asking in return, how is it that T. G. A. O. T. U. conceals from mankind the secret mysteries of his providence? For the wisest of men cannot penetrate into the arcana of heaven, nor can they divine to-day what to-morrow may bring forth.

"We endeavour to sustain our character as Masons creditably, by avoiding all meanness and dissimulation; and, though we are tenacious of our secrets as a belted knight of his honour, yet we have no wish to keep them entirely to ourselves, or to withhold information from any worthy man who may desire to participate legitimately in the benefits to be derived from the Craft. On the contrary, we are ever ready to communicate our mysteries to all candidates who are freeborn and of good report, if they be willing to accept the conditions. For, though we close our Lodges against impertinent curiosity, they are always open to the researches of liberal and consistent inquiry.

"To this argument our impervious cowan turns a deaf ear, and cries out—Bah! we don't want to know any thing about either you or your mummery, for we consider it to be a wretchedly selfish and exclusive pursuit.

"A most lame and impotent conclusion," said the Square. "There is nothing selfish about it. It is an open letter, which every one may read—a rich mine, more valuable than the gold of Ophir, which every worthy Brother may explore, and bear away its exhaustless treasures without diminishing its intrinsic value; nor did any one ever commence an earnest search into its hidden stores without reaping an ample reward.

"Another class of Antimasons object," the Square proceeded to say, "that we are Levellers, and strive to bring down every class of society to an equality of rank, and, therefore, they denounce the Institution as a dangerous nuisance, which ought to be abolished.

"So prejudice misrepresents truth," replied my communicative mentor. "It is admitted that, in masonic inquiries, there is a perfect equality—not that equality which would level the distinctions of civil and social life, but a moral equality, which places all mankind on a level in the eye of God, with whom there is no respect of persons. Can that be a levelling system which teaches, both by precept and example, that every man must consider himself subject to the higher powers? The very construction of Masonry forms a practical commentary on its teaching, for there is no other institution which is so stringent in exacting a due subordination to its rulers and governors, supreme and subordinate. We meet on the level in our mutual search after the hidden secrets of science; but our moral equality, even in the Lodge, is moderated by the dictates of justice and reason; for honour and respect are uniformly awarded to those who deserve them, and it is the industrious and sober inquirers who realize the benefit, and not the idle and dissolute.

"Our privileges and advantages are strictly equal," the Square continued. "We all start from one common point. But the face of things changes as we proceed; and individuals who have shown themselves earnestly desirous of meriting the esteem of the Fraternity, are sure to rise to offices of distinction; while those who are careless and indifferent, and do not improve their advantages, or who turn back, and, like Pliable in the Pilgrim's Progress,' *leer away on the other side*, being ashamed of what they have done, will remain all their life long on the threshold, and never emerge from the slough of despond in which their energies have been concentrated and swallowed up.

"I remember," said the Square, "a curious scene which took place in the Lodge-room, before the Lodge was opened, which it may be useful to record. It was in the month of March, 1797, the tyler having disposed the Lodge in order, and laid the Officers' Jewels on their respective cushions, when I was surprised by the entrance, unusually early, of a zealous Brother, who looked cautiously round the Lodge-room to ascertain, as I conjectured, whether any other person were present; and, being satisfied that he was alone, he slipped quietly into the Master's chair, and thus soliloquized:—

"'Well, I think I have half an hour free from interruption, and I will, therefore, rehearse a section of the Lecture. Bro. S. W., where did you and I first meet? On the Level. Where hope to part? On the Square. And what did you come here to do?'—A pause.—'No, that's incorrect—let me see—from whence come you? From the West. Whither going? To the East. What for? Pish! My memory is once more at fault. I wish I knew the ritual as well as our excellent R. W. M. Aye, now I have it. What induced you to leave the West and go to the East? In search of a Brother, by whom I might be instructed in Masonry. Capital! I hope I shall not be detected. What next? O—who are you that want instruction? A Free and Accepted Mason. If I was Master of the Lodge, how I would astonish the Brethren! And then, only think of being addressed by the honourable title of Right Worshipful—R. W. Sir this, and R. W. Sir that; and, it is the R. Worshipful's will and pleasure; and, your commands shall be obeyed, R. W. Sir. This is the glory that I covet; and I trust the day is not far distant when these honours and distinctions will be conferred upon me.'

"And then he proceeded," said the Square, "with his agreeable amusement, sometimes right, and sometimes wrong, till he was interrupted by the entrance of Brothers Shelton and Marshall.

"'Ha! Bro. Bell,' said the new-comers, 'you are early.'

"It will be needless to tell you," the Square interposed, "that Bro. Bell vacated the chair when he heard them coming up stairs; and he replied, 'I should like to know who would not be early when such a treat is provided for him as the proceedings of a Masons' Lodge. And I have been anticipating the pleasure by endeavouring to repeat a portion of the Lecture.'

"'Misspent time, misspent time,' Bro. Shelton responded. 'Who cares about the Lectures now-a-days, except, perhaps, the Masters and Wardens, whose business it is to know them perfectly; but to those who have no ambition for office, they are little better than a bore.'

"At this observation," said the Square, "Bro. Marshall rubbed his hands with pleasure, in the hope of seeing Bro. Bell's enthusiasm lowered; for he was known to be a zealous young man, who entertained a very exalted opinion of the Order; while such men as Brothers Shelton and Marshall were mere sensualists, and embraced Freemasonry for the sake of its convivialities only. His glee was not unobserved by Bro. Bell, although he was at a loss to account for it; and he replied—'I am sorry to hear this, because I can scarcely believe that you are speaking the true sentiments of your heart. And if such really be your opinion, I am bound to conclude that it is singular, and not likely to have many abettors. The generality of our Brethren would unequivocally repudiate such a doctrine, and entertain a very indifferent opinion of those that avow it.'

"'You are quite mistaken,' said Bro. Marshall, full of mischief. 'A clear majority of our Brethren think with Bro. Shelton and myself on this subject.' And he gave a self-gratulatory sniff with his nose, as if conscious that he had said a good thing.

"Bro. Bell appeared to be in the land of dreams," said the Square. "He muttered to himself—'Is this real? Are these men hoaxing me? Or am I truly hearing stern though unpalatable truths?' At length he replied, 'I sincerely hope and trust you are joking, else why do you attend the Lodge—what other inducement can you possibly have?'

"The two new-comers looked at each other and smiled, as though they would have said, if they had been alone, that their companion was rather verdant in his ideas. At length Bro. Shelton returned—'It is the refreshment, my dear Brother, the refreshment, the cheerful glass, the song and toast, the laugh, the joke, the sparkling conversation when labour is suspended. In our opinion, to quote the words of a favourite chorus—

"A bumper, a bumper, a bumper of good liquor,
Will end a contest quicker
Than justice, judge, or vicar;
So fill each cheerful glass,
And let good humour pass.

"But if more deep the quarrel,
I'd sooner drain the barrel,
Than be that hateful fellow,
That's crabbed when he's mellow.
So fill each cheerful glass,
And let good humour pass."

Besides, what is Freemasonry intrinsically, that you would so earnestly entreat us to fall down and worship it?'

"'I'll tell you what it is,' Bro. Bell replied; 'it is a beautiful system of morality, veiled in allegory, and illustrated by symbols.'

"'Illustrated,' said Bro. Shelton, with a sneer. 'Symbols are *mentioned*, I admit, in what you term the Lectures, but not by any means *illustrated;* and I should like to know, if you can tell me, why, in that technical code on which we are expected to pin our faith, the illustrations are so meagre?

"'A fair question,' Bro. Bell responded, 'and shall be fairly answered. It would be difficult, and perhaps impossible, to give a complete explanation of our symbols in any course of Lodge Lectures, because they are necessarily compressed into as narrow a compass as may be consistent with perspicuity, that human ingenuity may be able to devise. The emblems are so numerous and diversified, and admit of such an extensive application, that volumes would be required to contain all that might be said on this interesting subject. And, therefore, those who aspire to a superior knowledge of Masonry, and are desirous of becoming distinguished Members of the Craft, will not be contented with simply mastering the Lodge Lectures, ample though they be, but will aspire, by using the accessories of reading, study, and serious meditation, to something of a higher character, which may enable them to enlighten the Brethren, when they shall be called on to rule the Lodge, by imparting the fruits of their own experience, and by amplifying and explaining, in detail, the recondite mysteries embodied in types and symbols, as well as the doctrines of morality, which are veiled and hidden under an expressive series of significant allegories.'

"'Allegories, indeed!' Bro. Marshall interposed. 'Such as neither you nor I, nor any other person can possibly understand. And what benefit can be derived from such an unprofitable course of study and research?'

"'None whatever,' chimed in Bro. Shelton.

"'I crave your pardon, Brethren,' said Bro. Bell; 'on the contrary, the profit will do infinitely more than compensate for the labour. It is clear to me, that whoever shall pursue this laudable course earnestly and assiduously, may very reasonably expect that it will be attended with success. It will make him a wiser and a better man, and secure for him a place amongst the venerated names by which our Society is dignified, and whom we delight to honour. The Craft will respect him; the world will admire him; and his name will descend to posterity, crowned with glory and immortality.'

"'Pshaw!' said Bro. Shelton. 'It is nothing but an unsubstantial shadow. Concealment is useless. The convivialities of Masonry are the only inducements which draw us to the Lodge. And as the Welsh peasantry are seldom absent from the sermon, on account of a subsidiary dance which follows the service, so we are willing to endure the tiresome Lecture, because we know that, like all other inflictions, each clause must have an end, and the Lodge be called from labour to refreshment. The sections are not very lengthy; and, at the close of each, our forbearance is rewarded with an appropriate toast and song. And now you know the reason why we attend the Lodge.'

"Having said this, Bro. Shelton turned away, and walked to the fire with an air which indicated that, after such an avowal, nothing further could be advanced on the subject.

"Now, you will understand," said the Square, "that

Bros. Shelton and Marshall belonged to a certain party in the Lodge which constituted a feeble and uninfluential minority; and they all entertained similar opinions on the uses and enjoyments of Masonry. It is also probable that every Lodge in the kingdom might exhibit a few—some more and some less—of the same species; men who entertain no respect for the science, and care little about the honours of Masonry. Their sole enjoyment centres in its convivialities, and they are callous to every other incitement. Each of these worthies could swallow, and carry off, without much inconvenience, his two bottles of wine on festive occasions, although, thanks to the general regulations of the Craft, this was practicable only at the quarterly suppers, and they seldom failed to take advantage of so favourable an opportunity. Now, although these propensities were no secret to the Brethren with whom they were associated, yet, as they were sufficiently discreet to appear orderly and attentive during the delivery of the Lectures, it was scarcely supposed that they held them in contempt; and, therefore, when Bro. Shelton made the above explicit acknowledgment, Bro. Bell exclaimed, in the utmost surprise, at an open avowal which had never so much as entered into his imagination—in fact, he believed all Masons to be as enthusiastic as himself—'As the Irishman says, this beats Bannagher, if you be really in earnest!'

"'Never was more earnest in my life.' Bro. Shelton replied, as he stood with his hands behind him, and his back to the fire; 'and more than that, many of our Brethren entertain the same feeling. What say you, Mike?'

"'I, for one, quite agree with you,' Bro. Marshall responded. 'I do not care a fig for the Lecture, or any such trumpery The stoup, the flagon, and the bicker are my favourite symbols, and I love them better than Square, Level, and Plumb. And no exercise is so agreeable to me as charging, firing, and driving piles.'

> 'Give us some punch, and let it be strong,
> And we'll drink to the man that sang the last song.'

"'Hip! hip! hip! Three times three! Hurrah! That's my taste!'

"'Then,' replied Bro. Bell, 'you have opened my

eyes to an astounding fact, which nothing short of your own confession could have induced me to believe. But since you are so intensely devoted to these pursuits. perhaps you are able at least to tell me the masonic origin of this three times three, which seems to monopolize your enthusiasm.'

"The two Brethren were perplexed," said the Square. "It was a puzzling question, and they looked rather sheepish at being obliged to confess their ignorance respecting their own estimate of the peculiar excellence of Freemasonry. At length they acknowledged that they could not tell.

"'I thought as much,' said Bro. Bell. 'It was scarcely to be expected, with such views and propensities, that you would be able to say your own catechism. And I dare say you will thank me for enlightening you on the subject.'

"'They should gladly acknowledge the obligation,' they replied, 'although the enjoyment was not lessened because they were ignorant of its origin.'

"'You must know then,' Bro. Bell resumed, 'that in ancient times the E. A. P. degree was alone prevalent amongst the generality of our Lodges; for no Brother could be *passed* and *raised* except in the Grand Lodge, and few availed themselves of the privilege. Hence they had only one sign, one token, and one word, and these three constituted the honours. But the Members of the Grand Lodge had three signs, three tokens, and three words, and, therefore, three times three were appropriately termed the Grand honours. By subsequent arrangements the power of conferring all the degrees has been conveyed to every Lodge under the Constitution of England, and the Grand honours have passed along with this privilege. Hence, all private Lodges are now at liberty to use them at their pleasure. But you would not surely have me to understand that you really prefer toasts and songs, and such rubbish, to the sublime speculations of pure masonic inquiry.'

"'I should be glad to know,' replied Bro. Shelton, 'what you call pure masonic inquiry, apart from the *rubbish*, as you ignominiously term it, of the elements of conviviality? Or, in plainer language, what, in your opinion, is the distinguishing characteristic of a Mason?

"'Virtue and decency, which ought always to be found in every true Mason's breast,' answered Bro. Bell, in the very words of the Lecture.

"'And how do you describe virtue, as a Mason?' Bro. Marshall asked.

"'Virtue is the highest exercise of the mind,' said Bro. Bell, with some degree of enthusiasm in his manner; 'the integrity, harmony, and just balance of affection; the health, strength, and beauty of the soul. The perfection of virtue is to give a full scope to reason; to obey with alacrity the dictates of conscience; to exercise the defensive passions with fortitude, the public with justice, and the private with temperance, each in its due proportion. To love and adore God, and to acquiesce in his kind Providence with calm resignation, is the surest step towards testing our virtue, and an approach to perfection and happiness; as a deviation therefrom is to that of vice and misery. Such is virtue as it is described in the Lectures of Masonry. But independently of this, have you no pride in the privilege of meeting friends and Brothers in a just and perfect Lodge, where we feel that we are companions of princes and Brothers of kings?'

"'Absurd!' exclaimed Bro. Shelton. 'How can we be the Brothers of kings?'

"'Because,' said Bro. Bell, 'a king, like ourselves, is but a man; and though a crown may adorn his head, and a sceptre his hand, yet the blood in his veins is derived from the common parent of mankind, and is no better than that of his meanest subject. But Freemasonry teaches us to regard our superiors with peculiar esteem when we see them divested of external grandeur, and condescending, in a badge of innocence and bond of friendship, to trace wisdom, and to follow virtue, assisted by those who are of a rank beneath them. Virtue is true nobility; wisdom is the channel by which virtue is directed and conveyed; wisdom and virtue only can distinguish us as Masons.'

"'You said, if I understood you rightly,' Bro. Shelton replied, 'a just and perfect Lodge. Now, I should like to know what you mean by a just and perfect Lodge?'

"'It is technical,' Bro. Bell answered, 'and is thus explained by a passage in our ordinary Lectures, which

I should have thought, as you must have frequently heard it, would have been perfectly familiar to you. The Holy Bible, which is the primary supreme grand archive of Masonry, renders a Lodge *just*, because it contains that Sacred History which has been handed down to us by Moses, the Grand Master of the Lodge of Israel, and an inspired writer of God's commands. It also contains the writings of the prophets and apostles, together with a revelation of all the most eminent virtues, both moral and divine; the incitement of our love and fear of God, the origin of all wisdom. It inspires us with spiritual discernment, enables us to practise the above virtues, which will confer the blessings of peace and comfort here, with a full assurance of celestial happiness in the world to come. The *perfection* of a Lodge relates to number; and, as you well know, cannot be held in the absence of its R. W. M., Wardens, and certain other Brethren.'

"'However this may be,' said Bro. Marshall, 'you cannot deny but the custom of renunciation by a shoe is childish and unmeaning.'

"'I am not prepared to make any such admission,' Bro. Bell replied. 'It is a good custom, and an ancient. In the eastern parts of the world, when an inferior person paid his respects to a prince or noble, he took off his shoes, as a symbol of humility, and left them outside the door of the apartment where the audience was granted. This custom was also observed during the performance of religious worship, and probably originated in the interview which Jehovah vouchsafed to Moses at the Burning Bush, where the latter was commanded to take his shoes from off his feet, because the ground on which he stood was holy. You have truly observed, that taking off a shoe is a token of renunciation. Amongst the Jews, when a man died childless, his nearest relation was bound to marry the widow. If, however, it was inconvenient to perform this duty, he took off his shoe in the presence of competent witnesses, and passed it to the next of kin, as a legal token that he renounced his claim; and thus the inheritance was transferred. We Free and Accepted Masons copy the usage, to intimate that we renounce our own will and pleasure in all matters of Masonry, and undertake to render due obedience to its excellent laws and regulations.'

"'And you call this a sublime speculation,' said Bro. Marshall. 'Heaven defend me from the misery of such far-fetched elucidations!' And the recusants indulged themselves in a hearty laugh.

"Bro. Bell was thunderstruck," said the Square. "He looked earnestly, first at one, and then at the other, being uncertain what argument to apply in a dilemma that he had never so much as contemplated. As a lover of pure Masonry, he did not believe it possible for any Brother, who had been regularly initiated, had attended the Lodge meetings with moderate punctuality, as the two Brothers before him had uniformly done, and, consequently, had heard the sublime doctrines which were periodically promulgated there,—the pure morality,—the strong incentives to virtue—the teaching of active benevolence and God-like charity, accessible by the steps of faith and hope—he had never reflected, I say, on the possibility of a nature capable of proving callous to these impressions, or impervious to the salutary workings of a course of discipline so fructifying to the soul of man. He could scarcely believe his ears.

"It never occurred to him," the Square continued, "that these men were specimens of a class—that, as confirmed *bon vivants*, and wedded to the habits of hard drinking which characterized the period, they had no taste for the refinements of science, or the beauties of virtue. What! he thought to himself, is it possible that the husk should be preferred to the fruit—the chaff to the grain—brass to gold? Can a Mason be so perfectly insensate as to turn a deaf ear to the most sublime precepts ever offered to the consideration of a being designed for immortality? Can the carnal so far preponderate over the spiritual as to stupify the feelings, and make them insensible to the aspirations of such a pure and holy morality as is enunciated in the teaching of a Masons' Lodge?

"He looked at them again, supposing he might be under some disagreeable hallucination, that cast a baleful influence over his judgment; but there they stood visibly before him, with the broad grin of undisguised amusement still upon their faces, enjoying the unmistakable marks of astonishment which he so visibly displayed. How long he would have stood, or what might have been the ultimate result of his mental deliberations, it may be difficult to say, for they were cut short by Bro. Shelton, who said, as if for the purpose of diverting the conversation into a new channel, 'You know that noisy and troublesome fellow Browne, don't you?'

" 'Of the Corinthian Lodge, No. 188, Strand,' said Bro. Bell.

" 'The same.'

" 'I know him for no good,' Bro. Bell responded. 'I am told that his chief pleasure consists in keeping the Lodge in hot water, by fomenting disputes among the Brethren.'

" 'And proposing subjects for discussion,' added Bro. Marshall, 'on which he knows there exists a diversity of opinion, for the purpose of gloating, like the agent of evil, over the confusion which he has himself created.'

" 'A delectable amusement truly,' said Bro. Bell; 'but what of him?'

" 'He was ambitious of becoming Master of the Lodge at the last election of officers,' returned Bro. Shelton; 'but the Members, under the apprehension of a stormy year, if the power were placed in such dubious hands, rejected him in favour of a much younger but more peaceable Brother; and he was so exasperated by defeat, that he withdrew himself from the Lodge.'

" 'To the unfeigned satisfaction of all the Brethren,' Bro. Bell interposed.

" 'You may truly say that,' added Bro. Shelton; 'but further—in revenge, he threatens to disclose the secret.'

" 'He may threaten with safety,' said Bro. Bell; 'but fortunately it is not in his power to execute any such design. Let him make the attempt, and he will know, by experience, how few persons are to be found who will extend their credit to a self-proclaimed perjurer. Besides, he cannot betray a secret which he does not know.'

" 'Not know!' exclaimed Bro. Shelton, in unfeigned amazement, 'what do you mean? With all his faults he has the reputation of being a clever and intelligen Mason.'

" 'Granted,' Bro. Bell replied; 'but he stll may be

profoundly ignorant of the peculiar secrets of the Order.'[2]

"'Explain, explain,' said Bro. Marshall, 'you speak in riddles.'

"'That is easily done. I dare say you both think, as he doubtless does, that you are acquainted with the secret of Masonry, and that you could easily divulge it if you were so inclined. It is quite a mistake, my dear fellows. You know nothing about the matter. The true secrets are of a deep and recondite nature, and not so easily mastered.'

"The two Brothers," said the Square, "looked the picture of surprise and incredulity, while Bro. Bell went on.

"'You would like me to tell you what the secrets are; but I am in great doubt respecting my ability to gratify you. Ask Franklin whether he understands the secrets of electricity, and he will promptly answer in the negative. He has devoted his life to its improvement, but the secret remains undiscovered. Ask Watt whether he knows the secret power of steam, and you will receive the same reply. What did the learned Bishop Sanderson say about the secret or mystery of godliness? Why, he said that we may as well think to grasp the earth in our fist, or to empty the sea with a pitcher, as to comprehend these heavenly mysteries within our narrow understanding. *Puteus altus;* the well is deep, and our buckets, for want of cordage, will not reach near the bottom.[3] No, no; I am under no apprehension of any untoward consequences from the revelations of such a stupid fellow as Bro. Browne.[4] Besides, what sort of character at-

[2] Browne himself tacitly acknowledges this in his Introduction; where he says, "to those who are not Masons the author is well convinced that he has by no means revealed any of the masonic mysteries; and by printing it in this abstruse manner he defies them to make out any part. And were even that possible, they would be just in the situation of one who should attempt to fire a pistol without powder, or erect a stately fabric without tools or materials."

[3] Sermon, ad Aulam, on 1 Tim. iii., 16.

[4] There had already been published an attempted revelation of certain mysteries of Masonry in a work entitled "Remarkable Ruins and Romantic Prospects of North Britain, by Charles Cordiner, of Banff." London, Taylor, 1795. In this book the author founds a

taches to a man who attempts to divulge the mysteries of Masonry? Horace is very explicit on this point. He says,—

> ———— 'Vetabo, qui Cereris sacrum
> Vulgarit arcanæ, sub iisdem
> Sit trabibus, fragilemque mecum
> Solvat phaselum;'

and so say I. And he adds, '*est et fideli tuta silentio merces;*' there is a certain reward for a faithful silence.'

"'But my good Brother,' said Bro. Shelton, 'whether he be capable of disclosing the secret or not, he may publish the Lectures and ceremonies.'

"'You mean his version of them,' replied Bro. Bell; 'but who will vouch for their accuracy?[5] He is not

theory of initiation on the device of the Abbey Seal of Arbroath, in the following words:—"This seal, of which I have given an engraving, evidently represents some formidable ceremony in a sacred place. Where a pontiff presides in state, one hand on his breast, expressive of seriousness; the other stretched out at a right angle, holding a rod and cross, the badge of high office; while he makes some awful appeals respecting a suppliant, who, in a loose robe, blindfolded, with seeming terror, kneels before the steps of an altar, as undergoing some severe humiliation; while several attendants, with drawn swords, brandish them over his head. As some explanation of the above, it may be observed that there is a remarkable concurrence of design and resemblance of persons and attitudes, in the figures of the above seal, with those in a print accompanying a pamphlet on Masonry, published by an officer at Berlin; and this is the more worthy of notice, because he there gives an account of the ceremonies of initiation; and the prints are apposite representations of them. That which exhibits the manner of administering the tremendous oath of secresy, and of receiving the rudiments of the occult science at the communication of the first beams of light, is a pretty exact counterpart of the figures on the seal." The original seal of the abbey is in my possession, and represents the death of Thomas à Becket, to whom the abbey was dedicated.

[5] Browne executed and published his trumpery under the title of "Browne's Masonic Master Key throughout the Three Degrees, by way of Polyglot, under the sanction of the Craft in general. Containing the exact mode of working, initiation, passing, and raising to the sublime degree of a Master. Also the several duties of the Master, Officer, and Brethren while in the Lodge; with every requisite to render the accomplished Mason. An Explanation of all the hieroglyphics. The whole interspersed with Illustrations on Theology, Astronomy, Architecture, Arts, Sciences, &c.; many of which are by the Editor. By John Browne, P. M. of six Lodges, and M. A.' London, Printed and sold by the Editor, No. 60, Snowhill. Price Five Shillings and Sixpence, interleaved. First Edition, 1798. Second Edition, with additions, 1802.

the first, nor will he be the last, who has decried, and attempted to expose to public contempt, our flourishing Institution; as evil birds always prey on the sweetest fruit. Like Virgil's harpies, they endeavour to spoil what they have not the taste to enjoy.

> 'At subitæ horrifico lapsu de montibus adsunt
> Harpyiæ, et magnis quatiunt clangoribus alas:
> Diripiuntque dapes, contactuque omnia fœdant
> Immundo; tum vox tetrum dira inter odorem.'
>
> ÆN., iii., 225.

"'I shall not certainly vouch for the accuracy of his disclosures,' said Bro. Shelton; 'for in the ordinary affairs of life his veracity is by no means to be relied on. And if he anticipates that the profits of his threatened publication will be sufficiently remunerative to liquidate his debts, he may probably find himself mistaken.'

"'O,' replied Bro. Bell, 'as to the profit of his experiment, I should conceive it would be the very last consideration that would influence a man like Browne. His principal object would be to gratify his egregious vanity by the indulgence of his pique against a Society which has virtually repudiated him. His vain-glorious promises may be classed in the same category with those of Dean Swift's Rosicrucian, who thus addresses his besotted dupes. 'Look here, ye blind and ignorant neophytes, and be enlightened by me. I have couched a very profound mystery in the number of Os multiplied by seven, and divided by nine. Also, if a devout Brother will pray fervently for sixty-three mornings, with a lively faith, and then transpose certain letters and syllables according to prescription, in the second and fifth sections, they will certainly reveal into a full receipt of the *Opus Magnum*. Lastly, whoever will be at the pains to calculate the whole number of each letter in my MASTER KEY, and sum up the difference exactly between the several numbers, assigning the true natural cause for every such difference; the discoveries in the product will plentifully reward his labour. But then he must beware of *bythus* and *sige;* and be sure not to forget the qualities of *acamoth; à cujus lacrymis humecta prodit substantia, à risu lucida, à tristitia solida, et à timore mobilis.*"

"'Ha! ha! ha! very good!' exclaimed Brothers Shelton and Marshall together. 'I could almost fancy,' the former added, 'I see Bro. Browne standing on a barrel-end in the midst of an indiscriminate mob, and vending his wares, like a miserable quack doctor, in the very words you have put into his mouth. Did you never see such an empiric, Bro. Bell, with a score or two of gaping rustics about him, recommending his trumpery nostrums for all the ailments of life, by an unwearied repetition of the same unintelligible gibberish?'

"'There is no want of quacks,' Bro. Bell replied, 'to batten on the simple gullibility of John Bull; and I should not be surprised if he eagerly swallows the impositions of our faithless Bro. Browne, and confers upon him the questionable distinction of an unenviable notoriety.'

"'But it is no matter,' Bro. Shelton chimed in. 'The very possibility of committing such a base encroachment on our rights and privileges, forms, in my opinion, a cogent argument against allowing every Brother to become master of the secret. Bro. Marshall and I have no such ambition. We are fully contented with our share of the convivialities, without wishing to understand more of Masonry than is contained in the songs and toasts.'

"'The rest,' said Bro. Marshall bluntly, 'is all humbug!'

"'Humbug!' exclaimed Bro. Bell, his blood rising to boiling heat,—and I do not know what might have ensued," said the Square, "if the entrance of the R. W. M., and several Brethren, who had been waiting for him in the Tyler's room, had not put an end to the conversation. Brothers Shelton and Marshall were amused by his excitement; for it is quite true that they were kept in countenance by many Brethren, who were unfortunately more attached to refreshment than to labour."

CHAPTER XIII.

BEGGING MASONS.—STEPHEN JONES.

1798—1800.

"Old men for the most part are like old chronicles, that give you dull but true accounts of time past, and are worth knowing only on that score."—SWIFT.

"Late hours, irregularities that impair the health of the body, and much more the faculties of the mind, create and increase family dissensions, and reflect a dishonour on Freemasonry, from which its intrinsic excellence cannot at all times redeem it in the public opinion."—STEPHEN JONES.

"There's a difference between
A beggar and a queen,
And I'll tell you the reason why;
A queen cannot swagger,
Nor get drunk like a beggar,
Nor be half so happy as I."
BRO. JAMES ROBERTSON.

"IT was said by a periodical writer of the eighteenth century," the Square observed, in continuation of his interesting remarks, "while describing the abuses of science,—'As this supposititious learning diffuses itself, the manner in which it operates upon the new provinces of life on which it encroaches, how soon it accommodates itself to a new range of subjects, elevates the low, amplifies the little, and decorates the vulgar. There is now no occupation so mean into which it has not found its way, and whose consequence it has not raised, from the maker of geometrical breeches, to the manufacturer of manuscript sermons. We all begin to exalt our tones and pretensions, and adopt a prouder language. Mr. Powell, the fire-eater, is a singular genius; and Mendoza has more science than Johnson. I have heard of hieroglyphical buckles; so that our very shoes will want deciphering, and the Coptic language must soon make part of the education of our Birmingham buckle-makers. Alphabetical buckles are become common; insomuch that, in teaching ourselves to talk with our fingers, we may begin with learning to spell with our toes. Our wigs are made upon principles, which used to be made upon blocks. Our chimneys are cured of smoking by professors; and a dancing-master engages to teach you the nine Orders of the Graces, and if you take forty lessons, will throw you in an eleemosynary hornpipe. Our servants are beginning, as my correspondent tells me, to read behind our carriages; and the Bond street lounger, with his breeches cut by a problem, has as much of the language at least of learning, as any servitor in black logics at Oxford.'

"There is much truth in these quaint observations," continued the Square, "and the principle was unfortunately extended to Freemasonry, as will be apparent before my Revelations are concluded; for a case in point occurred during the presidency of our new R. W. M., Bro. Stephen Jones, the friend, pupil, and admirer of Bro. Preston, who had been recently restored to the Craft with all his blooming honours thick upon him.

"Bro. Jones was an active man, and had acquired, under the persevering instructions of this sincere friend, a competent knowledge, not merely of the ceremonies and lectures, but of the real object and design of the Order, which imparted a brilliancy to his other qualifications for judicious government; and he became one of our numerous good Masters, on whose breast I was proud to be seen glittering, like the morning dew on a rose-leaf in the merry month of June.

"At his inauguration," continued the Square, "he gave evidence of such a correct knowledge of his duty as gave ample promise of a career of future usefulness; for he was but a young man, and though his Wardenship had passed over irreproachably, it was quite uncertain how he would execute the complex duties of the Chair. Bad officers make bad members. There never was an inefficient Lodge, but it owed its imperfection to the blunders or carelessness of its officers. If the Society be feeble, depend upon it the officers are naught. If the Master be mild and quiet in his manners, the Lodge will, most likely, be well governed and prosperous.

"After the installation of Bro. Jones, the confidence of the Brethren was confirmed by a most eloquent inauguration speech; in the course of which he made a proposition which he admitted might be considered Utopian; *i. e.* to draw together, by the pure principles of Masonry, a select number of Brethren from the Fraternity at large, who, properly impressed by the tenets of the profession, shall have courage to carry them into practice, and make them the unerring guide of their conduct through life.

"'Our Society, my Brethren,' he added, 'can only acquire its proper rank in the scale of human institutions, by a general and faithful observance of its own precepts; and if this cannot be effected in its corporate capacity, very much may be expected from the junction of well-disposed individuals, who shall be inclined by the constant tenour of their lives to recommend the profession, and to prove that Freemasonry is only another term for inflexible virtue.'

"Although the R. W. M. was desirous of inducing all the Members of the Lodge to be strictly zealous in the discharge of their respective duties," said the Square, "yet he never failed to caution them in friendly terms against the indulgence of an enthusiastic spirit, because, as he told them, they had other important demands on their time and talents, besides those which are imposed by Masonry, that ought not to be neglected. He would say to the younger and more ardent Brethren, 'that when a man becomes a Mason, he sees, if he be a sensual man, the pleasures of the table to indulge his appetite, and the splendour of decoration to gratify his sight; if, on the other hand, he be a thinking man, he enters an ample field for contemplation; he receives the lessons of morality and of virtue, and is taught, by an easy and pleasant process, to diffuse its blessings among mankind; if he be a good man, he will illustrate the precept by his own conduct in life. But mark! to do this, it is not necessary that he should enroll his name among the members of I know not how many Lodges and Chapters, to shine a Z. in one, a R. W. M., a P. M., a S. W., a J. W., a T., and Heaven knows what, in others. Distinction, to be sure, is flattering; but distinctions of this nature can only have charms for weak minds.

"'Is your knowledge increased,' Bro. Jones continued, 'or your power of doing good to your fellow-creatures enlarged, in a just ratio with the number of offices you fill, or the number of societies to which you belong? Are not the sage tenets and maxims transmitted to us from our ancestors by oral tradition all comprehended in one regular series of doctrines, made memorable by the ancient simplicity of their style, universally prevalent, and adapted alike to the minds of all nations and sects? What is there new, that is not innovative? What fanciful, that is not corrupt?

"'If, then, one general system comprehend all that is valuable, all that is genuine, and that system be to be attained, in its primitive purity and perfection in one Lodge, whence results the need of attending others?'

"During this period," the Square observed, "the literature of Masonry assumed a lofty position, which empiricism found it difficult to reach. Some of the Lodges were fitted up with a philosophical apparatus, and scientific lectures were delivered, to the great edification of the Members. In others, the Brethren held special meetings for mutual improvement, which were termed Masonic Councils, and were usually holden on a Sunday evening. I disapproved of the practice, I assure you, but was compelled to be a consenting party. This system, I am inclined to think, was carried out in the provinces with greater spirit than in the metropolitan Lodges, although it is true that occasionally the discussions were deformed with untenable hypotheses, and speculative facts unsupported by authority, and altogether unreasonable and absurd.

"However, we were not without our literary reunions," the Sqyre playfully continued, and he solaced himself with a scientific twirl on his dexter limb, to display his satisfaction; "one of which occurred in 1799, the chair being occupied by Bro. Hannan, the author and actuary of the Masonic Benefit Society, which was matured and brought to perfection by his own individual exertions. And his zeal in its behalf ceased only with his life. He watched its progress carefully, and strained every nerve to make it instrumental in producing the welfare and happiness of the Fraternity. Bro. Preston terms its establishment an event of real importance, and so it was; for what can be more important than the institution of a society for the relief of sick, aged, and imprisoned

Brethren, and for the protection of their widows and orphan children? H. R. H. the Prince of Wales, G. M., became its patron; and the Earl of Moira, and the other acting officers of the Grand Lodge, its President and Vice-Presidents, and it was strongly recommended to the notice of the Provincial Grand Masters. Several thousand names were speedily enrolled; and the contributions amounted to a very considerable sum of money.

"But this is a digression," said the Square; "we were speaking (*we* indeed!) of literary re-unions as applied to Masonry, one of which was holden under the presidency of Bro. Hannan. And there were present, Brothers Preston, Jones, Blackman, Meyrick, Shadbolt, Inwood, Henry Bell, Daniell, Deans, Lambert, and many other eminent Brethren.

"The conversation was opened by a remark of the President, that he had been reading for the first time, although the book had been published more than ten years, 'A Recommendation of Brotherly Love on the Principles of Christianity,' by Bro. the Rev. James Wright, of Maybole;[1] in which, amongst many other sensible remarks, he judiciously observes that the office-bearers in every Lodge ought to take good heed to the characters of those whom they admit into the Society; because an Accepted Mason is held by all foreigners, as well as by us, to be a term which implies a man of honour and virtue; one who has a right to be admitted into the company of gentlemen of every description, and of the highest rank. By granting a man the privilege of being an Accepted Mason, ye do virtually give him a letter of recommendation to the acquaintance, and friendship, and confidence of a certain number of the most respectable characters that are to be found in every part of the world.

"'Bro. Wright is perfectly correct in his recommendation,' said Bro. Bell; 'for the absence of such caution may, and often does, introduce confusion into a Lodge, which it is difficult to allay. But Bro. Wright bears the

[1] "A Recommendation of Brotherly Love upon the Principles of Christianity; to which is subjoined an Inquiry into the True Design of the Institution of Masonry." In Four Books. London, Murray 1786.

character of an experienced Mason, and his example has produced many genial and beneficial effects in the locality which enjoys the advantage of his presence.'

"The Chairman then commended Bro. Sketchley, of Birmingham, for having done good service to Masonry by the publication of a useful little manual,[2] which contains some valuable little papers, particularly a curious lecture on Moral Geometry,[3] which contains a beautiful view of the ancient principles of the Art; and was written, as was thought, by Bro. Dunckerley; and also a Funeral Oration, which has some good points, and is worthy of a perusal.[4]

"'I have been much pleased,' said Bro. Jones, 'with two sermons, by my friend Turner, of Woolwich,[5] in which are many beautiful passages. What can be finer than this description of brotherly love?—'Verbal love is but painted fire; therefore, let His example, who went about doing good, be the pillar so elegantly adorned with lily-work, kindly directing and inflaming your humanity towards the Brethren. Meet the very lowest of them on the level of condescension, nor venture to despise the man for whom a Saviour died; that so you may be able to hold up your heads when justice is laid to the line, and righteousness to the plummet. Let your pure benevolence spread every way, like the more than gem-studded arch of heaven, expanding even over your enemies when in distress, that you may prove yourselves to be the children of the Most High, who is benign to the unthankful, and to the evil. Philanthropy is not confined to name or sect, to climate or language. Like the power of attraction, which reaches from the largest to the smallest bodies in the universe, it unites men from the throne to the cottage.''

"Bro. Blackman added his testimony to the superior excellence of Bro. Turner's preaching. But the crown

[2] "The Freemason's Repository, containing a Selection of valuable Discourses, Charges, Aphorisms, and Letters." Birmingham, Sketchley, 1786.

[3] Printed in the "Golden Remains," vol. i., p. 157.

[4] "An Oration on the Death of James Rollason," delivered by a Brother at the St. Paul's Lodge, Birmingham, 1789.

[5] "Two Discourses delivered at Woolwich." By the Rev. Daniel Turner. 1788.

of his character is, that he is a good man as well as a worthy Mason—indeed, the one can scarcely exist with out the other—and practises what he preaches.

"Bro. Deans begged to call the attention of the Breth ren to an interesting discussion in print between the Rev. H. E. Holder and Dr. Maryat, on the Philosophy of Masons,[6] in which it is satisfactorily proved that the masonic philosophy includes the practical doctrines of Christianity; the Cardinal and Theological Virtues; a firm belief in the atonement of Christ, leading to a resurrection from the dead, and eternal happiness in a future state.

"'In the absence of which doctrines,' Bro. Inwood observed, 'no true Christian would be found in the ranks of Masonry; which, though it be confessedly an institution professing the principles of pure morality, yet, without some more recondite reference, it would be like the dry bones mentioned by Ezekiel the Prophet; and it might, with equal propriety, be asked—Can these bones live? And the answer would be, They cannot live unless vitality be infused into them by the Great Architect of the Universe.'

"'Turn we now to another part of the kingdom,' said Bro. Lambert, 'and we shall find Dr. Jieans enlightening the Brethren of Southampton by an Oration at the Audit House,[7] in which the instruments of architecture, or moral Jewels of Masonry, are ably illustrated. Freemasonry, he says, deals in hieroglyphics, symbols, allegories; and to be qualified to reveal their meaning, a man must know more than a mere nominal Mason: the full interpretation of them, like that of the mysteries of old, is in select hands—has been committed only to those of tried

[6] "The Philosophy of Masons, in several Epistles from Egypt to a Nobleman." By Thomas Maryat, M. D., of Bristol. London, Ridgway, 1790. "A Brief, but it is presumed a Sufficient Answer to the Philosophy of Masons." By the Rev. H. E. Holder. Bristol, Pine, 1791. "A Letter to the Rev. H. E. Holder, on his Brief and Sufficient Answer." By a Layman. Bristol, Rough, 1791. "An Answer to the Layman's Letter." By H. E. Holder. Bristol, Pine, 1791.

[7] "An Oration pronounced at the Audit House in Southampton, on the occasion of laying the chief corner-stone of a building consecra ted to the worship of God." By Bro. Thomas Jieans, M. D. South ampton, 1792.

fidelity, who conceal it with suitable care: others, if not deficient in intellect, yet wanting industry or inclination to explore the penetralia of the Temple, are not qualified, if willing, to betray it. Hence the secresy which has so long distinguished the Fraternity. This secresy, however, has been urged against our Institution as a crime, but the wise know that secresy, properly maintained, is one of the best securities of social happiness: there is more private misery arising from an unqualified communication of words and actions, than from the anger of the heavens.'

"'The Oration or Lecture in defence of Masonry,' said Bro. Meyrick, 'pronounced at Liverpool by Bro. McConochie,[8] successfully combats the wild assertions of Professor Robison, who accuses the Fraternity of a deeply-concocted plot to overturn all the religions and governments in the world. He contends, on the contrary, that it contains nothing but a lovely display of benevolence to the distressed of every clime, without the distinction of birth, colour, or religion. Independent of every other consideration, he says, Masonry holds out two weighty arguments in its favour;—a universal language, understood by the Fraternity in every quarter of the globe; and a universal fund, for the relief of the distressed, whatever may be their religion, or country, or complexion. Our language is understood by every country, pretending to the slightest degree of cultivation, under heaven. The Mason needs but to speak it, and he is fed, and clothed, and comforted by men who never saw his face before.'

"'In a review of the literary productions of our country Brethren,' Bro. Preston observed, 'we must not overlook the Rev. James Watson, P. M., of St. John's Lodge, Lancaster, who has published two excellent Addresses on Taking and Resigning the Chair.[9] They entitle him to our highest consideration, although I can

[8] "A short Defence of British Freemasonry; being the substance of a Lecture delivered to Lodges No. 20, 25, and 299, Liverpool.' By Bro. James McConochie.

[9] "An Address to the Brethren of St. John's Lodge, Lancaster." By the Rev. James Watson, on his Installation into the Chair of the Lodge, Dec. 27, 1794. "An Address to the same Brethren, on quitting the Chair," Dec. 28, 1795.

scarcely subscribe to his distribution of the three Degrees. He says, the three Degrees into which Masonry is divided, seem to have an obvious and apt coincidence with the three progressive states of mankind, from the creation to the end of time. The first is emblematic of man's state of nature, from his first disobedience to the time of God's covenant with Abraham, and the establishment of the Jewish Economy. The second, from that period to the era of the last, full, and perfect Revelation from Heaven to mankind, made by our Great Redeemer. The third, comprehending the glorious interval of the Christian Dispensation, down to the consummation of all things.'

"'I believe,' Bro. Shadbolt observed, 'that our learned and intelligent Brother Hutchinson first promulgated that opinion, for I am not aware that it can be traced to any higher antiquity. A reference to the three ages of man would, I think, be more orthodox.'

"'I am rather inclined,' Bro. Preston replied, 'to make the reference scientific. According to my view, the First Degree enforces the duties of morality, and imprints on the memory the noblest principles that can adorn the human mind. The Second Degree extends the plan, and comprehends a more diffusive system of knowledge by the study of the liberal sciences, especially geometry, which is established as the basis of our Art. While, in the Third Degree, every circumstance that respects government and system, ancient lore and deep research, curious invention and ingenious discovery, is collected and accurately traced."

"'Who is to decide when doctors disagree?' Bro. Daniell asked, laughingly.

"'My dear sir,' Bro. Preston replied, 'this is an open question, on which every Brother is entitled to form his own opinion.'

"'I am afraid we are slightly wandering from our subject,' Bro. Hannan interposed, 'and we must not omit to do justice to the production of a Rev. and esteemed Brother, although he be present, when masonic literature is the theme. I allude to Bro. Inwood's volume of sermons, just published,[10] which would be creditable to any body

[10] "Sermons; in which are explained and enforced the Religious,

of men in the kingdom, not excepting the profession to which he himself belongs, teeming, as it does, with the brightest emanations of learning and talent. If the enunciation of the purest principles of Masonry and Christianity, expressed in chaste and beautiful language, and enforced by unadorned eloquence, be entitled to commendation, then Bro. Inwood's Masonic Sermons will receive the universal welcome of the Craft.'

"'I beg to be permitted to add my testimony,' said Bro. Preston, 'to the exceeding beauty and excellence of these Sermons, which dignify and adorn the literature of Masonry.'

"'And I,' said Bro. Jones. A mark of approbation which was echoed by every person present.

"'Dear Brethren,' said Bro. Inwood, 'your eulogium is greater than my simple compositions merit. I have endeavoured to preserve unimpaired what I conceive to be the general and particular bearings of the Order, and it is not my fault if I have been unsuccessful. But the encomiums which you have thought proper to bestow in the presence of such a company of distinguished Brethren, convince me that I have not had the misfortune to fail. I am proud of your favourable opinion, and the value of the discourses will be enhanced in my own estimation, after having been thus honoured with your approbation.'

"A few evenings after this literary reunion," continued the Square, "the subject of begging Masons, and the impositions practised on the liberality of the Craft by mendicants travelling with false certificates, was introduced by Bro. Arthur Tegart, during the hour of refreshment; and the Treasurer of the Lodge communicated some interesting facts which had occurred to him in the discharge of his official duties since the previous Lodge.

"But to make the subject intelligible," said the Square, "you must understand, that at this period begging Masons, and pretended Masons, abounded in this metropolis; and by their importunity gave the Treasurers a great deal

Moral, and Political Virtues of Freemasonry. Preached, upon several occasions, before the Provincial Grand Officers, and other Brethren in the counties of Kent, Essex, &c." By the Rev. Jethro Inwood, P. G. Chaplain for the county of Kent. London, Crosby and Letterman, 1799. Published in the "Golden Remains," vol. iv. Spencer, 1849.

of trouble. The Athol Lodges initiated unworthy persons for a trifling fee, and having furnished them with certificates, they converted their Masonry into a regular trade. If one of these men died in a lodging-house, there was sure to be a fierce struggle among the survivors for his diploma. Others gambled away their certificates at all-fours or dice; and hence numbers of common beggars, who had never seen a Lodge, were spread over the country, soliciting charity on the strength of these documents. The Treasurers and Masters of Lodges were obliged, therefore, to exercise the utmost caution in their examinations, lest these unprincipled scamps should glean any hint which might be usefully employed in other places to favour their imposture.

"This being premised, I proceed in my Revelations. The Treasurer *loquitur*:—

"'About a fortnight ago,' he said, 'I was applied to by a Brother in deep distress, who described himself as a stonemason out of work. He was a man of medium height, neither tall nor short, with light hair, and a beard of a month's growth. His dress was a light-coloured fustian jacket, with horn buttons, a long leather apron, with the skirts tucked under his belt to allow free motion for his legs in walking; and on his head a dirty white hat, with a broad brim and a low crown. Altogether, his appearance was that of a common working mason. He had a mallet in one hand, and a piece of rough stone in the other, and humbly begged relief.

"'In the exercise of my discretionary power of relieving any indigent Brother to the amount of one shilling, without reference to the R. W. M., I proceeded to ascertain whether the applicant were really a Mason, for I had some doubts about his certificate. I was, however, soon satisfied on that point, for he met all my inquiries very adroitly.

"'"Your name is ——?" I said.

"'"John Wilkins," he replied; "or Lewis, if you like it better. But here, some would probably answer by using the word Caution."

"'"Then I am to understand that you are a Mason?" I rejoined.

"'"I am so taken and accepted," was his prompt reply.

"'"Where were you made a Mason?" I asked.

" 'His answer was perfectly orthodox, although it was accompanied by a sardonic smile, which indicated, if it did not absolutely express, knavery.

" ' 'What is that in your left hand?'

" ' 'If I answer as a *Free*-mason,' he replied, 'it is a rough ashlar or broached thurnel; but as a working mason I should say it is a boulder-stone.'

" ' 'So far, so well,' I thought; and said aloud—'Since you appear so confident, can you tell me what that stone smells of?'

" 'The rogue put it to his nose scientifically, and, with another smile, gave me a direct and proper answer.

" ' 'What recommendation do you bring?' was my next inquiry.

" 'The fellow knew his points, however he might have become acquainted with them, and told me without the slightest hesitation. And, being satisfied that he was a Mason, I gave him the shilling, and he thanked me, and went about his business.

" 'A few days afterwards, a poor shoemaker applied to me for assistance, with hammer in hand, apron before him, buttoned up to his chin, and an awl stuck in his girdle, which was fastened with a wax end. His hair was black, his face dirty, his hat divested of its brim, and fitting close to his head; ribbed worsted stockings, and shoes very much the worse for wear. Divested of his apron, he might have passed for a respectable chimney-sweep, or a worn-out coal porter. Altogether he was a disgusting object, and redolent of the combined odour of stale tobacco and shoemaker's wax. He said he was on tramp, and could not fall into work. He was averse to begging, as he had not been used to it, and the necessity was galling to his feelings. But being hard up, he was obliged to have recourse to the liberality of his Brother Masons for assistance.

" 'I asked his name, and he answered the question by inquiring whether I alluded to his paternal or his masonic appellation.

" ' 'Your Christian and surname, sir?' I replied, sternly, for I was piqued at the fellow's pertinacity.

" ' 'James Patchett.'

" ' 'And your place of abode?'

" ' 'Faith,' said he, 'I can scarcely tell you that; for

my whereabouts has been sufficiently diversified of late, but I was born and brought up at Hinckley, in Leicestershire.'

" ' 'You say you are a Mason,' I continued; 'will you do me the favour to describe the mode of your preparation?'

" ' 'Describe to *you*, sir!' he said, with some humour. 'Come, that is a prime joke. As if you did not know all about it! If you must have it, it was thus;' and he satisfied the inquiry correctly. 'Certes,' he added, 'I remember my initiation as well as if it had occurred only yesterday.'

" 'I then tried him with a few of Grand Master Sayer's quaint examination questions, and found him *au fait* even there.

" ' 'Will you give or take?'

" ' 'Both, or which you please.'

" ' 'Are you rich or poor?'

" ' 'Neither.'

" ' 'Change me that?'

" ' 'With pleasure.'

" 'The fellow knew his catechism, and I failed to puzzle him.

" 'Seeing in his hand a hammer,' the Treasurer continued, 'I asked him whether it had any moral or masonic reference.

" ' 'Call it a mallet, if you please,' he answered with a knowing smile. 'Crispin's hammer is the Mason's gavel, though one is made of wood, and the other of iron; but iron tools ——' and he gave me an orthodox illustration of the implement.

" 'I then observed, for the purpose of hearing his reply,—'I see you wear an apron *out* of the Lodge as well as *in* it.'

" ' 'I belong to the Gentle Craft,' he replied, 'which is the designation of my *trade* as a cobbler, as well as of my *profession* as a Mason. The apron, sir, is common to both. I cannot, indeed, say much in favour of the whiteness or purity of my present badge, but, for all that, I may be as innocent as a new born babe,' laying a peculiar emphasis on the word *may*.

" ' 'You carry your awl about with you, I observe.'

" ' 'My *all*, sir,' he replied, 'is under my hat, and a

shocking bad hat it is! and my *end* will soon overtake me, if not prevented by the exercise of your kindness and commiseration.'

" 'The fellow's ready wit amused me, and I freely tendered him the usual amount of relief, which he pocketed, and took his leave.

" 'The next day I had another and very different appli cant. He was a man of rather fashionable appearance, well dressed, and his brown glossy hair neatly arranged; a round hat, nearly new, tight pantaloons, with hessian boots well polished and tasselled, and in his hand a dragon cane. He introduced himself by the aristocratic name of Walter Beauchamp, and apologised profusely for troubling me; but, he added, '*Necessitas non habet legem;* and here I am—a free and accepted Mason in deep distress.'

" 'I was not at leisure to dally with this gentleman, and, therefore, I determined, after having ascertained that he was really a Mason, to relieve and dismiss him. I asked him successively—What is the first point in Masonry?—What is the chief point—the original point—the principal point—the point within a circle?' He answered these questions without the slightest hesitation or mistake; and I then said carelessly, to catch him tripping, if possible—'By the bye, supposing a Brother to be lost, where might we hope to find him?'

" 'He said nothing, but with his cane traced a square and compass on the office floor. I then asked him whether he had seen a Master Mason to-day?

" 'He laughed, and answered curtly by another question—'Do I see one now?'

" 'I was perfectly satisfied, and while I took out my purse, I inquired what was his trade or profession.

" ' 'A short time ago,' he said, 'I was the conductor of a flourishing academy in the west of England, and my circumstances were promising. I filled the chair of the Rural Philanthropic Lodge, at Huntspill, with credit and success, though I say it myself, who ought not to do so, because the poet tells us—On their own merits modest men are dumb. You have heard the anecdote of a schoolmaster, who, being sea-sick when crossing the Bristol Channel, and seeing the waves run mountain high, hiccupped over the side of the vessel—'It's all very well to say 'Britannia *rules* the waves,' but, for my part, I wish she would rule them straight.' You have heard this? Very well. I am the man, sir. True, upon my honour. But *quid rides?* If I did not sound my own trumpet, there is no one here to lend me his breath, and, therefore, you must excuse my blushes. Being foolishly kind-hearted,' he rattled on, 'I was persuaded to become security for a Brother Mason, *hinc illæ lachrymæ*, who was a Mason in word but not in deed, for he vanished in some mysterious manner when the bills became due, *non est inventus*, and left me to bear the responsibility at my own discretion. As I was not in circumstances to meet the payment, I had no alternative but to copy his example—d'ye take? In a word, I absconded without beat of drum, leaving birchen rods, dunces' caps, and a whole troop of little boys and girls to satisfy my imperious creditor. Being unmarried, I occupied furnished lodgings, and consequently had no available assets to leave behind. Rather hard upon me, was it not; sir? But *jacta est alea*, and I must bide the result.'

" 'Thus he went on,' the Treasurer added, 'and talked so fluently and well, that I became rather prepossessed in his favour. To test his qualifications, however, I produced pen, ink, and paper, and desired him to write the word ——, I mentioned the pass-word.

" ' 'Pardon me, sir,' was his modest reply, 'I cannot conscientiously do that. Do you think poverty can ever induce me to disregard my O. B.? Fie on it! How poor soever a man may be, let him be honest. Does not the O. B. forbid us to——he repeated the clause. But to convince me of his calligraphic attainments, he wrote half a dozen lines applicable to his own circumstances, in a free and beautiful hand, which excited my admiration. I never bestowed a shilling with greater pleasure, and the poor fellow's agreeable conversation drew an additional half-crown out of my pocket. And I must say I never met with a begging Mason who acquitted himself so creditably throughout an examination as either of these three poor fellows did.

" 'About a week after this interview,' the Treasurer continued, 'I was walking down the Strand with a friend and Brother, who is Treasurer of the St. Alban's Lodge Dover-street, Piccadilly, and the above transaction formed the subject of our conversation, so much had I been charmed with the poor schoolmaster's address. My friend observed that applications for charity had been rather numerous of late; and the last person he had relieved was a poor carpenter out of work, who proved himself to be a clever and intelligent Mason; 'and, if my eyes do not deceive me, yonder he is, with his square and rule under his arm. Let us cross the street and question him; you will be pleased with his answers.'

" 'As we were passing over to the other side, the fellow appeared to eye us suspiciously, as though he wished to avoid the meeting. But when he found it impracticable, he saluted us respectfully, and was moving on. But my companion stopped him by saying,—' Well, my poor fellow, you have not succeeded in finding employment?'

" ' 'Why, the truth is,' he replied, 'Master Carpenters, as well as Master Masons, are rather shy of engaging with a perfect stranger, without a written character in his pocket; for you know, sir, the old canon—*all preferment among Masons is grounded upon real worth and personal merit only;* and who could discover my worth and personal merit without a certificate from my last employer, which I unfortunately neglected to procure? And, perhaps, they are right; for there are many impostors in this Great Babylon, as I myself have good reason to know.'

" 'I could scarcely believe my ears,' said the Treasurer. 'I looked in his face, and he smiled. I knew that smile, and the peculiar twinkle of his keen grey eye. It was no other than my accomplished schoolmaster!

" ' 'Why, you rascal,' I began—but he interrupted the explosion by saying, in his calm and quiet manner,—

" ' 'Don't abuse me, sir, I beseech you. Spare your precious breath for a better purpose. You cannot tell how soon you may have occasion for it. Your dull ass, as the grave-digger says, will not mend his pace with beating. As to being a rascal—if I was ignorant of that fact, I must be the stupidest ass breathing, for I am reminded of it twenty times a day. Everybody tells me so—and what everybody says, must be true. I am, indeed, something like the man Snake, in Sheridan's play, which I saw the other night, and most earnestly entreat you not to ruin my bad character, for it is all I have to depend on. Shakespeare informs his hearers, and his readers too, that each man in his turn plays many parts, and it is perfectly impossible for me to tell how many have fallen to my share.'

" 'The cool impudence and self-possession which the fellow displayed,' continued the Treasurer, 'amused me exceedingly, and I asked him how he managed to get a living, as he appeared to be disinclined to work?'

" ' 'Why, sir,' he said, 'the truth is, I sometimes live luxuriously, and sometimes starve; for mine is but a precarious employment at the best. At one time I dine off a noble haunch of venison, and wash it down with claret, and at another I am obliged to do penance with Duke Humphrey, or amuse myself by taking an account of the number of trees in the park, to allay the cravings of hunger. And sometimes, *Si fortuna perit, nullus amicus erit*, I am greeted with kicks instead of halfpence.'

" ' 'Why, then, do you not exchange such a degrading mode of life for some honest and regular employment?' I inquired. 'You appear to have some talent, and by the aid of industry and application, you might become a useful member of society.'

" ' 'It can't be done, sir,' the fellow replied; 'it can't be done. I have already tried it on without success. A dull droning life won't do for me.' And he began to sing, in a clear tenor voice,—

'Of all the trades in England,
A beggar's life's the best,
For whenever he's a weary,
He can lay him down to rest.
'And a begging we will go!

'I fear no plots against me,
I live in open cell,
Then who would be a monarch,
When beggars live so well?
'And a begging we will go!'

" ' 'No, gentlemen, it can never be. I live only in an atmosphere of fun and excitement; and even starving for a season is not without its pleasures. Sometimes, indeed, the joke becomes serious; and if it were not for such kind-hearted persons as yourselves, i' faith, I am afraid I should be obliged to work, which, to say the truth, would be very distasteful, and go woefully against the grain. But long life to the Freemasons! They are a liberal set of men, and not very discriminating, and, therefore, I have but little trouble with them. I shall never be reduced to the hard necessity of working, thank goodness, while we have Lodges in every street, and open-handed Treasurers. They are fruitful milch-cows, and a bountiful Goshen when the land of Canaan reduces me to famine.'

"'Then you are not a schoolmaster, after all?' I said.

"'Bless your heart, no,' the fellow replied, with his pleasant smile. 'A schoolmaster! Faugh! To be shut up the live-long day with a flock of dirty urchins, and no escape—it is not to be thought of. Besides, I never could endure confinement. I have been twice in Bridewell, and once in Newgate, not for making an illegal conveyance of property, mind, but, as the big wigs technically term it, as a rogue and a vagabond—for begging, in short; and in my daily Litany I pray to be delivered from all restraint. A schoolmaster! Ha, ha, ha! I have had many a laugh about that, and your beautiful new half-crown. It is clear that you believed my story.'

"'I certainly did, my good man,' was my reply.

"'Nay,' said he, 'now you call me good, when in fact it was not I, but the acting that was good.'

"'The fellow's taunt stung me to the quick, and I asked sternly, for I felt piqued at his unblushing effrontery—'What, then, in the name of the devil, are you—a daring thief, I warrant?'

"'Not a thief, your honour,' he replied, with the utmost composure. 'I have never yet been reduced to that dodge. Craving your pardon, begging is the safest employment of the two. I can sleep with a quiet conscience when I have no sins under my belt of greater burden than a few innocent white lies.'

"'You have a trade, I suppose, if you were compelled by necessity to work? Tell me at once what it is.'

"'That is a question which will be rather difficult to answer,' he replied. 'At this moment, as you see, I am a distressed carpenter; but what I shall be to-morrow is in the womb of fate. I have been the round of all known trades and professions. A horsedealer to-day, a lawyer to-morrow; this day a chimney-sweep, the next a distressed clergyman. For instance, do you recollect—for further concealment is unnecessary,' he continued, with the merry twinkle of his eye to which I have already referred—do you recollect a poor cobbler who paid you a visit a week or two back, whose *all* was beneath his hat, and his *end* certain unless you relieved him?'

"''Why,' I ejaculated, in astonishment, 'surely—'

"''Your humble servant, sir, and no mistake,' he coolly replied, with a low bow. 'And perhaps you have not altogether forgotten a distressed stonemason, who satisfied your scruples by telling you what the rough ashlar smelt of?'

"''And was that one of your performances also?' I inquired.

"''The same, sir. I am Proteus. Ever ready *tourner casaque*, as the Parisian gamins would say.'

"''Then you have been in Paris?'

"''I have been everywhere. It would be difficult to say where I have not been. Experience is a faithful instructor, and I have been some years under its tuition. And you shall hear what an apt scholar I have been. I once bet a guinea with a pal—you may stare, sir, but I sometimes have a fugitive guinea in my pocket to sport with, as well as my betters. Where was I? O!—I was saying, I bet a guinea that I succeeded in obtaining relief from the Treasurer of a certain Lodge, which shall be nameless, six times within the compass of fourteen days. Having at my command the choice of every species of disguise at the rate of sixpence a day, I accomplished the feat, and the poor dupe remains in perfect ignorance to the present moment that he has been imposed on. And sir,' he said, lowering his tone of voice, 'excuse me, sir, but I flatter myself, if I had not been so unfortunate as to encounter both of you together, that the experiment might have been safely and successfully repeated, although the representative of Wisdom in your Lodge does possess the Jewel of Sir Christopher Wren.'

"'The clever scamp chuckled over his reminiscences, and suddenly turning on his heel, and looking me full in the face, he said, in a half-whisper,—'By the bye, you don't happen to have such a thing as half a crown about you?'

"''Why? you impudent rogue—'

"''Stop a moment, if you please, dear Brother,' he said, with his usual quiet smile and twinkle of the eye, accompanied by the most unruffled composure—'don't be impatient, I beseech you. I was about to add, that if you have such a thing to dispose of, I am ready to purchase it by communicating a secret which is worth its weight in gold.'

"'This proposal,' continued the Treasurer, 'under the circumstances, I thought peculiarly insulting, particularly as the fellow had assumed that remarkably knowing look which seemed to indicate that he intended mischief. I had no wish to be victimized; but as the risk was trifling in amount, even if I got nothing in exchange for my coin, I consented to the proposal, simply for the purpose of ascertaining how far the fellow's impudence would carry him; and while he pocketed the gratuity, I heard him mutter,—'Well, you're a trump any how—*you* are—and no mistake! I *will* say that; and I'll not lose sight of you.' And then he said aloud,—'The secret I have to communicate is dirt cheap at half a crown. Listen to it:

"''TAKE CARE WHO YOU ADMIT AS CANDIDATES, AND YOU WILL HAVE FEWER BEGGING MASONS.'''"

"You will be at no loss to conclude," said the Square, "from these Revelations, that things went on very pleasantly with us. We had changes of Masters, it is true; but they all possessed average ability, and some were distinguished by superior attainments. Nothing further occurred, however, worthy of a special notice till the commencement of the nineteenth century, when the Rev. Jethro Inwood was unanimously elected to fill the Chair of the Lodge."

CHAPTER XIV.

LEGENDS.—REV. JETHRO INWOOD.

1800—1803.

"To Heaven's high Architect all praise,
All praise, all gratitude be given;
Who deign'd the human soul to raise
By mystic secrets sprung from Heaven."

HENRY DAGGE.

'There is no violation of truth in affirming that, in London especially, propositions for initiation into Masonry are often too easily, if not eagerly received, on the bare general recommendation of the proposer, and payment of the customary fees. But if character and circumstances were cautiously weighed in the qualification of candidates, though the Society might not be quite so numerous, the members of it would, in proportion, be more respectable, both as men, and as Masons."—NOORTHOUCK.

"Masonry has no principle but what might still more ornament the purest mind; nor any appendage but what might give additional lustre to the brightest character. By the exercise of the duties of Masonry, the rich may add abundantly to the fund of their eternal inheritance. The wise may increase their knowledge of the nature of God, in all his best perfections, and thereby daily grow still more wise unto eternal salvation. The pure in heart may be always advancing in the divine likeness; and they who walk in this path of the just, with zeal and activity, will find it as the shining LIGHT, which shineth more and more unto the perfect day."—INWOOD.

"I AM about to exceed the limits of our covenant," said the Square, swinging scientifically round on its dexter limb, with a slow and even motion, as if trying to describe some imaginary circle in the air, "in which, on certain conditions, I promised to reveal some of the peculiar practices of our Brethren in the eighteenth century; and as you have adhered so faithfully to the preliminary contract, by suffering me to proceed without interruption, I shall reward your constancy by continuing my Revelations for a few years longer, that I may have an opportunity of describing the causes which produced the extinction of the schism that divided the Fraternity into two hostile sections for three quarters of a century; and it is probable that I may be able to furnish a few new facts which may prove interesting to you."

I replied to my gossiping companion by a nod, and the sign of silence; for, to say the truth, I had become so accustomed to his lively conversation, that I shall regret its termination, whenever it may happen to cease.

"Aye," said he, "you are at liberty to employ our universal language, but not to speak; and I am glad to find that you have learned your lesson so perfectly.

"I have already told you," he continued, "that our present Master was the Rev. Jethro Inwood, curate of St. Paul's, at Deptford; and his opening address, delivered after his installation, was directed at a very prevalent objection of the Antimasons, that the Institution is deistical. He began thus:—

"'When the Almighty found it expedient to promulgate a code of laws for the especial government of the Israelites, after their deliverance from Egyptian bondage, to preserve them as a nation distinct from the idolatrous people amongst whom they were placed, he gave them a religious institution, formed upon exclusive principles, which was intended to be the cement of his ordinances, himself being the chief Ruler and Governor both of the civil and religious polity; and he constituted Aaron his authorized deputy over the one, and Moses over the other. On this model Freemasonry has been formed, but at an unapproachable distance. To render the parallel as complete as circumstances would admit, our ancient Brethren made the degrees of Masonry to correspond with the permanent and strongly-marked divisions of the Tabernacle, where the system was enunciated by a regular series of symbolical machinery. In a word, everything connected with the Tabernacle and its services, was typical of a better dispensation, whose builder and maker is God.

"'It is not my intention, however, to detain you on the present occasion with an explanation of all the emblems which were embodied in this primitive temple; and, indeed, the attempt would exceed the limits of a single oration, confined, as it must necessarily be, within a very circumscribed space of time. I shall merely allude to a few brief particulars which appear to be apposite in their application equally to Freemasonry and Christianity. The Tabernacle was built due east and west, in commemoration of that great and mighty wind which first blew east and then west, to divide the Red Sea for their safe transit, and the total destruction of the Egyptian army. For the same reason our Lodges are placed due east and west, in common with all Christian places of worship, for Wisdom sprang out of the east, and thence spread over the western parts of the world.

"'Our Lectures refer to Christianity in the same manner as the Jewish dispensation did, viz., by types and significant references. The First Great Light is the very basis and pillar of Christianity. The Theological Ladder is invested with a Christian reference; the Two Parallels in our system of Masonry are Christians. Those who aim at neutralizing these and other similar references, or, in other words, of preserving the universality of Masonry by depriving it of its allusions to our holy religion, little think that, by such arguments, they deny the truth of God's dispensation to Moses, and refuse to acknowledge with the Apostle, that it was intended as a schoolmaster to bring us to Christ. If the Jewish religion was truly a type of Christianity, so is Freemasonry. The conclusion is inevitable, because the Lectures of Masonry embody many of the historical facts, ordinances, and types of that ancient religion which was communicated to man by the Deity himself.'

"These orthodox sentiments," said the Square, "proceeding from the mouth of a reverend divine who had distinguished himself as a zealous and learned Mason, were highly applauded, and anticipations of an edifying year were indulged by all the members of the Lodge without exception. Their hopes were amply realized; and the popularity of his government formed a theme of congratulation, which extended beyond the four walls of the Lodge. His quiet and gentlemanly manners, and his method of imparting instruction to newly-initiated candidates by a free conversation with other members who proposed such questions for elucidation as they themselves might be inclined to ask, brought a host of visitors every Lodge night, and a marked increase of initiations.

'One evening, I remember it well," the Square continued, "after the business of the Lodge had been disposed of, a candidate, recently initiated, whose name was Lambert, rose and said—'R. W. Sir, if I am not taking too great a liberty—and as I have had very little experience, I am, of course, unable to determine whether I am in order or not—I should be glad if you would inform me by what process you acquired such a perfect insight into the mysteries of Masonry, that I may steer my course by your example, for I confess to the soft impeachment of an ambition to become a good practical Mason.'

"'And a laudable ambition it is,' replied the R. W. M.; 'nor can I have the slightest objection to gratify your curiosity by delineating the pursuits of my early masonic career. When I was but a boy, having been made a Mason, as a Lewis, at eighteen years of age, I determined to fathom the very lowest depths of Masonry; and for that purpose I commenced a regular course of study in the principles of the Order, under the instructions of my father; and, as it was a labour of love, I made a rapid progress. In fact, I am not ashamed to say that I entered on the pursuit with an alacrity, equal, at least, if not superior, to that of reading for my degree at the university. I soon became thoroughly master of the Prestonian Lectures in all the degrees, and capable of going through the ceremonies of making, passing, and raising with equal promptitude and precision.'

"'And you had sufficient resolution to persevere in this dry study?' said Bro. Lambert, inquiringly.

"'Resolution!' the R. W. M. responded. 'To be sure I had. And so far from finding it what you term a dry study, I became enthusiastically fond of it; and, in about four years after my initiation, I found myself in circumstances of great popularity with the Craft, and became Master of the Lodge in which I had been admitted a Mason.'

"'I should like to know,' said Bro. Lambert, 'whether you had any extraneous assistance—I mean, whether you had the advantage of printed publications to facilitate the acquirement of the Lodge Lectures?'

"'In answer to this home question,' the R. W. M. said, 'the truth is—and I name it by way of caution—

that, immediately after receiving my First Degree, I was invited to spend a few weeks in Leicestershire; and a masonic friend, perceiving my eagerness to acquire information in the Lectures and ceremonies, placed in my hands a pamphlet called "Jachin and Boaz."'

"'"Jachin and Boaz!"' exclaimed Bro. Lambert, eagerly; 'aye, I have seen the book—I have read it. But, surely, that work does not contain a correct portraiture of Freemasonry?'

"'You shall hear,' replied Bro. Inwood. 'Did you ever read about the mirage in the arid steppes of the desert, which mocks the thirsty traveller with hopes that are destined to be disappointed? Well, thus it was with me. At first, the possession of this pamphlet appeared to be a God-send; and I felt as much gratified by its acquisition as Gil Blas, when he was constituted critic in ordinary to the Archbishop of Grenada. I applied myself to its study with great earnestness, and read it for whole days together under the umbrageous shade of trees—*recubans sub tegmine fagi*—with the full determination of making myself perfectly master of its contents. Professing to be a complete exposition of the Lectures and ceremonies, instead of consulting my father, as I ought to have done, I entered heart and soul into its merits, and ultimately succeeded in fixing every line tenaciously in my memory. I liked the excitement. It was a rich treat. I had as great an affection for this trumpery book as a young mother for her first child, and always carried it in my bosom. I was delighted with the possession of such an easy means of becoming acquainted with the details of the Order. But, alas! it was all a delusion; and I have frequently had occasion to lament the sacrifice of so much valuable time to so little purpose.'

"'Well, and how did it end?' Bro. Lambert asked.

"'The result may be a useful lesson to you,' replied the R. W. M., 'and to all others who seek for a royal road to the knowledge of Masonry; or, in other words, who are desirous of becoming learned Masons without a devoted application of the adjuncts of time, labour, and serious meditation. When I received the Third Degree of Masonry, I found that all my pains and anxiety had been wasted, and that the pretended revelations, like the forgeries of poor Chatterton, were a gross imposition Nay, it was worse than leisure misapplied, for the impressions already produced interfered materially with the subsequent study of our legitimate Lectures; and I found the task of obliterating from my memory that which is false, more difficult than acquiring a perfect knowledge of that which is true. It was a work of retrogression, and mortified me exceedingly. I had been deceived on the threshold of Masonry, and the wonder is, that I did not relinquish the pursuit in disgust, as numbers do every day from causes infinitely less influential.'

"'But you persevered?'

"'I did; for there is a springiness in the ardent nature of youth which is not easily discouraged. On a reference to my venerated father, I found I had been duped; but I did not allow the imposition to quench the spirit of inquiry which had been excited in my bosom. I made the best use of the means at my disposal, and, by dint of severe application, I became at length fully indoctrinated in the ceremonies, rituals, and genuine Lectures of the Order. And if you will pursue the same process, I doubt not but your exertions will be rewarded with the same success.

"'Then huzza for a tough spell of masonic study without the assistance of "Jachin and Boaz!"' Bro. Lambert exclaimed, 'for I am determined to be, in the strictest sense of the word, a Mason.'

"You will at once conclude, from this description," the Square continued, "that Bro. Inwood was an assiduous Mason; and he permitted no opportunity to pass unimproved of storing his mind with useful knowledge, or of imparting instruction to those who needed it. At his first quarterly supper, a remarkable instance of this disposition occurred. Amidst the intervals of song and toast, a private conversation was going on between Bro. Dent and a visiting Brother from the country, by which the former seemed greatly interested. At length, during the brief silence which succeeded a song, Bro. Dent was heard to say—'Are you really in earnest, when you tell me that such a belief prevails extensively in the provinces?'

"This was heard by the Chair, who immediately said

—'Bro. Dent, have you forgot that excellent Charge, which forbids you to hold separate conversations, without leave from the Master? If your communication with our visiting Brother be on the subject of Masonry, I am sure you will not deprive us of any benefits which may be derived from it. If important, let us hear it; if not, I call on you for a song.'

"On this challenge from the Chair," the Square continued, "Bro. Dent rose and said—'R. W. Sir, whether the conversation between myself and friend, whom I have already introduced to you by the name of Bro. the Rev. Samuel Oliver, from Leicester,' (your respected parent,)" said the Square, parenthetically; "but it happened before you were initiated, and, therefore, you are probably, ignorant of the circumstance."

I gave a nod, to signify that it *might* be new to me; but I thought it scarcely probable, as, indeed, it proved when the Revelation was made, for I had heard the greater part of it from my father's own lips.

The Square, however, went on with Bro. Dent's reply —"'Whether Bro. Oliver's communication be or be not worthy of your attention, is not for me to determine. I can only say that he was detailing a series of facts, if facts they be, which have astonished me not a little.'

"'Let us hear, let us hear,' said the R. W. M. 'If the matter be interesting, as you represent, we can afford to suspend our convivialities for a few minutes to share in your surprise.'

"'Nay,' Bro. Dent responded, 'I have only heard the commencement of the strange recital; but it appears that there are some mysteries in each of the Three Degrees, of which we Metropolitan Masons are profoundly ignorant.'"

At this point the Square, with one of his quaint twirls on the point of his dexter limb, interrupted himself by a reference to a remark of the witty Dean of St. Patrick's, who said that some people are much more dexterous at pulling down and setting up, than at preserving what is fixed; and they are not fonder of seizing more than their own, than they are of delivering it up again to the worst bidder, with their own into the bargain. And to this observation he might have added, that it is doubtful whether what they set up is half so useful or half so true as what they pull down. You shall judge for yourself, when I have repeated the following conversation.

"Bro. Dent went on to say,—'From what I have heard this evening, some of the country Lodges are *disposed* on a novel principle, which appears to militate against our preconceived notions; and the Entered Apprentices are instructed to entertain the doctrine as a matter of faith.'

"Bro. Preston declared that the information would be peculiarly interesting to him, should it contain anything new; as he had already bestowed infinite pains in the collection of facts on all subjects connected with the usages and customs which exist amongst the Craft in every part of the world.

"Bro. Oliver was then requested by the Chair to recapitulate his communications, that the Brethren might have an opportunity of judging whether they are in accordance with ancient custom.

"Bro. Oliver rose and said, 'He was not aware that the conversation with his friend Bro. Dent would have had the effect of bringing him out so prominently before the Lodge, nor did he believe that an assembly of Brethren so well versed in the usages of the Craft, would be edified by anything he might have to say. It is true,' he continued, 'that some R. W. Masters, but not in the Lodge to which I belong, make a point of instilling into the minds of the Apprentices the form of the Lodge and the disposition of its furniture; because they think this knowledge constitutes an excellent foundation for any superstructure which they may find occasion to erect upon it. And I shall have great pleasure in communicating all I know on the subject, with this proviso, that the detail will be found to embrace many doubtful facts, to which I cannot conscientiously subscribe.'

"'First, then,' Bro. Preston said, 'let us hear the hypothesis respecting the form and disposition of the Lodge.'

"'Willingly,' returned Bro. Oliver. 'The form of the Lodge is said to be in length, double its height and breadth, as a representation of the Altar of incense in the Tabernacle of Moses, which was a double cube. The Bible, Square, and Compasses are placed upon the Tressel-board before the Master, in the east; with the former open at the book of Ruth. The Constitutions lie before the Past Master; the Globes before the Senior Warden; the rough Ashlar in the north-east for the use of the Apprentices; the perfect Ashlar in the north-west for the use of the Fellowcrafts; the Master Masons in the south-west, and the Past Masters in the south-east. The Mosaic pavement, Blazing star, and Tessellated border, with the emblems of science, are deposited in the east for the use of the R. W. M.'

"'There is certainly something new and ingenious in this,' Bro. Preston observed, 'and I should also say, partially heterodox. But will you allow me to ask you one question? Are you an ancient or a modern?'

"'In answer to this question,' Bro. Oliver replied, 'I must honestly say that I am both. Or I should answer more correctly were I to tell you that I am acquainted with the peculiarities of both. I was made in a modern Lodge, but afterwards became a member of another Lodge, which had just exchanged its Athol warrant for a Constitutional one, and still continued to practise the ancient system. And in that Lodge I acquired the marvellous information, which is very much at your service, if you think it worth hearing.'

"'This preliminary being understood,' said Bro. Preston, 'you will now permit me to ask whether you have any varieties to recount respecting the Second Degree?'

"'We teach our Fellowcrafts,' replied Bro. Oliver, 'the particulars of a curious legend touching the Pillars of the Porch. When the Ark of Noah rested on Mount Ararat, and its inmates came forth, the Patriarch erected a Pillar, which was highly venerated by his descendants, who added thereto many ornamental decorations. After the migration from Shinar, the wandering tribes built pillars in imitation of this great prototype in every country which they planted, to commemorate the universal Deluge, whence the custom originated. Many years after the deliverance from Egypt, Boaz erected two Pillars on his estate near the town of Bethlehem, one of which he called by his own name, and the other Jachin, after the son of Simeon, one of the twelve tribes of Israel. These two Pillars supported an arch or gateway, under which he married Ruth, after she had been formally renounced by a nearer kinsman; who took off one of his shoes as a pledge of his sincerity, and gave it to Boaz for a testimony, in the presence of competent witnesses, that he was at liberty to stand in his shoes as the legal claimant to the hand of Ruth.'

"'I have heard something of this,' said Bro. Inwood; 'but have ever considered it too absurd to merit any serious attention, as it rests on no authority whatever; and I am curious to know in what manner this gateway is connected with the Pillars of Solomon's Porch.'

"'The connection is thus explained,' replied Bro. Oliver:—'Boaz was the great grandfather of David; and Solomon's Pillars were called by the above names to commemorate his marriage with Ruth; for whose memory Solomon is said to have entertained such a respectful veneration, that when David anointed him King, he requested that the ceremony might be repeated under the gate at Bethlehem, which was supported by the two Pillars that Boaz himself had erected. The legend further says that *he was sleeping under this gate, and between the Pillars*, when he was favoured with that remarkable vision where the Most High condescended to offer him his choice of wisdom, long life, or riches, when he preferred the former. Between these Pillars he married his Egyptian wife; and here Hiram Abiff was first introduced to him by the noble prince Adoniram. In the same place he received the Queen of Sheba, when she came to view the magnificent Temple of Jerusalem, and to ascertain by personal communication whether the miraculous traditions of his wisdom and penetration were founded in fact.'

"'And this is the legendary lore which is taught in the Lodges of our ancient Brethren!' exclained Bro. Pigou. 'I do not envy their pretensions to superior knowledge. After this explanation we find no difficulty in understanding the boast of Lawrence Dermott, that *ancient Masonry contains everything valuable amongst the moderns, as well as many other things that cannot be revealed without additional ceremonies.* These absurdities, I conclude, constitute a portion of those *other things which cannot be revealed.*'

"'Your observation is very appropriate,' said the R.

W. M.; 'but let us have the whole case before us, ere we venture to express an opinion on its merits.'

"'I feel considerable interest in this communication,' interposed the D. G. M., Sir Peter Parker, who happened to be present, 'and trust our visiting Brother will favour us with the remainder of these curious legends.'

"'The next point,' Bro. Oliver replied, 'appertains to the Third Degree. The Temple of Solomon is represented as having two foundations, one beneath the other, in the form of an oblong square. The lower foundation is said to have been composed of compact rows of stones, in number 900; while the upper consisted of only twelve stones, to represent the tribes, which were placed in three rows, and were inlaid with upwards of nine hundred costly precious stones. It is further taught that, in order to perpetuate the infamy of the Tribe of Dan, which perpetrated the first apostasy, King Solomon commanded that the stone which appertained to that tribe should be defaced, and a certain cubical stone, which had formed the basis of Enoch's subterranean Temple, should be substituted for it, as it occupied a situation immediately beneath the centre of the Most Holy Place.'

"'I have heard,' said Bro. Meyrick, 'another version of the above legend, which contains a more noble and rational reference. According to my account, the Temple of Solomon had three foundations, the first of which contained seventy stones; five courses from north to south, and fourteen from east to west. The centre course corresponded with the upright of a cross, whose tranverse was formed by two stones on each side of the eleventh stone, counting from the east end of the centre row, which constitutes the upright beam, and the fourth stone from the west. The stone which occupied the place where the beams cross each other, was perpendicularly under the centre of the S. S.; a design which contained an evident reference to the Cross of Christ; and it was so placed, that the portion where the heart of Christ would be at the time of His Crucifixion was exactly beneath the Ark of the Covenant and the Shekinah of Glory.'

"Bro. Eamer, afterwards Sir John Eamer, Lord Mayor of London, and S. G. Warden in 1798, hoped that Bro.

Oliver had something more to communicate, and might be allowed to proceed.

"Bro. Oliver replied, 'that he had very little to add, except on the subject of the Temple decorations, which probably are known to every Brother present, and which it may, therefore, be unnecessary to detail.'

"'Go on, go on,' was heard from every part of the Lodge; and Bro. Oliver proceeded to say that the number of precious stones in the Holy Place is said to have been 22,288, arranged in symbolic figures by Hiram Abiff. In the most Holy Place were 603,550 precious stones, in commemoration of the offerings of the children of Israel towards the construction of the Tabernacle. The centre of the ceiling was decorated with a hierogram of the Sacred Name, curiously wrought with precious stones. in the form of a circle, inscribed within a square; which produced a more dazzling effect than the most superb rose-window in one of our richest cathedrals.

"Now, what value do you suppose our sapient Brethren place on these precious stones?" said the Square, parenthetically. "Open your mouth wide, and I will fill it. Why no less a sum than sixty-two thousand six hundred and seventy-five millions of pounds sterling!!!

"Our erudite visitor proceeded to inform us—and you will not be surprised to hear that we listened with due attention—although he personally repudiated the facts as being too incredible for belief—yet he had heard them insisted on with great pertinacity in a Lodge that he could name. 'In the Temple were 10,480,000 gold and silver vessels, which cost 6,904,832,500 pounds sterling. The workmen's wages amounted to 140,000,000 sterling; and the inferior materials to 150,000,000 pounds. The expense of the whole building was 69,869,832,500 sterling pounds!

"'After all these expenses had been incurred and satisfied, as the legend asserts, the funds subscribed by David, Solomon, Hiram, the Queen of Sheba, and others, were unexhausted; for David himself contributed 911,416,207 pounds; and the Queen of Sheba eighty thousand millions of pounds! It appears, therefore, that the sum of 11,041,583,707 pounds remained as an available surplus after the work was finished, for Solomon to amuse himself with, in the erection of palaces and towns at his pleasure!'

"This perilous stuff," the Square observed, "which is indebted for its origin to the Jewish cabalists, has very properly become obsolete. Freemasonry has been judiciously weeded since the union, and all such glaring improbabilities cancelled. But, sir, as my sole object in making these revelations is to display Masonry as it was in actual operation during the last century, a brief notice of these puerilities could not be consistently avoided. I think I have already told you that they were originally imported from the continent, like a cargo of smuggled merchandize, and were openly practised in the Athol Lodges as a constituent part of the system. Some of the constitutional Masons followed this pernicious example, in defiance of the repeated cautions of the Grand Lodge.

"The harmony of the evening," continued the Square, "was not disturbed by these communications; and Bro. Oliver, though a very indifferent singer, at the request of the R. W. M., favoured the Lodge with an original song of his own composition, which was highly applauded, to the old tune of 'Balinamona ora,' which you shall hear.

'As journeying in darkness through life's toilsome way,
The cheerful light darting not one feeble ray;
No friendly companion my sorrows to smother,
Kind fortune at last sent a true-hearted Brother.

'Sing Balinamona ora, &c.
A Mason's the guardian for me.

'His words smooth as oil, and as honey were sweet;
He guided my path and directed my feet;
He mysteries and dangers with me did explore,
Through a lab'ryuth of horrors I ne'er trod before.

'The terrors of darkness encompass'd me round:
But light, truth, and friendship I speedily found.
No suspicion of falsehood can ever appear,
To proceed from a Mason who acts on the square.

'By signs and words guarded, like Argus's eyes,
All guile and deceit a Freemason defies;
He lives within compass, he works with his tools;
And levels his ways by the Grand Master's rules.

At length quite enlighten'd, experience and truth
Beam'd rays of refulgence from East, West, and South;
I never beheld so resplendent a scene;
And none but a Mason can tell what I mean.

'No longer in darkness I now grope my way,
Illum'd by the beauty and glory of day,
The dense mists of error that clouded my sight
Are dispersed and destroyed by the Science of Light.

'So now, being fearful I trespass too long,
I beg to conclude with my thanks and my song;
Your praises, dear Brethren, I'll sing while I've breath,
May we meet in the Grand Lodge above after death!'

"A few evenings afterwards—it was in the month of November, if my memory does not deceive me," my amusing companion proceeded to say, "when we had some initiations coming off, I was entertaining myself with certain profound[1] reflections on the peculiar situation of a candidate, as I lay reposing on the cushion of the pedestal before the Brethren assembled, which were interrupted by the entrance of the R. W. M., and a very numerous company of Brethren.

"After the Lodge was opened, and the minutes read and confirmed," pursued the Square, "our Rev. Brother produced from a small casket a medal, which he handed round the Lodge that all the Brethren might see it, observing 'that it was intended to strike off a sufficient number of them for distribution amongst the Craft, to commemorate the appointment of their R. H. the Prince of Wales (afterwards George IV.) as Grand Master of Masons, and the Duke of Clarence (afterwards William IV.) as Grand Principal of the Royal Arch. He was acquainted,' he said, 'with the artist, who had entrusted the proof to him for a few hours to exhibit to the Lodge.' After the beauty of the design and chasteness of the execution had been sufficiently admired, the business of the Lodge proceeded.[2]

"We had three initiations; and after the ceremonies were completed, and the Prestonian Charge read, the R.

[1] Profound! The Square vaunteth itself! What an egotistical nonentity it is! Umbras falsæ gloriæ consectatur!—P. D.

[2] See the Lithograph of this beautiful Medal, which will be more satisfactory than the most elaborate description.

W. M., turning to the north-east, said, with great solemnity and effect,—

"'Brethren and friends, the usual routine prescribed by our ritual at the initiation of candidates into Masonry having been accomplished, it may be necessary to enter on some special explanation of our rites; that you may not esteem them to be frivolous or trifling; for the minutest observance, which you have this evening witnessed, has its peculiar reference to some dignified virtue; or to some ancient observance which points out a moral duty.'

"'Perhaps, R. W. Sir,' said Bro. Jones, rising from his seat, 'I humbly venture to suggest—perhaps you would be kind enough first to explain to the candidates what a Freemason is; for, although they may have heard a great deal about Masonry, and may have desired admittance amongst us from a sincere wish of being serviceable to their fellow-creatures, yet, from a hint which I have just received across the table, they are anxious to know what are the exclusive privileges and characteristics of a worthy Brother.'

"'I shall have much pleasure,' Bro. Inwood replied, 'in attending to your recommendation.' Then turning once more to the north-east, he said, 'A Fremason, my Brethren, is a free man, born of a free woman, a brother to kings, and a companion to princes, if they be Masons; an assumption which will be illustrated by the Senior Warden, if you will give him your attention.'

"The Senior Warden then rose, and said,—'Brethren, by command of the R. W. M., I will endeavour to explain the hypothesis of our perfect freedom, and our jealousy lest the vicious habits of slavery should contaminate the true principles on which Masonry is founded. You will observe that many of our usages and customs originated at the building of the Temple of Jerusalem. Now our ancient Brethren, who were employed by King Solomon to work at this famous edifice were declared free, and exempted from all imposts, duties, and taxes for them and their descendants. They were also invested with the privilege of bearing arms. At the destruction of the Temple by Nebuchadnezzar, the posterity of these Masons were carried into captivity with the Jews. But when the time of their humiliation was expired, by the good-will of Cyrus they were permitted to erect a second Temple, being declared free for that purpose. Hence we are called Freemasons. The custom of *accepting* as candidates none but the sons of free women, dates its origin from a much earlier period; even from the time when Abraham held a solemn festival at the weaning of his son Isaac, when Ishmael amused himself by teazing and perplexing the young child. When Sarah was acquainted with this, she remonstrated with Abraham, requesting him to put away the bond-woman Hagar and her son, as they were not competent to inherit with the free-born. She spoke by divine inspiration, as she knew that from Isaac's loins would spring a great and mighty people, who would serve the Lord with freedom, fervency, and zeal; and she feared that if the lads were brought up together, Isaac might imbibe some of Ishmael's slavish principles; for it is well known that the minds of slaves are more contaminated than of those who are born free.'

"The R. W. M. then resumed his instructions, by calling the attention of the candidates to the fact that 'these two persons, Ishmael and Isaac, to whom the Senior Warden has referred, are typical of the Law and the Gospel; the one given by Christ; the other by Moses; and the circumstance has been embodied in Freemasonry to show, that although a person may have been born of a free woman—although he may have been made a Mason, and entitled to all the privileges of initiation—yet if he undervalues these privileges, and neglects to improve his mind by an application of the doctrines and precepts which he hears in the Lodge, instead of profiting by his freedom as Isaac did, he will be no better than a profane bond-slave like Ishmael, who was cast out from his father's house as unworthy of any share in the inheritance. It was by the same carelessness and inattention that the Jews forfeited their freedom, and suffered their privileges to be transferred to others. By their wilful rejection of the Messiah, they have been excluded from the Covenant of Grace—have taken the place of the Sons of Slavery—have been cast out of the vineyard of promise, and are aliens from the true Israel of God.'

"'The candidates have remarked, I doubt not,' Bro.

Tegart observed, 'with no little curiosity, how careful we were to prevent them from bringing anything offensive or defensive into the Lodge. With submission, R. W. Sir, it may be useful to explain the reasons for a caution which might otherwise be considered rude and inexplicable.'

"'You are aware,' said the R. W. M., addressing himself to the newly-initiated Brethren, 'that in the earliest ages of the world there was a peculiar pollution attached to the contamination of metal tools. T. G. A. O. T. U., speaking of the construction of an Altar, commands it to be made of earth or rough stones; observing that if a metal tool were used in its fabrication, it would be polluted. In like manner the Temple of Solomon was built by the divine direction, without the noise of metallic tools; the stones being hewn in the quarry, then carved, marked, and numbered; the timber felled in the forest of Lebanon, there carved, marked, and numbered also. They were then floated down to Joppa, and from thence conveyed upon wooden carriages to Mount Moriah at Jerusalem, and there set up with wooden mauls made for that purpose; so that there was not heard the sound of axe, hammer, or metal tool throughout the whole building, for fear the Temple should be polluted.'

"'The sense of this is plain,' Bro. the Rev. S. Colman observed, 'and the excellence of the Craft thereby proved; for though the stone and timbers were prepared at so great a distance, yet when they were put together, each part tallied with such exact nicety, that the Temple appeared to be constructed of a single stone. From this result the Jews, and some Masons, have adopted the fancy that they were not cut and polished by any instrument; but that a worm, called Samir by the Jews, and Shermah by the Masons, accomplished the work under the Divine direction, and that they were fitted into their respective places on Mount Moriah by the agency of angels. It may, however, be remarked, that the transaction was an emblem of the peace and quietness which ought to exist in the Christian Church, where all things should be done decently and in order. But, R. W. Sir, the most important point that it will be necessary to enlighten our young Brethren upon is the peculiar state in which they made their first appearance in the Lodge, which may otherwise be the cause of some misapprehension on the nature and occult practices of the Order.'

"'Thank you, Bro. Colman, for the suggestion,' said the R. W. M., 'which I had nearly overlooked. You will observe then, my young friends, that the complicated preparation for the ceremony you have just witnessed, is intended to impress upon your minds how dependent you are on others for every comfort, as well as for every advantage you enjoy. The state of mutual subordination in which God has placed His creatures ought to exclude an inordinate regard for self, and annihilate its influence by a desire to promote the happiness and welfare of others. Man was not born for himself alone, but to contribute his quota towards the general benefit of the community. When, therefore, you see a worthy Brother reduced, by unavoidable misfortunes, to a state of distress—poor and penniless—if you be impressed with a due sense of your responsibility as Masons, pity will flow from your hearts, attended with that relief which his necessities may require, and your own circumstances will admit. But you are never expected to extend your charity beyond what you can conveniently afford. And after all, this is not masonic charity, but relief, and there is a wide distinction between the two, which I would recommend you never to lose sight of.'

"'Perhaps you would favour the Lodge with your own definition of masonic charity,' said Bro. James Deans. 'The candidates would be edified by the recital, and the Brethren cannot hear it too often.'

"'With pleasure, Bro. Deans. The universal charity of a Mason is like the charity of the Mason's God, and his God is the God of love. Within the Compass of his mind, he measures and draws the Square of his conduct and within that Square, having honestly provided for his own household, he forms his little angles of benevolence and charity to the distressed of all communities. He visits the fatherless and the widow, not out of idle curiosity, to know the extremity of distress, but, from the impulse of a loving heart, to cherish and to relieve. He searches out the secret and concealed cottages of distress; pours the balm, and oil, and wine of consolation into the bosom of sorrow, affliction, and misery; and through the influence of the love of God and of his Brother, he thus keeps himself unspotted from the evil of the world. This is true Masonry; this is true religion, and the conduct of every true Mason. Masonic charity is the charity of the heart; he thinks no evil of his Brother; he cherishes no designs against him. It is charity upon the tongue also; he speaks no evil; bears no false witness; defames no character; blasts no reputation; he knows that to take away a good name is to commit an evil, the damage of which no wealth can repay—it is of more value than great riches—rubies cannot repurchase it—the gold of Ophir cannot gild it again to its original beauty. It is the charity of the hand also; he anticipates his Brother's wants, nor forces him to the pain of petition; he enters the house of woe, and there finds the mouth he ought to feed, the sickness he ought to cure, and, perhaps, also, the very mind he ought to instruct before it can be fitted for an eternal world. Thus the heart, the tongue, the hand of the really Free and Accepted Mason, are warmly engaged and diligently exercised in all those grand principles of the Royal Order which render it in its nature and effects so much like the Order of that amiable band, whose love to each other so forcibly convinced their adversaries as to draw from them that honourable acclamation—"See how these Christians love!"'

"At this point, one of the candidates said, inquiringly, 'But the secresy, R. W. Sir; I am anxious to hear your reasons for it.'

"The R. W. M. replied, 'My dear Brethren, you must not be too eager in your inquiries. The secret of Masonry, and the reasons for it, will be communicated in due course. You are at present only on the threshold of Masonry, and must not expect to attain to a full development of our mysteries till you have not only passed through all the degrees, but have employed much study and research in their attainment. At present you have received the keys of our treasure in the signs, words, and tokens of the First Degree, and the Lodge is now employed in giving you a lesson on its philosophy. You must, therefore, at present be contented with knowing that you are bound to observe the strictest secresy respecting the occult points of the masonic science. In the ordinary transactions of life, as in Masonry, an apprentice is bound by his obligation to keep his master's secrets. Before your admission you were in a state of darkness, as a member of the profane world, and hence you are to learn that it is one part of your duty to keep all mankind in the darkness of ignorance respecting the secrets of Masonry, unless they come to the knowledge of them in the same lawful manner that you have done—*i. e.*, by initiation; for it is a necessary preparation, that the heart should be taught to conceal before the eyes are suffered to discover any valuable and recondite information.'

" 'These remarks on the several points of your preparation,' the R. W. M. continued, 'will, I have no doubt, satisfactorily point out that our ceremonies are neither trifling nor unimportant, but have a moral reference to something of a higher and more dignified character than the observances themselves would appear to indicate. Do you think it improbable that simple rites should convey a complex meaning, or that they cannot be significant because they are not complicated? Why, the distinguishing peculiarity of the masonic ritual is the unsophisticated character of its construction. It is very possible, however, that you may have formed certain frivolous conjectures respecting some few particulars connected with the mode of your preparation, which may not square with your preconceived views of the probable mode of your reception; but I trust that the explanations you have heard will turn the channel of your ideas into a more favourable construction of our plan. I am anxious that you should not quit the Lodge this evening without a competent knowledge of the ultimate reference of our proceedings; and for this purpose, though at the risk of being accounted tedious, I shall now give you a Lecture on our Tressel Board, which, added to what has been already said, will convey such a meed of instruction as will at least enable you to reflect without regret on the scene of your first introduction into a Masonic Lodge.'

"The Lecture was given in Bro. Inwood's best style," said the Square; "and when the Lodge was closed, the Brethren returned to their respective homes, delighted and edified with the instruction they had received from the Chair."

CALIFOR

CHAPTER XV.

LADY MASONS.—WILLIAM MEYRICK, JOSEPH SHADBOLT

1803—1810.

"——————Freemasonry
Is like the Ladder in the Patriarch's dream,
Its foot on earth, its height above the skies,
Diffus'd its virtue, boundless is its pow'r;
'Tis public health, and universal cure.
Of heavenly manna 'tis a second feast,
A nation's food, and all to every taste."—PRIOR.

"Kepe your rule. And then care not who se youre rule, who rede your rule, who knowe your rule. Rede it your selfe, knowe it your selfe, preche it, teche it, and openly shewe it. Be nothyng afrayd ne daungerous therof so ye fyrst kepe it and werke it."—RICHARDE WHYTFORDE. (m.cccc.xv.)

"Masonry is one of the most sublime and perfect institutions that ever was formed for the advancement of happiness and general good to mankind; creating, in all its varieties, universal benevolence and Brotherly love. It teaches us those useful, wise, and instructive doctrines upon which alone true happiness is founded; and at the same time affords those easy paths by which to attain the rewards of virtue; it teaches us the duties which we owe to our neighbour; never to injure him in any one situation, but to conduct ourselves with justice and impartiality; it bids us not to divulge the mystery to the public, and it orders us to be true to our trust, to be above all meanness and dissimulation, and in all our avocations to perform religiously that which we ought to do."—H. R. H. THE DUKE OF SUSSEX.

THE Square, being a primitive implement, exhibited at the building of Solomon's Temple, and used at a much earlier period, as no fine piece of architecture could be completed without its assistance,—my companion and instructor occasionally adduced Old World incidents and anecdotes in illustration of his historical and moral maxims; and he now broke off abruptly, to edify my mind by a simple anecdote of ancient times:— "When Eudamidas, the Lacedemonian general," he observed, "first saw Xenocrates, the philosopher, with a beard as white as snow, reaching below his girdle, he inquired of a friend who that venerable old man was. '*A wise man*,' was the reply, '*seeking after truth*.' The next question was, 'When does he calculate on reducing it to practice, after it is found, if he be still employed in the search?'

"The same may be said of those who defer the study of Freemasonry to a late period of life—they will have little time left to enjoy the benefit of its acquisition. Whoever is desirous of becoming a birght and active Mason, let him take advantage of the spring time of life, when ardent spirits predominate, and joy, and love, and hope unite to animate his soul to active enterprises, and fill it with genial aspirations."

After he had applied this little anecdote to his satisfaction, the Square gave a triumphant twirl, and then went quietly on.

"Bro. W. Meyrick," he said, "was elected R. W. M. of our Lodge on St. John's day, 1802, and proved an active and zealous Officer, and his services to Masonry, uniformly conceded for a series of years, elevated him at length to the proud distinction of Senior Warden in the Lodge of Reconciliation at the Union between the two sections, termed *ancient* and *modern* Masons, and Grand Registrar in the United Grand Lodge of England, after that event had restored perfect harmony to the English Craft.

"I was much pleased," the Square continued, "at his Installation Banquet or annual festival of the Lodge, with the brief, but very comprehensive manner in which he returned thanks for the handsome reception his name met with from the assembled Brethren, when his health was proposed by Bro. Inwood, the Past Master. I drew from it a favourable presentiment of what his government would be.

"'Brethren,' he said, 'I beg leave to return my best thanks for this additional mark of your esteem. Some years have now elapsed since I enjoyed the gratification of sitting with you at the festive board of Masonry. During that period, prejudices of long standing have yielded to the voice of truth. Like the dense vapours which darken the atmosphere, and obscure the face of the sun, they have been broken by a bright ray from the glory in the centre; they float before the reason as the light and impalpable clouds chequer the clear expanse of heaven, and will at length be wholly dissipated, and leave our science before the world's eye, clad in all its glories of wisdom, strength, and beauty. Permit me to offer, not only my thanks, but my best and most heart-felt wishes. As *men*, may you enjoy every happiness and prosperity this world can afford; as *Christians*, may you have peace in this world, and happiness in the next; as *Masons*, may you enjoy the intellectual supremacy which the science you profess is so well calculated to bestow; may your Brethren always speak as well of you in your absence as in your presence; may no slanderous tongues, like the assassins of Tyre, destroy your fair fame; may no cold-hearted envy efface in your breasts the excellent and invaluable precepts and principles imparted by our Lectures; may you practice morality and justice by the Square, equality by the Level, and integrity by the Plumb; like the Perfect Ashlar, may your mind be so true in all its feelings and propensities, as to be able to undergo the ordeal of the Square of God's word, and the Compass of your own conscience; that when death, the Grand Leveller of all human greatness, shall have drawn his sable curtain round your bed, you may receive possession of an immortal inheritance in those heavenly mansions veiled from mortal eye by the starry firmament, and be admitted by the Grand Master of the whole universe into His celestial Lodge, where peace, order, and harmony shall eternally reign.'

"During this period," the Square continued, "the true friends of masonic literature were neither few nor idle; and the beginning of the century was marked by several published Addresses and Sermons. The names of Samuel Oliver,[1] Killick, and Bryan,[2] Dr. Orme,[3]

[1] "A masonic Sermon, preached in St. John's Church, Peterborough, July 26th, 1802; being the day appointed for the Consecration of the Lodge of St. Peter within that city. By the Rev. S. Oliver, Chaplain of the same Lodge, Member of the Union Lodge, Nottingham, and Honorary Member of the Scientific Lodge, Cambridge. Cambridge, Nicholson, 1803."

[2] "Two masonic Addresses delivered in the Lodge of Freedom, Gravesend, Dec. 27, 1803; being the Anniversary of the Festival of St. John the Evangelist. By Brothers Killick and Bryan. London, Asperne, 1804."

[3] "A Sermon preached in the Church of Louth, at a Provincial Grand Meeting of Free and Accepted Masons, Aug. 13th, 1804. By

Stephen Jones,[4] and Hyppolita Da Costa,[5] were familiar to the London Craft, and their several productions were read to the Brethren as Lectures.

"Meantime our Lodge continued to prosper under the Mastership of Bro. Meyrick; and well it might, as you may judge from the part he took in an interesting conversation which occurred at a meeting when the Lodge was remarkably well attended, and in which his knowledge of the tendency of genuine Masonry became apparent to his hearers.

"He had been explaining the supporting pillars of the Lodge, in connection with the three rounds of the masonic Ladder, and concluded by saying—'The great and distinguishing principle on which Freemasonry is founded, as you all know, is Brotherly Love—a principle which was equally unknown both to Jews and heathens, either in youth or age. Many of the latter spent their whole lives in search of virtue, but without success, for they failed to discover the chief of all virtues—charity and love towards each other.'

"When the R. W. M. had concluded his Lecture, Bro. Shadbolt rose and said—'R. W. Sir, it strikes me that the sole reason why heathen nations did not practise the pre-eminent virtue of Brotherly Love, was, because they did not understand it. And hence when it was first brought practically under their notice by the early Christians, they expressed their surprise by asking one another whether they were acquainted with the mysterious link which cemented the Christians together, or the process by which they arrived at that display of mutual

the Rev. Thomas Orme, D.D., F.S.A., Prov. Grand Chaplain for the county of Lincoln. Louth, Sheardown, 1804."

[4] "A Vindication of Masonry." "Cursory Thoughts on the Masonic Institution; being part of a Letter addressed to the Author of the Illustrations of Masonry." "A Friendly Remonstrance to a skilful but over-zealous Mason." "A short Hint to the Fraternity at large." With many other orations and addresses by various Brethren. "Masonic Miscellanies in poetry and prose. In three parts. 1. The Muse of Masonry, comprising nearly two hundred masonic Songs, adapted to familiar tunes. 2. The Masonic Essayist. 3. The Freemason's Vade Mecum." By Stephen Jones, P. M. of the Lodge of Antiquity. London, 1797. Second Edition, 1811.

[5] "Narrative of his Persecution in Lisbon by the Inquisition, for the pretended crime of Freemasonry. By M. Hyppolita Joseph da Costa, Representative of the Portuguese Lodges in the Grand Lodge of England. 2 vols., 8vo. London, Sherwood, 1811."

love and charity which distinguished them from all people amongst whom they lived? And when the Emperor Decius commanded them to produce their treasures, they brought the lame, the blind, the diseased, the widows and fatherless children that were supported at the common expense of the Church, and said, These are our treasures; they are the only wealth which Christ bequeathed to His followers. The same may be said of Freemasonry, when practised in accordance with the doctrines enunciated in its Lectures.'

"'But if this view of the matter be correct,' Bro. Tegart observed, 'how are we to account for the instances that did actually occur, of such disinterested affection, both amongst Jews and heathens, as undoubtedly existed between David and Jonathan, Nysus and Euryalus, Damon and Pythias, and others in the same category?'

"'The solitary exceptions,' replied Bro. Meyrick, 'serve to make the rule more evident. *Exceptio probat regulam.* They did not occur once in a century; and in every recorded instance, the sentiment was not practised as a principle, but as a passion, seldom witnessed, little understood, and barren of fruits to the rest of mankind.'

"'True,' said Bro. Inwood; 'and this very observation places the system of Freemasonry in a new and beautiful point of view. That Sacred Volume which consecrates the Master's pedestal, and enlightens and sanctifies our proceedings, has its corresponding doctrines embodied in the Lectures.'

"'Otherwise,' the R. W. M. interposed, 'the Lectures would be inanimate, vapid, and useless. Our frequent appeals to the Grand Architect for favour and protection, display our firm belief in the Most High, whilst the first and third steps of the winding staircase are referred to the Trinity in Unity, both displaying our renunciation of the cold and repulsive principles of deism, which are clearly denounced in the Ancient Charges.'[6]

[6] In which it is distinctly provided that "a Mason is obliged by his tenure to believe firmly in the true worship of the eternal God, as well as in all those sacred records which the dignitaries and fathers of the Church have compiled and published for the use of good men; so that no one, who rightly understands the rite, can possibly tread in the irreligious path of the unhappy libertine, or be induced to follow the arrogant professors of atheism or deism; neither is he to

" 'And an evidence of the same truth,' said Bro. Hemming, 'is afforded in a series of tests that were used by the four old Lodges before the revival in 1717; a portion of which ran in this form:—'How many precious jewels has a Mason? Three; a square Ashlar, a diamond, and a square.—How many lights? Three; a right east, south, and west. What do they represent? Three divine persons; Father, Son, and Holy Ghost.—How many pillars? Two; Jachin and Boaz.—What do they represent? The Strength and Stability of the Church in all ages.—How many angles in St. John's Lodge? Four, bordering on squares, or a perfect cross.'

" 'And yet,' Bro. Inwood responded, 'strange to say, notwithstanding these distinct and unequivocal avowals, our opponents appear determined to make our Lodges so many nests to mature and disseminate the filthy dogmata of infidelity. Our protestations to the contrary they affect to disbelieve, in order that they may have the gratification of keeping up a kind of guerrilla war against us; for if they were deprived of that hackneyed objection, which has been refuted a thousand times over, they would have no excuse for the discharge of their splenetic diatribes against the Order.'

" 'The above representation,' said the R. W. M., 'shows their utter disregard of the plainest facts. It is well known that our rituals eschew every system of unbelief and false worship which are forbidden in the former portion of the Decalogue. The first lesson that a candidate receives at his initiation, teaches him never to pronounce the sacred name of God but with that reverential awe which becomes a creature to bear to his Creator; to look upon him as the Summum Bonum which we came into the world to enjoy, and to regulate all our pursuits according to that unerring principle. To act upon the square with our neighbours, by doing as we would be done by; and by avoiding all intemperance and excess,

be stained by the gross errors of blind superstition, but may have the liberty of embracing what faith he should think proper, provided at all times he pays a due reverence to the Creator, and deals with honour and honesty towards his fellow-creatures; ever making that golden precept of Christianity the standing rule of his actions, which engages him to do unto all men as he would have them do to him."—See the Ahiman Rezon, Ed. 1813, p. 18.

whereby we ourselves may be rendered incapable of following our work, or be led into any behaviour which is unbecoming to our laudable profession.'

"'This recommendation,' the R. W. M. continued, 'which is taken *verbatim* from the Lectures, forbids a breach of the third commandment. And the following examination questions equally evince our punctual observance of the fourth.—'Have you ever worked as a Mason? Where? How long?' 'Six days in the week.'—'And why not on the seventh?' 'Because the Almighty has strictly commanded that day to be kept holy.'—Nor has the latter portion of the Decalogue been overlooked in the construction of our very comprehensive system. The duty of children to their parents is taught by the Lewis. We are warned of the evil consequences and sin of murder by the remorse and punishment of certain Tyrian assassins, when the Temple at Jerusalem was completed; of adultery, by the O. B. of a M. M.; of covetousness and theft, by the four original Signs; of slander and false witness, by the Key; and of interfering with the property of others by the Moveable Jewels.'

"'But, notwithstanding the purity of these doctrines,' said Bro. M'Gillivray, 'which can neither be denied nor controverted, and their undoubted efficacy in promoting the practice of virtue and morality, it is to be lamented that they have not been of sufficient efficacy to prevent the sacred floor of the Lodge from being occasionally polluted by unworthy men.'

"'And for this cogent reason,' the R. W. M. replied, 'while such men outwardly comply with the letter of the Constitutions, we cannot pronounce sentence of expulsion against them; nor can they be subjected to censure without the clearest proof of some wilful violation of masonic law. Philip of Macedon, it is true, having two subjects whom he suspected of treason, ordered one of them, without any proof, to leave the country, and the other to follow him; but we have no law which decrees expulsion from a Lodge, without ample evidence of some determinate offence.'

"'This truth is illustrated,' Bro. Stephen Jones observed, 'in the conduct of the impostor Cagliostro, who conducted his masonic innovations with so much tact and judgment, as to steer clear of the laws then in force on the continent of Europe; for they were not sufficiently stringent to prevent the encroachments of designing empirics, and hence such characters became numerous and successful, both in France and Germany, and by their mercenary dealings brought great discredit on the Order.

"'The true principles on which Masons ought to govern their life and conduct,' the R. W. M. observed, 'are very simple, and plainly chalked out in the FIRST GREAT LIGHT, which, being the Tracing Board of the Most High, presents a perfect idea of the excellent plans and moral designs by which our commerce with the world ought to be regulated. Indeed, when we look at Freemasonry, and consider its antiquity, its usefulness, its vast aggregate of simple piety and unostentatious benevolence, its countless host of enthusiastic champions, its unburdensome support, its innumerable charitable institutions, we ought cordially to unite in the preservation of such a beneficent Order from the attacks of envious Cowans, when, like the wild boar out of the woods, they would break down its fences, and destroy its fruits.'

"'The SECOND GREAT LIGHT of Masonry,' the R. W. M. continued, 'is the Master's Jewel,'—exhibiting me," said the Square—"'and hence our ancient Grand Master, King Solomon, has left it on record, that the lips of knowledge are a precious Jewel.[7] And as its operative use is to bring rude matter into due form, so it is appropriated to the chief Officer and Ruler of the Lodge, as an allegorical emblem, suggestive of his numerous and paramount duties, and to indicate, that to preserve harmony among the Brethren, his chief care should be to suppress promptly and firmly, by the certain process of morality and justice, every attempt at insubordination, and to cause all animosities to cease, should any unfortunately exist, that order and good-fellowship may be perfect and complete.'

"'And R. W. Sir,' Bro. Inwood added, 'every conscientious Master, who consults his own credit equally with the reputation and stability of his Lodge, will emulate the qualities which are symbolized by the Square; and,

[7] Prov. xx., 15.

when judiciously exercised, they will add dignity to the office, and convey an influence which cannot fail to produce a salutary effect on the community under his jurisdiction, and elevate the Order to its proper rank in the opinion of mankind.'

"'Nor ought the THIRD GREAT LIGHT to be overlooked,' said Bro. Hemming, 'for without its assistance the expert architect could not complete his magnificent designs, or bring his plans to perfection. And hence it constitutes in Speculative Masonry the appropriate badge of the Grand Master, because the government of the entire Order is committed to his charge, and he is required, not only to be true and faithful, but, in the exercise of his office, to adopt such judicious plans and designs as may gradually and effectually advance its private interests and public popularity, and contribute to the general benefit of its Members, both in and out of the Lodge.'

"'This significant symbol,' Bro. Shadbolt observed, 'possesses, as I am inclined to think, a further and still more important reference. It should suggest to the Grand Master a due caution not to be biassed or led astray, by the advice of interested or injudicious friends, from that cause which his judgment pronounces to be the best adapted to promote the universal prosperity of the Craft; for not only in Masonry, but in every other institution, whether scientific or political, many councillors will arise, whose deliberations, like those of Achitophel, are influenced more by a regard to their own personal interests than the benefit of the Society which they profess to entertain an anxious desire to improve. In the words of Dryden, slightly altered,—

'To further this the charlatan enlists
The malcontents of all the separatists,
Whose differing parties he could wisely join,
For several ends to serve the same design,
He heads the faction while their zeal is hot,
And popularly prosecutes the plot.'

"'The Theological Virtues,' said Bro. Deans, 'which you, R. W. Sir, have so ably illustrated, and are so highly esteemed among Masons as to assume a prominent situation amongst our symbols, will admit, I venture to suggest, of a more extended illustration than is assigned to them in our Lectures; and I am sure the Brethren present would be gratified to hear your sentiments on that interesting subject.'

"The R. W. M. being thus appealed to," said the Square, "replied without hesitation, 'That their reference might be safely extended to other topics of the utmost consequence to the best interests of man on this side the grave, as preparatory to a more perfect state of existence in another and a better world. They may be likened to the Three Pillars of the Lodge, which point out the three ages of man, and the three prismatic colours, blue, purple, and crimson. The initiatory rite of baptism amongst Christians, and admission into the Lodge amongst ourselves, are symbolized by the White, as the representative of external purity, and internal truth, embodied in the Apron of lambskin—that animal being the personification of innocence. Blue, the colour of Faith, represents the First Degree, because it is an emblem of Creation, the first work of T. G. A. O. T. U., and hence, in the cosmogonies of all nations, the Creator is painted blue, in reference to his perfect wisdom.'

"'Purple, the colour of Hope,' continued Bro. Meyrick, 'denotes the Second Degree, as well as the second stage of life, and the Pillar of Strength. It was royal, and formed the usual clothing of kings and princes. Thus, Xenophon says in the "Cyropædia," that his royal hero was clad in a vest of a purple colour, half mixed with white. His outer robe was wholly of purple, and on his legs he had yellow buskins. This description naturally reminds us of the yellow jacket and blue breeches of our ancient Brethren. Purple was adopted as the colour of a Fellowcraft, which was the highest degree acquired by the Fraternity in ancient times, and even qualified a Brother for the office of Grand Master. It also referred to the middle stage of life, through which every one passess in his progress from infancy to old age, or from birth to death. This colour was placed on tombs in Christian symbolism, to illustrate the solemn doctrine—"*In the midst* of life, we are in death."'

"'Charity was represented by the Crimson or Rose, which is the colour of beauty, and belonged to the closing stage of human life, and the Third Degree of

Masonry. In the spurious Freemasonry of Greece and Rome, the rose was a symbol of death and resurrection, which were imitated in the ceremonies of initiation. And it was used by our Fraternity for much the same reason. An unfailing Charity is the ever-burning fire of the heart; and Freemasonry enlightens the mind of the candidate, by opening it to the influence of divine love, and instilling that degree of purity, which is the chief end of masonic regeneration.'

"'This combination,' the R. W. M. concluded, 'of the Three Degrees of Masonry, the Three Colours and Pillars of the Lodge, with the Three Ages of Man, will fairly place the Free and Accepted Mason, through the medium of Faith, Hope, and Charity, on his way to those celestial mansions which are veiled from mortal eye by a canopy of clouds; and if he shall continue in this effectual walk of Faith, he has a promise of shining like the stars for ever and ever.'

"'I should rather have been inclined to transpose these remarkable coincidences,' said Bro. Inwood, 'and make the infant to represent Beauty, the man Strength, and old age Wisdom.'

"'I had some conversation a short time ago,' said Bro. M'Gillivray, 'with a Hebrew Mason, who had been on the continent; and he informed me that his Brethren there reject and totally repudiate our application of Faith, Hope, and Charity, to Freemasonry, because they are the peculiar virtues of Christianity, and belong to no other system of religion that ever existed on the face of the earth. The staves or rounds of the Ladder, which we term innumerable, they limit to seventy-two. These, they say, refer to so many branches of science, over which JEHOVAH presides, because they all derive their essence from the Divine power. But they subjoin no account of its origin or symbolical use, and simply say that it is called by the allegorical cabalists l'Echelle de Jacob.'

"'The argument is evidently delusive,' replied Bro. Hemming; 'because, if that be the name which they assign to it, their explanation falls to the ground; for it cannot, in that case, have any other reference than to the Theological Ladder of our system of Freemasonry, which has the Holy Bible for its basis, Faith, Hope, and Charity for its supporters, Jehovah for its president, and Heaven for its end.'

"'The true masonic philosopher,' said the R. W. M., 'sees in all things an ever-present Deity, as the Governor and Director of those magnificent works which proceeded from His hand, all guided by the celestial dictates of these Theological virtues. If the trees of the field bud and blossom under the influence of a genial sun—if the teeming earth is irrigated with gentle showers—if

> 'Fleecy flocks the hills adorn,
> And valleys smile with wavy corn;'

it is the blessed ordinance of a benignant Divinity. If the great ruler of the day rise in the morning to call the inhabitants of the earth from their slumbers, and commence their labours—if the ruler of the night move majestically through the heavens, partially enlightening the darkness with her silver light, and dividing the year into twelve equal portions for the convenience of man;—if the stars and planets with which the firmament is studded, like an azure canopy charged with sparkling knobs of burnished gold, pursue their accustomed courses century after century without the slightest deviation—it is to display the power and goodness of the Great Architect, and His provident care in making all the works of the creation subservient to one object—the comfort and happiness of His creatures. And we ought reverentially to bow the knee, and exclaim with our Ancient Grand Master, "Lord, what is man that thou art mindful of him, or the son of man that thou visitest him?"'

"'Excellent!' said Bro. Tegart; 'this is the true poetry of Freemasonry, and an able illustration of the ordinary labours of a well-conditioned Lodge.'

"'But this is not all,' said Bro. Inwood. 'The R. W. M. will tell you that our labours and investigations extend also to many sublime branches of science and philosophy, human and divine, which admit of ample discussion under the care of a judicious and talented Master, when performing the paramount duty of his high station—the instruction and improvement of the Brethren in Masonry.'

"'It is quite true,' Bro. Hemming observed; 'and in the absence of such researches, Freemasonry will be but a name without a substance, and will fail to convey any peculiar benefits. Without a proper attention to its poetry and philosophy, the Lodge would sink to the level of an ordinary club-room, and the Brethren into mere members of a convivial society. And it may be for this reason that so many of the Fraternity appear to entertain an indifferent opinion of the Order, because their attention has not been drawn to these prominent beauties which are applicable to the best interests of man, whether in this world, or in that which is to come.'

"During the course of this discussion," the Square parenthetically observed, "Brothers Shelton and Marshall frequently cast a significant look at each other, in which weariness and dissatisfaction were combined; but they wisely held their peace.

"'The Free and Accepted Mason,' replied the R.W.M., 'who is really desirous of deriving benefit from the practice of Masonry, will never entertain any doubts respecting the intrinsic excellency of the lessons he receives in open Lodge, because doubt leads to despair, and despair to renunciation. Let him take a lesson from honest John Bunyan, who very judiciously makes the giant Despair the occupant of Doubting Castle, in which the pilgrims atoned for their doubts by imprisonment in one of its deepest dungeons. Hope, however, revived, and they opened the gates of the dreary cell with the Key of promise.'

"'The most effectual safeguard,' Bro. Inwood observed, 'against the encroachments of doubt, is prayer, which constitutes an essential element in the system of Freemasonry. Our Lodges are opened and closed with prayer; and the same holy exercise accompanies the ceremonies of every degree. And if the Mason hopes to attain the summit of the Ladder which terminates in the Cloudy Canopy, it must be by the prayer of Faith and Hope, and the exercise of Charity; for these are the only steps by which he can have access to the glories that lie beyond it, and lead to the regions of everlasting Light.'

"'And yet,' said Bro. Hemming, 'some of our adversaries contend that the Society is anti-Christian. But to mark more strongly the utter absurdity of the imputation, another class of opponents, with Professor Buhle at their head, assert that we exclude anti-Christians from our assemblies! His words, as we learn from a paper, read only last year before the Philosophical Society of Göttingen, are, '*Women, children, those who are not in full possession of civil freedom, Jews, anti-Christians, and Roman Catholics, are excluded from the Society of Freemasons.*'

"'So conflicting and unscrupulous,' the R. W. M. replied, 'are the assertions of all who decry Masonry, without understanding either what they say, or whereof they affirm. Freemasonry, however, furnishes a series of rules by which every true-hearted Brother may easily surmount the difficulties which impede his progress in the pursuit of knowledge. And if he adheres, amidst evil report and good report, to the precepts which are promulgated from the Master's Chair, and applies them steadily to his masonic and Christian duties, he will be at no loss to steer his course, be the vituperations of the Antimason ever so loud, or the conjectures of the cowan ever so absurd; and with the promised land in view, he will go on his way, rejoicing in the hope of attaining to its never-fading glories.'

"In the year 1808," the Square continued, "viz., on St. John's day, Bro. Shadbolt was installed into the Chair, and proved worthy of the honour conferred upon him. I remember an amusing conversation which took place in the Lodge on the subject of female Freemasonry, during his year of office, which may be interesting to you.

"In order to make it intelligible, you will observe that the Lodges of Adoption on the continent of Europe, which admitted females to share in the celebrations, resumed their meetings after the excitement occasioned by the French Revolution had subsided. On a notice to that effect issued by authority, the Members assembled in full force, the badges were furbished up or renewed with great alacrity, and the initiations were numerous. A Grand Festival of the Order was celebrated in Strasburg, over which the Empress Josephine presided; and another in Paris, under the presidency of the Duchesse de Vaudemont, which were attended by many of the chief nobility of France, both male and female.

"On the evening to which I have referred," said my entertaining instructor, "a visitor was introduced by Bro. M'Gillivray, who had been residing some time at Paris.

He informed us that he had attended several meetings of the Adoptive Masonry, and found them conducted with remarkable order and propriety.

"The R. W. M. asked him if he had witnessed an initiation?

"He replied, that he had enjoyed the good fortune of being present when each of the Five Degrees was conferred.

"'Do you recollect the names of the Degrees?' Bro. M'Gillivray inquired.

"'Perfectly. They are, 1. Apprentie. 2. Compagnone. 3. Maîtresse. 4. Parfait. 5. Eluc. Under this arrangement, the Jewel of the Order is a Golden Ladder, with five rounds or staves. Originally, however, the Androgyne Lodges had only Four Degrees, which were denominated l'Apprentissage, la Compagnonnage, la Maîtrise, and la Maîtrise parfaite; but this arrangement has been discontinued for many years.'

"'Are you at liberty,' said Bro. Meyrick, 'to communicate the ceremonies?'

"'I was allowed to witness them,' our intelligent visitor replied, 'without any injunctions of secresy; for I believe all Freemasons, who have passed the degree of a Fellowcraft, are eligible for admission.'

"'I am afraid,' Bro. Inwood suggested, 'that there must be some degree of indelicacy in the proceedings.'

"'Not the slightest, I assure you,' said the visitor. 'The ceremonies are conducted with the most laudable decorum. We are, of course, totally ignorant of the proceedings of the dark room, as none but females are admitted to that penetralia, and the preparations are conducted by females only. But when these are completed, and the trials of fortitude come on, the novice is conducted through the process by a lady and gentleman together.'

"'The lady candidates, I presume, are not subjected to any very severe tests,' Bro. S. Jones observed.

"'By my faith,' said the visitor earnestly, 'but you are mistaken. The trials they have to undergo would be sufficient to make many of our more robust sex tremble.'

"'Their powers of endurance, however,' Bro. Tegart observed, 'cannot be very strictly dealt with, or many of them would shrink from the infliction, and the number of initiations would be considerably reduced.'

"'On the contrary,' the visitor replied, 'their trials are urged to the severest extremity, and the novices endure them bravely. Occasionally, indeed, a timid female may faint during the harrowing process, and I am told it does sometimes happen. An anecdote is related of an event of this kind which occurred at the Revolution, just before the Lodges were closed.'

"'Which you will perhaps do us the favour to relate,' the R. W. M. interposed.

"'With the greatest pleasure,' our visitor replied. 'But to make the detail clearly intelligible, I ought first to inform you that the Adoptive Lodges are fitted up with scenery and machinery like a theatre prepared for one of our most complicated pantomimes. This being premised, you will have no difficulty in comprehending the following extraordinary scene.

"'A young lady, of somewhat irritable temperament, was introduced as a candidate for admission. During the preparatory examination, she exhibited a degree of nervous excitement, which attracted the observation of the Venerable, or R. W. M., and he asked her kindly whether she had any confidence in her own fortitude?'

"''I know,' she replied, 'that there is danger to be encountered; but I am not afraid of it.'

"''Not to deceive you in this matter,' responded the Venerable, 'I think it right to add that your person will be exposed to the most imminent perils; and if you feel any misgivings, it would be better for you to retire unscathed than to fail in courage and resolution; for if you should be so unfortunate as to shrink from the actual presence of danger, you will expose yourself to the contempt and derision of the Lodge.'

"''You insult me by your doubts,' said the lady; 'exhibit your terrors, and see if I shall blanch under them.'

"'She was accordingly conducted through all the usual trials of fortitude, and endured them with the courage of a martyr; and even at last, when placed on the summit of the symbolical mountain, and told that she must cast herself down from thence into the abyss below, where she saw a double row of bright steel spikes, long and sharp.'

"'Mimic spikes, of course,' interposed Bro. Inwood.

"'No, indeed,' said the stranger; 'they were real, substantial spikes, that would have killed a horse, if he should have been impaled thereon. The word was given to throw herself down, and, with a suppressed shriek, she made the required plunge; and so unexpectedly sudden was her obedience, that the *Frère terrible*, or guide, who had charge of the machinery, was scarcely allowed time to touch the spring, before she fell recumbent at the bottom of the abyss.'

"'Poor creature! What became of her?' asked Bro. Inwood, highly interested.

"'You shall hear. The machinery is so contrived, that, at the very moment when the final leap is taken, the scene changes to an Elysium of green fields and shady trees, bubbling fountains and purling streams; and beneath the velvet herbage is placed a bed of the softest down, to receive the fair body of the exhausted novice as she falls. In the present case the lady fainted, and lay for a time without motion; but she was soon restored and tranquillized by the application of essences and perfumes, and the soft and soothing influence of delicious music. Being afterwards introduced into the Lodge, her constancy was rewarded by witnessing, and forming a part of, one of the most beautiful and captivating scenes I ever beheld.'

"'You mean the Lodge, I presume,' said Bro. M'Gillivray.

"'I do. And my description, I am afraid, will do it imperfect justice. Imagine a lofty room of ample dimensions, magnificently fitted up and decorated; the richly-ornamented walls adorned with a profusion of costly pictures in massive gilt frames, and garlands of sweet-smelling flowers; and at either end of the room superb mirrors reaching from the ceiling to the floor; the hangings of crimson velvet and gold; statues and busts disposed in convenient situations; the floor covered with a rich Turkey carpet; and the room brilliantly lighted by cut-glass chandeliers. The R. W. M., or Venerable, and the Grand Maîtresse occupy two gorgeous thrones in the east, and the sisters, alternately with well-dressed men, are seated around, uniformly habited in pure white robes, relieved by aprons and scarfs in sky blue, from which jewels of gold are suspended; and they are crowned with bouquets of roses.

"'Imagine all this, and still it will be impossible to understand the effect which this brilliant scene produces in the mind. It almost realizes the luxurious description of the palace of pleasure in the groves of Shadaski, by which the merchant Abudah was ensnared.'

"'The French ladies are, of course, enchanted with Freemasonry,' Bro. Crespigny observed.

"'Why, to say the truth,' the stranger replied, 'there are but few that embrace the opportunity. A vast majority of the women are pefectly indifferent to initiation and all its privileges; and even those who have been admitted, are very remiss in their attendance except on occasions where some extraordinary excitement is anticipated—as a gala, an initiation, a ball, or some other species of amusement that is in character with the anomaly of Lady Masons. And some who have evinced a feverish anxiety, before their admission, to know the secrets, have professed themselves grievously disappointed. I am acquainted with an instance of this kind, which is not uninteresting.'

"'And no secret, I presume,' said the R. W. M.

"'By no means,' our entertaining visitor replied. 'An English young lady of good family, residing at Paris, received the addresses of a French gentleman with the concurrence of her parents. Matters had been satisfactorily arranged; and as they sat together on the sofa, he pressed her to name the happy day.'

"''If you would but give up that nasty Masonry,' she listlessly replied, 'you should have my permission to name it yourself.'

"''Or admit you into the Lodge,' he suggested.

"''Ah,' she sighed, 'that is a different affair. If that could be accomplished indeed——'

"''We'll see what can be done,' he replied.

"''Well, Adolphe,' she eagerly responded, 'if you can manage *that*,—why then'—she hesitated.

"''Then what?' the gentleman asked.

"''Why, then, I promise that the marriage shall be solemnized within a week.'

"''Agreed,' said the gratified lover, 'you shall be made a Mason this very night.' And he left her to arrange the necessary preparations.

"'In the evening he escorted her to the Lodge-room, and she was formally initiated by the celebrated Madame Vaudencourt, assisted by the Venerable of the Lodge of St. Caroline, and permitted to ascend even to the third step of the Adoptive Ladder; was invested with the symbolical apron and sash; intrusted with the signs, tokens, and words; and after having heard from the orator the usual explanations of the antiquity (?), the nature and design of the Institution, the banquet was introduced, and our curious novice was instructed in the mystical signification of the cabalistic words—*red oil, trim your lamp, snuff your lamp, lift up by fire, &c.*; which being uttered by a sweet and musical voice, possess an indescribable charm, of which those who have not heard it can form no adequate idea.'

"'I have no doubt but your fair friend was immensely gratified,' said Bro. Crespigny.

"'You shall hear,' replied the visitor. 'The next morning our eager lover called on his affianced bride early, impatient to receive her thanks and congratulations for procuring her such an unexpected treat. But in answer to his inquiry how she liked Freemasonry, she only exclaimed, in a tone of voice resembling the whine of a noble hound, which receives a smart cut of the whip instead of the expected crust—'L—a—w! Adolphe! and is this a—ll?'

"''All! To be sure it is. What more did you expect?'

"''If that is really all,' she continued, in a listless tone of voice; 'I half repent my promise; for although the *tout ensemble* is very beautiful—as a show—I confess I am woefully disappointed.'

"''Why, what in the name of wonder could you hope to see? Grinning goblins—speaking pictures—or statues weeping blood? Or did you expect any magical performances—evoking spirits, or raising the dead?'

"''Be quiet, Adolphe,' the lady pettishly replied, 'and do not be ridiculous. I can't tell you what I expected. All I can say is—that it is unsatisfactory Heigho! If this be *all*—you will be at liberty to attend the Lodge at your pleasure; but for myself—I shall go no more.'

"'What a practical lesson does this anecdote furnish,' said Bro. Meyrick, 'to those cowans who affect to term the exclusion of females from the celebrations of Masonry a blot in our escutcheon!'

"'Aye,' replied Bro. Tegart, 'and I believe every genuine Englishwoman would exhibit the same noble feeling, if she were to be forced into Masonry. It is not to her taste.'

"'She would be more agreeably employed,' said Bro. Simpson, 'in making shirts for her husband, or puddings for her children; or in pickling walnuts and preserving plums.'

"'A Frenchwoman,' Bro. Tegart resumed, without attending to Bro. Simpson's homely remark, 'may be pleased with such frippery, and gratified by the adulation and subserviency which accompanies it; but our countrywomen look forward to the more rational pursuits and amusements of their sex; to the pleasure of domestic happiness, surrounded by their beloved children; to the delights which flow from the practice of Christian benevolence; visiting the sick; relieving the distressed; comforting the afflicted; and last, though not least, of superintending the morals of their poor neighbours, and crowning their humble dwellings with industry and content; practising, in a word, all the moral duties of Masonry, without being troubled with its details. This is the glorious career of an Englishwoman, which she would not barter for all the Masonry in Christendom, if it were freely offered for her acceptance. Nor can I be led to believe that if Freemasonry were thrown open to the females of this land to-morrow, any educated or respectable woman would consent to be a candidate for initiation.'

"'I am acquainted with a lady,' said Bro. M'Gillivray, 'who knows all the signs, words, and tokens of the First Degree, having, I am sorry to say, been enlightened by her husband, at the expense of his O. B.; but she is a woman of honour, and makes no use of the information, but to astonish young candidates of her acquaintance, by giving them the grip, and whispering in their ear the E. A. P. word; which proves clearly that a woman is capable of keeping a secret; for I am confident that she has never betrayed it to any person of her own sex, or to a man who had not been previously initiated.'

"'But we are all this while waiting to hear the ceremonial described,' said Bro. Simpson.

"The visitor hesitated," said the Square, "and the R. W. M. came to the rescue, by saying,—'Come, come, Bro. Simpson, I think it will be unfair to press our worthy Brother too far. I can easily conceive, although he may be under no particular injunctions of secresy, that it would be repugnant to the feelings of a conscientious man to reveal what he honestly believes ought, in strict justice and propriety, to be kept secret. Let us not, therefore, pry too narrowly into the recondite mysteries of our fair sisters; but show by our conduct that—

'We are true and sincere,
And just to the fair,
Who will trust us on any occasion;
No mortal can more
The ladies adore,
Than a Free and an Accepted Mason.'"

CHAPTER XVI.

THE SCHISM HEALED.—DR. HEMMING.

1810—1813.

"———The grand debate,
The popular harangue, the tart reply,
The logic, and the wisdom, and the wit,
And the loud laugh—I long to know them all,—
I burn to set the imprisoned wranglers free,
And give them voice and utterance again."
COWPER.

"Take care always to choose a good president; and then follow your leader. An army of stags is more to be feared under the command of a lion, than an army of lions led by a stag."—OLD PROVERB.

"Lo! see from Heav'n the peaceful dove
With olive-branch descend;
Augustus shall with Frederic join
All rivalry to end;
And taught by their fraternal love,
Our arms and hearts shall intertwine,
The Union to approve."
GLEE, *sung at the Union.*

"SINCE the revival of Freemasonry at the death of Sir Christopher Wren," the Square continued, "every consecutive period has been enlightened by the lucubrations of some intelligent expositor, whose suggestions have received the sanction of the Grand Lodge, and increased the value of masonic literature. The laudable exertions of Desaguliers, Anderson, and Bathurst (who was Grand Master of the York Masons), were followed up by Brothers Oakley, Martin Clare, Cole, and Dermott (ancient), Entick, Calcott, Bagnall, Dunckerley, Hutchinson, Thompson, Smith, Noorthouck, Preston, Jones, and Inwood, all well-known names amongst the Fraternity, and many others, whose writings have adorned the Order, and whose lives have been a running commentary on their works.

"I do not enumerate these brilliant masonic characters," said the Square, "for the purpose of conveying an idea that they stand alone in their several periods as the renovators and pillars of the Craft, because their cotemporaries were numerous and active. These are merely the worthy band of Brothers, to whom at different periods the sanction or countenance of the Grand Lodge was extended as an encouragement to their activity, and an incitement to their zeal in augmenting and displaying the capabilities of Masonry, that it might proceed in its onward march in a line parallel with social and scientific improvement, and prevent the Society from falling back on the moral and intellectual darkness of unrecorded times.

"Such were the observations of Dr. Hemming," said the Square, "when he was elevated to the chair of the Lodge on St. John's day, 1811; and he pursued the same train of thought at great length, to the edification of several eminent scientific Brethren who were present on the occasion. He proved to be an excellent Master, and ever attentive to his duties in the Lodge; strict, even to severity, in his discipline, and watchful over the conduct of his officers in the punctual and orderly performance of their respective functions.

"During this year, a noble and learned peer of the realm was proposed as a candidate for initiation; and our R. W. M. performed the ceremony with such seriousness and effect, as produced a genial impression on his lordship's mind; and when in due course he was raised to the sublime degree of a Master Mason, Dr. Hemming subjoined the following apposite remarks to the Prestonian Charge:—

"'As the foundation-stone of every magnificent edifice,' he said, addressing the newly-raised Brother, 'is usually deposited at the north-east angle of the building, so you, my Lord and Brother, as a masonic postulant, when you had taken your first degree, were placed in the same situation, because you then represented the foundation-stone of a new masonic structure, which, it is hoped, you will beautify and adorn with the rich materials of Wisdom, Strength, and Beauty. In this sense, the degree which was then conferred upon you, represents the outer court of the Tabernacle of Moses, and the court of the Gentiles in the Temple at Jerusalem; for in either case the uncircumcised could penetrate no further. A similar disposition prevailed in the early ordinances of Christianity; for penitents were only allowed to seat themselves in the *atrium*, outside the western portico of the church.

"'Again,' the R. W. M. continued, 'your lordship will do well to observe another extraordinary coincidence. The Rite or Sacrament of Baptism, which introduced the penitent into the nave of the Church, corresponding with the privilege that enabled a Jew to enter into the second division of the Tabernacle or Temple, is represented by the Degree of a Fellowcraft, which qualifies the candidate to enter into the Holy Place, and be invested with the highest honours and privileges of Masonry; and as this part of the Tabernacle was called Holy, so the advanced Mason is said to stand on Holy Ground. It was denominated by St. Paul a worldly sanctuary; and, therefore, at this step of your progress, you became eligible for instruction in worldly knowledge, and received the rudiments of scientific acquirement. You were taught the elements of the seven liberal sciences, including geometry, with its application to architecture, which may be said to constitute the secular design of the Order, in which your name has now been fully enrolled.'

"'But it is only when a Mason has been raised to the Third Degree, that he can form an accurate judgment of the real tendency of our mysterious Association. Up to this point, all has been preliminary, and consequently superficial. But now the whole scheme of Masonry becomes revealed to the enlightened eye of the Master Mason. Like the High Priest of Israel entering the S. S. of the Tabernacle and Temple, he beholds, with steady gaze, the Shekinah of glory;—like the perfect Christian admitted to communion with his God and Saviour, he enters the Church Triumphant, and beholds insuperable things, which it is not lawful for him to reveal; and, like St. Paul in the third heaven, he hears unspeakable words, which to utter would be death.'

"At this period," the Square continued, "the conduct of the Athol Masons formed the all-absorbing subject of conversation throughout the entire Craft, and the unpopularity of the schism was every day increasing. I remember very well—it was about the year 1755—that Dr. Manningham, our R. W. M., attended a Lodge at the Ben Jonson's Head, for the purpose of ascertaining, by ocular demonstration, the practices of certain Brethren meeting there, which had become objects of suspicion amongst the regular Craft. It had been publicly announced that this Lodge was principally composed of *ancient* Masons, though under the *modern* constitution, and that *some of the Brethren had been on the continent, and had witnessed extraordinary manifestations in ancient Masonry in some of the foreign Lodges,* which it had been agreed by the Members to practise on every third Lodge night there.[1]

"It was at one of these privileged meetings that our R. W. M. offered himself as a visitor; and holding the high office of D. G. M., he could not decently be refused admission, although many other Masons had already suffered the disappointment of exclusion from these mysterious celebrations. Dr. Manningham did not assert his right to occupy the chair as D. G. M., but consented to take his place as the R. W. M. of his Lodge.

"The business went on, and we found ourselves in a new atmosphere, which presented much that we were at a loss to comprehend; and Dr. Manningham at length ascertained, by repeated examinations—and his questions were answered with evident reluctance—that this pretended ancient Masonry consisted of nothing more than a reconstruction of Ramsay's Royal Arch, adapted by the genius of Craft Masonry, the principal feature of which was a transfer of the real Landmarks of a Master Mason to a new degree, unknown to the Fraternity before the date of this unnatural schism.

"Dr. Manningham expressed, in very strong terms, his uncontrollable surprise at this discovery; and told the Brethren plainly that they were practising an imposition on the public. While taunting the constitutional Masons with using a *modern* system, he said, and tampering with the old Landmarks, they themselves were distinguished by an apparatus which could not substantiate an antiquity of more than ten or a dozen years; and were making fearful havoc with the Landmarks, by subdivid-

[1] See the Ahiman Rezon, p. xii., Ed. 1813.

ing the Third Degree into two separate and distinct portions, to lend a sanction to the new and untenable doctrine that Freemasonry consists of four Degrees; the latter of which, called the Holy Royal Arch, was conferred upon no Brother who could not prove himself to be well-versed in the three preceding Degrees,[2]—a very unstable foundation to support the fiction of an ancient establishment.

"After making these wholesale innovations," the Square continued, "Lawrence Dermott, the then Grand Master, boasted that 'Ancient Masonry contains everything valuable amongst the moderns, *as well as many other things that cannot be revealed without additional ceremonies.*' And again, 'a person made in the modern manner, and not after the ancient custom of the Craft, *has no right to be called Free and Accepted,* according to the intent and meaning of the words.' And further, that '*the number of Ancient Masons abroad, compared with the moderns,* prove the universality of the old Order, &c., &c.'[3]

"Now," said the Square, "the offensive appellation of *moderns* was inflicted on the original body by the seceders, because, in the year 1740, the Grand Lodge, in order to detect these impostors, as I heard Bro. Noorthouck explain from the Chair when he was R. W. M. of our Lodge, and debar them and their abettors from the countenance and protection of the regular Lodges, made a slight but unimportant variation in the established forms. This afforded a subterfuge at which the refractory Brethren eagerly grasped. They at once, and invidiously, assumed the distinctive appellation of *Ancient Masons,* and stigmatized the constitutional Brethren with the title of *moderns.* This artifice served to strengthen their party; the uninformed were readily caught by the specious deception; and in an age when thousands of people assembled together with the firm belief that they were about to see a man inclose himself in a quart bottle, we need scarcely wonder that a few persons should believe in the plausible fiction that a knot of expelled Members constituted the original Society, and the Brethren who discarded them were the innovators. And the boldness and pertinacity by which the plea was

[2] Ahiman Rezon, p. 113. [3] Ibid., p. xix.

urged, ultimately secured the adhesion of the Sister Grand Lodges of Scotland and Ireland.

"And what was this variation," the Square inquired, "which produced such important results? Why, I'll tell you in the words of Bro. Daniell. 'I would beg leave to ask,' he said, 'whether two persons standing in the Guildhall of London, the one facing the statues of Gog and Magog, and the other with his back towards them, could, with any degree of propriety, quarrel about their situation, as Gog must be on the right of one, and Magog, on the right of the other?' Such, then, and far more insignificant, was the alteration complained of, and bore not the slightest comparison with the wholesale mangling of the Third Degree, that had been perpetrated by the Brethren who had adopted the style of *Ancient Masons.*

"At the ensuing Grand Lodge, Dr. Manningham communicated the above-mentioned irregularities, and stated his opinion that immediate measures ought to be adopted to discountenance the schism, as he considered it to be an open and gratuitous insult on the Grand Master and the whole Fraternity. After a short debate, in which there was scarcely a difference of opinion, it was unanimously resolved, 'That the meetings of Brethren, under any denomination of Masons, other than as Brethren of this our ancient and honourable Society of Free and Accepted Masons, is inconsistent with the honour and interest of the Craft, and a high insult on our Grand Master, and the whole body of Masons.'[4]

"The D. G. M. then moved, and it was agreed to unanimously, that the consideration of the irregular proceedings of the said Brethren be postponed till the next Quarterly Communication, that a thorough sense of their misconduct, and a determination not to be guilty of the like for the future, may induce them to acknowledge their transgression, and reconcile them to the Grand Lodge.

"But, alas!" the Square apostrophized, "the scheme was too promising to be hastily abandoned. Instead of confessing their fault, the seceding Brethren openly defied

[4] Minutes of Grand Lodge, March 20, 1755. See also Noorth. Const., p. 264.

the power of the Grand Lodge; and, therefore, at the succeeding Quarterly Communication, it was ordered 'that, as the delinquents persisted in their disobedience the Lodge, No. 94, held at Ben Jonson's Head, in Pelham street, Spitalfields, be erased from the list of Lodges, and that such of the Brethren thereof as shall continue those irregular meetings, shall not be admitted as visitors in any Lodge under the Constitution of England.'[5]

"Lawrence Dermott," the Square continued, "was an intelligent fellow, and cared very little for the above denunciation. He proceeded to form a Grand Lodge of his own, elected himself its Grand Master, and performed, without the slightest hesitation, all the functions of an independent body, granting warrants, and exacting fees, with all imaginable coolness; and his imposition was more successful than those of many of the continental innovators, for it enjoyed a supremacy, although not unquestioned, of seventy years' continuance; and, which appears still more strange, his Royal Arch Degree was ultimately adopted by our own Grand Lodge, and formally incorporated into the system, with this essential difference, however, that while the schismatics declared, in their Book Constitutions, that ancient Masonry consists of Four Degrees, the Constitutional Grand Lodge retained the primitive tradition, that Freemasonry contains Three Degrees only, including the Royal Arch.[6]

"At the very beginning of the nineteenth century," the Square continued, "viz., in November, 1801, a charge of a very serious nature was exhibited in Grand Lodge, by Bro. Daniell, S. W. of the Grand Stewards' Lodge, who had been complimented by authority, as a reward for his activity and zeal, with the title of *Defender of the ancient rights and privileges of Masonry*, against Thomas

[5] Minutes of Grand Lodge, July 24, 1755.

[6] The difference between ancient and modern, when divested of all technicalities, was simply this:—The modern, so called by the innovators, retained the original system, consisting of three degrees, in all its integrity; the ancient, so called by themselves, mutilated the third degree, by dividing it into two parts, and pronounced in the Book of Constitutions that *genuine Ancient Masonry consists of four degrees*. They boasted of the sanction of the Grand Lodge at York but I never heard that that Grand Lodge extended its countenance to them; and, indeed, if that assertion had been true, why did they establish a Grand Lodge of their own?

Harper, a D. G. M. of the adverse party, and others, for patronizing and becoming principals in a Society calling themselves Ancient Masons, and acting in direct violation of the laws of the regular Grand Lodge.

"When the complaint was heard, Bro. Harper, pursuant to a summons which had been served upon him, appeared personally; and, in the joint names of himself and his associates, read a rambling defence, in Cromwellian style, which failed either to disprove or justify the charge, and was rather calculated to display the gullibility of mankind, than to exculpate himself. Taking advantage of the Hudibrastic aphorism, that

> '——— the pleasure is as great
> Of being cheated as to cheat,'

he converted the principle to his own advantage, and found it rather a successful ruse. But Bro. Daniell, in his reply, dissipated all his arguments, and substantiated the original accusation by new facts, drawn from Bro. Harper's own defence. He practically applied the above principle by a humorous allusion to the passage, and pursued his illustrations by quoting a few additional lines from the same inimitable burlesque. 'Some with a noise,' he said, amidst loud peals of laughter—

> 'Some with a noise, and greasy light,
> Are snapt, as men catch larks by night;
> Ensnar'd and hamper'd by the soul,
> As nooses by the leg catch fowl.
> Some with a med'cine and receipt,
> Are drawn to nibble at the bait;
> And tho' it be a two-foot trout,
> 'Tis with a single hair pulled out.

'As for Bro. Harper's arguments,' he continued, '*valeant quantum*—there they are—take them for what they are worth—I myself attach no value whatever to them.'

"It was at length resolved, that the laws of Masonry shall be strictly enforced against the offenders unless they promptly withdraw their countenance from the irregular assemblies.

"This resolution having been carried by a very large majority, Bro. Harper threw himself on the mercy of the Grand Lodge, and requested time to consult his officers, which, he said, if the Grand Lodge would be considerate enough to grant, he pledged his honour that he would use all his influence to secure their consent to a reunion of the two sections, and promised to furnish a definite answer at the next Quarterly Communication.

"After this solemn declaration," continued the Square, "the Grand Master, H. R. H. the Prince Regent, felt so certain, that the seceding Brethren would be no longer contumacious, but, like the repenting prodigal, would return to their allegiance with olive branches in their hands, and *peccavimus* in their mouths, that he instructed his A. G. M., the Earl of Moira, to form a committee, with ample powers to receive the erring Brethren with all honour, and bring them back into the fold. And that noble Brother publicly declared, when reporting the Constitution of his committee, that *his heart was devoted to the work*, and that he would use every means in his power to bring it to a satisfactory termination.

"The Fraternity throughout England participated in the enthusiasm of the A. G. M., and were animated with the same hope. Our P. G. Chap., Bro. Inwood, wrote a congratulatory epistle to Bro. Daniell on the subject, in which he expressed his unfeigned pleasure at hearing 'that a union of the two masonic Societies is likely to be accomplished through the medium of our highly amiable and talented A. G. M.; and,' he continued, 'it will impeach the character of any Brother in either division, who shall cast an impediment in the way, which may obstruct such a measure of peace and harmony; for it will prove an hindrance to the growth of brotherly love, and subvert all the genial and beneficial effects which arise, not only from the principles of Masonry, but also from those of our most holy religion.

" 'My hearty wish and sincere desire is,' Bro. Inwood continued, 'that the contemplated union may be speedily effected; that the masonic Temple of universal love and concord may raise its beautiful head, not only above all opposition of those who are unacquainted with its excellences, but also that all its avenues of brotherly love may be occupied by Brethren of one heart and one mind, all aiming, according to the true painciples of masonic union, to love each other with a pure heart fervently, that the gazing world, admiring to see how we Brethren love, may anxiously desire to increase our numbers, and our means of doing good.'

"Notwithstanding all these favourable anticipations," said the Square, "the negotiation signally failed. Bro. Harper's influence was not exerted to restore peace and order to the Fraternity, in redemption of his pledge, nor was his answer delivered at the Quarterly Communication; and, therefore, he was again summoned, more than once or twice, to appear before the Grand Lodge, and show cause why he should not be expelled, but without effect. His contumacy being thus clearly established, and his irregularities undenied, the Grand Lodge, after much forbearance, proceeded to more vigorous measures; and, on the 9th day of February, 1803, the A. G. M. being on the throne, and between three and four hundred Brethren present, the matter was discussed *seriatim;* and after a debate, if it can be properly called a debate where all the speakers are of one opinion, Bro. Harper's conduct was unanimously pronounced to be altogether unjustifiable; and the following resolutions were passed *nem. con.:*—

" 'Resolved, that the said Thomas Harper be expelled the Society, for countenancing and supporting a set of persons, calling themselves Ancient Masons, and holding Lodges in this Kingdom without authorization from H. R. H. the Prince of Wales, the Grand Master duly elected by this regular Grand Lodge.

" 'Resolved also, that this resolution be inserted in the printed accounts of the Grand Lodge, to prevent the said Thomas Harper from gaining admittance into any regular Lodge.

" 'And it was further resolved, that, whenever it shall appear that any Masons, under the Constitution of this Grand Lodge, shall in future attend or countenance any of the Lodges or meetings of persons calling themselves Ancient Masons, under the sanction of any person claiming to be Grand Master of England, and not duly elected by this Grand Lodge, the laws of the Society will be strictly enforced against them, and their names will be sent to the several Lodges under the Constitution of England."[7]

"These decisive resolutions," continued the Square, "operated on the adverse faction very powerfully; and many private Lodges, under the Athol system, trans-

[7] Minutes of Grand Lodge, Feb. 9, 1803.

mitted their spurious charters to our Grand Lodge, requesting that they might be exchanged for regular warrants under the Constitution of England, which was uniformly complied with, free of expense.

"Exasperated by these proceedings, which the principal leaders of the Athol section incorrectly attributed to the original motion on the subject made by Bro. Daniell, they resolved to punish him for the consequences of their own delinquency; and for that purpose they committed a furious onslaught on his pet Lodge, which was then in the height of its popularity; and I have heard Bro. Daniell assert that its numerous initiations had yielded upwards of a thousand pounds in Grand Lodge fees; and its finances were so flourishing, that no member was ever permitted to apply to the fund of benevolence for pecuniary assistance, but was invariably relieved with sums ranging from five to twenty pounds out of its own charitable fund. It was called the Royal Naval Lodge of regular Freemasons, held at their own hall, Burr street, near the Tower. The Brethren held their general assembly on the first Wednesday in every month, and a masonic council every Sunday evening, from six to ten o'clock.

"I do not approve of Sunday evening councils," said the Square parenthetically, "but they were of very common occurrence in those days, both in London and the provinces, and excited neither attention nor remark from the public in general. They have now been judiciously replaced by Lodges of Instruction, meeting on a more appropriate day.

"It was against this Lodge," the Square continued, "that Bro. Harper and his colleagues fulminated an anathema in the shape of a circular forwarded to all their 350 Lodges, in these words:—'W. Sir, and Brethren,—Beware of certificates with the following inscription engraven under an arch at the top, viz., *Lodge No. 57. of the most ancient and honourable Society of Free and Accepted Masons of all England, according to the old Constitutions.* We have no such Lodge, nor ever had any uch under our Constitution. These certificates are, in other respects, an imitation and piracy, taken from our Grand Lodge certificates. It has become necessary to guard you against imposition and the designs of those who, to gratify the ambition of some, or cover the nefarious practices of others, are most sedulously employed to destroy your existence as a Lodge. Signed, Robert Leslie, G. Sec.'

"Bro. Daniell was the R. W. M. of the Royal Naval Lodge at that time, and the last man in the world to submit quietly to such an insult. He, therefore, replied to this fierce attack by taking the bull by the horns, and determined to fathom the very bottom of the mystery by making the Duke of Athol an actual party to the proceeding. For this purpose he published, and circulated extensively, a pamphlet of more than a hundred pages, in the form of an address to the Duke of Athol, in whose name, and under whose authority, all the abovementioned acts were committed.[8] It was written in flowing language, and exhibited a series of stubborn facts, which were calculated to excite his grace's attention, and dispose him to listen to the pressing solicitations of the writer for an union of their mutual interests, in order to promote the general peace and prosperity of the Craft at large.

"'The Grand Lodge of England,' he said, 'were ready to receive their Brethren with open arms, to register them free of expense, and to let them hold their funds sacred to their own widows and children; or in such manner as a committee, composed of an equal number of Brethren from both the discordant sections, might decide.

"'That your grace,' he continued, 'may proceed on the information of higher and more respectable authority

[8] "Masonic Union. An Address to his Grace the Duke of Athol on the subject of an Union between the Masons that have lately assembled under his Grace's sanction, and the regular Masons of England, of which H. R. H. George, Prince of Wales, is the Grand Master. To which is added an Appendix, containing authentic sources of masonic information, compiled from ancient records; with an Account of the Grand Patrons and Officers of the Grand Lodge from time immemorial to the present period; and a correct list of all the regular Lodges under the sanction of the ancient Grand Lodge of all England. Also, an account of a projected Union lately commenced between the Grand Lodges of Scotland and England, by means of the Right Hon. the Earl of Moira, A. G. M. With invaluable extracts from Inwood's 'Masonic Sermons.' By a Member of the Fraternity. London, printed by J. Shaw, Whitefriars; published by Asperne, Cornhill; and sold by Symonds, Paternoster Row; Hatchard, Piccadilly, and others; and may be had of the Tylers of Lodges, and all Booksellers in Town and Country."

than that of a humble individual like myself, I rejoice to have it in my power to name the Right Hon. the Earl of Moira, whose knowledge of Masonry is equalled only by the goodness of his heart.

"'Under all these circumstances,' he concluded," said the Square, "'can it be supposed that you, my lord, as a regular Mason, when you are informed of the origin of the Institution, which I am fully persuaded that you have hitherto patronized from the purest motives; can it, I say, be supposed that you, or any other nobleman, would lend his name to support or countenance a society, however praiseworthy its motives may appear, which holds its meetings in direct violation of the laws of the original establishment, and the government of the Fraternity? No, my lord, your public character is too well known—your zeal for the welfare of the country is too manifest—and your attachment to the royal family too deeply rooted to admit of wilful deviation. Therefore, my lord, I trust your feelings coincide with my own, and that you really conceive what honour, what peculiar satisfaction, and what heartfelt pleasure it would give you, to bring that society, which you have lately patronized, under the royal banner.'

"This address," continued the Square, "did not fail to produce the intended effect on the mind of the noble duke, as I shall soon have the pleasure of recording; and I have related these anecdotes for the purpose of showing that the attention of our masonic rulers was now more particularly directed to the question of extinguishing the schism, which, like a tower built on sand, was tottering to its fall. The time was rapidly approaching when the delusion should be unmasked; and our R. W. M. was a party to the detection of the imposture. A hope was confidently entertained that the re-admission of the seceders into the pale of genuine Masonry, by the mediation of mutual friends, would be speedily accomplished; although few were acquainted with the particular process by which so desirable a result was to be effected.

"I have already told you," said the Square, "that a committee had been appointed, consisting of several distinguished members of the Grand Lodge, of which the Earl of Moira was president; and his lordship declared, after accepting that appointment, that if he was fortunate enough to secure the great object of a coalition between the two parties, he should consider the day in which it was ratified and confirmed to be one of the most brilliant of his life.

"The first preliminary step towards the readmission of the refractory Brethren, for they still openly resisted every overture towards a compromise, and even continued to pursue aggressive measures against the regular Lodges, was taken by the A. G. M. on the 30th of November, 1803, at the festival of the Grand Lodge of Scotland. It is acknowledged by Laurie, in his history of the Scottish Craft, 'that the Masons calling themselves *ancient*, are much to be blamed as the active promoters of the English schism. But having chosen for their G. M. the Duke of Athol, who held the same office in the Grand Lodge of Scotland, an alliance between the two parties was the necessary consequence; and the Scottish Masons hence imbibed a strong prejudice against the Grand Lodge of England, arising from an alleged alteration in ceremonial observances.' It was to remove the prejudice that the Earl of Moira now directed his attention.

"On the above-mentioned day he attended the annual grand festival of Scottish Masons, and an opportunity being thus afforded for the discussion of this interesting subject, he detailed the entire history of the schism, and dwelt on the repeated failures of the Grand Lodge to convince the seceders of their error, and receive them back into the bosom of their common mother. He further explained that the trifling alteration which it had been judged expedient to make in the ceremonies, was more an imaginary than a real defect; and that the English Craft had ever entertained that affection and regard for their northern Brethren, which it is the object of Freemasonry to cherish, and the duty of Freemasons to feel.

"This explanation was received with plaudits, and the Earl of Dalhousie, G. M. of Scotland, expressed his gratification at hearing that measures were at length contemplated to effect an union which would restore harmony, promote activity and vigour, and invest the Order with its primitive purity and usefulness.

"These proceedings," added the Square, "furnished

copious matter for reflection and speculation in every Lodge throughout the entire length and breadth of the land; and in 1809, our Grand Lodge, with the design of neutralizing all objections, resolved: 'That it is not necessary any longer to continue in force those measures which were resorted to in or about the year 1739, respecting irregular Masons; and do, therefore, enjoin the several Lodges *to revert to the ancient Landmarks of the Society*.' This measure was completed by the appointment of the Lodge of Promulgation, with powers to put in practice certain instructions preparatory to a final union between the two societies.

"Matters continued in this state," said the Square, "till 1813, when Dr. Hemming was re-elected our R. W. M.; and at the very commencement of the year he communicated the fact in tyled Lodge, which afforded the Brethren unmixed gratification. He said that the preliminary steps had been already taken to bring this controverted dispute to an issue; and that several Brethren were then present who were parties to the conciliatory measure. 'It appears, indeed,' he added, 'to be the almost unanimous opinion of the whole Fraternity of both sections, that the removal of the unimportant differences which have so long kept the Brotherhood asunder, will be a means of establishing in the metropolis of the British empire one splendid edifice of ancient Freemasonry, to which the whole masonic world may confidently look for the maintenance and preservation of those pure principles of the Craft which have been handed down to them from time immemorial, under the protection of the illustrious branches of the royal house of Brunswick,—the practice of loyalty, morality, brotherly love, and benevolence, which it has been the great object of Masonry to inculcate, and of its laws to enforce.'[9]

"'As this subject has been opened by the R. W. M.,' said Bro. Meyrick, 'it may be no breach of confidence on my part to add, that the present unhappy state of the Craft, divided into two hostile sections, in open and undisguised rivalry with each other, having received the attention of Brethren in the highest quarters, they have

[9] See Minutes of Grand Lodge, Dec. 27, 1813.

resolved, at all hazards, to remedy the evils which have, for so long a period, resulted from this unnatural opposition—*civile avertite bellum*—by the interposition of measures which cannot fail to be successful. The Duke of Athol has been prevailed on to resign the office of Grand Master at the ensuing election, and H. R. H. the Duke of Kent is expected to be his successor. This being accomplished, an union between the two parties is inevitable; and arrangements are actually in some degree of forwardness to bring this long-controverted dispute to an amicable termination.'

"Bro. Shadbolt then rose, and intimated 'that H. R. H. had graciously consented to accept the office of Grand Master, and certain Brethren have been already nominated on both sides to arrange the details of the projected union, several of whom are now present. I make this communication in perfect good faith, assured that it is in safe hands, and in no danger of being repeated beyond the walls of the Lodge, until it shall be officially announced.'

"The R. W. M. observed, that 'such a breach of faith was not likely to happen, and as he saw the principal Brethren who were in the secret then present, viz., Brothers Washington Shirley, Rodwell Wright, Shadbolt, Meyrick, Tegart, Deans, and Stephen Jones, and as the Lodge, in other respects, was remarkably thin of Members, with no business of importance to transact, it would be a favourable opportunity to communicate to each other the results of our private reflections or active agency in the prosecution of this important measure, and to deliberate on the terms of re-union which it may be expedient to propose to the adverse party, as he was aware that objections, apparently insuperable, must be met and obviated before the erring Brethren could be induced to acknowledge their schism, and sue for readmission into the ample fold of genuine Masonry.'

"'I have already had several conversations with Bro. Harper, and his under spur-leathers, Perry, Agar, and Cranfield on the subject,' said Bro. Tegart, 'and they take very high ground at present. Their demands are so unreasonable, that unless their influence be extinguished by some authority superior to their own, our attempts will fail, and the projected union will never be accomplished. Bro. Agar was bold enough to insinuate that our only object was to increase our annual income by the fees for the registration of their numerous Members, and that, consequently, while we are avowedly acting for the benefit of Masonry, we are, in reality, seeking an advantage to ourselves.'

"'I hope,' said Bro. Wright, 'you repudiated the charge promptly, without descending to a vindication, because they know better; for it has been repeatedly intimated to them that we never contemplated the imposition of new fees, or of alienating any existing funds from the purposes of their original appropriation.'

"'The assumption is too absurd to merit any serious notice,' Bro. Deans observed; 'but I am anxious to know what Bro. Harper says to the measure.'

"'Why, the fact is,' replied Bro. Tegart, 'that he says very little, but appears distant and reserved. While declaring that he should not object to the proposed union, if it can be effected on grounds consistent with the honour of the ancient Grand Lodge, he pertinaciously attributes views and motives to our party utterly at variance with the truth, as if he was afraid that an union of the two sections would swallow up and annihilate his own personal power, and reduce him to a mere unit.'

"'His power and influence,' said Bro. Hemming, 'will, of course, be superseded; for a person in his rank of life can have no legitimate claim to the government of such a vast and influential body as the Society of Freemasons; and, indeed, it is the name of the Duke of Athol alone that imparts or confirms the influence which he possesses.'

"'The Duke of Athol seldom attends in person, I presume?' said Bro. Deans, inquiringly.

"'Very seldom,' Bro. Meyrick answered; 'yet every act is published in his name, and is consequently invested with his authority, which will be scattered to the winds of heaven when the Duke of Kent proposes the union from the throne. *Quo more pyris vesci Calaber jubet hospes.* No one, how interested soever he may be in the present state of things, will be bold enough to oppose the projected reform, which is anxiously anticipated by nine out of every ten Brothers in both sections: and as this, motion will assuredly be made, it only remains for us, who are intrusted by the Grand Master with the management of this delicate negotiation, to determine finally on what conditions their section of the Fraternity shall be re-admitted to all the privileges of constitutional Masonry. And I should be glad to have the benefit of your deliberate opinions on the subject.'

"'In the first place,' said Bro. Rodwell Wright, 'and as an indispensable condition, Brothers Tegart and Deans, who have been associated with me by authority to arrange the preliminary negotiations, have agreed, firmly, and with brotherly affection, to uphold and maintain the ancient Landmarks, and the rights, privileges, and dignity of the Grand Lodge, and the several Lodges under the Constitution of England; founding the negotiation on principles of perfect equality, and unity of obligation, discipline, and working; that the edifice of the union may be constructed on a basis constituted of such materials as must be rendered more firm and compact by revolving years, and on which the hand of time can work only to prove that Masons possess the art of raising a structure which storms cannot destroy.'

"'The great difficulty will be,' Bro. Tegart observed, 'about the disposal of the funds of the Athol section; and I am not aware that we have any other course open on this litigated point, than to declare openly and fairly that the property of both sections of the Fraternity shall never be alienated from the benevolent purposes for which it was originally intended; but shall together form one common fund, to be appropriated equally to the distressed of the united community, without respect of persons, or to the education of the orphan children of Masons, as the case may be; that the names of the trustees shall not be changed; but in case of death or withdrawal, the United Grand Lodge shall possess the power of nominating successors, who shall be instructed to take a special care that the property be not diverted to any other use or purpose whatsoever.'

"'And with respect to rites and ceremonies,' Bro. Deans added, 'I suppose we shall have to deal with them summarily, so as to secure a perfect uniformity, according to the old Gothic Landmarks, Charges, and Traditions; for I shall never consent to depart from these authentic precedents under any circumstances or conditions whatever.'

"'It will be absolutely necessary that we make it clearly understood at the very outset,' said the R. W. M., thoughtfully, 'that it must be publicly acknowledged, without any mental reservation or self-evasion of mind, that *genuine ancient Masonry consists of Three Degrees, and no more*, viz., those of Apprentice, Fellowcraft, and Master, including the Royal Arch; and a declaration to this effect must be insisted on as a *sine quâ non*, before we can enter on the details.'

"'The question is,' Bro. Shirley replied, 'how will the ancients swallow this bitter pill, after having asserted in their Book of Constitutions, that the Order is composed of Four Degrees?[10] This doctrine has become incorporated so essentially into their system, as to constitute an absolute article of faith, and, in reality, is the sole difference between us and them. They plume themselves upon it, and have passed strong censures on the Constitutional Grand Lodge, because we repudiate it as an innovation. The question is, Can they consistently acknowledge themselves to be in error?'

"Dr. Hemming," continued the Square, "here produced an elaborate engraving of the (so-called) High Degrees, and explained it to the Lodge as being a complicated diagram, published by the ancients about the year 1790, of several Degrees of Masonry which they had derived from France. It was entitled *Mysticum Sapientiæ Speculum*, and contained numerous symbols of the different Orders of Continental Masonry, and also illustrations of the acknowledged Masonic Cypher. It consisted of a Cross, inscribed in a Circle, the former containing eight Squares, completely charged with emblems of certain Degrees, not generally known in this country. 'The first Square, beginning at the top,' he said, 'is the carpet or floorcloth of the Degree of Knights of the East and West, surrounded by the letters B, D, S, H, P, F, G, which signify Beauty, Divinity, Strength, Honour, Power, Fidelity, Glory.[11] The second, on the left hand, represents the Birth of Light from Darkness; the next con-

[10] Ahiman Rezon, p. 113, Harper's ed., 1813.

[11] See the Hist. Lmks., vol. ii., p. 117, for an explanation.

tains the emblems of the Degree of Rose Croix;[12] and the fourth is an allegorical representation of the Order of Harodim.[13] The fifth is the Brute Stone (our Rough Ashlar) symbolizing the elements of Blue Masonry. Then we have the Arches of Enoch, as illustrative of the Degree of Knights of the Ninth Arch;[14] and after it the Cubical Stone (Perfect Ashlar), which, according to a legend at the foot, contains the Sacred Name; and, last of all, a diagram of the Degree of Prussian Knights, or Noachites;[15] and in the lower spandrils are vestiges of the Spurious Freemasonry. In the circle we have a brief exposition of the Seven Liberal Sciences, and at the four cardinal points are appropriate Latin mottoes. The crest, or surmounting symbol, is a hierogram appended to the Degree of Knights of the White Eagle and Pelican.'[16]

"After this extraordinary engraving had been examined," the Square continued, "the R. W. M. observed that, 'as it was their intention to confine ancient Masonry to its primitive category of Three Degrees, he entertained an idea of republishing this curious document at the union,[17] with certain alterations, as a testimony of the exclusive claims of Blue Masonry to the sole consideration of the United Fraternity. Thus he would enliven the dark angles of the Brochure with the words—No RARCH—No KTPS—No HRDM—No KADH, &c., as a standing proof that our Grand Lodge acknowledges Three Degrees only; and that, if other Degrees or Orders are tolerated, they must be entirely disconnected with the United Grand Lodge of Ancient Free and Accepted Masons, and work under Grand Lodges of their own.'

"'This will be a most judicious step,' said Bro. Shirley, 'as it will point their own artillery in the proper direction.'

"'But,' said Bro. Wright, 'they have not only put on record their conviction that genuine ancient Masonry consists of Four Degrees, but they have publicly, in the

[12] See Hist. Lmks., vol. ii., p. 347. [13] Ibid. vol. ii., p. 14.
[14] See Ant. Mas., p. 83. [16] See Hist. Lmks., vol. i., p. 63.
[15] Ibid. vol. ii., p. 139.

Ahiman Rezon, declared that they abhor and detest the unconstitutional fopperies of cunning, avaricious tradesmen, invented and introduced among the *moderns* with no other design than to extract large sums of money, which ought to be applied to more noble and charitable uses,[18] when, in point of fact, if venality really exists, it is all on their own part. But the real delinquent often joins the hue and cry, and is the first to call out, "Stop thief!"'

"'True,' Bro. Deans replied; 'and they have given equal publicity to the avowal that there is an essential difference between us in makings, ceremonies, knowledge, masonic language, and installation,[19] when, in reality, if there be any difference between the systems, it is to be attributed solely to the liberties they have taken with the Third Degree.'

"'Bro. Laurie has justly observed, in his "History of Freemasonry,"' said Bro. S. Jones, 'that much injury has been done to the cause of Masonry by a book entitled "Ahiman Rezon," written by one Dermott, their Secretary, and very imprudently republished by Thomas Harper, in 1800. The unfairness with which he has stated the proceedings of the Regular Masons, the bitterness with which he treats them, and the quackery and vain glory with which he displays his own pretensions to superior knowledge, deserve to be reprobated by every class of Masons who are anxious for the purity of their Order, and the preservation of that charity and mildness which ought to characterize all their proceedings.'

"'The *ex parte* observations and censures against the regular Craft,' the R. W. M. replied, 'might be excusable at the first breaking out of the schism, when prejudice ran high, and the disgrace of expulsion was tingling in their minds, as vents for the discharge of superfluous bile, and props to sanction their own designs at the expense of a powerful rival; but why has Bro. Harper reasserted these calumnies at the present moment, when the negociations are in such a state of forwardness, by the publication of a new edition of the "Ahiman Rezon" even in this very month? This conduct will scarcely admit of an

[18] Ahiman Rezon, p. xxvi. [19] Ibid. p. xxx.

apology; for it is evidently a device to stave off the approaching union, by a final appeal to the passions and prejudices of his Brethren.[20] But the remedy is at hand. An authority will be interposed that is irresistible, and the private interests of a few must give way to the general benefit of the Fraternity. We shall take our stand on the ancient Landmarks; and that is a position from which it will be difficult to dislodge us. Besides, most of Bro. Harper's immediate colleagues, including Brothers Perry and Cranfield, are as desirous of a reconciliation and general amnesty as ourselves, and, therefore, we do not anticipate any difficulty when the subject comes fairly before a Committee, composed of an equal number of members from either party.'

"'I presume,' Bro. Jones asked, 'that all the Athol Fraternity must be re-obligated before their admission amongst us?'

"'It will be unnecessary, I should think,' Bro. Meyrick replied.

"'And yet,' said the R. W. M., 'it will be stipulated as an express condition on our part, that, before their names are entered on our books, the O. B. shall be administered. And for this purpose it has been suggested, that a certain number of expert Brethren from each section of the Craft shall meet together at some convenient central place in London, when each party having opened, in a separate apartment, a just and perfect Lodge, agreeable to their peculiar regulations, they shall give and receive, mutually and reciprocally, the obligations of both Fraternities, deciding, by lot, which shall take priority in giving and receiving the same; and, being thus all duly and equally enlightened in both forms, they shall be empowered and directed to hold a Lodge under the warrant or dispensation to be entrusted

20. These conversations may be considered by living Masons as an exaggerated picture of the feelings and sentiments of the Fraternity. But, in reality, they are a subdued representation of the very high state of excitement which prevailed amongst both sections for several years before the union was effected. And it would be utterly impossible for any person, who had not witnessed the operation of these feelings, as I have done, to form the slightest estimate of the extent to which the rivalry was carried.

to them, and to be entitled the Lodge of Reconciliation.'

"Accordingly," said the Square, "the Duke of Kent being elevated to the throne, and the preliminaries having been mutually arranged, the Articles of Union were signed at Kensington Palace by the contracting parties, viz., the Dukes of Sussex and Kent, and by Brothers Waller Rodwell Wright, Arthur Tegart, and James Deans, on the part of the constitutional Masons; and Thomas Harper, James Perry, and James Agar, on the part of the Athols; and the Great Seal of each Grand Lodge was affixed on the first day of December, 1813.

"The thirteenth article of union provided that, 'after the day of reunion, certain worthy and expert Brothers shall be appointed to visit and attend the several Lodges for the purpose of promulgating the pure and unsullied system, that a perfect reconciliation, unity of obligation, working, language, and dress, may be restored to the English Craft.'

"On St. John's day, in the above month and year," the Square continued, "this important measure was consummated at Freemasons' Hall by a general assembly of the whole English Craft, and the representatives of several foreign Lodges. As I was suspended from the collar of one of the Masters on this august occasion, I am able to give you a particular account of the ceremony. It was a most magnificent scene, and, unfortunately, the last masonic celebration I was ever destined to witness; for, a new description of jewels being now adopted, I was laid up in ordinary, and have been in obscurity ever since. I'll tell you how it was."

"You need not give yourself the trouble," I exclaimed, forgetting our compact at the moment; "for I am already acquainted with every detail of that memorable ceremony."

I saw my error at once; for, while I was yet speaking, my companion fell prone upon the table, where he lay silent, and, without any token of animation, a simple silver Square, and nothing more. I started—rubbed my eyes—the clock struck two—the candles were burning in the sockets, and I thought I must have been asleep.

I regretted my premature exclamation, which had, probably, deprived me of some interesting anecdotes of the illustrious Brothers who were principally concerned in that celebrated movement; for, as to the transaction itself, it had been already laid before the public in Preston's "Illustrations," and in my own letter to Dr. Crucefix on the "Origin of the Royal Arch."

LIST OF BOOKS

PUBLISHED AND FOR SALE BY THE

MASONIC PUBLISHING AND MANUFACTURING CO.,

430 Broome street, New York.

☞ *Postage prepaid, on printed books, on receipt of the price. The money must, in all cases, accompany the order.*

THE GENERAL AHIMAN REZON AND FREEMASON'S GUIDE, containing Monitorial Instructions in the Degrees of Entered Apprentice, Fellow-Craft and Master Mason, with explanatory notes, emendations and lectures: together with the Ceremonies of Consecration and Dedication of New Lodges, Installation of Grand and Subordinate Officers, Laying Foundation Stones, Dedication of Masonic Halls, Grand Visitations, Burial Services, Regulations for Processions, Masonic Calendar, etc. To which are added a Ritual for a Lodge of Sorrow, and the Ceremonies of Consecrating Masonic Cemeteries: also an Appendix, with the forms of Masonic Documents, Masonic Trials, etc. By DANIEL SICKELS, 33°. Embellished with nearly 300 Engravings.

Bound in fine Cloth—extra—large 12mo.................. $1 50

" " Morocco, full gilt, for the W. Master's table, with appropriate insignia of the East...... 3 00

Freemason's Monitor, containing all the Degrees in the Lodge, Chapter, Council, and Commandery. By Daniel Sickels. *(An enlarged edition of Macoy's Masonic Manual.)*

.... Tucks. 1 50

Same work, bound in cloth.............................. 1 00

The Historical Landmarks and other Evidences of Freemasonry Explained in a series of Practical Lectures, with copious Notes. By George Oliver, D. D. 2 vols. Large Duodecimo—with Portrait of the Author.

BINDING —	Cloth—Uniform Style	$5 00
	Half Morocco—Uniform Library Edition	7 00

Signs and Symbols, Illustrated and Explained in a Course of Twelve Lectures on Freemasonry. By Geo. Oliver, D. D. Large Duodecimo.

BINDING —	Cloth—Uniform Style	1 50
	Half Morocco—Uniform Library Edition	2 50

The History of Initiation, in Twelve Lectures; comprising a Detailed Account of the Rites and Ceremonies, Doctrines, and Discipline of the Secret and Mysterious Institutions of the Ancient World. By George Oliver, D. D. Royal Duodecimo—300 pages.

BINDING —	Cloth—Uniform Style	1 50
	Half Morocco—Uniform Library Edition	2 50

The Symbol of Glory, showing the Object and End of Freemasonry. By George Oliver, D. D.

BINDING —	Cloth—Uniform Style	1 50
	Half Morocco—Uniform Library Edition	2 50

The Lights and Shadows of Freemasonry; consisting of Masonic Tales, Songs, and Sentiments never before published. By Rob. Morris, K. T.

BINDING —	Cloth—Uniform Style	1 50
	Half Morocco—Uniform Library Edition	2 50

The Theocratic Philosophy of Freemasonry, in Twelve Lectures on its Speculative, Operative, and Spurious Branches. By George Oliver, D. D. Large Duodecimo.

BINDING —	Cloth—Uniform Style	1 50
	Half Morocco—Uniform Library Edition	2 50

The Revelations of a Square, exhibiting a graphic display of the Sayings and Doings of Eminent Free and Accepted Masons, from the Revival in 1717, by Dr. Desaguliers, to the Reunion in 1813. By George Oliver, D. D. Royal Duodecimo.

BINDING —	Cloth—Uniform Style	1 50
	Half Morocco—Uniform Library Edition	2 50

The Mystic Tie; or Facts and Opinions, illustrative of the Character and Tendency of Freemasonry. By Albert G. Mackey, M. D.

BINDING — { Cloth—Uniform Style.................... $1 50
Half Morocco—Uniform Library Edition. 2 50

Traditions of Freemasonry and its Coincidences with the Ancient Mysteries. By A. T. C. Pierson. Large Duodecimo—fine cloth.................................... 2 00

Manual of the Order of the Eastern Star, containing Symbols, Scriptural Illustrations, Lectures, etc., adapted to the system of Adoptive Masonry. Beautifully Illustrated. Gilt Edges and Illuminated Cover...................... 1 00

Signet of King Solomon; or, the Freemason's Daughter. By Aug. C. L. Arnold, LL.D. Splendidly Illustrated..... 1 25

Ancient Constitutions of Freemasons. By James Anderson. A verbatim copy of the original edition of 1723......... 1 00

Taaffe's History of the Knights of Malta. 8vo. 4 vols. bound in 2.. 5 00

Text-Book of Masonic Jurisprudence, by A. G. Mackey..... 2 00
Book of the Chapter, by A. G. Mackey.................... 1 50
Manual of the Lodge, by A. G. Mackey................... 1 50
Lexicon of Freemasonry, by A. G. Mackey................ 3 00
Familiar Treatise on the Principles and Practice of Masonic Jurisprudence, by John W. Simons..................... 1 50
Digest of Masonic Law, by G. W. Chase.................. 1 50
Origin and Early History of Masonry, by G. W. Steinbrenner 75
Book of the Commandery, by John W. Simons............ 75
Manual of the Chapter, by Sheville & Gould.............. 75
Freemason's Monitor, by Webb.......................... 75
Freemason's Hand-Book, by Wm. H. Drew...........Tuck. 1 00
Masonic Manual, by J. Ashe............................ 1 00
Moral Design of Freemasonry, by S. Lawrence............ 1 00
Freemason's Pocket Library and Working Monitor, by G. W. Chase ....Tuck. 1 50
Rationale and Ethics of Freemasonry, by A. C. L. Arnold... 1 00
Masonic Advocate, containing Mackey's Lexicon and Oliver's Masonic Dictionary.................................. 1 50
Des Freimaurer's Handbuch *(German)*.................. 75

Manual of the Ancient and Accepted Rite, by William M. Cunningham....................................$2 00
Manual de la Masoneria, (*Spanish,*) by A. Cassard.......... 8 00
Craftsman and Freemason's Guide, by C. Moore............ 1 50
Freemason's Manual, by K. J. Stewart.................... 1 50
Masonic Trestle-Board, by C. W. Moore.................. 1 50
Masonic Text-Book, by J. L. Cross....................tuck. 1 50
Masonic Chart, by J. L. Cross.......................... 1 50
Templar's Chart, by J. L. Cross........................ 2 00
Star in the East, by George Oliver..................... 1 00
Revelations of a Square, by George Oliver............... 1 50
History of the Ancient and Accepted Rite, by Robt. B. Folger. 5 00
Antiquities of Freemasonry, by George Oliver............ 1 25
Statutes and Regulations of the Ancient and Accepted Rite, by A. Pike.. 2 00
Beauties of Freemasonry Examplified, by George Oliver.... 20
Outlines of Speculative Freemasonry, by Salem Town...... 20
Mason in High Places, by an English Rector.............. 20
Juryman Mason, by an English Rector.................... 25
Masonic Vocal Manual, by Robt. Macoy............per doz. 3 00
Masonic Harp, by George W. Chase...................... 1 00
Ancient Constitutions of 1723, by James Anderson......... 75
Keystone of the Masonic Arch, by Charles Scott........... 1 25
Master Workman, by James K. Hall..................tuck. 1 25
Do. do. do. ....cloth. 1 00
Book of Marks for Chapters............................ 4 00
Ode Cards for the Lodge..........................per doz. 1 50
Ode Cards for the Chapter.......................... " 1 50
Proposition Book...................................... 3 00
Receipt Books for Lodge and Chapter.................... 3 00
Lodge Register... 2 00
Draft Books for Lodge and Chapter...................... 3 50
Question Book for Commandery.......................... 4 00
Visitors' Book... 3 50
Petitions for Membership..........................per 100, 1 25
Black Book.. 3 50
Ledgers and Minute Books. Large and Small Bibles.

☞ *All Masonic Books now published, and not named in this List on hand, or furnished to order at the lowest market prices.*

www.ingramcontent.com/pod-product-compliance
Lightning Source LLC
Chambersburg PA
CBHW021125270326
41929CB00009B/1044

9783337711917